KB175194

옥기
玉器

中國 西安(長安)의 문화유산

Xi'an Relics Essence_Jade Articles

초판인쇄 2016년 1월 29일
초판발행 2016년 1월 29일

엮은이 시안시문물보호고고학연구소
옮긴이 중국문물전문번역팀
펴낸이 채종준
진 행 박능원
기 획 지성영
편 집 백혜림 · 조은아
디자인 조은아
마케팅 황영주 · 김지선

펴낸곳 한국학술정보(주)
주 소 경기도 파주시 회동길 230(문발동513-5)
전 화 031-908-3181(대표)
팩 스 031-908-3189
홈페이지 http://ebook.kstudy.com
E-mail 출판사업부 publish@kstudy.com
등 록 제일산-115호(2000. 6. 19)

ISBN 978-89-268-7070-9 94910
　　　 978-89-268-6263-6 (전11권)

 한국학술정보(주)의 학술 분야 출판 브랜드입니다.

옥기
玉
器

中國 西安(長安)의 문화유산

시안시문물보호고고학연구소 엮음
중국문물전문번역팀 옮김

한눈에 보는 중국 시안(西安, 長安)의 문화유산

시안(西安, 長安)은 중국 고대문명의 발상지로 역사상 13왕조의 왕도인바 중국 전통문화의 산실이라고 할 수 있다. 주(周)·진(秦)·한(漢)·당(唐)나라 등의 수도로서 청동기(靑銅器)를 비롯한 각종 옥기(玉器)와 금은기(金銀器), 불교조각상(佛敎彫刻像), 당삼채(唐三彩), 도용(陶俑), 자기(瓷器), 회화(繪畵), 서예(書藝) 등 수많은 문화유산을 남기고 있다. 그러나 이러한 문화유산은 여러 박물관이나 문화재연구소에서 분산 소장하고 있어 한눈에 감상할 수가 없다.

시안을 답사했을 때 중국의 지역연구기관으로서 시안 지역의 유적·왕릉·건축물 등 역사문화유적의 보호와 연구를 담당하고 있는 시안시문물보호고고소(西安市文物保護考古所)에서 정리하고, 세계도서출판시안유한공사(世界圖書出版西安有限公司)에서 발행한 『西安文物精華(시안문물정화)』를 접한 바 있다. 이번에 출간된 『中國 西安(長安)의 문화유산』 시리즈는 이를 번역·출판한 것으로, 이를 통하여 시안의 문화유산을 한눈에 감상할 수 있게 되었다. 이 책은 전문가들이 몇 년간에 걸쳐 시안의 문화유산 가운데 에센스를 선정, 회화·금은기·옥기·당삼채·불교조각상·자기·청동거울·도용·청동기·서예·도장(圖章) 등으로 분류하여 집대성한 것이다. 중국어를 해득하지 못하는 이들을 위해 각종 문화유산에 대한 상세한 해설을 실어 이해를 돕고 있으며, 화질이 좋아 원서보다도 선명하게 문화유산을 접할 수 있게 되었다.

특히 회화편은 원서보다도 화질이 선명하여 그림의 색감이 더 살아나며, 청동기와 동경(銅鏡)도 세밀한 부분이 더 입체적으로 드러나고 있다. 회화편의 경우, 그림을 보고 있노라면 한국화의 주제나 기법이 어디서 영향을 받았는지를 확연하게 알 수 있어 한국의 회화를 이해하는 데도 많은 도움이 될 것이다. 청동기와 동경의 경우, 한국의 그것과 공통점과 차이점을 비교해보는 재미를 느낄 수 있으며, 불교조각상과 자기의 경우에도 중국과 한국의 공통점과 차이점을 한눈에 살펴볼 수 있다. 이와 같이 『中國 西安(長安)의 문화유산』 시리즈는 중국의 문화유산을 감상하고 이해하는 것뿐만 아니라 한국의 문화유산과의 비교를 통하여 두 전통문화 간의 공통점과 차이점을 느낄 수 있다.

실크로드의 기점인 시안은 중국뿐만 아니라 서역의 많은 문화유산을 소장하고 있으나 이곳의 문화유산을 감상하려면 박물관이나 미술관에 직접 가야만 하고, 중요한 유물을 모두 보기 위해선 여러 번 발품을 팔아야 한다. 이에 『中國 西安(長安)의 문화유산』 시리즈는 한눈에 중국의 우수한 문화유산을 감상하면서 눈의 호사를 누리고, 중국의 전통문화를 제대로 이해하는 계기가 될 것이다.

2015년
前 문화체육관광부 장관
現 고려대학교 한국사학과 교수
최광식

중국 시안(西安, 長安)의 유구한 역사를 보여주다

　　시안(西安, 長安)은 중국의 역사에서 다양한 별명을 갖고 있다. 중화문명의 발상지, 중화민족의 요람, 가장 오래된 도시, 실크로드의 출발지 등이 그것이다. 시안의 6천 년 역사 가운데 왕도(王都, 혹은 皇都)의 역사가 1천 2백년이었다는 사실도 시안을 일컫는 또 다른 이름이 될 수 있다. 즉, 시안은 남전원인(藍田原人)의 선사시대부터 당(唐) 시기 세계 최대의 도시 단계를 거쳐 근대에 이르기까지 중화의 역사, 종교, 군사, 경제, 문화, 학예 등 분야 전반에 걸쳐 가히 대륙의 중심에 서 있어 왔다고 할 수 있다. 그만큼 시안은 역사의 자취가 황토 고원의 두께만큼 두껍고, 황하의 흐름만큼 길다고 할 것이다.

　　시안시문물보호고고소(西安市文物保護考古所)에서 엮은 『西安文物精華(시안문물정화)』 도록 전집은 이와 같은 시안의 유구한 역사와 그 문화사적인 의미를 잘 보여주고 있다. 첫째, 발굴 및 전수되어 온 문화재들이 병마용(兵馬俑), 자기(瓷器), 인장(印章), 서법(書法), 옥기(玉器), 동경(銅鏡), 청동기(靑銅器), 회화(繪畵), 불상(佛像), 금은기물(金銀器物) 등 다양할 뿐 아니라, 시안만이 가지는 역사 배경의 특징을 심도 있게 관찰할 수 있는 분야의 문화재가 집중적으로 수록되어 있다. 각 권의 머리말에서 밝히고 있듯이 이 문화재의 일부는 시안 지역의 특징을 이루는 것들을 포함하면서 다른 일부, 예컨대 자기는 당시 전국의 물품들이 집합되어 있어 그 시기 중국 전체의 면모를 보여주기도 한다는 것이다. 둘째, 당 이후 중국 역사의 주된 무대는 강남(江南)으로 옮겨갔다고 할 수 있는데, 이 문화재들은 시안이 여전히 역사와 문화의 중심축에서 크게 벗어나지 않고 있음을 보여준다. 문인 취향의 서법, 인장 및 자기들이 이를 말해준다고 할 수 있다. 셋째, 이 문화재들은 병마용의 경우처럼 대부분이 해당 예술사에서 주로 다루어질 수준의 것들이지만 다른 일부, 예컨대 회화 같은 경우는 그러한 수준에서 다소 벗어난 작품들로 보이기도 한다. 그러나 이 경우 이 문화재들은 해당 예술사 분야에서 대표성을 갖는 작품들이 일류 작가의 범작(凡作)들과 이류 작가의 다른 주제와 기법을 통하여 어떻게 조형적 가치와 대표성을 가질 수 있는가를 되비쳐줌과 동시에 중국적인 조형 의식의 심층을 엿볼 수 있게 한다는 사료적 가치가 있다고 평가할 수 있다.

　　이러한 시안의 방대하고 의미 있는 문화재를 선명한 화상과 상세한 전문적 설명을 덧붙여 발간한 것을 한국학술정보(주)에서 한국어 번역본으로 출간, 한국의 관련 연구자와 문화 애호가들에게 시의적절하게 제공하게 된 것은 매우 다행스럽고 보람된 일이라 생각한다. 향후 이를 토대로 심도 있는 연구가 진행되고, 이웃 문화권에 대한 일반 독자들의 이해가 깊어질 수 있기를 기대하면서 감상과 섭렵을 적극적으로 추천하는 바이다.

2015년 관악산 자락에서
서울대학교 미학과 교수
박낙규

시안시문물보호고고소(西安市文物保護考古所)에서 편저한『시안문물정화(西安文物精華)』「옥기(玉器)」편의 출판에 즈음하여 쑨푸시(孫福喜) 박사님께서 서언을 써달라고 부탁하였다. 이 자리를 빌려 본서의 출판을 진심으로 축하하는 바이다.

시안은 중국역사에서 서주(西周), 진(秦), 서한(西漢), 서위(西魏), 북주(北周), 수(隋), 당(唐) 등 왕조의 도읍지이자 정치, 경제, 문화의 중심지이며 자연히 옥기가 제조ㆍ유행되었던 주요 지역이었다. 지난 몇십 년간 시안에서 역대 옥기가 연이어 출토되었는데 그중 대부분이 시안시고고소에 소장되었다. 본서에 수록된 백여 점의 옥기는 그중의 정수이다. 예를 들면 시안 라오뉴포(老牛坡)에서 출토된 대옥창(大玉戈)은 상대(商代) 말기의 대표적인 옥기이다. 진나라 아방궁(阿房宮) 유적지 내 처장촌(車張村)에서 출토된 곡문구연운문옥배(谷文勾連雲文玉杯)는 조형, 장식문양, 제조기법 등에서 모두 당시 옥기 조각의 최고수준을 보여준다. 서한시기 장안성(長安城) 건장궁(建章宮) 유적지에서 출토된 청백옥(青白玉)인 칠절수두철예대대구(七節獸頭鐵蕊大帶鉤)도 기법이 보기 드물게 뛰어나다. 시안시 남쪽 교외 한묘(漢墓)에서 출토된 한 쌍의 옥악저(玉握豬)도 한대 옥돼지[玉豬] 중에서 형상이 가장 생동감 있고 크기가 가장 큰 것이며 시안시 북쪽 교외 한묘(漢墓)에서 출토된 옥검수(玉劍首)도 한나라 옥검구(玉劍具) 중 뛰어난 작품이다. 당대(唐代) 대명궁(大明宮) 유적지에서 출토된 옥매[玉鷹] 및 당대 곡강지(曲江池) 유적지에서 출토된 옥룡수(玉龍首) 모두 당시 옥기 중에서 예술성이 가장 뛰어난 작품이다. 당대 대명궁 유적지 내 쑨자완촌(孫家灣村)에서 출토된 감금백옥패(嵌金白玉佩)는 중앙아시아와 서아시아의 풍격을 띠었는데 이는 당왕조와 서역 간 문화교류의 실질적 증거이다. 시안 시에서 출토된 옥대구(玉帶鉤), 옥안(玉雁), 목동기우(牧童騎牛) 등 원대(元代) 옥기는 전부 기백이 넘치고 가공기술이 정교한 보기 드문 예술 작품이다.

이 책의 저자는 시안 시에서 출토된 옥기에 대한 연구를 거쳐 자기만의 견해를 내놓았다. 본서의 다른 한 특징은 구성이 참신하고 세부적인 부분까지 살피고 있다는 점이다. 최대한 다양한 측면에서 옥기를 설명함으로써 사람들이 옥기를 심도 있게 연구하는 데 충분한 자료를 제공하였다. 이 책은 독자들에게 추천할 만하며 중국 고대 옥기를 감상하고 연구하는 데 참고할 만하다.

2004년 11월 시안

류윈후이(劉雲輝)

　　由西安文物保護考古所編寫的《西安文物精華、玉器》即將出版發行，孫福喜博士囑我寫個序言，謹在此對該書出版表示衷心的祝賀。

　　西安是中國歷史上西周、秦、西漢、西魏、北周、隋、唐等王朝建都之地，是當時政治、經濟、文化中心、自然也是其時玉器制作和流行的主要地區。近几十年來，西安地區不斷有歷代玉器出土，絕大部分玉器都收藏在西安市考古所。本書中選用的百余件組玉器，是它們藏品中的精品。如西安老牛坡出土的大玉戈，屬商代晚期代表性的玉器。秦阿防宮遺址范圍内車張村出土的谷紋勾連雲紋玉杯，從造型、裝飾文樣，乃至制作工藝均代表了當時玉器雕琢的最高水平。西漢長安城建章宮遺址出土的青白玉七節獸頭鐵蕊大帶鉤，工藝精湛，十分罕見。西安南郊漢墓出土的一對玉握豬，是迄今爲止所見的漢代玉豬中造型最爲生動且形体最大的。西安市北郊漢莫中出土的玉劍首也是漢代玉劍其中的精品。唐大明宮遺址出土的玉鷹和唐曲江池遺址出土的玉龍首均是唐代玉器中藝術性特强的珍品。唐大明宮遺址内孫家灣村出土的嵌金白玉佩具有中亞和西亞的風格，是唐代與西域文化交流的實物見證。西安市出土的元代玉器如玉帶鉤、玉雁、牧童騎牛均氣魄宏大、作工精細，爲罕見的藝術珍品。

　　《西安文物精華、玉器》的作者，對西安市出土的玉器進行了較爲深入的研究，提出了自己的見解。該書另一個特點是設計新穎，并且充分利用特寫鏡頭，突出了細部，最大限度的展示了玉器各方面的信息，爲人們深入研究提供完整的資料。因此，此書是一部值得向讀者推荐的鑒賞和研究中國古代玉器重要的參考書，此爲序。

2004年11月 西安

劉雲輝

'장안(長安)'이라고 불렸던 시안(西安)은 기후가 온화하고 산천이 수려하며 물자가 풍부해 예로부터 '천부(天府)'라는 이름을 얻은, 중화문명의 발상지 중 하나이다. 일찍이 석기시대부터 중국인들은 이곳에 정착하여 살아왔다. 기원전 11세기에 이르러 서주(西周)왕조가 이곳을 도읍으로 정하면서 3천여 년 간 발전을 거듭했다. 특히 주(周), 진(秦), 한(漢), 당(唐) 시대 이곳은 전국의 정치중심지였을 뿐만 아니라 수공업, 상업, 교육, 예술의 중심지이기도 하였다. 이처럼 유구한 역사와 찬란한 문명은 이곳에 무궁무진한 유물을 남겨 놓았다. 20세기 들어 이곳에서는 다양한 고대유물이 출토되었는데 그중에서도 옥기는 눈부신 걸작이다.

현재 시안시문물보호고고소(西安市文物保護考古所)에는 1950년대 들어 시안에서 출토, 수집된 고대 옥기 4천여 점이 소장되어 있다. 이들은 종류가 다양하고 체계적으로 정리되어 있어 시안지역 옥기의 역대 발전 상황을 충분히 알 수 있게 해준다.

1

시안은 남전옥(藍田玉)의 고향이다. 남전옥은 오래전부터 이름난 옥이라고 할 만한데 전하는 바에 의하면 헌원황제(軒轅黃帝)가 남전옥으로 병부(兵符, 고대에 명령을 전달하거나 병력을 이동시키고 장수를 파견할 때 사용했던 증표)를 만들어 각 씨족부락의 수령들을 통솔하였다 한다. 시안지역의 신석기시대 및 선진(先秦)시기 유적지, 고분 중에서도 남전옥으로 만들어진 예기(禮器), 병기, 도구 및 장신구가 출토되었다.

남전옥이라는 이름은 『한서(漢書)』「지리지(地理志)」에서 가장 처음 보이는데 아름다운 옥은 '경북(京北, 오늘날 시안 북쪽) 남전산(藍田山)'에서 난다고 적혀 있다. 그 뒤로 『후한서(後漢書)』「외척전(外戚傳)」, 장형(張衡)의 『서경부(西京賦)』, 『광아(廣雅)』, 역도원(酈道元)의 『수경주(水經注)』 및 『원화군현도지(元和郡縣圖志)』 등 수많은 고서에도 남전에서 옥이 난다는 기록이 있다. 훗날 원래 광산의 매장량이 소진되고 양질의 재료가 더는 나오지 않자 한때 채굴을 중지한 듯하다. 이로 인해 송응성(宋應星)은 『천공개물(天工開物)』에서 "남전이라 함은 옥이 나는 총령[蔥嶺, 곤륜산(崑崙山)]의 또 다른 이름일 뿐, 후대 사람들이 서안의 남전으로 오해한 것이다"라고 적기에 이르렀으며 남전을 다만 옥석을 저장하고 운송하는 곳으로 추정하였다. 이는 후대 사람들의 분분한 논쟁을 일으켰는데 일부는 남전에서 옥이 전혀 나지 않았다고 주장했으며 다른 일부는 옥이 났다 하더라도 채옥(茱玉, 남새 잎의 빛이 나는 옥석)이었을 것이라고 하였다. 최근 산시(陝西) 지역 지질학자들은 남전에서 사문석화대리암(蛇文石化大理岩)을 발견하였는데 이것이 곧 고서에 기록된 남전옥이라고 추정하였다. 이 발견은 옥석 재료를 찾고 있던 지질학계뿐만 아니라 고고학자들의 관심을 끌기에 충분했다. 이러한 옥석 재료는 강렬한 사문석화 작용이 일어날 때 일부분이 수옥(岫玉)과 비슷한 옥석으로 변한다. 재질은 외관으로 볼 때, 녹색 얼룩무늬 및 녹색 운무(雲霧) 모양의 무늬가 보이고 부분적으로는 분홍색을 띠며 또한 연한 백색 대리암도 섞여 있다. 이런 옥석은 연마한 후 운무 속의 아침노을과 같은 느낌이 있어 아름답고 절묘하다.

옛사람들은 부드럽고 윤기가 흐르는 아름다운 돌을 전부 옥, 즉 '돌 가운데 아름다운 것은 옥'이라고 간주하였다. 시안지역에서 출토된 선사 및 선진시기의 각종 옥기들은 남전옥 외에도 마노(瑪瑙), 옥수(玉髓), 수정, 대리석, 방해석(方解石), 활석(滑石), 유리(琉璃), 녹송석(綠松石) 및 자수정, 계혈석(鷄血石) 등도 사용하였다. 상대(商代) 말기 이후, 신장(新疆) 화전옥[和闐玉, 연옥(軟玉)의 일종, 속칭은 진옥(眞玉)] 등 각지에서 양질의 옥 재료들이 연이어 중원으로 들어옴으로써 이곳에는 화전옥으로 조각한 옥기들이 점차 많아졌다. 시안지역에서 출토된 한대(漢代) 이후 옥기는 대부분 화전옥을 가공하여 만든 것이고 극히 일부분만이 마노 혹은 기타 옥석 재료를 사용하였다. 비취는 18세기에 미얀마로부터 중국에 유입되면서 신속히 보급되었으며 빛깔이 우아하고 윤기가 나며 매끄러워 옥석 재료 중에 상품(上品)에 속했다.

2

선사 및 선진(先秦)시대, 시안(西安)이 위치한 진(秦)왕조 지역은 옥공예가 발달하였으며 옥기의 조형과 무늬는 선명한 지역적 특징을 띠었다.

지금까지 산시(陝西)에서 발견된 선사시대 옥기는 그다지 많지 않으며 주로 시안 부근과 산베이(陝北) 일대에 집중되어 있다. 그중 앙소문화(仰韶文化) 지역인 시안 반포(半坡), 위화자이(魚化寨), 린퉁(臨潼) 덩자좡(鄧家莊) 및 바오지시(寶鷄市) 푸펑현(扶風縣) 안반촌(案板村) 등 유적지에서는 옥벽(玉璧), 옥비녀와 패식(佩飾)이 출토되었고 용산문화(龍山文化) 지역인 시안 커성좡(客省莊), 산베이 석묘(石峁) 유적지에서는 옥벽, 옥도끼, 옥창이 포함된 예기(禮器) 및 옥 장신구가 출토되었다. 이러한 선사시대 옥기의 주요특징은 기법이 단순하고 평범하며 두께도 일정치 않고, 대부분 기물(器物)의 조형도 불규칙적이다. 그리고 구멍은 그 크기가 상ㆍ주(商ㆍ周)시기보다 조금 크며 마흔(磨痕) 중앙에 위치하지 않는 경우가 종종 보인다.

선사시대 옥기 가운데 가장 특색 있는 것은 앙소문화 지역에서 출토된 '丁(정)'자형 옥석 비녀라 하겠다. 1954년 시안시 바차오구(灞橋區) 반포 유적지에서는 이러한 석제(石制) 장식품 2점이 출토되었다.[1] 1978년 린퉁 덩자좡의 앙소문화 지역 묘저구(廟底溝) 유형의 유적지에서 역시 같은 종류의 장식품 8점이 출토되었는데 그중 하나는 묵옥(墨玉)을 연마하여 만든 것으로 맨 끝은 짙은 녹색을 띠며 재질은 투명하고 빛났다.[2] 1986년 푸펑현 안반촌의 앙소문화 지역 반포 Ⅱ기 유적지에서는 돌로 만든 丁자형 비녀 1점이 출토되었고,[3] 2002년 시안시 옌타구(雁塔區) 위화자이 유적지에서도 옥벽 및 옥비녀가 출토되었다. 상술한 丁자형 비녀는 옥, 돌 외에 도자기로 만들어진 것도 다수 있다. 시안시 반포 유적지에서는 도자기 비녀 백여 점이 출토되었는데 선사시대 산시(陝西) 지역에서 이러한 비녀가 유행하였음을 알 수 있다.[4] 주목할 만한 것은 대다수 丁자형 비녀는 모두 산시 지역에서 발견되었고 기타 지역에서는 보기 힘들다는 것이다. 형태를 보면 산시에서 출토된 옥석 비녀는 산둥(山東)의 대문구문화(大汶口文化),[5] 강남(江南) 지역의 양저문화(良渚文化)[6] 및 광둥(廣東)의 석협문화(石峽文化)[7] 지역에서 출토된 옥석 비녀와 전혀 다른데 이 세 지역의 옥석비녀는 모두 가늘고 긴 원뿔 모양으로 굵은 쪽(손잡이 부분)에 간혹 구멍을 뚫었다. 이를 보면 丁자형 옥석 비녀는 산시 지역의 지방특색을 띤 선사시대 옥석 장신구였음을 알 수 있다.

3

산시에서 발견된 상대(商代) 옥기 역시 적은 편이다. 그중 1972년 시안시 바차오구 라오뉴포에서 출토된 옥창, 1986년 란톈현(藍田縣) 쓰포촌(寺坡村)에서 출토된 옥도끼, 옥삽은 산시 지방에서 출토된 대표적인 상대 옥기이다. 이들은 형태가 반듯하고 가공이 정교하며 날이 예리하고 직선 변과 호형(弧形) 변 모두 단단하고 힘이 있다. 전체적인 광택뿐 아니라 구멍도 모두 세세하게 연마하였다.

주대(周代) 옥기의 조각공예는 전과 비교해 더욱 정교해졌다. 연마한 선이 거침없고 복잡한데 굽은 선이 많아짐으로써 선이 뚜렷하고 매끈하였다. 기물 종류가 늘어난 것 외에 옥 조각기법이나 조형 또한 발달하였다. 기물의 수정(修整) 및 연마기술도 개선되어 날로 아름다워졌다.

서주(西周)의 도읍지였던 시안과 주원(周原, 주나라의 발원지)을 대표로 한 산시의 서주시대 옥기는 뚜렷한 지역적 특징을 가지고 있다. 예컨대 사다리꼴 봉문 혹은 용문 옥패식, 기이한 모양의 봉문옥황, 철식이 있는 봉문병형옥식, 인룡합조옥식 등이다. 이러한 옥기들은 시안 또는 산시 지역의 주대 무덤이나 유적에서 흔히 보이며 기타 지역에서는 거의 보이지 않는다. 구체적으로는 아래와 같다.

1) 사다리꼴 봉문(鳳紋) 또는 용문(龍紋) 옥패식(玉牌飾)

1976년 치산현(岐山縣) 평추촌(鳳雛村) 서주 종묘(宗廟) 건축물 터에서 표면에 한 쌍의 등진 봉황이 음각된 사다리꼴 옥패식 조각 한 점이 출토되었다. 봉황은 눈이 둥글고 볏이 높으며 주둥이가 길고 굽었으며 꼬리 역시 길고 굽었다. 패식의 양 끝에는 각각 한 줄로 배열된 작은 구멍들이(뚫지 않은) 있는데[8] 그 연대는 서주 초기로 추측된다.[9] 이러한 옥패식은 산시에서만 볼 수 있어 주대의 유물일 것으로 추정된다.

2) 기이한 모양의 봉문옥황(鳳紋玉璜)

1954년 창안현(長安縣) 푸두촌(普渡村) 서주 중기 2호 묘지에서 출토되었다. 기체(器體)는 납작하고 얇으며, 평면은 활 모양이고, 활 모양 양측의 넓은 변과 한쪽 좁은 끝에는 각각 '八(팔)'자 모양 볼록 무늬가 있는데 외형의 윤곽으로 보았을 때 마치 파충류인 듯하다. 윤곽 안에는 서 있는 봉황 하나를 음각(陰刻)하였다. 머리를 처든 봉황은 관(冠)이 높고, 긴 꼬리는 위로 말렸으며, 발이 굵고 단단해 보이며, 발아래에는 용머리가 있다. 그 밖에, 푸펑현(扶風縣) 백가묘(白家墓) M9,[10] 바오지시(寶鷄市) 루자좡(茹家莊) 1호 묘지[11]에서도 이와 같은 옥황이 출토되었는데 모두 서 있는 봉황이 음각되어 있다.

이는 지금껏 산시에서만 발견되었으며 기타 지역에서 출토된 고대 옥기 가운데서는 아직 이런 유형이 보이지 않으므로 이를 산시 지역 고유의 옥식(玉飾)으로 여겨도 될 듯하다. 비록 이런 종류가 지닌 상징적 의미를 정확히 알 수 없지만 옥황패식으로 추정된다.

3) 철식(凸飾)이 있는 봉문병형옥식(鳳紋柄型玉飾)

이러한 옥기 중 다수는 긴 꼬리 봉문(鳳紋)이 장식되어 있다. 형태는 상술한 옥황과 비슷한데 앞부분 및 좌우 양 끝에 모두 八자형 볼록 무늬를 새겼다. 다만 기체(器體)가 곧고 평평하며 또한 앞뒤 양 끝에 구멍을 뚫지 않았으므로 패식(佩飾)은 아닌 듯하다. 바오지시 루자좡 서주 묘지의 출토 상황을 보면 장식용 손잡이일 가능성이 크다고 추정된다.[12] 이런 종류의 옥식은 산시에서 가장 많이 발견되었는데 예컨대 창안현 푸두촌 서주 묘지,[13] 바오지시 루자좡 1호 묘지,[14] 푸펑현 창자촌(强家村) 1호 서주 묘지[15] 등지에서 모두 출토되었다. 산시를 제외하고, 유사한 옥기는 여태까지 단지 산둥성(山東省) 지양현(濟陽縣) 류타이쯔(劉臺子) 서주 묘지에서 1점이 출토되었는데 이는 당시 주나라 귀족들이 산시에서 산둥 지역으로 가져간 기물일 가능성이 높다.[16]

4) 인룡합조옥식(人龍合彫玉飾)

산시 지역 특유의 서주시대 옥기이다. 1981년 푸펑현 창자촌 1호 서주 묘지에서 출토된 옥기 중 4점이 바로 이런 종류의 옥식이다.[17] 그중 1점은 무릎을 꿇고 있는 인물 측면 흉부에 용의 머리와 몸(또는 사람 손)이 있고 두부 및 발

아래에 용의 꼬리가 있다. 두 번째 옥식은 조형은 이와 비슷한데 다른 점이라면 사람 발아래에 용머리 하나가 있다. 세 번째 옥식은 조형이 좀 더 복잡하다. 정중앙에는 무릎을 꿇고 있는 인물 측면상이 있는데 흉부에는 혀를 내민 용머리가 있고 엉덩이 아래에는 굽은 꼬리 하나가 있으며 발 앞 끝에는 발톱이 조각되어 하반신이 마치 호랑이 뒷모습과 흡사하다. 사람 머리 위쪽에는 또 다른 혀를 내민 용머리가 있고 용머리 위에도 굽은 꼬리가 하나 있다. 네 번째 옥식은 대체적으로 직사각형 모양인데 주요 부분은 S형 쌍두룡(雙頭龍, 머리와 꼬리에 각기 한 개씩의 용머리가 있음)이다. 용머리는 모두 혀를 내밀었고 혀끝에는 사람머리가 있다. 이 밖에, 우궁현(武功縣) 황자허(黃家河) 서주 묘지 M40에서도 이런 유형의 옥식 한 점이 출토되었다. 용의 몸통은 S형인데 한쪽 끝에는 비교적 큰 용머리가 있고 다른 한쪽 끝에는 이보다 작은 사람머리가 있다.[18]

고고학 연구에 의하면, 푸펑현 창자촌 1호 묘지 및 우궁현 황자허 서주 묘지 M40은 모두 서주 중기에 조성된 것으로 이로써 이같이 사람과 용을 같이 조각한 옥식의 연대를 추정하는 근거가 된다. 지금까지 이러한 옥식은 산시에서 다수 출토되었고 연대 또한 빨라 이러한 옥식이 산시 지역 특유의 옥식일 것으로 추정할 수 있다.

1976년 허난성(河南省) 신정현(新鄭縣) 당호(唐戶) 서주 말기 묘지에서 이런 종류의 옥기 2점이 출토되었는데 산시의 서주 중기 옥기공예를 계승했을 가능성이 높다. 다른 점이라면 사람형상이 상당히 두드러진 반면, 용의 형상이 잘 드러나지 않아 단순한 옥인(玉人)으로 여겨지기 쉽다는 것이다.[19] 옥기 중 1점은, 사람 머리, 몸체 및 하반신에 각각 용머리를 음각하였는데 몸체 부분의 용머리가 좀 뚜렷하고 사람 머리 및 하반신 부분의 용머리는 식별이 어려웠다. 다른 1점도 마찬가지로, 비록 몸체부분의 용머리는 뚜렷하지만 하반신 부분의 용머리는 거의 다 없어지고 다리 중간부위에만 눈썹(뾰족한 모양으로)이 남아 있으며 사람 머리 부분의 용머리도 이미 없어졌다. 이러한 현상은 사람과 용이 같이 조각된 옥기 조형이 점차 쇠락하는 추세였음을 말해 준다.

4

동주(東周)시기에는 사회의 혼란, 예법의 파괴, 왕실의 쇠퇴, 제후들의 분란, 정치상의 장기적 대립 등 원인으로 문화예술은 지역성을 띠게 되었으며 이러한 상황은 옥기 풍격에도 일정 부분 영향을 미쳤다. 예를 들면 진(秦)나라 옥기와 예(豫)·초(楚)·월(越)나라 옥기를 비교할 때 전체적으로 비슷하지만 일부 다른 점도 있었다.

전체적으로 비슷하다는 것은 종류가 기본적으로 같다는 것으로, 대부분 용문(龍紋) 위주의 규(圭), 벽(璧), 황(璜), 형(珩), 결(玦) 등 예기(禮器) 및 패식(佩飾)이다. 이는 춘추(春秋)시대 옥공예의 주류이자 중국의 전통문화 및 예술을 계승한 것이다.

다른 점은 형태 및 무늬의 특이성이다. 다시 말해 진의 옥기는 조형과 무늬가 예, 초, 월 등지의 옥기와 다르다. 이런 차이점의 식별은 매우 중요하며 춘추시대 옥기의 연구에 도움이 된다. 구체적으로 보면 아래와 같다.

1) 옥벽(玉璧)

춘추시대 진(秦) 옥벽의 용문(龍紋) 조형은 모두 기하무늬인데 네모난 머리에 긴 삼각형 모양의 몸과 꼬리를 가졌으며 일부는 전체가 거의 긴 삼각형 모양으로 간소화된 것도 있다. 다른 지역 옥기와 현저히 다른 용문은 특유의 풍격을 충분히 반영하였다. 일부 용문은 도문(綯紋)을 기준으로 나뉘는데 이는 사실상 전국(戰國) 및 양한(兩漢) 시대 용문(혹은 용봉문), 곡문(谷紋), 포문(蒲紋) 등 옥벽 무늬의 원형이다.

2) 옥계벽(玉系璧)

간소화된 용문(龍紋)으로 장식된 작은 계벽은 진(秦) 옥기 중 가장 특색 있는 유형이다. 기하 S형의 용문은 극히 추상화되어 구상적(具象的) 용문과 비교하지 않으면 그 의미를 설명하기 힘들다.

3) 옥결(玉玦)

진(秦) 옥결 중 일부분은 형태 및 무늬가 특이하다. 특징으로는 중간 구멍이 매우 작고, 끊어진 부분은 바깥이 넓고 안쪽이 좁으며, 추상적인 기하 모양 용문(龍紋) 가운데 변형된 운문(雲紋)을 장식하거나 외연에 추상화된 용문을 새겼다. 이런 유형의 옥결은 다른 지역에서 보기 드문 것으로 지역 특색이 짙다.

4) 옥황(玉璜)과 옥형(玉珩)

진(秦) 옥황과 옥형의 가장 뚜렷한 특징은 기하형 용문(龍紋) 또는 용머리로 장식하거나 기하형 S무늬로 간략하게 표현한 것이다. 형태를 보면 어떤 것은 호도(弧度)가 커 긴 막대기에 가까운가 하면 어떤 것은 양쪽 끝이 뾰족한 모양을 이루고 전체적으로 물고기와 비슷하다. 이런 기이한 모양의 옥황은 진의 옥기에서만 보인다.

5) 옥휴(玉觿)

진(秦) 옥휴는 형태적으로 기타 지역에서 출토된 옥휴와 마찬가지로 모두 굽은 짐승의 이빨 모양을 이룬다. 다른 점이라면 기하형 용문(龍紋) 또는 용머리[방형(方形)]를 새긴 것이다.

6) 직사각형 투조용문(透彫龍紋) 옥패식(玉牌飾)

이런 유형의 진(秦) 패식은 직사각형의 표면에 세 줄의 기하형 용문(龍紋)을 수평방향으로 음각하였다. 사각형의 좁은 양 옆과 넓은 윗부분에는 투조 및 음각으로 새긴 기하 모양의 용이 둘러싸고 있다. 다른 지역에서는 볼 수 없는 유일무이한 옥패식으로 매우 진귀하다.

7) 원형(圓形) 투조용문 옥패식

두 마리 용의 머리와 꼬리가 서로 이어진 것으로 중간에 용 발을 투조하고 굽은 용 몸에는 기하형 용문(龍紋)을 가득 음각하였다. 이런 유형 역시 기타 지역에서는 거의 보이지 않는다.

상술한 춘추시대 진(秦) 옥기는 비록 종류는 다르지만 무늬는 거의 같은 모양으로 복잡하거나 간소화된 기하형 용문이다. 이런 유형의 무늬는 산시에서 출토된 도자기[20][21]나 청동기[22][23]에서도 볼 수 있는데 실은 춘추시대 진나라에서 유행하던 공예미술품 장식무늬이다. 이로 볼 때 진대 옥공이 이를 장식무늬로 사용한 것은 당연한 일이었다.

전국(戰國)시대 진의 옥기는 발견된 것이 상당히 적어 시대를 연결하는 역할이 불가능해 예술풍격도 자기만의 특색이 결여되었다. 이는 당시 진나라와 관동 여러 나라들과의 교류가 날로 빈번해졌음을 반영하는 동시에 당시 진나라 사람들이 옥기에 대한 관심이 적어졌음을 말해 준다.

서한(西漢)은 장안(長安)에 도읍을 정하였으며 유적지는 오늘날 시안의 서북부에 위치한다. 여기에는 유명한 미앙궁(未央宮), 건장궁(建章宮), 명광궁(明光宮), 무고(武庫), 상림원(上林苑) 등 유적지가 있으며 주위에 다수의 고분 군(群)이 있다. 여기서 출토된 다량의 유물 중 옥기도 다수 발견되었다.

한대(漢代) 옥기는 재료를 중시해 당시 교통의 발달로 신장(新疆) 화전옥(和闐玉)이 중원으로 끊임없이 유입되었다. 기형(器形)은 옥벽(玉璧), 옥환(玉環), 계심패(雞心佩), 검패(劍佩), 대구(帶鉤) 외에 부장품으로 쓰였던 각종 '명기(明器)' 및 다양한 용기, 감상용 기물도 대량으로 나타났다. 이 밖에 각종 기형(器形)과 무늬에 신화(神話), 고사(故事) 등을 차용하여 신비한 색채를 띠게 되었다. 대형 옥기는 풍격이 소탈하고 도법(刀法)이 단순하며 날이 힘차 보여 '한팔도(漢八刀)'라 불리기도 한다. 소형 옥기는 전체적인 모양이 자연스럽고 간결하며 또한 선이 가늘고 아름답다. 재료는 청옥(青玉), 황옥(黃玉), 묵옥(墨玉) 외에 백옥(白玉)이 당시 옥 중 상품(上品)으로 유행하였다.

위·진·남북조(魏·晉·南北朝)시대는 4백여 년에 이르는데 당시 병법가들이 쟁탈했던 전략적 요충지인 장안과 주변의 관중 지역에는 전쟁이 그치지 않았다. 이곳은 전조(前趙), 전진(前秦), 후진(後秦), 서위(西魏), 북주(北周)의 도읍으로 당시 중국 남·북방 문화 교류의 중심지이기도 하였다. 전쟁이 끊이지 않아 현학(玄學) 및 불교가 성행하고 박장(薄葬)이 점차 풍속으로 되어가면서 옥기의 신비한 색채가 점차 사라지고 수요도 점차 줄어들어 전체적으로 쇠퇴하게 되었다. 시안 지역에서 출토된 당시 옥기는 그 수가 매우 적은 동시에 민무늬 옥패, 옥수(玉獸), 옥선(玉蟬) 및 뉴인(鈕印) 등이 대부분이었으며 조각기법이 단순하고 연마기술도 거칠다.

6

581년, 수(隋)왕조가 전국을 통일함으로써 3백여 년 동안 지속된 할거상태가 끝나게 되었는데 이는 옥기의 발전에 사회적 기초가 되었다. 또한 비단길이 다시 열려 교통이 편리해지면서 신장의 화전옥을 더 용이하게 사용할 수 있게 되었다. 이 시기는 중국 역사에서 보기 드문 전성기로, 특히 초당(初唐) 및 성당(盛唐)시기에는 경제와 문화가 고도로 발전하고 영토도 넓었으며 각 민족이 서로 융합하고 비단길도 열려 광범위하고 심도 있는 대외 문화 교류가 가능해져 심지어 '속국이 알현하고, 외국에서 공물을 바치기'도 하였다. 중국문화의 정수인 옥기 또한 최초로 외래문화의 영향을 받기 시작했다. 예를 들어, 당대(唐代) 옥기 재료는 주로 화전옥을 사용했지만 외국에서 공물로 바친 옥도 사용하였으며 재료뿐만 아니라 외국에서 직접 제작한 옥기도 적지 않았다. 이 밖에, 당대 옥공들은 외국 옥기의 조형을 모방하여 중국인들이 좋아하는 문양을 조각함으로써 당시 옥기는 중국과 외국 문화가 결합된 특징이 나타났다. 또한 당시 옥기는 예부터 이어온 예옥(禮玉)과 장례용 옥이 위주였던 전통에서 벗어나 실용성과 아름다움을 함께 갖춘 장신구용 옥을 위주로 하여 당대 이후의 옥기 발전에 기반이 되었다.

시안 시내에 자리 잡은 당(唐) 흥경궁(興慶宮), 대명궁(大明宮) 유적지 및 주변의 당묘(唐墓)에서는 옥기가 다량 출토되었는데 생활정취가 가득한 화조(花鳥) 및 인물문양이 주를 이룬다. 또한 실용적인 배(杯), 완(盌), 충(盅, 손잡이가 없는 작은 잔) 및 품계를 나타내는 옥대(玉帶) 패식(佩飾)도 나왔다. 옥기는 종류가 풍부하고 당초문(唐草紋), 과일, 날짐승과 길짐승, 하늘을 나는 사람, 벌레와 물고기 등의 도안으로 이루어져 있다. 당대 옥 조각품은 옥대판식(玉帶板飾)에 악기를 든 소수민족이 눈에 띄고 연마기술은 도법이 난잡하지 않고, 배치가 균일하며, 가늘면서도 무게감 있는 것이 특징이다.

7

당대(唐代) 이후 장안(長安)은 비록 도읍의 지위를 상실하였지만 송·원대(宋·元代)에는 여전히 서북 및 서남지역에서 중요한 지리적 역할을 하였다. 당시 옥기의 가장 큰 특징은 세속화 경향이 나타나 생활의 정취가 짙은 것이다.

북송(北宋) 및 남송(南宋)시기 옥기는 꽃, 새, 들짐승과 용봉(龍鳳) 도안이 많았다. 실용품으로는 배(杯), 세(洗), 대판(帶板)이 있으며 장식품은 들짐승과 물고기 모양이 주를 이루었다. 이 밖에, 선진(先秦), 한(漢), 위(魏) 시기의 청동기, 검식(劍飾), 대판, 패식(佩飾)을 모방한 옥기도 성행하였다. 당시 옥기는 조각기술이 정교하고 섬세하며 소형 기물의 수량이 늘어났다.

원대(元代) 옥기는 조각기술이 거친 것도 있고 섬세한 것도 있다. 거친 것은 비록 투박한 듯하지만 도법이 능숙하여 예스러움이 있다. 섬세한 것은 매우 정세(精細)하게 표현되어 옥기에 새긴 털도 도법이 거침없을 뿐만 아니라 운문(雲紋) 또한 아래위로 출렁이는 듯한 것이 기세가 드높다. 당시에는 정세한 부조법과 여러 층의 투조법(透彫法)이 나타났다. 특히 부조법에 사용되는 세공 연마 기법은 당대나 명대(明代)에는 볼 수 없는 원대 옥기만의 특징이다.

원대 옥기는 문양의 미를 추구하기 위하여 재료의 특징을 이용하여 정교한 기물을 가공하기 시작하였다. 도안은 노루, 호랑이, 두루미, 용, 화훼, 소나무 등 무늬를 다량 차용하고 기물종류는 대구(帶鉤), 잔탁(盞托), 향로(香爐), 패식, 말과 각종 조류를 더하였다.

8

명·청대(明·淸代)에 이르러, 장안(長安)은 서안부(西安府)라고 불렸으며 서북지역의 정치, 경제, 문화의 중심지가 되었다. 당시 경제가 고도로 번영하고 시민계층이 신속히 증가하여 옥기의 사용 계층 및 범위도 늘어났으며 기법 수준도 크게 높아졌다. 당시 옥기는 수량, 종류가 많고 재료와 조각이 우수하며 무늬가 아름다워 한대(漢代)와 수·당대(隋·唐代) 이후 다시 한 번 전성기를 맞았다. 또한 후세에 전해지는 것이 많은 반면 출토되는 경우는 상대적으로 적다.

명대 옥기는 도법이 소박하고 힘이 있으며 조각이 섬세하였다. 특히 옥대판(玉帶板)의 예술성이 매우 뛰어났으며 당시 투조기법은 장인들의 독창적인 풍격이다. 문양의 종류도 어느 때보다 다양해 소나무, 대나무, 매화, 꽃과 과일, 송록(松鹿), 인물, 조수(鳥獸), 당초문(唐草紋) 등을 고루 다루었다. 그중에서 용문(龍紋), 송록문 대판이 가장 많다. 흔히 보이는 옥기 종류로는 쟁반, 배(杯), 완(盌), 장식품, 진열품 및 고대패식 모방품, 각종 화편(花片), 교사탁(絞絲鐲) 등이 있다. 명대 말기에 이르러 도교가 성행하였는데 옥 조각공예도 이의 영향을 받아 운학(雲鶴), 송학(松鶴), 복괘(卜卦) 등 도교를 상징하는 도안을 새긴 기물들이 많이 나타났다. 누공(鏤空)은 회전 숫돌로 양면 모두 구멍을 내는 방법을 사용했기 때문에 직사각형 구멍 안에서는 반달 모양 맷돌 흔적을 흔히 볼 수 있다. 이 밖에 명대 옥기는 평평하게 다듬어 기물의 가장자리와 안쪽의 무늬가 똑같이 평평하다. 그러나 마지막 제작 순서인 연마세공(碾磨細工)은 정교하게 다듬은 것과 달리 거친 편이다.

청대 중기에 이르러, 옥 조각공예는 더욱 발전했다. 건륭(乾隆)연간, 베이징(北京)이 전국 옥 제작의 중심지가 되어 수많은 숙련공들이 베이징으로 진출하면서 시안에서 유행하던 옥기들도 대다수 베이징에서 제작하게 되었다. 재료 선택, 가공, 연마 등 제조공정 수준도 더욱 높아졌다. 도안은 보다 풍부해졌으며 고대 청동기 문양 외에 암팔선(暗八仙), 팔보(八寶) 등 도안도 다수 눈에 띄는데 길상(吉祥)을 뜻하는 무늬와 글자들이 자주 쓰였다. 본 연구소에 소장된 청대 옥기는 대부분 후세에 전해진 것들이다.

주석

1) 石興邦, 楊建芳, 金學山：《西安半坡》, 文物出版社, 1963年9月.

2) 趙康民：《臨潼塬頭, 鄧家莊遺址勘查記》,《考古與文物》, 1982年第一期.

3) 西北大學歷史系考古專業實習隊：《陝西扶風縣案板遺址第三, 四次發掘》,《考古與文物》, 1988年第 56期.

4) 同注1.

5) 山東省文物管理處, 濟南市博物館：《大漢口》, 文物出版社, 1974年12月.

6) 南京博物院：《江蘇嗚縣張陵山遺址發掘簡報》,《文物資料叢刊》, 第6集, 1982年7月.

7) 廣東省博物院, 曲江縣文化局：《廣東曲江石峽墓葬發掘簡報》,《文物》, 1978年7期.

8) 陝西周塬考古隊：《陝西岐山鳳雛村西周建筑基址發掘簡報》,《文物》, 1979年10期.

9) 陳全方：《周塬與周文化》上海人民出版社, 1988年9月.

10) 陝西省文物管理委員會：《陝西扶風, 岐山岐代遺址和墓葬調查發掘報告》,《考古》, 1963年第12期.

11) 盧連成, 胡智生：《寶鷄强國墓地》, 文物出版社, 1988年10月.

12) 楊建芳：《一種造型奇特的西周玉牌飾》,《中國文物世界》(香港), 1988年2月.

13) 五省重要出土文物展覽籌備委員編：《陝西, 江蘇, 熱河, 安徽, 山西五省出土重要文物展覽圖錄》, 文物出版社, 1958年3月.

14) 同12.

15) 周塬扶風文管所：《陝西扶風强家一號西周墓》,《文博》, 1987年第4期.

16) 德州行署文化局文物組, 濟陽縣圖書館：《山東濟陽劉台子西周早期墓發掘簡報》,《文物》, 1981年第9期.

17) 楊伯達, 周南泉主編：《中國美術全集・工藝美術編(9)》, 1986年7月.

18) 中國社會科學院考古研究所武功發掘隊：《1982-1983年陝西武功黃家河遺址發掘簡報》,《考古》, 1988年第7期.

19) 開封地區文管會等：《河南省新鄭縣唐戶兩周墓葬發掘簡報》,《文物資料叢刊》, 第2集, 1978年12月.

20) 嗚鎭烽, 尙志儒：《陝西鳳翔八旗屯秦國墓葬發掘簡報》,《文物資料叢刊》, 第3集, 1980年5月.

21) 嗚鎭烽, 志儒：《陝西鳳翔高莊秦墓地發掘簡報》,《考古與文物》, 1981年第1期.

22) 中國科學院考古研究所寶鷄發掘隊：《陝西寶鷄福臨堡東周墓葬發掘記》, 1963年第10期.

23) 李學勤：《秦國文物的新認識》,《文物》, 1980年第9期.

西安，古稱“長安”。這里氣候溫和，川原秀麗，卉物滋阜，自古就有“天府”的美譽，是中華文明的發祥地之一。早在遙遠的石器時代，華夏的祖先就在這里繁衍生息。公元十一世紀西周王朝卽建都于此，從而開始了西安三千多年持續不斷的城市發展史，特別是周、秦、漢、唐時期，這里不但是全國政治中心，而且是手工業、商業、教育、藝術中心。悠久的歷史和燦爛的文明給這座古城留下了數不盡的文物寶藏。二十世紀以來，這里先後出土了數以万計的各類古代遺物，玉器就是其中一束格外璀璨的奇葩。

我們西安市文物保護考古所文物庫房現收藏有二十世紀五十年代以來西安出土、征集的古代玉器四千余件。這些玉器種類齊全，序列完整，可以反映西安地區各時代玉器發展的基本狀況。

一

西安是藍田玉的故鄉。藍田玉可謂久負盛名，相傳軒轅黃帝曾用藍田玉制作兵符，統領各氏族部落的首領。在西安地區的新石器時代和先秦時期的遺址、墓葬中就出去過用藍田玉制做的禮器、兵器、工具和佩飾。

藍田玉的名稱初見于《漢書·地理志》，美玉產自“京北(今西安北)藍田山”。其後，《後漢書·外戚傳》、張衡《西京賦》、《廣雅》、酈道元《水經注》和《元和郡縣圖志》等衆多古籍中都有藍田產玉的記載。後來舊礦窮竭，不出佳材，似乎曾一度停采，以致宋應星在《天工開物》中稱：“所謂藍田，卽葱岭(昆侖山)出玉之別名，而後也誤以爲西安之藍田也。”并推論藍田爲儲運玉石之地，從此引起後人的紛爭，有的說藍田根本不產玉，有的說卽使產玉也應是菜玉(色綠似菜葉的玉石)。近年，陝西地質工作者在藍田發現了蛇紋石化大理岩玉料，認爲它就是古代所記載的藍田玉。這一發現不僅引起了尋找玉石原料的地質界的重視，也引起了考古工作者的興趣。這種玉石料在蛇紋石化強烈時，局部就變成與岫玉相似的玉石。玉質從外觀上看，呈綠色斑紋和綠色雲霧狀紋，局部有粉紅色，并伴有淺白色的大理石，抛光後有似雲霧中的朝霞之感，美倫美奐。

古人視一切溫潤有光的美石爲玉，卽“石之美者爲玉”。西安地區出土的史前和先秦時期各類玉器，用材除藍田玉外，還有瑪瑙、玉髓、水晶、大理石、方解石、滑石、琉璃、綠松石及紫晶、鷄血石等。商代晚期以後，和闐玉等各地優質玉材陸續進入中原地區，本地以和闐玉雕琢的玉器漸漸增多。至漢以後，西安地區出土的玉器几乎都用和闐玉加工而成，僅有少量采用瑪瑙或其他玉材。翡翠玉十八世紀由緬甸傳入我國并迅速普及，其色莊重典雅，滋潤細膩，屬各類玉材中的上品。

二

史前和先秦時期，西安所處的秦地爲玉雕發達地區之一，其造型和紋飾具有明顯的區域特征。

迄今爲止，陝西發現的史前玉器并不多，主要集中在西安附近和陝北一帶。其中仰韶文化的西安半坡遺址、魚化寨遺址、臨潼鄧家莊遺址以及寶鷄的扶風案板村遺址，先後出了玉璧、玉笄和佩飾；而龍山文化的西安客省莊遺址、陝北石峁遺址出土了包括玉璧、玉斧、玉戈在內的禮器和玉飾品。這些史前玉器的主要特點是：工藝簡單平素，磨制厚薄不一，大部分器物造型不規則，鑽孔較商周時期稍大，孔洞往往不在磨痕正中。

史前玉器中最具特色的當屬仰韶文化的丁字形玉石笄。1954年西安市灞橋區半坡遺址出土二件此種飾物，材質爲石質[1]。1978年臨潼縣鄧家莊仰韶文化廟底溝類型遺址又出土八件此種飾物，其中一件爲墨玉磨制，尖端呈深綠色，質地晶瑩[2]。1986年扶風縣案板村仰韶文化半坡Ⅱ期遺址，出土一件石質丁字形笄[3]。2002年西安市雁塔區魚化寨遺址也出土了玉璧和玉笄。上述丁字形笄，除玉、石質外，尚有大量屬陶制。西安半坡遺址曾出土一百余件此類陶笄，足見此種笄實爲陝西地區史前時期流行的飾物[4]。值得注意的是，丁字形石笄大多數發現于陝西境內，其他地區稀見。從形制方面來看，陝西出土的玉石笄與山東大汶口文化[5]、江南地區良渚文化[6]及廣東石峽文化[7]出土之玉石笄迥然不同，後三者之玉石笄皆呈細長園錐狀，粗端(柄部)間或穿孔。顯然，丁字形玉石笄爲陝西地區一種極富地方特色的史前玉、石飾物。

三

陝西發現的商代玉器也很少，1972年西安市灞橋區老牛破出土的玉戈，1986年藍田縣寺坡村出土的玉斧、玉鏟是本地商代玉器的代表。其形制規整，加工精細，鋒刃犀利，直邊、弧邊均鋼勁有力。拋光碾磨精細，甚至連穿孔和扉芽的間隙都作了仔細碾磨。

周代玉器的琢工，精細程度較前代進了一大步。琢制線條流暢、復雜，彎曲線條增多，線條顯的清晰、挺拔。除器物品種有所增加外，琢玉技法、造型設計也不斷改進。器物修整以及拋光技術均有長足進步，器物日趨美觀。

西安爲西周的都城所在地，以這里和周原爲代表的陝西西周玉器具有鮮明的區域特點，如梯形鳳(或龍)紋玉牌飾、鳳紋異形玉璜、帶凸飾之柄形玉飾、人龍合雕玉飾等。此等玉器僅見或常見于西安或陝西境內的周代墓葬或遺迹，不見或少見于其他地區。具体論述如下：

1、梯形鳳(或龍)紋玉牌飾：1976年，岐山縣鳳雛村西周宗廟建筑基址出土一件片狀梯形玉牌飾，它的表面陰刻一對背向鳳鳥，園眼、高冠、長彎啄、長尾卷曲。牌飾上下端分別有排成一列的小園孔(未穿透)[8]，其年代爲西周早期[9]。這種玉飾迄今只見于陝西，當爲周人之遺存。

2、鳳紋異形玉璜：1954年，長安縣普渡村西周中期二號墓出土一件鳳紋異形玉璜。器体扁薄，平面呈弧形，弧形兩側寬邊及一狹端分別有八字形凸飾，其外形輪廓彷彿爲爬行動物。輪廓內有一陰刻立鳳，昂首、高冠、長尾上卷，足粗壯，鳳足下爲一龍頭紋。此外，扶風白家墓M9[10]、寶雞茹家莊一號墓[11]亦曾出土此種玉璜，後者同樣有陰刻立鳳紋。

上述鳳紋異形玉璜迄今僅在陝西發現，其他地區出土古玉中尚未見到，故可認爲是一種具强烈地方色彩的玉飾。此種玉飾的象征意義不明，然充作玉璜挂佩則應無疑問。

3、帶凸飾的鳳紋柄形飾：這種玉器多飾長尾鳳紋，其形制與上述鳳紋異形玉璜近似，前端及左右側端皆有八字形凸飾，只是器身平直，且前後兩端無穿孔，當非挂佩飾品。由寶雞茹家莊西周墓的清理與發現，可知這種器物很可能是作爲裝飾性器柄使用的[12]。此種玉飾以陝西發現最多，比如長安普渡村西周墓[13]、寶雞茹家莊一號墓[14]、扶風強家村一號西周墓[15]等均有出土。陝西之外，類似的玉器迄今僅于山東濟陽劉臺子西周墓出土一件，這极可能是周人貴族由陝西携帶到山東地區的器物[16]。

4、人龍合雕玉飾：這是陝西出土的另一類具有地區特色的西周玉器。1981年，扶風強家村一號西周墓出土一批玉器，有四件此種玉飾[17]。其中一件爲屈膝蹲姿的側面人像，其胸部有一龍頭及龍身(兼作人手)，龍尾則在人之臀部及足下端。另一件造型與此相似，惟足下接一龍頭。第三件造型較復雜，正中爲一屈膝蹲姿側面人像，它的胸部有一吐舌龍頭，臀下有一卷尾，足前端雕爪，整個下半身似虎後半部；人頭上端爲另一吐舌龍頭，此龍頭之上尙有一卷尾。第四件的輪廓大致呈長方形，主體爲一S形的雙頭龍(首尾各有一龍頭)。龍頭均吐舌，舌末端連接一人頭。此外，武功黃家河西周墓M40亦出土一件人龍合雕玉飾，龍身呈S形，一端爲較大龍頭，另一端爲較小人頭[18]。

考古研究表明，扶風強家村一號墓及武功黃家河M40均屬西周中期，這爲此類人龍合雕玉飾年代的推定提供了可靠的依据。目前所知，人龍合雕玉器以陝西出土較多，且年代亦較早，故有理由推定其爲陝西富于特色的玉飾。

1976年，河南新鄭縣唐戶西周晚期墓出土兩件人龍合雕玉器，這應是陝西西周中期人龍合雕玉器工藝的延續。只是其人形頗爲突出，而龍的形象則較爲隱晦，一致易遭忽略，而被視爲單純的玉人[19]。其中一件的人頭、身軀及下肢分別加陰刻龍頭，且以身軀部分的龍頭較顯著，人頭及下肢部分的龍頭則難以辨識。另一件身軀部分的龍頭也极顯著，但下肢部分的龍頭則消失殆盡，僅于腿中部殘留眼眉(呈尖狀)，而人頭部分的龍頭已不存在。這種現象說明人龍合雕造型開始趨于式微。

四

東周時期，社會動蕩、禮崩樂壞、王室哀落、諸侯紛起，政治上的長期對立導致了文化藝術上地域性的出現。這一狀況在玉器風格上也有所反映。秦國(秦式)玉器與豫、楚、越等地玉器比較，于大同中具小異。

所謂大同，指秦式玉器的各種與豫、楚、越等地玉器的種類基本相同，多爲圭、璧、璜、珩、玦等禮器及佩飾，且都以龍紋爲主要紋飾。這旣是春秋玉雕的主流，又堪稱中國傳統文化及藝術的延續。

所謂小異，指形制與紋飾方面的特殊性。換言之，秦式玉器的造型及紋飾，于豫、楚、越等地玉器不盡相同。這種差異的辨識至爲重要，有助于我們對春秋玉器的深入研究。具體而言，可略述爲：

1、玉璧：春秋秦式玉璧上的龍紋造型均呈几何圖案化，頭呈方形，身尾爲長三角形，一些龍紋几乎全形簡化爲長三角形。此等形象與其他地區玉器上的龍紋大相徑庭，充分顯示了它特殊的紋飾風格。有的龍紋以絢紋分隔，這種作法實爲戰國及兩漢龍紋(或龍鳳)、谷紋(或蒲紋)等玉璧紋飾構圖的淵源。

2、玉系璧：飾有簡化龍紋的小系璧，是秦式玉器中最具特色的一種，其龍紋呈几何S形，极抽象化，若不與具象龍紋比較，很難說明其涵義。

3、玉玦：秦式玉玦中有的形制與紋飾較特殊，其特點爲：中孔极小，缺口外寬內窄，抽象的几何形龍紋中飾變形雲紋，間或于外側邊緣加刻抽象龍紋。這類玉玦在其他地區很少見，極富地域特色。

4、玉璜與玉珩：秦式玉璜與玉珩最顯著的特點，是以几何形龍紋或龍頭爲飾，間或簡化爲几何形S紋。形制方面，有的弧度极大，几乎近于長條形；也有兩端呈尖狀，全形似魚者。這類奇形怪狀的玉璜，爲秦氏玉器所獨有。

5、玉觿：秦式玉觿形制與其他地區玉觿相似，皆呈彎曲的獸牙狀，所不同的是以几何形龍紋或龍頭（方形）爲紋飾。

6、長方透雕龍紋玉牌飾：這種秦式牌飾的主体爲一長方塊狀，表面飾三橫列陰刻几何形龍紋。長方塊左右兩狹端，及上側寬端，有透雕及陰刻的几何圖案化龍形圍繞。這種玉飾未見于其他地區，亦爲迄今所僅見。

7、園形透雕龍紋玉牌飾：這種牌飾爲二龍首尾相接而成，中間透雕出龍足，彎曲的龍身滿飾陰刻几何形龍紋。此種玉飾亦不見于其他地區。

以上列舉的春秋秦式玉器，盡管種類有異，而紋飾則基本相同，爲繁縟或簡化的几何形龍紋。此類紋飾亦見于陝西出土的陶器[20][21]及青銅器[22][23]，實爲春秋時期秦國流行的工藝美術品裝飾紋樣，故秦國玉工以之作爲玉器紋飾是十分自然的事。

戰國時代秦的玉器發現量少，時代環節也不夠完整，藝術風格缺乏自身特色，這既反映出此時秦與關東諸國交流的日益頻繁，同時也表明當時秦人對玉器較少着意。

五

西漢帝國建都于長安，其遺址在今西安城的西北部，有著名的未央宮、建章宮、明光宮、武庫、上林苑等遺址，其周圍有很多墓葬區。出土的文物較丰富，玉器也很多。

漢代玉器非常重視選材，由于交通方便，新疆和闐玉源源不斷流入中原。器形除玉璧、玉環、鷄心佩、劍佩、帶鉤外，各種用于殉葬的"明器"和各式容器、玩賞品種大量出現，而且各種器形和紋飾多摹擬神話故事，富有神秘色彩。大件玉器比較粗擴，刀法簡單，見鋒有力，有"漢八刀"之稱。小件玉器線條流暢簡潔，刻出的線條非常纖細、美觀。玉材除青玉、黃玉、墨玉外，白玉開始流行，成爲當時玉中上品。

魏晉南北朝，連綿近四百年，長安與其周圍關中地區烽火不斷，兵連禍結，成爲兵家爭奪之地，先後爲前趙、前秦、後秦、西魏、北周的京都，是當時中國南北方文化的交流中心。由于戰爭頻繁，玄學流行，佛教興盛，薄葬成俗，玉器的神秘色彩逐漸消失，玉器需求量明顯減少，整個玉器的制作雕琢呈現出一派停滯衰敗的狀態。西安地區出土的此時期玉器數量較少，主要有素面玉佩、玉獸、玉蟬和鈕印等，其中多數雕工簡單，碾磨粗率，拋光不精。

六

公元581年，隋王朝統一了全國，結束了三國魏晉南北朝三百余年的分裂割据狀態，爲玉器的發展尊定了基礎。絲綢之路的重新開通，爲隋朝使用新疆和闐美玉提供了交通上的便利。唐代是中國歷史上少有的鼎盛時期，特別是初唐和盛唐，經濟和文化高度繁榮，疆域遼闊，民族融合，絲綢之路的暢通使中外文化交流廣泛而深入，曾出現了"万邦來朝，絶域入貢"的盛況。而最具中國文化特質的玉器也首次受到外來文化的影響和冲擊，唐王朝使用的玉除主要來自新疆和闐外，還有不少域外的貢玉，不僅有玉材，而且還有域外制作的玉器。另外，唐朝的玉工還模仿域外玉器的造型，雕琢中國人喜聞樂見的紋樣，使得此期玉器具有中外文化結合的特征。且玉器擺脱了上古以禮爲中心、以喪葬用玉爲主的傳統，開創了以實用玉器爲中心、以美觀爲主的人体裝飾用玉的新時代，爲唐代以後玉器的發展尊定了良好的基礎。

西安市内的唐興慶宮、大明宮遺址和周邊唐墓出土了大量高品質的唐代玉器，它們主要以花鳥、人物紋爲飾，富有濃郁的生活氣息。并出現了有實用价值的杯、碗、盅以及表示統治者官階高下的玉帶飾物等。玉器的品種丰富，圖案多采用纏枝花卉、瓜果、鳥獸、人物飛天、蟲魚爲主要題材。玉帶板飾中的人物大多數爲少數民族手持樂器，這是唐代玉雕的獨特風格。刀法不亂，布局均勻，細而厚重，爲唐代玉琢的一大特點。

七

唐代以後，長安雖然失去了國都的地位，但在宋元時期仍是控制西北和西南地區的重鎮。此時期玉器的最大特點是强烈的世俗化傾向和濃郁的生活氣息。

兩宋玉器，以花、鳥、獸類爲主，以龍鳳祥圖案爲多。實用品有杯、洗、帶板，陳設品主要有獸、魚。此外，仿古玉器開始盛行，以仿先秦漢魏的青銅器、劍飾、帶板、佩飾爲主。此時玉器雕工細膩靈巧，小件增多，大件减少。

元代玉器的雕工有粗、有細，粗琢的器物粗獷，但刀法深厚，頗有古風；細致的器物細得出奇，就連獸件上雕刻的毛發也刀法流暢，刻出的雲紋上下翻騰，氣勢磅礴。這一時期還出現了細致的凸雕法和二三層的透雕法，尤其是凸雕的細工碾磨技法，在唐代或者是明代器物中是無法找到的，這是元代玉雕器物的一個主要特征。

元代玉器在紋飾技巧上，爲了美觀，開始利用玉材的特點加工巧琢的器物。圖案設計大量采用鹿紋、虎紋、鶴紋、龍紋、花卉、松樹等。另在器物品種上增加了帶鈎、盞托、香爐、佩飾、馬及各種鳥類等。

八

明清時期，長安稱爲西安府，是西北地區的政治、經濟、文化中心。當時經濟高度繁榮，市民階層迅速擴大，玉器的服務對象與范圍也相應擴大，工藝水平大爲提高。當時玉器的數量之多，品種之繁，玉質之佳，雕琢之精，紋飾之美，可謂空前絕後，成爲繼漢和隋唐之後的又一高峰。此期玉器以傳世的居多，出土的相對較少。

明代玉雕刀法粗獷有力，雕琢十分精細，特別是在玉帶板上表現得淋漓盡致，藝術性很高，這種透雕技法是明代藝人的獨創風格。紋飾之多爲前代所不及，常見的有松竹梅、花果、松鹿、人物、鳥獸、纏技花卉等，以龍紋、松鹿紋的帶板最多。常見的玉器品種有盤、杯、碗、裝飾用品、陳設品和仿古佩飾、各種花片、絞絲鐲等。到了明代晚期，道教盛行，玉雕工藝在其影響下有制琢出很多雲鶴、松鶴、卜挂一類標志道教圖案的器物。由于縷空方法是用釺砣雙面鏤孔，在長方形孔洞內常見半月形的砣痕。另外，明代玉器是平整磨面，琢出的器物邊框和里邊的花紋一樣平整。與琢工精細不相稱的是，最後一道工序(碾磨細工)比較粗糙。

清代，特別是清代中期，玉雕工藝發展到了一個新的高峰，乾隆年間北京成爲全國的制玉中心，各路能工巧匠紛紛進京獻藝，西安流行的玉器多由北京制成。當時，對玉材選用、加工、磨光等工序，也進一步提出了更高的要求。玉器圖案丰富多彩，除仿古銅器紋飾盛行外，暗八仙、八寶等圖案也活躍在玉器上，吉祥寓意的紋飾、字樣是當時的主要題材，我們收藏的清代玉器多爲傳世品。

注释

1) 石興邦、楊建芳、金學山：《西安半坡》，文物出版社，1963年9月。

2) 趙康民：《臨潼塬頭、鄧家莊遺址勘查記》，《考古與文物》，1982年第一期。

3) 西北大學歷史系考古專業實習隊：《陝西扶風縣案板遺址第三、四次發掘》，《考古與文物》，1988年第56期。

4) 同注1。

5) 山東省文物管理處、濟南市博物館：《大漢口》，文物出版社，1974年12月。

6) 南京博物院：《江蘇吳縣張陵山遺址發掘簡報》，《文物資料叢刊》，第6集，1982年7月。

7) 廣東省博物院、曲江縣文化局：《廣東曲江石峽墓葬發掘簡報》，《文物》，1978年7期。

8) 陝西周塬考古隊：《陝西岐山鳳雛村西周建築基址發掘簡報》，《文物》，1979年10期。

9) 陳全方：《周塬與周文化》上海人民出版社，1988年9月。

10) 陝西省文物管理委員會：《陝西扶風、岐山岐代遺址和墓葬調查發掘報告》，《考古》，1963年第12期。

11) 盧連成、胡智生：《寶鷄强國墓地》，文物出版社，1988年10月。

12) 楊建芳：《一種造型奇特的西周玉牌飾》，《中國文物世界》(香港)，1988年2月。

13) 五省重要出土文物展覽籌備委員編：《陝西、江蘇、熱河、安徽、山西五省出土重要文物展覽圖錄》，文物出版社，1958年3月。

14) 同12。

15) 周塬扶風文管所：《陝西扶風強家一號西周墓》，《文博》，1987年第4期。

16) 德州行署文化局文物組、濟陽縣圖書館：《山東濟陽劉台子西周早期墓發掘簡報》，《文物》，1981年第9期。

17) 楊伯達、周南泉主編：《中國美術全集・工藝美術編(9)》，1986年7月。

18) 中國社會科學院考古研究所武功發掘隊：《1982-1983年陝西武功黃家河遺址發掘簡報》，《考古》，1988年第7期。

19) 開封地區文管會等：《河南省新鄭縣唐戶兩周墓葬發掘簡報》，《文物資料叢刊》，第2集，1978年12月。

20) 吳鎮烽、尙志儒：《陝西鳳翔八旗屯秦國墓葬發掘簡報》，《文物資料叢刊》，第3集，1980年5月。

21) 吳鎮烽、尙志儒：《陝西鳳翔高莊秦墓地發掘簡報》，《考古與文物》，1981年第1期。

22) 中國科學院考古研究所寶雞發掘隊：《陝西寶雞福臨堡東周墓葬發掘記》，1963年第10期。

23) 李學勤：《秦國文物的新認識》，《文物》，1980年第9期。

Xi'an is know as "Chang'an" in the ancient times. With mild climate, beautiful landscape, abundant plants and animals, this place became the cradle of Chinese civilization and has always been called "heavenly place". Early in the stone Age, the forefathers of Huaxia nation had lived here. In the eleventh century BC, the West Zhou Dynasty set its capital here. Thus started the over three thousand years of civil phylogeny for Xi'an. In Zhou, Qin, Han and Tang Dynasties, this place had been the center for handicraft industry, commerce, education, art, and religious belief of the whole country. Long history and brilliant civilization has left this place with countless cultural treasures. Since the twentieth century, tens of thousands of various antiques had been excavated from here, among which, jade article is an extraordinary resplendent flower.

The collections in the depositary of Xi'an Cultural Relic Protection Archeology Institute have more than four thousand pieces of jade articles that were excavated since 1950s. These jade articles are complete in category, intact in list sequence and can reflect the basic information of the jade article development in Xi'an indifferent periods of time. The following is the brief introduction of jade articles in Xi'an from several aspects.

I

Lantian Jade has enjoyed great reputation since long ago. It is said the early emperor Xuanyuan had used Lantian jade to make military tally to rule the leaders of different tribes. Ritual articles, weapons, tools and pendants that were made from Lantian jade had been excavated in the relics and tombs of the Neolithic Age and early Qin Period.

The appellation of Lantian jade was first seen in the <Book of Han>, which said that the beautiful jade was discovered in the Lantian Mountain of Jingbei(in the north of Xi'an now). After that, several ancient books had recorded that Lantian did have jade. Later, the old jade mines were exhausted and no fine jade could be found there. The mining seemed to come a halt for sometime. As a result, Song Yingxing said in his book <tian-gong-kai-wu>: "the so called Lantian, is the misnomer of Congling(Kunlun Mountain) which is the real place that produces jade. The later generations had mistakenly took it for Lantian in Xi'an." Song Yingxing even made the conclusion that Lantian is the place for the store and transportation of jade. Thus came the dispute among people. Some said Lantian doesn't have jade at all. Others said even if this place did have jade. it could be the vegetable jade (jade that has the green color like the leaf of the vegetable) Recently, some geologists discovered the serpentine marble jade material and believed that to be the Lantian jade described in the ancient times. This discovery not only was valued by the geologists, but also brought on the interests of the archeologists. When serpentine petrifaction process is strong enough, part if the stone material became jade that is similar to Xiu jade. From outer appearance, the jade has green spotty patterns and mist, part of it is in pink, accompanied by ivory colored marble. After polishing, the stone looks beautiful like the morning sunglow in the midst of cloud.

Ancient people regarded all smooth and glossy stones as jade. Among the jade articles that were excavated prehistorically and in the early Qin Dynasty, the material of those articles, besides Lantian Jade, are agate, chalcedony, crystal, marble, calcite, talcum, colored glaze, turquoise, purple crystal. blood chalcedony etc. Since late Shang Dynasty, fine jade materials such as Hetian jade continually entered the midland, jade pieces that were made of Hetian jade gradually increased and after Han Dynasty, almost all the jade articles excavated in Xi'an were made of Hetian Jade, the rest of which used agate or other materials. Emerald entered our country from Burma in the eighteenth century and soon became popular With the color venerable and elegant; texture moist and smooth, emerald is regarded as one of the best jade materials.

II

In the prehistorical and early Qin Dynasty, the Qin land, which is where Xi'an lies now, is one of the centers of jade carvings. The patterns and decorations also bear distinct regional traits.

There are not many prehistoric jade articles in Xi'an heretofore, most of which are ritual articles, tools and ornaments. The major characteristics are: simple craftworks, uneven thickness, irregular shape, larger bores(compared with that in Shang and Zhou Dynasties). Besides, the bores are often not in the center of the article.

The most characteristic prehistoric jade article in Shaan'xi Province is the t-shaped jade Ji(hair pin) in the Yang-shao Culture. In the l950s, two such ornaments were excavated in the Ban-po Relics in Xi'an. It was reported that the ornaments were made of stone. In l978, eight such ornaments were excavated in the Yang-shao Culture in Miaodigou Relics at Dengjiazhuang in Lintong County. One of them is made of celadon jade. The tip of which is deep green with glittering and translucent texture. Among the relic of Yang-shao Culture in Banpo at Anban Village, Fufeng County, a stone t-shaped jade Ji was also excavated in 1986 Beside jade and stone. such t-shaped Ji were also made of clay, Over one hundred such clay-made Ji were excavated in Banpo Relic in Xi'an, which shows that Ji was indeed the prevalent ornament in prehistoric period in Shaan'xi area. It is worth noticing that t-shaped stone Ji were most found in Shaan'xi, and were rarely seen in other areas. Compared with those excavated in Dawenkou Culture in Shandong, Liangzhu Culture in Jiangnan area, as well as Shi-xia Culture in Guangdong, the shape of jade and stone Ji in Shaan'xi is quite different. The Ji in those three areas were all in slender taper shape, the wide end (handle) of which may or may not have perforation. Apparently, the t-shaped Stone and jade Ji is a characteristic regional prehistoric ornament in Shaan'xi area.

III

Not many jade articles in Shang Dynasty were found in Shaan'xi, the representatives of which is the jade dagger-axe which was excavated in Laoniupo at east suburb of Xi'an in 1972 and the jade spade found ai Sipo Village in Lantian County in 1982. Those articles were regular in shape and meticulous in production. The blades are sharp and the ridges are strong and forceful. Not only were the two articles finely polished, but also the bores and crevices of the ridges were carefully grinded.

The carving technique had greatly improved in the degree of refinement in Zhou Dynasty The lines are smooth and intricate with more curves. The decoration looks clear and legible. Beside the increasing varieties, the carving technique and sculpt design has been ameliorated as well, together with improved repairing and polishing techniques. All these made the jade articles even more beautiful.

Xi'an is the capital city in West Zhou Dynasty, and the jade articles in West Zhou Dynasty in Shaan'xi had distinct regional feature, such as the trapezoid-shaped jade board pendant with phoenix (or dragon) patterns, irregular shaped jade plaque with phoenix pattern, handle shaped jade pendant with relief decorations, as well as jade ornament with human and dragon carvings. Such articles are mainly found in Xi'an or other Zhou Tomb Relics within Shaan'xi Province and seldom found elsewhere.

The following is the description of those West Zhou ornaments:

1. Trapezoid-shaped jade board pendant with phoenix (or dragon) patterns: a trapezoid jade board flake was excavated in the building site of Zong Temple in the West Zhou Dynasty at Fengchu Village in Qishan County in 1976, the surface of which is carved in intagliated lines with a pair of phoenixes standing back to back. The phoenixes have round eyes, tall crests, long and hooked beaks, as well as coiling long tails. A group of small holes(unpenetrated) were found on both upper and lower ends of the board. The time is early West Zhou Dynasty, and such ornaments were only found in Shaan'xi, and might be possessed by people in Zhou Dynasty.

2. Irregular shaped jade plaque with phoenix pattern: an irregular shaped jade plaque with phoenix pattern was excavated in the No.2 Tomb (middle Zhou Dynasty) at Pudu Village in Chang'an County in 1954. The ornament is thin and flat, with arc-shaped surface. The two wide ends of the arc and one pointed end have λ-shaped carvings in relief. The outline of it resembles reptile, inside the outline is a standing phoenix carved in intagliated lines. The phoenix has a lifted head, tall crest, upcoiled long

tail, and strong feet. Beneath the feet of the phoenix is a dragon head. In addition, such jade plaques were also excavated in the Baijia Tomb in Fufeng County and the No.1 Tomb in Rujiazhuang in Baoji City. These plaques are also carved with standing phoenixes in intagliated lines.

So far, such irregular jade plaques are found only in Shaan'xi and not in other areas. Thus it can be sure that such ornaments bear Strong regional features. The symbolizing significance of such object is not clear, yet undoubtedly it can he used the same as jade Huang. Such pendant excavated in the No.2 Tomb in Pudu Village was placed on the chest of the dead. as the ornament worn at the chest, same as jade Huang(plaque) in function.

3. Handle shaped jade pendant with phoenix patterns in relief: such jade articles are mainly decorated with long-tailed phoenix patterns, the shape of which is similar to the irregular jade plaque described above. It also have λ-shaped carvings in relief on the frontal and lateral ends. Only the body is flat and there is no bore on the surface. It is not the pendant for hanging. According to the study and discovery of the West Zhou Tomb in Rujiazhuang in Baoji City, such jade ornaments might well be used as the decorative handles. This kind of pendants are found mainly in Shaan'xi, such as West Zhou Tomh in Pudu Village in Chang'an County, No.1 Tomb in Rujiazhuang in Baoji city, No.1 West Zhou Tomb in Qiangjia Village in Fufeng County, etc. Only one piece of such jade article was found in the West Zhou Tomb in Liutaizi at Jiyang, Shandong Province, which was probably brought to Shandong from Shaan'xi by aristocracies of Zhou Dynasty.

4. Jade ornament with human and dragon carvings: this is another Jade article in West Zhou Dynasty that were excavated in Shaan'xi with strong regional features. A passel of jade articles were excavated in the No.1 West Zhou Tomb in Qiangjia Village in Fufeng County, among which, four belong to this type. One is the profile of a human with bending knees in squat position.

On its chest is a dragon head and body (also served as human hand) The tail of the dragon is at the buttocks of the man as well as beneath the feet. The second piece is similar to the first one; only the dragon head is beneath the feet of the human. The third one is more complicated. In the middle is the profile of a human with bending knees in squat position, on whose chest is a dragon head with tongue hanging out. Under the man's buttocks is a coiling tail, on the tip of the feet is the claws. The whole lower part of the human body resembles the hind part of a tiger. On the top of the human head is another dragon head with hanging tongue, on top of the dragon head is another coiling tail. The contour of the fourth one is approximately rectangular shaped, the main body of which is an S-shaped double-headed dragon(one dragon head in each end). The two dragon heads both have hanging tongues Each tongue-tip is connected with a human head. Beside that, another jade ornament with human and dragon patterns was excavated from the West Zhou Tomb M40 at Huangjiahe in Wugong County. The body of the dragon is S-shaped, the larger end of which is a dragon head and the smaller end of which is a human head.

The archeological research has proved that the No.1 Tomb at Qiangjia Village in Fufeng County and Huangjiahe M40 Tomb in Wugong County both belong to the middle period of West Zhou Dynasty. Thus reliable evidence was provided on determining the year of such jade pendants with human and dragon patterns. According to present knowledge, such jade articles are mainly found in Shaan'xi Province and are relatively early in the times. Therefore, we have reason to believe that this is another type of jade article that bears the regional features of Shaan'xi.

In 1976, two jade articles with human and dragon patterns were excavated at the late West Zhou Tomb in Tanehu at Xinzheng County in Henan province. This should be the extension of the human and dragon carving technique in the middle period of West Zhou Dynasty in Shaan'xi. Only the human character got prominent and the image of dragon became less recognizable. In fact, the dragon was easily neglected and article was often regarded as only jade human character. One article is carved with dragon heads in intagliated lines on the head, trunk and lower extremities of the human. The dragon head on the trunk of the body is still distinctive, while the dragon heads on the head and legs of the human is intelligible. The other jade article has distinct dragon head on the trunk of the human body, but the dragon head disappeared on the lower extremities with only point-shaped eyes and brows left on the middle part of legs The dragon head on the human head no longer existed This shows that human and dragon pattern had started to decline gradually.

IV

By East Zhou Dynasty, the society was unsteady, the rites and manners Collapsed, royal families broke up, leuds sprang up. The long-term political opposition resulted in the appearance of regional art and culture. This situation was also reflected in the style of jade articles. The jade articles in the ancient Kingdom of Qin is a little bit different from those in the other areas such as Midland, Chu Land and Yue Land. This variation represents the regional and national cultures.

In the broad sense, the Qin's jade articles are basically the same as those in the Middle Land, Chu and Yue areas. All belong to jade pendants and ritual objects like Jade Tablet(Gui), Jade Disk(Bi), Jade Plaque(Huang), jade Heng and jade penannular(Jue) etc. Besides, all has dragon pattern as the major decoration. This is the mainstream of jade carving in the Spring and Autumn Period and the extension of Chinese traditional art and culture.

The minor difference refers to the particularity of the shape and patterns In another word, the shape and decorative pattern of Qin's jade articles is different from that in other lands. The discrimination of such difference is very important and is helpful for the in-depth study of the jade articles in Spring and Autumn Period. Generally speaking, such differences can be summed up in the following:

1. Jade Disk(Bi): the dragon patterns on the Qin's jade disk took on geometric designs. The dragon head is square, the body and tail is elongated triangular shape. Some dragon patterns were even totally simplified to form the shape of acute triangle. Such a form is widely divergent with the dragon patterns elsewhere, which fully demonstrate the unique feature of the decorative patterns. Some dragon patterns are separated by Tao (rope) patterns. Such a practice become the origin of dragon (or dragon and phoenix) patterns and grain (or cattail) patterns in the Warring States as well as the West and East Han Dynasties.

2. Jade Disk Pendant: The small jade disk pendant decorated with simplified dragon patterns is most characteristic in Qin's jade articles. The dragon patterns take on S-shape and are very abstract. The denotations are hard to tell unless they are compared with visualized dragon patterns.

3. Jade Penannular(Jue): The shape and decorative patterns of the jade penannular in Qin style is very special. The characteristics are: the bore in the center is very small and the gap of the circle is wide outside and narrow inside. The abstract geometric dragon pattern is adorned with transfiguring cloud patterns. Such jade penannulars are rare in other areas and bear strong regional features.

4. Jade Plaque(Huang) and Jade Heng(top jade of group pendants): The most typical feature of Qin's jade plaque and jade Heng is the geometrical dragon pattern or dragon head pattern. occasionally simplified into S-shaped. In terms of the shape, some articles have such large radian that they are almost in rectangular shape. Some also have pointed two ends, resembling the shape of a fish Such grotesque shaped jade plaque is unique in West Zhou Dynasty.

5. Jade Xi(horny ornament): The jade Xi in Qin style is similar of those in other areas, all in the shape of bending beast teeth. The difference is that Qin's jade Xi is decorated with geometric dragon patterns or square dragon head patterns.

6. Oblong jade board ornament decorated with hollow-carved dragon patterns. On the narrow left and right ends as well as the wide upper end of the board is hollow carved and intagliated with geometric visualized dragon patterns. Such ornament is not found elsewhere. It is the only one found up till now.

7. Round jade board ornament with hollow-carved dragon patterns: This board is decorated with two dragons join together head to tail. with hollow-carved dragon claws in middle. The bending dragon body was intagliated with geometric dragon patterns. Such ornament is also not found in other areas.

The Qin's jade articles in Spring and Autumn Period, though different in Variety, have basically same decorative patterns, i.e., elaborated or simplified geometric dragon patterns. Such decorative patterns are also found on the crockery as well as bronze wares. It is the prevalent artistic decorative pattern in the Kingdom of Qin during Spring and Autumn Period. Therefore, it is natural to decorate the jade articles in the Kingdom of Qin with dragon patterns.

The Qin's jade articles were seldom excavated in the Warring Slates Period, nor is the temporal link complete. There is no characteristic artistic style. This shows that the Qin Kingdom at that time had more communication with kingdoms to the east, and that the Qin people then paid less attention to the jade articles.

V

The West Han Empire set its capital in Chang'an. the relics of which lies in the northwest of Xi'an City. A lot of famous sites were there, such as Weiyang Palace, Jianzhang Palace, Mingguang Palace, Wuku, and Shanglin Garden, etc., around which are a lol of burial and construction sites. Beside the Du Tomb and Ba Tomb, which lie in the southeast of Xi'an, all the rest emperor's tombs lie in northwest of Xian'yang City. A lot of antiques were found in those tombs, including many jade articles.

The choice of the jade materials was very careful in Han Dynasty. Because of the convenience of communication, nephrite in Xinjiang continuously entered the midland. The Jade articles include jade disk, jade ring, heart-shaped jade pendant. jade sword ornament, jade belt buckle as well as burial jade and all kinds of containers and ornamentals The shape of the jade articles and their patterns and motifs mainly simulate fairy tales and are full of mysterious colors. The big jade articles are comparatively rough, with simple but powerful carvings, hence the name "the eight cuts of Han". The small jade articles arc smooth and succinct in style. with delicate and beautiful carvings. In the choice of jade materials, beside green jade, yellow jade and celadon jade, white jade became popular and was the jade of top grade.

The Wei, Jin. South and North Dynasties stretched nearly 400 years from 300BC to 600BC. During that time. Chang'an and the neighboring areas were constantly in battle. It became the place that every army fought for and was made the capital of the early Zhao Kingdom, early Qin Kingdom, late Qin Kingdom as well as North Zhou Kingdom. All these made Chang'an the center of cultural communication between south and north in China. Because of the frequent warfare, metaphysics became popular. Buddhism prevailed and sparing burial became a convention. The mysterious color of the jade article gradually disappeared and the demand for jade articles distinctively reduced. The whole manufacture and carving technique of jade articles came to a halt. Few jade articles were handed down during that period except for some jade beasts. The carving of the jade beast is simple, and the beast looked ferocious with protruding chest and abdomens. Despite the simplicity, the carving was clear and elegant.

VI

In 581BC, the Sui Dynasty consolidated the whole country, thus ended the disrupted situation that last for more than three hundred years. The consolidation of the country formed the basis of the development of jade articles. What's more, the reopening of the Silk Road provided the traffic convenience for the using of Hetian jade in Xinjiang. The Tang Dynasty is the few period in history that enjoyed the height of power and splendor. particularly in the early and middle Tang Dynasty. The flourishing development of economics and culture, the broadness of the kingdom's territory, the union of the nations as well as the run-through of the Silk Road enabled the extensive and thorough cultural communication between China and foreign countries. The jade materials used in Tang Dynasty, besides the widely used Hetian jade in Xinjiang, also include the tribute jade from the foreign countries. Foreign-made jade articles were also paid as tribute to Tang Dynasty. Besides, the jade craftsman in Tang Dynasty also simulated the model of foreign jade articles and carved on them the patterns that were loved by the Chinese people. Thus the jade articles at this time possessed the combined feature of Chinese and foreign cultures. The jade articles ai this time had cast off the old functions in the ancient times, and jade articles was no longer limited to ritual ceremonies, nor mainly used in burial. Instead, a new era had started in which jade articles were used for practical usage, and jade ornaments for decorative and aesthetic purposes became the mainstream. This established good groundwork for the later development of jade articles.

The form of the jade articles in Tang Dynasty is different from that in the previous Dynasties. Large amount of flowers and birds, human character patterns appeared, which brought strong liveness to the jade implements At the same time, the jade utensils for practical usage like jade cup, bowl, wine cup also appeared, as well as the jade belt ornament symbolizing the ranking status of the ruling class. The varieties of jade articles got richer, with motifs of winding flowers and plants, melons and fruits, birds and beasts, human characters and flying fairies, insects and fishes, etc. A unique feature of jade carvings in Tang Dynasty is that the human images in the jade belt ornaments are mainly minorities holding musical instruments. The characteristic craftwork of Tang Dynasty includes the neat cuts, the well-proportioned Distribution, as well as the thin but clear lines.

After Tang Dynasty, Chang'an was no longer the capital city. But it was still important in northwest and southwest areas during Song and Yuan Dynasties. The biggest characteristic of the jade articles at this time is the strong secularizing tendency as well as intense liveness.

The jade articles in the South and North Dynasties arc mainly in the motifs of flowers, birds, beasts, as well as dragon and phoenix for auspiciousness. The utensils for practical usage include cup, washer, and belt plate. The displaying articles are mainly jade beast and jade fish. Besides, the archaized jade articles became popular, mainly imitating the bronze ware, sword Ornaments, belt plate and baldrics in the early Qin, Han and Wei Dynasties. The craftwork at this time is exquisite and delicate, with more small articles and few large ones.

There are both coarse and delicate craftworks of the jade articles in Yuan Dynasty. The articles that are coarsely carved does look rough, but the cuttings are deep and bear strong archaic style, while the articles that are delicately carved are rather diaphanous. The hairs on the jade beasts are fluently carved. and the cloud patterns look floating and majestic. The dedicate rilievi and multi-tiered hollow-carving techniques appeared at this time. The special refined grinding rilievi technique was unfound in the articles of Tang or Ming Dynasties. It is a major feature of the jade articles in Yuan Dynasty.

In the design of the decorative patterns, the peculiarities of the jade materials were utilized in the making of the jade articles. This is a new species particularly designed for aesthetic purpose. The design widely adopted the patterns of deer, tiger, crane, dragon. as well as flowers and pine trees. Besides, the variety of jade articles also increased. The added varieties are belt buckle, cup saucer, incense burner, baldric, horse as well as all kinds of birds.

In Ming and Qing Period, Chang'an was called "Xi'an prefecture". It was the center of politics, economics and culture in northwest area. At that time, the economy was highly developed and the civilian class rapidly expanded. Therefore, the serving scope of jade articles also expanded correspondingly. The technique of craftwork was also greatly improved. The quantity of the jade works, the variety of the species, the quality of the jade materials, the exquisiteness of the carvings as well as the beauty of the decorative patterns is incomparable. It became another golden age after Han and Sui, Tang Dynasties.

The carvings of che jade articles in Ming Dynasty is both powerful and delicate, as can be seen thoroughly in jade belt plates. Such hollow-carving technique is the unique style in Ming Dynasty and has high artistic values. The amount of the decorative patterns are unprecedented. The commonly seen patterns are: pine tree, bamboo and plum blossoms; flowers and fruits; pine tree and deer; human character; bird and beast: as well as winding flowers and plants etc. Most jade belt plates arc decorated with dragon patterns and pine tree and deer patterns. The commonly seen jade wares are dishes, cups, bowls, decorative objects, displaying ornaments as well as archaized adornments, flower flakes, twisted-thread bracelets and so on. By late Ming Dynasty, Taoism prevailed, under whose influence came forth many jade articles bearing taoistic patterns such as cloud and crane, pine and crane, as well as the Eight Diagrams. Because grinding drill was used to do the hollow carvings on both sides. The lunate-shaped grinding traces can be found in the rectangular apertures. In addition, because the jade articles in Ming Dynasty had the level-off grinding surface, the frame of the articles is in the same level of the decorative patterns in the center. What is incommensurate with the elaborate carving technique is that the last procedure (refined grinding) is not so meticulous.

During Qing Dynasty, especially in the middle period, jade carving technique mounted to a new height. In the Year of Qianlong, Beijing was the center of jade manufacture in China and all the skilled craftsmen went to Beijing to perform their outstanding skills. Higher demands were also brought forward for the choice of jade materials, processing and polishing procedures an so on. The patterns of the Jade articles were also abundant. Beside the archaized bronze ware patterns, motifs of hidden eight immortals, eight treasures also flourished on the jade articles. The main theme that time is the patterns and words showing auspiciousness.

　　西安は、昔、長安と呼ばれ、遥かなる昔の石器時代には、中国人の祖先がすでにこの地に生息し、生活を営んでいた、西周王朝がここに都を築いた紀元前十世紀より、西安は都会としてその三千年の発展史を始めたのである。特に周、秦、漢、唐においては、全国の政治中心だけでなく、手工業、商業、教育、芸術の中心でもあった。悠久なる歴史、燦爛たる文明によって、この古城に数知れない文物宝器を残した。二十世紀以来、数万点にものぼる古代遺物が出土し、玉器はその中の特に輝かしい逸品である。西安市文物保護考古学研究所の文物倉庫には二十世紀五十年代以来、西安で出土し、または募集した古代玉器を四千点も蔵し、その種類が豊富で、序列が完全である。これらの所蔵品からは西安地方における各時代の玉器の発展状況をうかがうことができる。

一

　　西安は藍田玉の故郷であり、藍田玉は昔からよく知られたのである。軒轅黄帝がかつて藍田玉をもって兵符を造ったといわれる。西安地方の新石器時代と先秦時代の遺跡、また古墳からは藍田玉で製造した礼器や兵器、道具、飾り物などが出土した。

　　西安地方の遺跡から出土した史前と先秦時代の各種の玉器は、その用材は瑪瑙、玉髄，水晶、大理石、方解石、滑石、琉璃、緑松石、紫水晶、鶏血石などである。商の時代後期になると、和闐玉など各地の良質玉材が中原に流入し、和闐玉で彫刻した玉器が次第に増え、西安地方で出土した漢の時代以後の玉器はほとんど和闐玉で加工したものである。瑪瑙などに材料で製造したものはほんのわずかである。

二

　　史前時代と秦の時代において、西安は秦の領地として、玉石加工術の発達した地方の一つであり、その製品の造形にせよ、紋様にせよ、明らかに地方の特色をもっている。今まで、陝西省内で発見した史前期の玉器はあまりおおくないが、主な発見地は西安の近辺と陝西省の北部である。仰韶文の遺跡である半坡遺跡、魚化寨遺跡、臨潼鄧家荘遺跡、宝鶏扶風の案板村遺跡などの遺跡から、玉璧、玉簪、飾り物が出土し、龍山文化の遺跡である西安客省荘遺跡、陝西省の北部の石峁遺跡などから、玉璧、玉斧、玉戈などの礼器と飾り物が出土した。

三

　　陝西省内で発見された商の時代の玉器も数少ない。一九七二、西安市灞橋区老牛坡で玉戈が出土した。一九八六年、藍田県寺坡村で出土した玉斧，玉鏟は商の時代の玉器の代表作である。その造形は整然であり、加工は精密であり、刃も鋭いである。曲線も直線も剛気有力で、艶出しもよくできている。穴と扉芽との間の隙間も丹念に磨いて見事に艶をだしている。

　　周の時代の玉器の彫刻の技法は前代より、かなり進歩した。線体は流暢且つ複雑で、曲線技法も多くされた。きわめて明晰で、峻抜な線体はその特徴と言える。その時代の玉器の種類は増えたばかりでなく、彫刻技法も、造形設計も改良され、総仕上げおよび艶出しの技術も長足に進歩し、できた器物も更に美しくなったのである。

四

　東周の時代に入ると、社会は動乱になり、従来の社会秩序に崩れ、王室の支配力は衰え、諸侯は相次いで反乱した。そのような政治上の長期対立によって、当然、文化芸術の地域特異性を醸成するのである。こういう現象は玉器製作の風格にも反映している。秦の国の玉器は豫、楚、越などの地のそれと比べると、大同小異なるものである。

　大同とは、秦の国の玉器の種類は豫、楚、越などの地方のそれとほぼ同じ種類である。圭、壁、璜、袂などの礼器と帯玉はその主な品目である。そして紋様は龍紋を主とされていた。これは春秋時代の玉彫刻品の主流を成し、また中国伝統文化を芸術の伝承ともいうことができる。

　小異というのは、その造形と紋様の特異性を指す。秦の地方の玉器の造形と紋様は豫，楚，越などの地方の玉器の紋様と比べると微小でありながらも、異なるところがある。このような微小な差異を見分けることはとても重要であり、春秋時代の玉器の研究の大事な手がかりにもなる。

　戦国時代の秦の国の玉器の発見点数は非常に少ないし、また、時代の断層もあり、その独特の芸術風格も欠けている。これはその当時、秦の国は東方諸国との交流が頻繁になったことを反映し、秦の国においては、玉器はあまり人気を呼ばないことをも物語っている。

五

　西漢帝国は長安に都を築き、その遺跡は現在の西安城の西北部に位置している。その周辺には古墳が多く、地下埋蔵文物も豊富であり、中には玉器も多いのである。漢の時代では、玉器製造にあたって、材料に非常に凝っていた。東西交通の発達により、新疆和田の玉材は大量に中原に流入した。出土したものは数が多くて、器物は玉壁、玉環、心佩、剣佩、帯玉のほかに、副葬品に用いる「明器」といわれるもの、さまざまな容器、賞玩品などがある。その造形と紋様は神話物語から取材したのが多く、神秘的な色彩に富んでいる。大型の器物の場合、その造形は豪放で、線体は簡潔且つ剛毅で、「漢の八刀」と言われている。小型の器物の場合、線体は流暢且つ洗練で、刻んだ線はとても繊細で、美しいのである。原材料は青玉、黄玉、墨玉のほかに、白玉も利用され、当時の玉の上品となった。

　魏、晋、南北朝になると、約四百年の間、長安とその周辺の漢中地方は兵家の争いの地となり、戦火が頻発した。長安に相前後して、前趙、前秦、後秦、西魏、北周の都となり、当時の南北文化交流の中心になった。戦乱の頻発、玄学の流行、仏教の興隆、埋蔵の簡素化などにより、玉器の神秘的な色彩がだんだん消え、玉器の需要量も著しく減ってきた。玉器の製作は衰退に状況に陥った。西安地方において、この時期の玉器出土品が少ないし、そのほとんどは玉佩，玉獣、玉蝉、紐印である。彫刻も粗末で、艶だしもよくなかった。

六

　隋王朝の統一で、三国魏晋南北朝の三百年にわたる分裂割拠の状態に終止符を打った。シルクロードの再開で、隋王朝の和闐の美玉を利用するに交通上の便をもたらした。

唐の時代は中国の歴史において、空前の隆盛な時期であった。特に初唐と盛唐には、経済と文化は高度繁栄し、国土の統一、民族の融合、シルクロード開通によって、中外の文化交流を一層促進し、「万方の来朝、絶城の入貢」の大盛況が現れた。もっとも中国文化の特色をもつ玉器芸術もはじめて外来文化の影響とショックをうけた。唐の時代の玉器雕刻師は外国の玉器の造形を模倣して、中国人に喜ばれる紋様を雕刻し、中外文化の合璧という特徴をもつ玉器を製作した。

西安市内にある興慶宮遺跡、大明宮遺跡とその周辺の唐の時代の古墳から大量の高品質の唐の時代の玉器が出土した。その紋様は主として花鳥、人物であり、濃厚なる生活の息吹に富んでいた、図案は主に蔓枝、草花、瓜、果実、鳥獣、人物飛天、虫魚から取材した。刀法が乱れることなく、配置がよく均整がとれ、鉄細かつ重厚であることは唐の時代の玉器作品の大きな特徴である。

七

唐の時代以後、長安は都の地位を失ったが、宋、元の時代においては依然として中国西北、西南部の重鎮であった。この時期の玉器の最大の特徴は強烈な世俗化と濃厚な生活息吹であった。北宋、南宋の両宋時代の玉器は花、鳥、獣を主とした。龍鳳吉祥図案も多くあった。実用品には杯、洗浄具、帯玉があり、置物には獣や魚の造形があった。また古代の玉器の模倣製作も流行っていた。主に先秦、漢、魏時代の青銅器、剣飾、帯玉、佩飾を模倣製作した。この時代の玉器の彫刻はきわめて繊細巧みで、小型の器物は多くなり、大型のものは少なくなった。

元の時代の玉器は、その彫刻は豪放なものもあるし、繊細緻密なものもある。豪放なものは飾り気なく、奔放でありながら、刀法は重厚であり、古風を帯びているのである。それに対して、繊細なものはきわめて繊細で。獣の毛まで厳密に刻んでいたのである。刀法は流暢で、刻んだ雲紋は動感があり、その勢いは雄大である。また、この時期に技法として、緻密な凸彫法と二、三層透彫法が現れた。元の時代の紋飾技法は、美しさを極めるために、玉石の材質に応じて、器物を製作することを考案した。図案紋様はほとんど鹿紋様、虎紋様、鶴紋様、龍紋様、草花紋様、松紋様であった。器物の造形には帯玉、燭台、香炉、佩飾、馬、各種鳥類があった。

八

明、清時代において、長安は西安府といって、西北地方の政治、経済、文化の中心となり、経済は高度繁栄し、市民階級は急速に拡大し、玉器の供給の対象と範囲も広くなり、技法水準も高くなった。当時の玉器の出産量、種類の豊かさ、玉質の優良さ、彫刻の精巧さなどは空前的なものであり、漢、隋、唐時代に継ぐ玉器の繁盛期であった。この時期の玉器は伝世品は多く、出土品はあまり見られなかった。

明の時代の彫刻刀法は豪放且つ剛毅で、彫刻も清細で、特に帯板にはその技法を悉くいかしている。このような透彫技法は芸術的価値が高く、明の時代に玉彫刻師の独特な風格をあらわしている。紋様の種類は前代を遥かに超え、よく見られるのは松竹梅、花、果実、松鹿、人物、鶏獣、草木などである。龍紋様、松鹿紋様はもっとも多く見られる。また器物の造形には盆，碗，装飾品がおおく、置物には模倣製作した配飾、各種の花びら、金糸入りの腕輪などがある。

　清の時代では、特に清の中期、玉彫刻の技術は更に新しい階段に入り、材料の選別、加工、艶だしなどの工芸技術は更に高く要求されるようになった。図案紋様も豊富多彩で、古銅器の紋様を真似た玉器のほかに、暗八仙、八宝なども玉器の図案になり、吉祥縁起の意味を表す紋様、文字は当時の主流題材であった。われわれが収蔵した清の時代の玉器の多くは伝世品である。

Contents

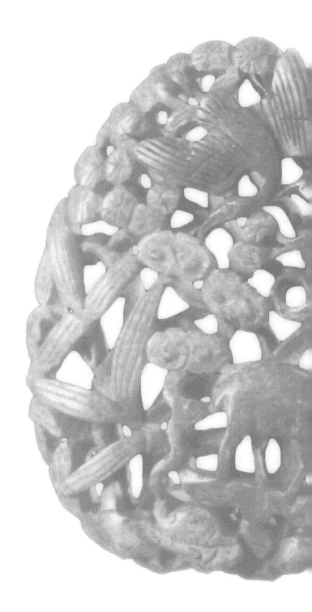

예옥
禮玉

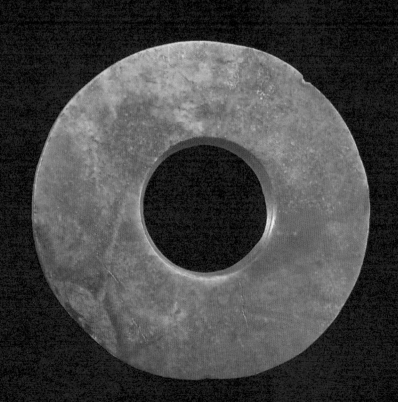

예옥(禮玉)은 고대 의례활동에서 사용했던 옥기이다. 상고(上古)시대, 사람들은 만물에 영혼이 존재한다고 믿었다. 아름다운 돌인 옥은 산천의 정수이고 천지의 귀신과 통하는 영성(靈性)이 있다고 여겼기 때문에 부족의 토템이자 수령의 상징으로 사용하였다. 상·주대(商·周代) 이후 옥기는 제사, 조향(朝享), 책봉 등 의례활동에서 매우 중요한 역할을 했는데 보통 각종 의례활동에서 사용하던 의장품(儀仗品), 토템을 나타내는 상징물, 권력과 등급을 상징하는 옥기는 전부 예옥이라 할 수 있다.

Jade Ritual Artifacts are the jade articles used in ancient ritual ceremonies. In the early times, people believed that everything had spirit. Thus jade, the quintessence of the mountains, was regarded to possess the spiritual power of communicating among the ghosts and gods in heaven and earth. Therefore, it was used as the totem of tribes and the symbol of headman. After Shang and Zhou Dynasty, jade articles began to play important roles in the ritual ceremonies such as sacrifice, imperial court banquets, official position conferments and so on. It is generally believed that all the jade articles used for ceremonial purposes, the sacrificial rites, court ceremonies, symbols of totems, as well as other jades representing power and status, could be regarded as jade Ritual Artifacts.

벽(璧)

　곡물을 연마하는 고리모양의 석기에서 발전한 옥벽은 원형의 편평한 모양이고 중간에 구멍을 냈다. 원형 벽면을 '육(肉)', 중심 구멍을 '호(好)'라고 칭하며 '육'이 '호'보다 크다. 벽(璧)의 조형은 고대 '천원지방(天圓地方)'이라는 우주관에서 출발하여 태양과 우주를 상징함으로써 제천예기(祭天禮器)에 속했다. 실제로 옥벽은 권력과 계급의 상징물이며 패식, 부장품으로 사용한 동시에 선물이나 신물(信物)로도 사용하였다. 옥벽은 대벽(大璧), 곡벽(谷璧), 포벽(蒲璧)으로 나뉜다. 대벽의 지름은 대략 20cm이고 재료는 청옥이며 원형으로 만들어 형태와 색상이 하늘과 대응된다. 대벽은 천자가 예천(禮天)할 때뿐만 아니라 제후들이 천자한테 헌납할 때도 사용했다. 곡벽의 벽면에는 종횡으로 정연하게 배열된 곡정(谷釘)이 가득 조각되어 풍조우순(風調雨順) 및 오곡풍등(五穀豐登)을 상징하고 포벽의 벽면에는 서초문(瑞草紋)을 새겨 초목의 번성과 생활의 번영을 기원하였다. 이로써 옥벽의 형태, 색채 및 문양은 예천과 연관이 있음을 알 수 있다.

　　Jade Disk evolved from the ring-shaped stoneware for grinding grain. It's round and flat, with a hole in center. The circular jade surface is called "flesh" (Rou), and the hole in the middle is called "goodness" (Hao). The jade whose flesh is bigger than goodness is called jade Disk. According to ancient people's cosmologic concept, heaven is round and earth is square. Thus the shape of jade Disc symbolizes the sun and heaven. jade Disk was used as ritual objects for presenting sacrifice to heaven. In actual practice, it was also used as an indicator of power rankings. It could either be worn or be used in burial. Meanwhile, it served as presents and keepsakes in the social activities. jade Disk includes Grand Disk, Grain Disk(Gu Bi), and cattail Disk(Pu Bi). the diameter of Grand Disk is approximately 20cm, made by celadon jade, in correspondence with the shape and color of heaven. It is the object used by emperors to worship the heaven. Leuds also use Grand Disk to give offerings to the emperor. The Grain Disk is carved with full grain spikes that are arranged vertically and great harvest. Cattail Disk, the Pu pattern on the disk is a kind of auspicious grass, emblematize the thriving and flourishing of trees and grass. The quality of the disk, it's color and luster, as well as the linings on the disk are all related to rituals in worshiping heaven.

001

옥벽(玉璧)

석영암(石英岩) ｜ 앙소문화(仰韶文化)
지름 6.4cm 구멍지름 0.6~1cm 두께 0.7cm
2002년 서안시 안탑구 어화채(西安市 雁塔區 魚化寨) 출토

Jade Disk

Quartzite ｜ YangShao Culture
D 6.4cm　Bore D 0.6~1cm　T 0.7cm
Excavated from Yuhuazhai Village in Yanta District, Xi'an in 2002

　　납작한 원형(圓形)으로 가운데에 구멍이 나 있다. 가장자리는 불규칙적인 원형이며 연마 또한 불규칙적이다. 중심에서 살짝 벗어난 나팔 모양 구멍은 한쪽이 크고 한쪽이 작다. 양면은 비교적 평평한데 두께가 불균일하며 광택처리가 되지 않았다. 이 옥벽은 약간 거칠며 크기가 작고 모양이 불규칙적이다. 또한 기법이 질박하고 대범하여 전형적인 초기 공예의 특징이 잘 드러난다.

002

옥벽(玉璧)

투섬석옥(透閃石玉) | 용산문화(龍山文化)
지름 11.7cm 구멍지름 5cm 두께 0.7cm
1983년 서안시(西安市) 수집

Jade Disk

Tremolite | LongShan Culture
D 11.7cm Bore D 5cm T 0.7cm
Collected in Xi'an in 1983

납작한 원형(圓形)이지만 모양이 불규칙적이다. 가운데에는 대롱 모양 도구로 단면(單面)을 뚫은 구멍이 나 있는데 한쪽이 크고 다른 한쪽이 작으며 아래위 모두 가공흔적이 남아 있다. 한쪽 면에는 곧고 굵은 경사선이 있어 한쪽이 높고 한쪽이 낮아 보인다. 전체적으로 민무늬이고 가장자리는 파손이 심하며 표면은 정교하게 연마되어 평평하고 매끈하며 빛이 난다. 이물질이 많이 섞여 재질이 거칠며 대부분 회갈색을 띠었는데 띄엄띄엄 청백색 얼룩무늬가 있다. 전체적으로 뚜렷한 원시적 특징을 띠었다.

003

포문벽(蒲紋璧)

청백옥(靑白玉) | 한(漢)
지름 12.8cm 구멍지름 4.5cm 두께 0.5cm
1976년 서안시 연호구(西安市 蓮湖區) 홍묘파(紅廟坡) 한묘(漢墓) 출토

Jade Disk with Cattail Patterns

Green and white jade | Han Dynasty
D 12.8cm Bore D 4.5cm T 0.5cm
Excavated from Han Tomb at Hongmiaopo in Lianhu District, Xi'an in 1976

납작한 원형(圓形)으로 양면 모두 포문으로 꾸몄다. '호(好)'에는 현문(弦紋)을 둘러 비교적 두꺼운 내곽(內廓)을 이루었고 '육(肉)'은 가장자리에 편사도(偏斜刀)로 안쪽을 향한 윤곽을 그려 경사진 외곽(外廓)을 이루었다. 포문은 먼저 표면에 능형(菱形) 망문(網紋)을 새긴 다음 다시 능형마다 두 예각을 경사지게 깎아내어 배열이 균일하고 정연하다. 벽의 표면과 안팎 가장자리 측면은 모두 정세(精細)하게 연마하였고 전체적으로 진갈색을 띠는데 띄엄띄엄 푸르스름한 얼룩이 있다.

포문은 옥기 가운데 정세한 문양으로 6각 방사형(放射形) 구조이다. 『주례(周禮)』「춘관(春官)」「대종백(大宗伯)」에는 "옥을 육서(六瑞)로 하여 제후를 표상하였다. ……남(男)은 포벽(蒲璧)을 지닌다"라고 적혀 있다. 이로부터 포문벽은 공(公), 후(侯), 백(伯), 자(子), 남(男) 가운데 '남' 등급의 제후를 상징하는 전문 예기(禮器)임을 알 수 있다. 포(蒲)는 돗자리를 짜는 데 사용되는 수초(水草)이므로 포문은 돗자리 무늬라 할 수 있다. 『주례』「춘관」「대종백」에서는 "포는 돗자리로서 사람이 앉을 수 있다……"라고 주석하였는데 이로부터 돗자리는 '자리'라는 뜻으로 확대 사용되었고 한자리를 차지한다는 길조(吉兆)로 간주되었다. 출토된 연대가 가장 이른 포문벽은 춘추전국(春秋戰國)시대의 것이며 이는 진·한대(秦·漢代)까지 이어졌다.

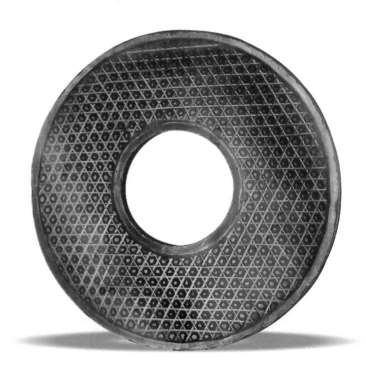

004

곡문벽(谷紋璧)

청옥(靑玉) | 한(漢)
지름 16.4cm 구멍지름 5.7cm 두께 0.4cm
1982년 서안시 미앙구(西安市 未央區) 홍기(紅旗)기계공장 출토

Jade Disk with Grain Patterns

Green jade | Han Dynasty
D 16.4cm Bore D 5.7cm T 0.4cm
Excavated from Hongqi Machinery Factory in Weiyang District,
Xi'an in 1982

　벽의 안팎 가장자리에는 각각 음각선을 둘러 곽(廓)을
이루었으며 안쪽은 저부조한 곡문으로 장식하였다. 곡문
은 먼저 표면에 능형이나 방형(方形)의 망문(綱紋)을 새긴
후 다시 격자 안에 곡문을 조각하여 배열이 정연하고 분
포가 균일하다. 표면과 안팎 가장자리 측면은 모두 정세
(精細)하게 연마하였다.
　『주례(周禮)』「춘관(春官)」「대종백(大宗伯)」에는 "옥을
육서(六瑞)로 하여 제후를 표상하였다. ……자(子)는 곡
벽을 지닌다"라고 적혀 있다. 이로부터 곡문벽은 공(公),
후(侯), 백(伯), 자(子), 남(男) 중 '자' 등급의 제후를 상징
하는 전문 예기(禮器)임을 알 수 있다. 곡(穀)은 백곡(百穀)
을 통틀어 일컫는 것으로서 녹봉을 의미하기도 하는데 옥
기에 사용되면 길상(吉祥)을 뜻한다. 출토된 연대가 가장
이른 곡벽은 춘추전국(春秋戰國)시대의 것으로서 이 문양
은 한대(漢代)까지 사용되었다.

005

봉문벽(鳳紋璧)

청옥(靑玉) | 한(漢)
지름 16.6cm 구멍지름 2.3cm 두께 1cm
1973년 서안시 연호구(西安市 蓮湖區) 704고(庫) 출토

Jade Disk with Phoenix Patterns

Green jade | Han Dynasty
D 16.6cm Bore D 2.3cm T 1cm
Excavated from 704 Warehouse in Lianhu District, Xi'an in 1973

　납작한 원형(圓形)으로 '호(好)'와 '육(肉)'의 가장자리에는 각기
현문(弦紋)을 둘러 비교적 두꺼운 내외 곽(廓)을 이루었다. 벽면(璧
面)은 음각(陰刻)한 도문(綯紋)에 의해 안팎으로 나뉘는데 안쪽에는
균일하고 정연한 포문(蒲紋)이 있고 바깥쪽에는 머리와 꼬리가 맞닿
은 봉황 세 마리가 있다. 엎드린 채 몸을 돌려 뒤돌아보고 있는 봉황
은 부리가 긴 갈고리 같으며 관(冠), 날개, 꽁지가 모두 굽었다. 문양
은 구조가 치밀하고 섬세하며 율동감이 강해 예술적 표현과 조각기
법이 조화를 이루었다.
　한대(漢代) 옥기의 봉문은 비교적 규범화되었다. 동한(東漢)시기
『설문(說文)』에는 "봉황은 신조(神鳥)이다. 천로(天老, 전설 속 황제의
좌신)는 봉황에 대해 '앞부분은 기러기, 뒷부분은 기린(麒麟) 같고 뱀
의 목, 물고기의 꼬리, 황새의 이마, 원앙새의 뺨, 용의 무늬, 거북의
등, 제비의 턱, 닭의 부리를 갖고 있으며 오색(五色)을 갖추었다'고
말했다"란 구체적인 묘사가 있다. 옥기에서 봉문은 대부분 변형된
모습이지만 머리만은 『설문』에 적혀 있는 것과 큰 차이가 없다. 특히
부리는 과장되어 대부분 홰를 치는 수탉의 부리와 닮아 있다.

006

기룡벽(夔龍璧)

청옥(靑玉) | 한(漢)
지름 18.8cm 구멍지름 3.3cm 두께 0.5cm
1983년 서안시 안탑구(西安市 雁塔區) 사파(沙坡) 한묘(漢墓) 출토

Jade Disk with Dragon Patterns

Green jade | Han Dynasty
D 18.8cm Bore D 3.3cm T 0.5cm
Excavated from Han Tomb at Shapo in Yanta District, Xi'an in 1983

벽은 납작한 원형(圓形)이고 '육(肉)'과 '호(好)' 가장자리에는 현문(弦紋)을 둘러 비교적 두꺼운 내외 곽(廓)을 이루었다. 벽면(璧面)은 가운데 음각(陰刻)한 도문(絢紋)에 의해 안팎으로 나뉜다. 안쪽에는 균일하고 정연하게 배열된 포문(蒲紋)이 있고 바깥쪽에는 구철법(勾徹法)과 가는 음각선을 결합하여 크기와 모양이 같은 쌍신(雙身) 기룡문 4조를 조각하였다. 기룡은 둥근 눈, 굵은 눈썹, 곧은 코, 넓은 주둥이를 갖고 있어 흉악해 보이며 양쪽 볼에는 'S' 모양의 파곡문(波曲紋)이 있다.

벽의 양면과 안팎 가장자리 모서리는 모두 정세(精細)하게 연마하였다. 자세히 살펴보면, 바깥쪽 기룡문에는 압지은기법(壓地隱起法, 무늬 주위를 사선으로 한 둘레 깎아내는 기법, 다만 무늬는 표면 위로 도드라지지 않는다)으로 조각한 얕은 규문(規紋)이 있다.

종(琮)

밖이 각지고 안이 둥근 옥기로 대부분 원기둥과 각기둥의 복합체이다. 종심(琮心)에는 원형의 구멍이 있고 바깥은 한 층 혹은 다층으로 조각했다. 신석기시대의 양저문화(良渚文化) 지역에서는 옥종이 대량 출토되고 대부분 신비한 문양들이 새겨진 반면, 상대(商代)에는 출토량이 극히 적고 문양도 없으며 주대(周代) 이후부터는 더욱 희소하다.

옥종은 용도가 매우 다양한데『삼례(三禮)』와 한대(漢代) 유학의 해석에 의하면, 제례의 제지(祭地)에 사용하거나 장례 때 죽은 자의 복부에 놓아두기도 하고 조빙(朝聘) 때 제후들이 군부인(君夫人)에게 바치기도 하였다. 그러나 현대에 들어서는 옥종의 모양과 문양에 근거하여 하늘과 땅을 연결하는 법기(法器)로 토템의 의미가 있거나 무당들이 신령과 통하려 할 때 사용했던 도구라고 추측하고 있다.

Cong is the jade article that is square outside and cylinder inside. It is the combination of cylinder and cuboid. The center of Cong is a round hole, the outside of which is carved with one or more layers. A lot of jade Cong with mysterious carvings were excavated in Liang Zhu Culture in Neolithic period. Few were excavated in Shang Dynasty and without any carving patterns. It went even rare after Zhou Dynasty.

Cong has many usages. According to the book San Li(the three rites), it is used when sacrificing to the earth, to be put on the belly when encoffining the dead body, it is also held by leuds to be given to the emperor's wife in the court engagement. Modern people, according to it's shape and carving pattern, believe that it is a sacred object which can run through heaven and earth. It could also serve as a totem column and an instrument used by necromancers to communicate with gods.

007

벽종(璧琮)

청옥(青玉) | 상(商)
높이 3.9cm 지름 6.7cm 벽두께 0.78~0.82cm
1974년 서안시 파교구(西安市 灞橋區) 노우파(老牛坡) 상대 유적지 출토

Jade Disk Cong(a long hollow piece of jade with rectangular sides)

Green jade | Shang Dynasty
H 3.9cm D 6.7cm T 0.78~0.82cm
Excavated from Shang Dynasty Relic At Laoniupo in Baqiao District, Xi'an in 1974

대롱 모양이며 구멍은 대롱 모양 도구에 모래를 더해 뚫은 것으로 벽이 비교적 얇다. 종면(琮面)은 감지법(減地法)으로 방호좌(方弧座) 세 개를 돌출되게 하였는데 좌면(座面)은 민무늬이고 빛이 난다. 종면과 구멍 내벽은 모두 연마를 거쳐 매끈하고 윤이난다. 자세히 살펴보면, 아래위 사(射, 양쪽에 본체보다 돌출된 부분) 높낮이가 일치하지 않는다.

소면종(素面琮)

청백옥(靑白玉) | 서주(西周)
높이 8.5cm 변(邊)길이 4.9cm 구멍지름 4cm
1987년 서안시 안탑구 산문구촌(西安市 雁塔區 山門口村) 출토

Plain Surfaced Cong(a long hollow piece of jade with rectangular sides)

Green and white jade | West Zhou Dynasty
H 8.5cm L 4.9cm Bore D 4cm
Excavated from Shanmenkou Village in Yanta District, Xi'an in 1987

종은 밖이 각지고 안이 둥글며 양쪽 끝부분에 사(射)가 있고 4면 모두 민무늬이며 빛이 난다. 내외 표면은 연마 가 잘 되어 매끈하고 윤이 난다. 구멍을 자세히 살펴보면, 안쪽 가운데가 살짝 볼록한데 이는 양면에서 마주하여 구멍을 뚫은 다음 세세하게 연마하고 광택처리하였음을 말해준다.

왜방종(矮方棕)

청백옥(靑白玉) | 서주(西周)
높이 5.4cm 구멍지름 6.8cm
1986년 서안시 장안현 신왕촌(西安市 長安縣 新旺村) 출토

Short Square Cong(a long hollow piece of jade with rectangular sides)

Green and white jade | West Zhou Dynasty
H 5.4cm Bore D 6.8cm
Excavated from Xinwang Village in Chang'an County, Xi'an in 1986

빛이 나는 민무늬 종은 비교적 낮은 편인 데 밖이 각지고 안이 둥글며 양쪽 끝부분에 짧은 사(射)가 있다. 구멍 가운데는 뚜렷하 게 볼록한데 이는 양면에서 마주하여 구멍 을 뚫은 다음 연마하여 턱진 부분을 고르고 다시 광택처리한 것으로 보인다.

황(璜)

옥황은 지금으로부터 7천여 년 전 신석기시대 하모도문화(河姆渡文化)에서 최초로 출현하였다. 본래 형태는 불균형적이고 이후 대부분은 원호형(圓弧形)이었는데 벽의 2분의 1 또는 3분의 1 정도이고, 일부는 철사를 이용해 한데 꿰면 온전한 모양이 되는 것도 있다. 황의 양쪽 구멍은 실로 꿰매서 착용하려는 목적으로 뚫은 것이다. 『주례(周禮)』에는 "현황(玄璜)으로 북방을 예(禮)한다"라는 내용이 있는데 이로써 옥황은 북방의 신을 제사할 때 사용하던 예기(禮器)임을 알 수 있다.

신석기시대의 옥황은 대부분 단면(單面) 조각인데 그중 대다수는 민무늬이고 간혹 용문(龍紋) 혹은 수면(獸面)이 조각되었다. 상대(商代) 및 서주(西周)시기 옥황에 조각된 용, 새, 물고기 혹은 기타 동물도안들은 대부분 양면의 대칭 조각으로 조패(組佩)의 윗부분이나 가운데에 사용되었으며, 소형 황은 패식(佩飾)에 주로 사용되었다. 춘추(春秋)시대의 옥황은 대부분 여러 부속물이 조합되어 하나의 패식을 이루는 형태이고 하나로 이루어진 옥황에는 용, 호랑이 등 동물도안을 주로 조각하였다. 전국(戰國)시대 옥황은 대부분 누공(鏤空)과 투조법(透彫法)을 사용하였다. 진·한대(秦·漢代)부터 옥황은 점차 줄어들어 위·진(魏·晉) 이후에는 완전히 사라졌다.

Jade Plaque was discovered in the He Mudu Culture in Neolithic Period more than 7,000 years ago. It's original shape was irregular. Later, it took on arc shape, some were half the disk, some were one third of a disk, some could also be stitched together by metal wires to from a disk. Usually, the both ends of the plaque have perforations in order to tie the string on. As Zhou Li had it, "Use dark jade Plaque to honor the North". This shows that it is used as ritual objects to worship the God in North.

The Plaques in Neolithic Period are mainly plain with no decorative patterns, some have the decoration of dragon patterns or beast face. The carvings are on one side. During the Shang and West Zhou period, the carvings of dragon, bird fish as well as other animals appeared on both sides in symmetrical patterns, and are used to make the upper middle parts of group pendants. Small Plaques are especially used in combination with other pendants. those who appear alone often have animal Patterns such as dragons or tigers on them. In the Warring States period, through-carved technique was adopted in carving the decorative patterns on the Plaque. Plaque got rare in the Qin and Han Dynasties and gradually disappeared after Wei and Jin Dynasties.

010

쌍룡문황(雙龍紋璜)

청옥(靑玉) | 서주(西周)
길이 8.5cm 너비 2.4cm 두께 0.3cm
1978년 서안시 장안현(西安市 長安縣) 풍서(灃西)구리망공장 출토

Jade Plaque with Double Dragon Patterns

Green jade | West Zhou Dynasty
H 8.5cm W 2.4cm T 0.3cm
Excavated from Fengxi Copper Netting Factory in Chang'an County, Xi'an in 1978

납작한 호형(弧形)으로 한 면에만 쌍룡문을 새기고 다른 한 면은 반질반질하고 빛이 난다. 용은 모두 머리가 크고 몸통이 작은데 서로 등지고 아래위로 엇갈려 있다. 문양은 음각(陰刻) 단선(單線)과 구철법(勾徹法)을 결합하여 조각하였는데 도법(刀法)이 힘 있고 유창하다. 황의 양쪽 끝에는 각기 돌기된 비릉(扉稜)과 구멍이 있다. 한쪽 구멍은 단면(單面)으로 뚫어 나팔 모양을 이루고 다른 한쪽 구멍은 막대기 모양 도구로 양면으로 뚫어 가운데 턱졌으며 입구가 말발굽 모양을 이룬다. 전체적으로 정세(精細)하게 연마되어 투명하고 윤이 난다.

옥황(玉璜)은 서주시기 각지 무덤에서 흔히 볼 수 있는데 대부분 죽은 자의 가슴이나 복부에 놓아둔다.

011

조문황(鳥紋璜)

청백옥(青白玉) | 서주(西周)
길이 9.1cm 너비 3cm 두께 0.4cm
1986년 서안시 장안현(西安市 長安縣) 풍서(澧西)부품공장 출토

Jade Plaque with Bird Patterns

Green and white jade | West Zhou Dynasty
L 9.1cm W 3cm T 0.4cm
Excavated from Fengxi Fittings Factory in Chang'an County, Xi'an in 1986

납작한 호형(弧形)이며 양면에 서 있는 모습의 조문(鳥紋)을 조각하였다. 정수리와 몸 앞쪽에 튀어나온 부분은 부리, 볏, 깃털을 나타낸다. 몸통에는 가는 음각선과 단철도법(單徹刀法)으로 여러 가지 형태의 운뢰문(雲雷紋)을 새겨 드리운 볏, 날개, 꽁지, 발을 나타냈다. 몸통 앞뒤는 모서리가 없게 다듬었고 볏의 가장자리는 윤곽이 뚜렷하다. 볏 위쪽 가운데와 부리의 굽은 부분에 나 있는 구멍은 단면(單面)을 막대기 모양 도구로 뚫어 만든 것이다.

이 옥황은 형태로 보아 상대(商代)의 것과 비슷하나 조각기법은 상대보다 많이 발전하였다. 문양은 선에 힘이 있고 유창하며 곡선처리가 자연스럽고 전체적으로 매끈하며 서주시기에 유행했던 단철(單徹)기법을 사용하였다.

012

조문황(鳥紋璜)

청백옥(青白玉) | 서주(西周)
길이 7.6cm 너비 2.9cm 두께 0.4cm
1972년 서안시(西安市) 수집

Jade Plaque with Bird Patterns

Green and white jade | West Zhou Dynasty
L 7.6cm W 2.9cm T 0.4cm
Collected in Xi'an in 1972

납작한 호형(弧形)으로 양면에 대칭되게 조문을 새겼다. 새는 동그란 눈, 굽은 부리, 짧은 꽁지를 가졌는데 서 있는 모습이고 볏, 날개, 깃털은 여러 가지 권운문(卷雲紋)으로 나타냈다. 몸통 앞쪽 모서리는 모두 연마하였고 다른 부분 모서리는 비교적 각지고 단단하다. 양쪽 끝부분의 구멍은 양면으로 뚫은 것으로 가운데는 턱이 졌다.

013

수수문황(獸首紋璜)

청옥(靑玉) | 진(秦)
길이 11.5cm 너비 4cm 두께 0.7cm
1971년 서안시 미앙구 대명궁공사 연지촌(西安市 未央區 大明宮公社 聯志村) 출토

Jade Plaque with Animal Head Patterns

Green jade | Qin Dynasty
L 11.5cm W 4cm T 0.7cm
Excavated from Lianzhi Village at Daminggong Community in Weiyang District, Xi'an in 1971

양쪽 끝에는 가는 음각선으로 짐승 머리를 양면 조각하였다. 똑같은 형태의 짐승 머리는 긴 입 밖으로 이빨을 드러내고 눈은 능형(菱形)이며 귀는 뒤로 젖혀졌다. 표면은 반듯하게 연마되었으나 광택처리가 그다지 정세(精細)하지 않다.

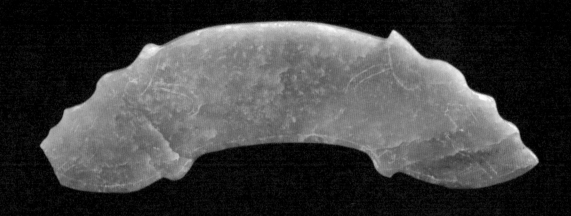

014

소면황(素面璜)

청옥(靑玉) | 진(秦)
길이 11.4㎝ 너비 2.6㎝ 두께 1.1cm
1971년 서안시 미앙구 대명궁공사 연지촌(西安市 未央區 大明宮公社 聯志村) 출토

Jade Plaque with Plain Surface

Green jade | Qin Dynasty
L 11.4cm W 2.6cm T 1.1cm
Excavated from Lianzhi Village at Daminggong Community in Weiyang District, Xi'an in 1971

납작한 호형(弧形)으로 민무늬이다. 위쪽 한가운데는 마주하여 뚫은 구멍이 있는데 구멍 속에는 턱이 남아 있으며 입구는 말발굽 모양이다. 모양이 가지런하고 연마가 잘 되었으나 광택처리는 정세(精細)하지 않다.

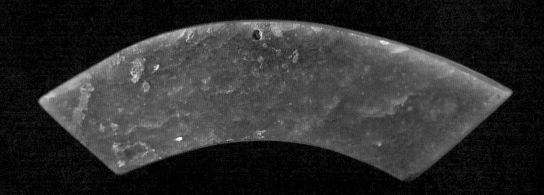

원(瑗)

원은 큰 구멍이 있는 벽(璧)이다. 고대에는 '호(好)'가 '육(肉)'보다 배가 큰 벽 모양의 기(器)를 원이라고 하였는데 문양 및 기법은 당시 옥 벽과 거의 같았다. 선진(先秦)시대, 천자가 제후들을 접견할 때 또는 제후들이 경대부(卿大夫), 사(士)를 접견할 때 모두 원을 증표로 하여야 했 다. "원으로 사람을 소견(召見)한다"라는 말에서 원이 접견 시 사용하던 증표였음을 알 수 있다.

Yuan is the disk with a large hole in center. Ancient people called the disk shaped Jade whose "goodness" is twice the size of "flesh" as "Yuan". It's decorative pattern and art craft are basically the same as the contemporary Jade Disk. During the early Qin period, when the emperor summoned to meet the leud, or the leud summoned to meet the senior officials or scholar officials, they all have messengers to carry Yuan as credentials. Yuan is the warrant for the summon of people.

015

도문원(絢紋瑗)

대리석(大理石) | 전국(戰國)
지름 7.6cm 구멍지름 4.5cm 두께 0.5cm
1976년 서안시 안탑구 금호타촌(西安市 雁塔區 金滹沱村) 출토

Jade Yuan with Tao Patterns

Marble | Warring States Period
D 7.6cm Bore D 4.5cm T 0.5cm
Excavated from Jinhutuo Village in Yanta District, Xi'an in 1976

납작한 고리 모양이며 '호(好)'가 '육(肉)'의 2 배이다. 전체적으로 도문을 새겼는데 구철법(鉤 徹法)으로 양면에 호선(弧線)을 사선으로 앞뒤가 맞물리게 새겨 나선모양을 이룬다. 호선은 굵기 가 같고 곡률도 일치하여 유창하고 자연스러우 며 율동감이 있어 보인다. 옥은 연황색이며 투명 하고 윤이 난다.

도문은 밧줄을 모방하여 만든 문양이다. 신석 기시대의 도기(陶器)에서 최초로 나타났고 그 후 청동기(靑銅器), 자기(瓷器), 석각(石刻), 옥기(玉 器) 등 기물(器物)에서 바탕문양으로 사용되었 다. 옛 옥기 중 도문은 일반적으로 기물이나 도안 의 가장자리에 장식되었으며, 일부 경우 짐승의 몸통을 새기는 데 사용되기도 하였다.

곡문원(谷紋瑗)

청백옥(靑白玉) | 전국(戰國)
지름 11cm 구멍지름 5.5cm 두께 0.5cm
1972년 서안시 장안현(西安市 長安縣) 위곡(韋曲) 북쪽 출토

Jade Yuan with Grain Patterns

Green and white jade | Warring States Period
D 11cm Bore D 5.5cm T 0.5cm
Excavated from the North of Weiqu in Chang'an County,
Xi'an in 1976

　납작한 원형(圓形)으로 '육(肉)'과 '호(好)'의 가장자리에는 각기 현문(弦紋)을 둘러 비교적 두꺼운 내외 곽(廓)을 이루었다. 앞뒤 면에는 사방연속(四方連續)으로 균일하게 분포된 곡문을 새겼다. 돌기 크기는 일치한데 그 위에 가는 음각선으로 나선문(螺旋紋)을 새겼으며 선의 끝부분은 인접한 곡문과 이어진다. 곡문의 윗부분은 뾰족하게 돌출되어 만지면 찌르는 감이 있는데 이는 전국(戰國)시대 옥기 곡문의 가장 큰 특징이다.

곡문원(谷紋瑗)

청백옥(靑白玉) | 진(秦)
지름 7.1cm 구멍지름 3.6cm 두께 0.5cm
1983년 서안시 안탑구(西安市 雁塔區) 섬서사범대학(陝西師範大學) 남문(南門) 밖 한묘(漢墓) 출토

Jade Yuan with Grain Patterns

Green and white jade | Qin Dynasty
D 7.1cm Bore D 3.6cm T 0.5cm
Excavated from Han Tomb outside the south gate of Shaanxi Normal
University in Yanta District, Xi'an in 1983

　납작한 원형(圓形)으로 '육(肉)'과 '호(好)' 가장자리에는 각기 현문(弦紋)을 둘러 비교적 두꺼운 내외 곽(廓)을 이루었다. 앞뒤 면에는 모두 곡문을 장식하였다. 곡문은 규칙적으로 배열되었는데 먼저 옥의 표면에 능형(菱形)이나 방형(方形)의 망문(網紋)을 새긴 후 다시 격자 안에 곡문을 새겼다. 이 원의 곡문은 윤이 나고 옹골진 것이 전국(戰國)시대 것처럼 뾰족하지도 않고 한대(漢代)의 것처럼 밋밋하지도 않다. 전체적으로 광택처리가 잘 되어 유리질감이 난다.

장(璋)

　상·주대(商·周代) 유행한 옥장의 형태는 편평하고 긴 막대기 모양의 사수(斜首), 네모난 기둥 모양의 평수(平首), 채찍 모양의 첨수(尖首), 단준(短隼, 매의 일종) 모양 죽절수(竹節首) 등이 있으나 일반적으로 수면문(獸面紋)을 많이 새긴다. 『주례(周禮)』의 기록에 의하면 장(璋)은 남쪽의 신을 제사할 때 사용했던 예기(禮器)인 동시에 천자가 여러 지방을 시찰하고 산천에 제를 지낼 때 사용하는 한편 결혼예물, 부장품으로 사용하였다. 몸체와 손잡이 사이의 양측에 튀어나온 난(闌) 혹은 이빨 모양의 비릉(扉棱, 청동기의 장식)이 달린 것을 아장[牙璋, 이빨 모양의 규(圭)의 반쪽처럼 생긴 옥기]이라고 칭하였는데 출병 시 증표로 사용하였다.

　Jade Zhang was prevalent in the Shang and Zhou Dynasties, which tool in different shapes: flat blade with inclined head, cuboid shape with flat head, whip shape with pointed head, short hawk beak shape with bamboo knots head and so on. Most of these are carved with decorative patterns. The most common pattern is beast face. According to Zhou Li, Zhang is the ritual object used in offering sacrifice to god of the South, it is also used by the emperor in hunting, offering sacrifice to mountains, wedding engagement as well as burials. Ya Zhang has a segment between its body and handle which has teeth-like protrusions on both sides. It is the credential for sending armies.

018

옥장(玉璋)

청옥(靑玉) | 진(秦)
길이 21.3cm 너비 6.6cm 두께 2.3cm
1971년 서안시 미앙구 대명궁공사 연지촌(西安市 未央區 大明宮公社 聯志村) 출토

Jade Zhang

Green jade | Qin Dynasty
L 21.3cm W 6.6cm T 2.3cm
Excavated from Lianzhi Village at Daminggong Community in Weiyang District, Xi'an in 1971

　납작한 직육면체로 윗부분은 경사지게 예각을 이룬 것이 반쪽 옥규(玉圭) 같다. 전체적으로 민무늬이고 면마다 반듯하고 빛이 나게 연마하여 표면 및 모서리 모두 매끈하고 윤이 난다. 이런 모양의 장은 대부분이 춘추전국(春秋戰國)시대 것이다.

규(圭)

신석기시대 용산문화(龍山文化) 시기에 출현한 규는 상·주(商·周)부터 진·한(秦·漢)까지 광범위하게 이용되었다.『주례(周禮)』에는 길(吉), 흉(凶), 군(軍), 병(兵), 가(嘉) 다섯 가지 의례활동에서 규를 가장 많이 사용하였다고 기록되어 있다. 이렇듯 중요한 예옥(禮玉)으로 계급제도를 상징하였을 뿐만 아니라 천지신령을 제사할 때, 알현 시, 결혼예물, 토지 측량, 시간 측정, 중량 표시 등 다양하게 사용되었다. 규의 표면은 일반적으로 민무늬이지만 수면(獸面), 인면(人面) 또는 문자가 조각된 것도 드물게 보인다.

Jade Zhang was prevalent in the Shang and Zhou Dynasties, which tool in different shapes: flat blade with inclined head, cuboid shape with flat head, whip shape with pointed head, short hawk beak shape with bamboo knots head and so on. Most of these are carved with decorative patterns. The most common pattern is beast face. According to Zhou Li, Zhang is the ritual object used in offering sacrifice to god of the South, it is also used by the emperor in hunting, offering sacrifice to mountains, wedding engagement as well as burials. Ya Zhang has a segment between its body and handle which has teeth-like protrusions on both sides. It is the credential for sending armies.

019

옥규(玉圭)

청옥(青玉) | 진(秦)
① 길이 8.5cm 너비 2.1cm 두께 0.9cm
② 길이 7.1cm 너비 2.5cm 두께 0.8cm
1971년 서안시 미앙구 대명궁공사 연지촌(西安市 未央區 大明宮公社 聯志村) 출토

Jade Tablet(Gui)

Green jade | Qin Dynasty
① L 8.5cm W 2.1cm T 0.9cm
② L 7.1cm W 2.5cm T 0.8cm
Excavated from Lianzhi Village at Daminggong Community in Weiyang District, Xi'an in 1971

두 점은 모양이 같으며 아랫부분이 직육면체이고 윗부분이 삼각형이다. 두께는 불균일하고 표면과 모서리는 연마만 하고 광택처리를 하지 않았다.

호(琥)

　호랑이 모양 옥기를 '호(琥)'라고 부르는데, 서쪽의 신을 제사할 때 사용하였던 제기(祭器)이다. 유가(儒家)에서는 호로 늦가을의 쓸쓸함을 표현하였는데 서쪽의 신(백호, 재앙을 쫓고 풍수를 기도하는 상징물)을 제사 지낼 때 신에 대한 경건함을 나타내는 도구였다. 전국(戰國)시대에 와서 호부(虎符)라 하여 용병술을 펼칠 때 증표로 하였고 이후 장식품으로 사용하였다.

　Tiger shaped Jade is called "Hu". It is used especially in sacrificing to the god of the west. Confucians use "Hu" to symbolize the solemnness of deep autumn, to show respect to the God of west, also to express a sense of piety. During the Warring States Period, it is Known as tally, called tiger tally, as the credential for deploying troops. Later, "Hu" is mainly used as ornaments.

020

옥호(玉琥)

청옥(靑玉) | 진(秦)
높이 4cm 길이 11.5cm 두께 0.7cm
1971년 서안시 미앙구 대명궁공사 연지촌(西安市 未央區 大明宮公社 聯志村) 출토

Jade Hu(Tiger-shaped jade)

Green jade | Qin Dynasty
H 4cm L 11.5cm T 0.7cm
Excavated from Lianzhi Village at Daminggong Community in Weiyang District, Xi'an in 1971

　실루엣으로 오린 듯한 납작한 호랑이 측면 모습이다. 양면에 대응되게 가는 음각선으로 호랑이의 입, 코, 눈, 귀, 사지, 꼬리 등을 새겼다. 호랑이는 입이 살짝 벌어졌고 눈이 올리브 모양이며 귀가 뒤로 젖혀졌다. 사지는 걷는 자세를 취하였고 꼬리는 위로 말려 등에 얹혔다.

옥병형기(玉柄形器)

　옥병형기는 상(商) 및 서주(西周)시기에 유행하였다. 상대의 옥병형기는 대다수 수면(獸面), 인면(人面), 양 머리 및 현문(弦紋) 등을 새기고 서주시기는 대부분 민무늬였지만 간혹 봉문(鳳紋) 혹은 용봉문(龍鳳紋)을 새긴 것도 있다. 고분에 부장된 옥병형기는 대부분 죽은 자의 허리 부위에 있었고 일부는 몸 옆 또는 손안에 쥐어져 있었다. 이러한 옥기에 대해 일부 학자들은 노루 이빨로 만든 갈고리 형태에서 변화되어 온 것으로 '아장(牙璋)'의 손잡이일 것이라고 추측하였다.

　Jade Handle-shaped Articles were very popular during Shang and West Zhou Dynasties. Most of the articles in Shang Dynasty are decorated with animal face, those in West Zhou Dynasty are mainly plain surfaced, occasionally with phoenix or dragon and phoenix patterns. Most of the jade handle-shaped articles found in the tomb were placed on the waist of the dead, and some were placed beside the body or held in the hand. Some archeologists believed that such jade articles could be originated from booked articles resembling the teeth of the river deer, and that they are the handle of certain jade Ya Zhang(teeth).

021

병형기(柄型器)

백옥(白玉) ｜ 상(商)
길이 17cm 너비 1.8cm 두께 1cm
1996년 서안시 미앙구(西安市 未央區) 출토

Jade Handle-shaped Article

White jade ｜ Shang Dynasty
L 17cm W 1.8cm T 1cm
Excavated from Weiyang District, Xi'an in 1996

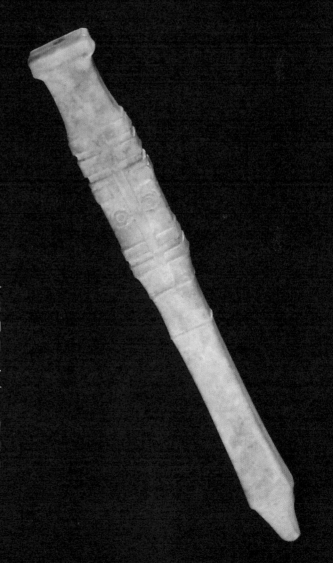

　단검(短劍) 모양으로 손잡이가 잘록하다. 끝부분 단면(斷面)은 직사각형을 이루는데 둥근 구멍이 나 있다. 가운데는 돌기된 넓은 띠 다섯 줄이 있으며 앞면 한가운데는 오목하고 넓은 띠가 세로로 뻗어 있다. 3, 4번째 넓은 띠 사이가 비교적 넓어 그 앞면에는 수목문(獸目紋)을, 측면에는 월(鉞) 도안을 선각(線刻)하였다. 앞부분 역시 잘록한데 철릉(凸棱) 두 줄을 장식하였으며 앞 끝은 뾰족하다.

　양건방(楊建芳)은 짐승 얼굴에서 눈의 특징으로 보아 이 병형기의 시대를 이리두문화(二里頭文化)시대로 추정하였다. 만약 정확한 판단이라면 이 기물(器物)은 중국에서 발견된 가장 이른 병형기이다.

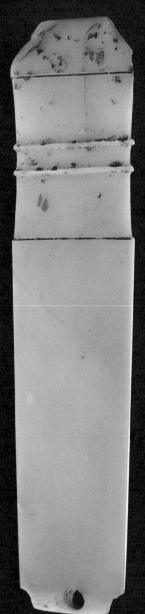

병형기(柄型器)

백옥(白玉) | 서주(西周)
길이 15.7cm 너비 3.7cm 두께 0.5cm
서안시 장안현(西安市 長安縣) 풍호(豐鎬) 유적지 출토

Jade Handle-shaped Article

White jade | West Zhou Dynasty
L 15.7cm W 3.7cm T 0.5cm
Excavated from Fenghao Relic in Chang'an County, Xi'an

편평한 직사각형 모양으로 위가 넓고 아래가 좁다. 위쪽 끝부분 두 모서리를 깎아내어 사다리꼴을 이루었고 아래쪽에는 짧은 돌기가 있으며 가운데에는 나팔 모양 구멍이 있다. 손잡이에는 앞뒤로 현문(弦紋)을 음각(陰刻)하였고 가운데는 감지법(減地法)과 구철법(鉤徹法)으로 돌기된 평행(平行) 현문 두 줄을 새겼다. 기신(器身)의 한쪽을 둥그렇게 갈고 다른 모서리도 연마하여 각을 없앴다. 윤곽선이 가지런하고 표면이 정세(精細)하게 연마되어 매끈하고 윤이 난다.

병형기(柄型器)

백옥(白玉) | 서주(西周)
길이 15.2cm 너비 2.4cm 두께 0.7cm
1970년 서안시 장안현 풍서향(西安市 長安縣 灃西鄉) 서안구리망공장 서주묘(西周墓) 출토

Jade Handle-shaped Article

White jade | West Zhou Dynasty
L 15.2cm W 2.4cm T 0.7cm
Excavated from the West Zhou Tomb in Xi'an Copper Net Factory in Fengxi Village in Chang'an County, Xi'an in 1970

편평한 직사각형 모양이며 위쪽 끝부분 두 모서리를 깎아내어 사다리꼴을 이룬다. 손잡이 부분에는 앞뒤로 각각 현문(弦紋)을 음각(陰刻)하였고 가운데는 감지법(減地法)과 구철법(鉤徹法)으로 돌기된 평행(平行) 현문 두 줄을 새겼다. 기신(器身)의 한쪽 앞뒤 모서리와 단면(單面)을 갈아 날로 만들었다. 이물질이 비교적 많으며 흙이 침투된 흔적이 있다.

부(斧, 도끼)

돌도끼는 석기시대 가장 주요한 생산도구이자 무기였고 원시사회 말기에 이르러 부족연맹 및 추장권위의 상징물이 되었다. 옥도끼는 돌도 끼로부터 변화 발전한 것이다. 신석기시대의 옥도끼는 상당히 많은 수량이 출토되었는데 주로 남자 묘지에 집중되고 대부분 편평한 모양이 다. 구멍은 단면만 뚫거나 양면 모두 뚫었는데 단면만 뚫은 곳은 나팔 모양이고 양면 모두 뚫은 곳에는 각뿔대가 있다. 상대(商代)의 옥도끼는 비교적 적고 이후 더 이상 보이지 않는다. 대부분 정교하게 연마되어 있고 칼날부분에 베거나 자른 흔적이 없는 것으로 보아 일종의 의장기 (儀仗器)였음을 알 수 있다.

Stone Axes are the most important productive instruments and weapons in the Stone Age. In the primitive society, stone axe is also one of the symbols of clan alliance and the authority of chieftains. Jade axe evolves from stone axe. The excavation of Jade axes in the Neolithic Period is very common. They are mainly found in the tombs of the males, most of which are flat. The borings on the Jade axe are either from one side or both sides. The boring that is made from one side takes a trumpet shape, the boring that is made from both sides have found in Shang Dynasty, and none was found after that. Most Jade axes that are excavated are finely crafted and the blade shows no sign of chopping. It is the ceremonial object not made for actual usage.

024

옥부(玉斧)

사문석(蛇紋石) | 용산문화(龍山文化)
길이 16.6cm 너비 4.9~7.8cm 두께 1cm 구멍지름 0.5~0.7cm
1965년 서안시 장안현 풍서향(西安市 長安縣 灃西鄉) 출토

Jade Axe

Serpentine | LongShan Culture
L 16.6cm W 4.9~7.8cm T 1cm Bore D 0.5~0.7cm
Excavated from Fengxi Village in Chang'an County, Xi'an in 1965

사다리꼴 모양으로 뿔은 좁고 날은 넓으며 중간부분은 볼록하고 둥 글며 단면(斷面)은 올리브 모양이다. 날은 호(弧) 모양으로 굽었는데 양면을 연마하여 만든 것이다. 끝부분과 가까운 곳에는 막대기 모양 도 구로 단면(單面)을 뚫은 나팔 모양 구멍이 나 있어 끈을 꿰어 나무 자루 를 고정시킬 수 있다. 이 옥도끼는 기법이 간단하고 소박하며 세부적으 로 두께가 고르지 않고 모양이 반듯하지 않다. 또한 구멍도 정중앙에 위치하지 않고 재질도 거칠며 파손된 흔적이 여러 군데 있어 원시적 특 징이 뚜렷하다.

옥부(玉斧)

사문석(蛇紋石) | 상(商)
길이 10cm 너비 5.1cm 두께 0.5cm 구멍지름 0.6~0.8cm
1986년 서안시 남전현 사파촌(西安市 藍田縣 寺坡村) 출토

Jade Axe

Serpentine | Shang Dynasty
L 10cm W 5.1cm T 0.5cm Bore D 0.6~0.8cm
Excavated from Sipo Village in Lantian County, Xi'an in 1986

납작한 사다리꼴 모양으로 날이 넓고 뿔이 좁다. 호형(弧形)의 날은 양면을 연마하여 만든 것이다. 양쪽 측면은 위쪽이 곧고 아래쪽이 밖으로 벌어졌으며 모서리는 매끈하다. 끝부분은 평평하게 깎았는데 표면이 거친 편이다. 이와 가까운 한가운데에는 막대기 모양 도구로 뚫은 나팔 모양 구멍이 나 있어 끈을 꿰어 나무 자루를 고정할 수 있다. 진녹색이고 재질은 섬세하고 온윤(溫潤)하며 광택처리가 잘 되었다. 날 부분에 파손이 없고 구멍에 끈을 묶었던 흔적이 없는 것으로 보아 실용품은 아닌 듯하다.

도(刀)

옥도(玉刀)는 신석기시대의 돌칼에서 발전되어 온 것이다. 당시의 석제도구 및 무기에는 도끼, 자귀, 칼, 낫, 삽, 월(鉞, 큰 도끼 모양의 고대 병기), 척(鏚, 도끼) 등이 포함되었는데 옥제 도구의 출현으로 용도가 변해 실용성에서 벗어나 상징성을 띠게 되었다. 신석기시대의 유적지에서도 옥도가 종종 출토되는데 뒷면의 구멍지름은 2~5cm 사이이고 가장 긴 것은 5.4cm에 달하였다. 고고학 발굴 중에서 발견된 이러한 옥도구, 옥무기는 대부분 죽은 자의 가슴이나 신체 주위에 놓여 있어 죽은 자의 신분을 짐작할 수 있다.

Jade Knives are evolved from stone knives in the Neolithic Period. At that time, the stoneware that were related to weapons were axes, adze blades, knives, sickles, spades, tomahawks, battle axes and so on. As time went on, Jade instruments appeared, and their usage experienced qualitative change. They are no longer for practical usage, but become a symbol indictor. In the Neolithic period sites, the excavation of such jade knife is common. The diameter of the perforations on the back are between 2cm to 5cm, the biggest could reach 5.4cm. Such jade instruments or jade weapons that are excavated from the tombs are often found to be placed on the chest and abdomen regions of the body or beside the body. The owner of the tomb should have special identity or enjoy high status.

026

삼공옥도(三孔玉刀)

사문석(蛇紋石) | 용산문화(龍山文化)
위길이 17.7cm 아래길이 19cm 너비 4.5cm 두께 0.3cm 구멍지름 0.7~1.1cm
1978년 동천시(銅川市) 수집

Jade Knife with Three Borings

Serpentine | LongShan Culture
Upper L 17.7cm Lower L 19cm W 4.5cm T 0.3cm Bore D 0.7~1.1cm
Collected in Tongchuan City in 1978

납작하고 기다란 사다리꼴 모양으로 날이 넓고 등이 좁다. 날은 단면(單面)을 사선으로 연마해 만든 것이며 홈이 여러 군데 나 있는데 이는 사용해서 생긴 자국이다. 등과 가까운 부분에 막대기 모양 도구로 단면을 뚫어 만든 나팔 모양 구멍 세 개가 있는데 끈을 꿰어 나무 자루를 고정시킬 수 있다. 앞면은 양쪽 모서리를 사선으로 깎아내고 윗부분을 평평하게 다듬었다. 날, 가장자리, 구멍은 모두 같은 면에서 가공하고 다른 한 면은 평면가공만 하였다. 자세히 살펴보면, 도면(刀面)은 섬세하게 연마되었으나 두께가 고르지 못하고 날과 모서리가 가지런하지 않다. 그리고 구멍도 크기와 간격이 일치하지 않고 대칭되지 않는 것이 신석기시대 옥기의 보편적인 특징을 띠고 있다.

산(鏟, 삽)

　돌삽으로부터 직접 발전된 것으로 옥산(玉鏟)의 형태는 옥월(玉鉞)보다 좁고 옥도끼보다 얇다. 그리고 대부분 정교하게 연마되어 있고 칼날 부위에도 손상이 없어 의장기(儀仗器)에 속한다는 것을 알 수 있다. 신석기시대 말기의 양저문화(良渚文化), 제가문화(齊家文化), 용산문화(龍山文化) 유적지에서 모두 발견되고 상대(商代) 것은 드물다. 상대 이후로는 더 이상 발견되지 않는다.

　Jade Spades are born out of stone spade. It is narrower than jade battle axe, and thinner than jade axe. Many of them are, and thinner than jade axe. Many of them are carefully crafted, without damage on the blade. It belongs to ceremonial objects. Jade spades are discovered in the Liangzhu Culture, Qi's Culture and Long Shan Culture in the late stage of Neolithic Period. Few were discovered in Shang Dynasty, and after that, it disappeared.

027

옥산(玉鏟)

사문석(蛇紋石) | 용산문화(龍山文化)
길이 14.5cm 위너비 6cm 아래너비 7cm 두께 0.5cm 구멍지름 0.7~0.8cm
1965년 서안시 장안현 풍서공사(西安市 長安縣 灃西公社) 객성장(客省莊) 유적지 출토

Jade Spade

Serpentine | LongShan Culture
L 14.5cm Upper W 6cm Lower W 7cm T 0.5cm Bore D 0.7~0.8cm
Excavated from Keshengzhuang Relic at Fengxi Village in Chang'an County, Xi'an in 1965

　납작한 사다리꼴로 날이 넓고 등이 좁다. 날은 호형(弧形)인데 단면(單面)을 갈아 만든 것이고 다른 세 변의 앞면 모서리는 모두 둥글게 다듬었다. 뒷면은 반들반들한 민무늬이며 윤곽이 분명하다. 끝부분과 가까운 한가운데는 막대기 모양 도구로 뚫은 나팔 모양 구멍이 나 있는데 끈을 꿰어 나무 자루를 고정시킬 수 있다. 구멍 양쪽 구연(口沿)에는 모두 가공흔적이 남아 있다. 날, 가장자리, 구멍은 모두 같은 면에서 가공하였고 다른 한쪽 면은 평면가공과 연마만 하였다. 진녹색이고 재질이 섬세하고 온윤(溫潤)하며 표면에는 반짝이는 결정체 조각이 보인다. 전체적으로 반질반질하고 날에 파손이 없으며 구멍에 묶었던 흔적이 없는 것으로 보아 실용품은 아닌 듯하다. 이 삽은 서안 서쪽에 위치한 객성장(客省莊) 유적지에서 출토되었는데 이곳에서는 대량의 용산문화(龍山文化) 유물이 출토된 바 있다.

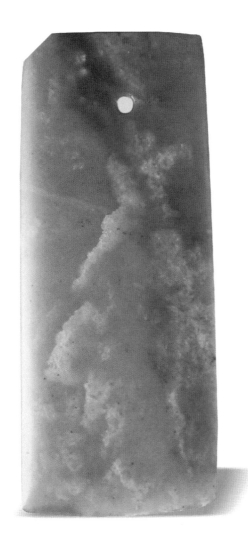

옥산(玉鏟)

사문석(蛇紋石) | 상(商)
길이 14.6cm 너비 6.2cm 두께 0.4cm 구멍지름 0.5~0.6cm
1986년 서안시 남전현 사파촌(西安市 藍田縣 寺坡村) 출토

Jade Spade

Serpentine | Shang Dynasty
L 14.6cm W 6.2cm T 0.4cm Bore D 0.5~0.6cm
Excavated from Sipo Village in Lantian County, Xi'an in 1986

　　납작한 직사각형으로 날 부분이 조금 넓고 살짝 호(弧) 모양으로 굽었으며 단면(單面)을 갈아 만든 것이다. 윗부분은 평평하게 다듬었고 앞면 한쪽 모서리를 경사지게 깎아내었으며 양쪽 측면의 앞쪽 모서리는 호각(弧角)으로 다듬었다. 뒷면은 반들반들한 민무늬로 윤곽이 선명하다. 윗부분과 가까운 가운데에는 마주하여 뚫은 구멍이 있는데 끈을 꿰어 나무 자루를 고정시킬 수 있다. 날, 가장자리는 같은 면에서 가공하고 다른 한쪽 면은 연마와 평면가공만 하였으며 진녹색에 재질이 섬세하고 온윤(溫潤)하다. 전체적으로 반들반들하고 날에 파손이 없으며 구멍에도 묶였던 흔적이 없는 것으로 보아 실용품은 아닌 듯하다.

옥산(玉鏟)

사문석(蛇紋石) | 상(商)
길이 11.5cm 너비 4.6cm 두께 0.4cm 구멍지름 0.4~0.5cm
1977년 서안시 파교구 모서공사(西安市 灞橋區 毛西公社) 출토

Jade Spade

Serpentine | Shang Dynasty
L 11.5cm W 4.6cm T 0.4cm Bore D 0.4~0.5cm
Excavated from Maoxi Village in Baqiao District, Xi'an in 1977

　　납작한 사다리꼴로 날이 넓고 등은 좁다. 날은 호형(弧形)으로 단면(單面)을 갈아 만든 것이며 위쪽과 한쪽 측면의 앞쪽 모서리는 둥글게 다듬어졌다. 다른 한쪽 측면의 모서리는 윤곽이 선명하고 그 윗부분에 안쪽으로 오목하게 들어간 구멍 반쪽이 있다. 이로부터 제작 당시 너비는 지금의 갑절이었으나 가공하면서 파손되어 구멍 부분에서 두 개로 나눈 것으로 추정된다. 뒷면은 반질반질한 민무늬로 4면 가장자리 모두 윤곽이 선명하다. 위쪽 가운데 막대기 모양 도구로 양면으로 뚫은 구멍이 나 있는데 뒷면 구연(口沿)이 크고 앞면 구연이 작다. 이 구멍은 끈을 꿰어 나무 자루를 고정하는 데 쓰인다. 이 삽은 서안시 파교구 모서공사 부근 노우파(老牛坡) 상대(商代) 유적지에서 출토되었는데 이곳에서는 상대 옥기가 여러 차례 발견된 바 있다. 제작기법으로 보아 상대 유물로 추정된다.

과(戈, 창)

상·주대(商·周代)에 유행하던 의장기(儀仗器)로 옥과(玉戈)는 원[援, 신(身)], 내[內, 병(柄)], 천[穿, 공(孔)], 난[闌, 호(胡)], 필[珌, 병(柄)] 등으로 나눌 수 있다. 원은 창의 긴 막대기형 칼날 부분이고, 내는 원과 연결되어 필(珌)에 삽입하는 부분이며, 호(胡)는 필과 인접한 하단의 연장부분이고, 그 위의 구멍은 고정시키기 위해 만든 것이다. 상대 초기의 옥창은 내에 직접 구멍을 뚫고 원 양측의 칼날은 예리하며 끝이 뾰족하다. 상대 중기, 말기에 와서는 크기가 30cm까지 커지고 척릉(脊棱, 등에 새긴 모서리) 및 홈을 조각하였다. 서주(西周) 이후부터 크기가 점차 작아지고 이빨 모양의 난(闌) 또는 운문(雲紋)을 주로 조각하였다.

Jade Dagger-axe is the ceremonial objects that is widely used in Shang, Zhou Dynasties. It is composed of Yuan(body), Nei(shaft), Chuan(perforation), Lan, Mi(handle) etc. Yuan is the bar shaped part containing blade, Nei is the section which joints the body with the handle, Hu is the place near the elongated lower end of Mi, with perforation on it for fixation. In the early West Zhou Dynasty, Chuan was in the Nei, blade appeared on both sides of Yuan, the fore edge is sharp. By the middle and late period, its size elongated to 30cm, and is carved with dorsal ridges and grooves. It gradually gets smaller after West Zhou Dynasty, and many are carved with tooth-like railings and cloud patterns.

030

옥과(玉戈)

사문석(蛇紋石) | 상(商)
길이 31cm 최대너비 8.1cm 두께 0.7cm 구멍지름 0.8~1.2cm
1975년 서안시 파교구(西安市 灞橋區) 노우파(老牛坡) 상대 유적지 출토

Jade Dagger-axe

Serpentine | Shang Dynasty
L 31cm Max W 8.1cm T 0.7cm Bore D 0.8~1.2cm
Excavated from Shang Dynasty Relic in Laoniupo, Baqiao District, Xi'an in 1975

원(援)이 넓고 조금 굽었으며 가운데에는 척릉(脊棱)이 있는데 앞쪽은 삼각형 모양이고 양측은 모두 날로 한쪽이 굽고 다른 한쪽이 곧다. 내(內)는 직사각형으로 구멍이 나 있으며 내와 원이 만나는 양측에는 호(胡)가 있다. 원과 가까운 부분에는 나팔 모양 구멍이 나 있고 뒤 가장자리에는 이빨 모양 비릉(扉棱) 네 개가 있다. 이 옥과는 진령(秦嶺) 일대에서 흔히 보이는 사문석으로 만들어진 것인데 서안 지역에서 출토된 상·주(商·周) 옥제(玉製) 도구와 패식(佩飾) 중에는 이런 재료로 만들어진 것이 적지 않다. 제작이 정교하고 날이 예리하며 직선 변, 호형(弧形) 변 모두 단단하고 힘 있다. 전체적으로 반듯하고 반질반질하며 아무런 손상이 없는데 광택처리가 정세(精細)하고 구멍과 비릉 사이마저도 세세하게 연마하였다. 곧은 내, 비릉, 긴 원과 척릉 등의 특징으로 보아 상대(商代) 말기 유물로 추정된다.

옥인(玉人)

옥인은 신석기시대의 용산문화(龍山文化) 시기에 처음 나타난 이후 각 시대마다 나타났지만 특징 및 의미는 모두 다르다. 선진(先秦)시대의 옥인은 평조(平彫)와 원조(圓彫) 두 종류가 있다. 당시 옥인 머리의 주요특징은 보통 선형(船形) 모자, 볼록한 코, 송곳니, 비첨식(飛檐式) 관(冠)이고 서 있거나 꿇어앉은 자세이며 모든 원조 옥인의 표정은 우울하고 생기가 없어 보인다. 진대(秦代) 옥인은 대부분 납작한 모양이고 가는 선을 음각하여 얼굴표정 및 옷차림을 표현하였다. 한대(漢代) 옥인은 사실성을 추구하여 인물 형상도 더욱 풍부해졌는데 특히 무인(舞人)이 많이 보인다. 위·진(魏·晉) 이후, 불교인물 형상도 점차 많아졌는데 당대(唐代)의 옥비천(玉飛天), 송대(宋代)의 옥동자(玉童子)가 그 예이다. 원·명·청대(元·明·淸代)에 옥인 조각기술이 크게 발전하였는데 그중 종교 조각으로는 여래, 관음, 종규(鐘馗), 미륵, 십팔나한(十八羅漢) 등이 있고 상서로움의 상징물로는 재신(財神), 화합(和合), 복녹수삼성(福祿壽三星), 유해희금섬(劉海戲金蟾) 등이 있다. 성현(聖賢) 및 신선을 표현한 것에는 공자(孔子), 노자(老子), 관우(關羽), 팔선(八仙), 낙신(洛神), 태백취주(太白醉酒) 등이 있다. 그리고 민간 고사에는 천녀산화(天女散花), 견우직녀, 항아분월(嫦娥奔月), 사대미녀(四大美女) 등이 있다.

진대 이전 옥인은 주로 제사 또는 벽사(辟邪)에 사용되었고 한대 이후 패식(佩飾) 또는 진열품으로 사용되었다.

Jade Human Characters already existed in the Long Shan Culture in the Neolithic Period. After that, jade human characters have been found in every dynasty, only with different features and connotations according to different period. The jade human characters in the early Qin Dynasty are either in flat carvings or round carvings. The head of the jade human at that time are featured with boat-shaped hat, garlic-shaped nose, bucktooth and flying-eave shaped hats. The jade man either stand on feet, or kneel, or sit on the ground. All the jade humans looked worried and unhappy, with dull expressions. The jade human characters in the Qin Dynasty are in flat flake, using slender intaglied lines in the Qin Dynasty are in flat flake, using slender intaglied lines to express face and dress. during Han Dynasty, the jade human characters get into a realistic style, with richer images. Dancers were especially common at that time. After Wei and Jin Dynasties, the Buddhist characters gradually increased. In the Tang Dynasty, there are jade flying fairies, and in the Song Dynasty, there are Jade boys. By Yuan, Ming, and Qing Dynasty, the figures showing religious beliefs have been greatly enriched, the figures showing relinguous beliefs include: Jade Rulai Buddha, Jade Lwan-yin Buddha, jade Zhong-kui, jade Mi-le Buddha, jade eighteen Luohan(Arhats, Buddha's disciples), etc; the images showing auspiciousness and good fortunes are jade He-he(god of reunion), jade Fu-Lu-Shou(the three gods in charge of good fortune, official career and longevity), jade Liu-hai Playing with gold toad etc; the images representing sages and legendary gods are jade Confucius, jade Laozi(founder of Taoism), Jade Guan-gong, Jade Eight Immortals, Jade Luo God, Jade drunken Tai-bai(the famous poet in Tang Dynasty), etc.; the images presenting folk stories are Jade flying fairy scattering flowers, Jade Niu-lang and Zhi-nv(the story of cowboy and weaving girl), jade Chang-e flying towards the moon, and Jade Four Ancient Beauties, etc.

The jabe human characters are mainly used in offering sacrifices and warding off evils before Qin Dynasty. After Han Dynasty, they are mainly used as ornaments or displaying objects.

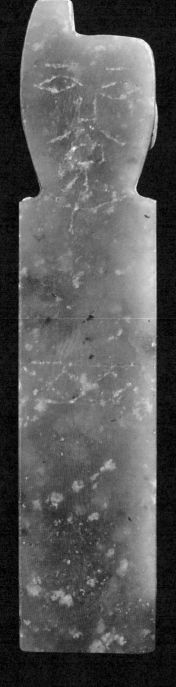 

남녀옥인(男女玉人)

청옥(靑玉) | 진(秦)
남자옥인: 높이 7.5cm 너비 1.5cm 두께 0.5cm
여자옥인: 높이 7.4cm 너비 1.4cm 두께 0.4cm
1971년 서안시 미앙구 대명궁공사 연지촌(西安市 未央區 大明宮公社 聯志村) 출토

Jade Man and Woman

Green jade | Qin Dynasty
Jade Man: H 7.5cm W 1.5cm T 0.5cm
Jade Woman: H 7.4cm W 1.4cm T 0.4cm
Excavated from Lianzhi Village at Daminggong Community in Weiyang District, Xi'an in 1971

옥인 2점은 조형이 비슷하며 둘 다 직사각형의 편(片) 모양이다. 윗부분은 머리와 상반신 윤곽으로 머리카락, 눈썹, 눈, 코, 입 등을 가는 선으로 음각(陰刻)하였다. 허리 부분에서는 가는 선으로 허리띠를 표현하였다. 입술 위에 팔자수염이 새겨진 것은 남성이고 다른 한 점은 여성이다. 조각기법이 질박하고 형상이 간단하며 끈을 끼워 착용할 수 있는 구멍이 없다. 선진(先秦)시대 옥인은 일반적으로 제사(祭祀)에 사용되었는데 이 한 쌍의 용도(用途)도 마찬가지인 것으로 추정된다. 이런 유형의 옥기는 진대(秦代)에 나타나기 시작했으며 형태는 기본적으로 같다. 남녀가 공통으로 뚜렷한 시대적 특징을 띠어 옥인 발전사 내지 당시 복식을 연구하기 위한 주요 유물자료이다.

패식

佩飾

중국 고대 옥기는 대부분 패식(佩飾)에 속하며 이러한 풍습은 신석기시대부터 줄곧 성행하였다. 옥기는 관식(冠飾), 머리장신구[髮飾], 귀걸이[耳飾], 목걸이[項飾], 팔찌[腕飾], 허리부위의 패식 등으로 나뉜다. 패식옥기는 결(玦), 환(環), 구슬 장식품[管珠串飾] 및 동물상이 많은데 대부분 착용하기 위한 구멍이 있다. 일반적으로 순도가 높은 옥으로 만들어졌고 조형이 아름다워 중국 고대옥기를 대표한다.

Most jade articles in ancient China belong to pendant ornaments. The practice of wearing jade on bodies and consumes for decoration has been popular since Neolithic Period. Jade pendants can be divided into hat pendants, hair pendants, ear pendants, neck pendants, wrist pendants and waist pendants. The jade articles for wearing are mainly Jue(penannular) Rings, tubular beads as well as those with animal patterns, most of which have bores for tying and fixation. Such jades are usually of pure quality and are elaborately crafted. They are the mainstream of jade artifacts in China.

계(笄, 비녀)

계는 고대인들이 머리를 묶을 때 사용하는 도구로 남자들이 쪽 찐 머리가 풀어지지 않도록 꽂는 장신구였다. 옥계(玉笄)는 양저문화(良渚文化)에서 처음 나타났는데 명 · 청대(明 · 淸代)는 물론, 현대 소수민족들도 여전히 사용하고 있다. 보통 긴 송곳 모양을 이루는데 상대(商代) 초기, 중기에 이미 형태가 완성되었다. 계의 자루는 대부분 길고 가느다란 원형의 송곳 모양이며 윗부분은 굵고 아랫부분은 가늘며, 평평하고 광을 냈다. 일부는 자루 윗부분에 무늬를 조각하였다. 옛날 남자들은 18세가 되면 성인식을 치르면서 길게 기른 머리를 계로 고정시키는 의례를 진행했기 때문에 18세를 급계지년(及笄之年)이라고 칭하였다. 옥으로 된 계는 일반적으로 귀족 남자의 머리장신구이다.

Ji is the ornament used by the ancient people to bind hair. At that time, man bound hair on calvaria and inserted Ji horizontally in the hair for fixation. Women also used Ji in the hair both for fixation and decoration.

032

옥계(玉笄)

석영암(石英岩) | 앙소문화(仰韶文化)
잔존길이 5.9cm 최대지름 0.7cm
2004년 서안시 안탑구 어화채(西安市 雁塔區 魚化寨) 출토

Jade Ji(Hairpin)

Quartize | YangShao Culture
Residue L 5.9cm Max D 0.7cm
Excavated from Yuhuazhai Village in Yanta District,
Xi'an in 2004

원뿔 모양으로 단면(斷面)은 타원형을 이루며 윗부분은 떨어져 나갔고 아랫부분은 뾰족하다. 자루는 곧고 표면은 정교하게 연마되었다. 계는 옛사람들이 머리를 묶는 장식품으로 당시 남성들은 머리를 쪽진 후 계를 가로 꽂아 고정시켰다. 여성들도 계를 꽂아 머리를 고정시켰는데 장식작용도 있었다.

033

옥계(玉笄)

사문석(蛇紋石) | 용산문화(龍山文化)
길이 14cm 최대지름 1.3cm
서안시 미앙구 미가애촌(西安市 未央區 米家崖村) 출토

Jade Ji(Hairpin)

Serpentine | LongShan Culture
L 14cm Max D 1.3cm
Excavated from Mijiaya Village in Weiyang District, Xi'an

기다란 송곳 모양으로 윗부분은 평평하고 아랫부분은 뾰족하다. 자루는 가지런하고 곧으며 반질반질한 것이 세심하게 연마되었다.

옥어(玉魚)

옥어는 중요한 고대 옥패식(玉佩飾)으로 상대(商代)에 처음 나타났다. 당시 옥어는 보통 단일한 얇은 편(片)으로 되어 있고 상대 중기, 말기의 은허(殷墟) 부호묘(婦好墓)에서 다량 출토되었다. 옥어는 조각이 단순하고 대충 만들어진 것 같으면서도 사실감이 있다. 주대(周代)에는 기법적으로 상대보다 발전하였는데 예를 들어 굽은 형태의 물고기가 늘어난 동시에 원호형(圓弧形) 비늘무늬가 출현하였다. 춘추전국(春秋戰國)시대부터 한대(漢代)까지는 옥어가 거의 보이지 않고 당대(唐代)에 와서야 다시 늘어나 옥어의 패식제도도 형성되었다.

당대에는 왕공(王公)이 옥어를 착용하는 제도가 나타났다. 예컨대 친왕(親王)은 옥어, 대신 및 훈척(勳戚, 공이 있는 황제의 가족과 친척)들은 금어(金魚)를 착용하였다. 송대(宋代) 엽몽득(葉夢得)이 쓴 『석림연어(石林燕語)』 7권에는 아래와 같은 내용이 나온다. "본조(本朝) 친왕들은 전부 금대(金帶)를 착용하였다. 원풍(元豐)연간 중관제(中官制)를 시행하면서 황제는 가왕(嘉王), 기왕(岐王)을 총애한다는 의미에서 둘을 불러들여 방단옥대(方團玉帶)를 하사하여 궁중의 예의를 표현하였다. 어용(御用) 옥대가 모두 배방(排方, 고대 허리띠 장식의 일종)이므로 방단(方團, 네모와 둥긂)으로 구분하였다. 두 왕은 극구 사양하다가 보배를 집에 숨겨 두고 착용하지 않았다. 황제가 이를 허락하지 않아 그제야 두 왕은 금어를 요청하였고 황제는 이들을 다시 불러들여 옥어를 하사하였다. 이때부터 친왕은 옥대에 옥어를 착용하기 시작하였다." 이로부터 물고기 모양 옥식이 송대에 크게 유행하였으며 요(遼) · 금(金) · 원(元) · 명(明) · 청(淸)까지 영향을 미쳤다.

Jade Fishes are very important jade pendants in Chinese history. The wearing of jade fish began in Shang Dynasty, during which period, jade fish usually came in single flake shape. Large number of jade fishes were excavated from Fuhao tomb in Yin Relic at mid and late Shang Dynasty. The carvings are quite simple, as if they were made casually in haste, yet they render a feeling of neatness and reality from those rough and sparse lines. The carving technique of the jade fish had been improved during Zhou Dynasty, with more curved fishes. Arc Shaped squama also appeared on the body of the fish. Jade fish got rare from Spring and Autumn and Warring States Period to Han Dynasty. During Tang Dynasty, jade fish again became popular and stipulations were made on the wearing of jade fishes.

During Tang Dynasty, lieges have the stipulation to wear jade fishes. Princes wire jade fish. ministers and meritorious relatives wore gold fish. According to the seventh volumn of Shih-lin yen yu by Yeh Meng-de: "All the imperil infantes wear gold belt, as was stipulated by Zhong Gong (bureaucracy in the imperial palace) in the year of Yuanfeng. The emperor tended to bestow favor on the two infantes jia and Qi, and instructed to bestow Fangtuan jade belt to them, and made the wearing of Fangtuan jade belt a convenance for court meetings. The two infantes insisted to decline, asking for permission to put the treasure away at home and not to wear them. Their request was rejected, and the two infantes then asked to be given gold fish instead. The emperor then dictated to bestow jade fish to them. And the practice of wearing jade fish by princes was started since then." As a result, jade fish pendants prevailed in Song Dynasty, and such vogue even affected Liao, Jin, Yuan, Ming and Qing Dynasties.

034

옥어(玉魚)

사문석(蛇紋石) ｜ 서주(西周)
길이 10.7cm 너비 2.5cm 두께 0.9cm
1978년 서안시 장안현(西安市 長安縣) 풍호(豐鎬) 유적지 서주묘(西周墓) 출토

Jade Fish

Serpentine ｜ West Zhou Dyansty
L 10.7cm W 2.5cm T 0.9cm
Excavated from West Zhou Tomb in Fenghao Relic in Chang'an County, Xi'an in 1978

전체적으로 납작하고 길며 머리는 삼각형을 이루고 몸통은 곧으며 꼬리는 좁아지다가 두 갈래로 나뉘었다. 뒷부분이 아래로 굽은 음각선으로 꼭 다문 입을, 동심쌍현문(同心雙弦紋)으로 눈을 표현했고 몸통에는 와문(瓦紋)을 새겨 비늘을 나타냈으며 등지느러미와 꼬리는 음각선으로 나타냈다. 입, 꼬리와 가까운 부분에는 각각 '亞(아)'자 모양 구멍이 있다. 등지느러미는 양면을 경사지게 깎아내어 뾰족하게 만들었고 머리와 배 부분은 둥글게 다듬었다. 한쪽 면에는 주사(朱砂)가 가득 묻어 있다.

035

옥어(玉魚)

사문석(蛇紋石) | 서주(西周)
길이 8,3cm 너비 2cm 두께 0,3cm
1972년 서안시 장안현(西安市 長安縣) 풍호(豐鎬) 유적지 출토

Jade Fish

Serpentine | West Zhou Dynasty
L 8,3cm W 2cm T 0,3cm
Excavated from Fenghao Relic in Chang'an County, Xi'an in 1972

납작한 편(片) 모양으로 입은 벌어졌고 몸통은 곧으며 꼬리는 갈라졌다. 움푹 파인 삼각형으로 벌어진 입을 표현하고 눈, 아가미, 아래위 지느러미는 모두 음각(陰刻)하였다. 입 쪽에 끈을 끼워 착용할 수 있는 구멍이 나 있다. 등지느러미와 꼬리 끝부분은 양면을 경사지게 깎아내어 날로 만들었고 다른 모서리는 사선으로 연마하였다. 표면은 정밀하게 연마되어 반들반들하고 온윤(溫潤)하다.

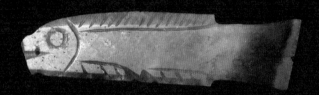

036

옥어(玉魚)

사문석(蛇紋石) | 서주(西周)
길이 12,5cm 너비 3,6cm 두께 1cm
1972년 서안시 장안현(西安市 長安縣) 풍호(豐鎬) 유적지 출토

Jade Fish

Serpentine | West Zhou Dynasty
L 12,5cm W 3,6cm T 1cm
Excavated from Fenghao Relic in Chang'an County, Xi'an in 1972

둥글납작한 막대기 모양으로 입은 둥글고 꼬리는 넓으며 몸통은 퉁퉁한데 양면을 조각하였다. 눈은 작은 동그라미로 표현하고 아가미는 평행(平行) 호선(弧線) 사이 짧은 평행 사선으로 나타냈다. 꼬리 부분은 세로로 그은 직선 뒤에 가로로 평행 직선 여러 줄을 그어 표현했다. 복부 한쪽 면에는 원재료를 절삭할 때 생긴 굵은 경사선이 남아 있다. 가장자리는 연마하여 둥글고 매끈하다.

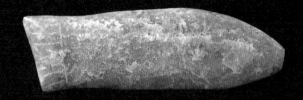

037

옥어(玉魚)

사문석(蛇紋石) | 서주(西周)
길이 8,7cm 너비 2,4cm 두께 0,7cm
서안시 장안현(西安市 長安縣) 풍호(豐鎬) 유적지 출토

Jade Fish

Serpentine | West Zhou Dynasty
L 8,7cm W 2,4cm T 0,7cm
Excavated from Fenghao Relic in Chang'an County, Xi'an

전체적으로 납작한데 머리가 좁고 꼬리는 넓고 갈라졌다. 크고 둥근 눈, 호형(弧形) 아가미, 커다란 등지느러미, 작은 배지느러미 2개를 가지고 있으며 입 부분에는 구멍이 나 있다. 눈, 아가미, 지느러미는 모두 가는 선으로 음각(陰刻)하였다. 표면은 정세(精細)하게 연마되었고 4면 가장자리는 양면을 경사지게 깎아내어 날로 만들었다.

038

옥어(玉魚)

사문석(蛇紋石) | 서주(西周)
길이 3cm 너비 0,8cm 두께 0,4cm
1981년 서안시 호현(西安市 戶縣) 출토

Jade Fish

Serpentine | West Zhou Dynasty
L 3cm W 0,8cm T 0,4cm
Excavated from Huxian County, Xi'an in 1981

둥글납작한 막대기 모양으로 입은 둥글고 꼬리는 넓고 갈라졌으며 배는 둥글고 볼록하며 양면을 조각하였다. 아가미, 지느러미는 가는 선으로 음각(陰刻)하고 꼬리의 갈라진 부분은 예각 삼각형으로 다듬었다. 눈은 천공(穿孔)이지만 양쪽 방향이 맞지 않아 만나는 부분만 뚫렸다. 몸통 아래위와 꼬리는 양면을 경사지게 깎아내어 날로 만들었다.

옥패선(玉佩蟬)

패선(佩蟬)은 허리나 가슴에 패용하는 장식품으로 보통 구멍에 끈을 끼워 사용한다. 양저문화(良渚文化)에서 최초로 나타났고 상(商) 및 서주(西周)시기에 와서 유행하였다. 당시 옥패선은 대부분 타원 기둥 모양이었고 머리 부위에 있는 둥근 구멍이 복부까지 이어졌다. 한대(漢代)에 이르러, 옥선(玉蟬)은 양과 질에서 모두 이전 시대를 능가하였다. 재료는 재질이 매끄러운 신강(新疆) 화전옥(和闐玉)을 사용하고 제작기법이 아주 정교하며, 납작한 모양을 이룬다. 매미의 두 눈은 튀어 나왔으며 꼬리와 날개는 볼록하게 튀어나와 세 개의 뾰족한 각을 이루고 등에는 간결한 선만으로 각 부위를 나타내었다. 배와 꼬리 부위는 3~5개의 횡선으로 꾸며 주었다. 칼날이 예리하고 윤곽이 뚜렷하여 전형적인 '한팔도(漢八刀)'의 풍격을 띠었다. 한대 이후에도 여전히 유행했으나 기법이 점차 쇠락하였다. 조형은 사실적으로 변하였고 세부적인 묘사가 지나쳐 형태를 중시하는 반면 운치를 잃었다. 당시 예술수준은 이미 한대와 비교하여 크게 뒤떨어졌다.

Jade Cicada Pendant is a kind of ornament that is worn at the waist or in front of the chest. They were usually perforated for attachment by strings. Such cicada pendants were first seen in Liangzhu Culture and became popular by Shang and West Zhou Dynasties. The cicada at this period usually takes on oval shape, with a round hole that goes from the head down to the abdomen. In Han Dynasty, The production of jade cicada exceeded other periods both in quantity and quality. The material of cicada in Han Dynasty used the fine and glossy Hetian jade in Xinjiang. The technique was also meticulous. The shape of the cicada was flat, with bulged eyes and three heaved sharp angled at tail and two wings. Different parts of the body was manifested by simple lines on the back, with three to five transverse line at the tail and belly. The carvings were trenchant and distinctive, with typical style of "eight cuts of Han". The wearing of jade cicada was also popular after Han Dynasty, but the carving techniques had waned. The shape of the cicada turned to a realistic style, overloaded with details, The emphasis of similarity in shape instead of verve has made the technique incomparable with that in Han Dynasty.

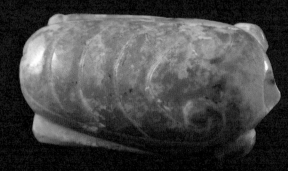

039

옥패선(玉佩蟬)

청백옥(靑白玉) | 서주(西周)
길이 3.8cm 너비 2cm 두께 1.6cm
1982년 서안시 호현(西安市 戶縣) 출토

Jade Cicada Pendant

Green and white jade | West Zhou Dynasty
L 3.8cm W 2cm T 1.6cm
Excavated from Huxian County, Xi'an in 1982

둥근기둥 모양으로 정수리가 꺼지고 턱이 나왔다. 두 눈은 볼록하게 융기되고 목은 관대문(寬帶紋)으로 장식되었으며 양 날개는 비탈 모양을 이루었다. 'U'형 음각선으로 복부 윤곽을 그렸는데 윗부분 양쪽 끝은 소용돌이 모양으로 새겨 발음기를 나타내고 아랫부분은 가로로 호선(弧線) 여러 줄을 그어 신축(伸縮)기능이 있는 배마디를 나타냈다. 몸통 한가운데에는 머리에서 꼬리까지 꿰뚫은 끈을 끼워 착용할 수 있는 구멍이 나 있다. 옥선은 장례용과 패식용으로 나뉘는데 이것은 착용하는 패식이다.

용형패(龍形佩)

용(龍) 문양은 일찍이 지금으로부터 약 5천~6천 년 전의 홍산문화(紅山文化) 유적지에서부터 발견된다. 관련 유물 중 상대(商代)부터 명·청대(明·淸代)의 용문(龍紋) 옥기가 대부분이다. 이들은 조형이 풍부하고 생동감이 있을 뿐 아니라 문양이 정교하고 다양하였다. 또한 각 시대의 작품들은 이전 시대의 풍격을 계승할 뿐만 아니라 각 시대의 독특한 특징도 가지고 있다.

The pattern of dragon appeared early in the "Hongshan Culture" relics 5000~6000 years ago. Among the cultural heritages that are excavated of handed down from ancient times, from Shang Dynasty to Ming and Qing Dynasties, dragon patterned articles took up considerable proportion. They are abundant and vivid in shape, with lines delicate and diversified. What's more, the style of the works in different period reflects both the inherited relationship and respective feature.

040

옥룡(玉龍)

청옥(青玉) | 서주(西周)
지름 3.8cm 두께 0.6cm
1979년 섬서성 봉상현 유담촌(陝西省 鳳翔縣 劉淡村) 출토

Jade Dragon

Green jade | West Zhou Dynasty
D 3.8cm T 0.6cm
Excavated from Liudan Village in Fengxiang County, Shaanxi Province in 1979

용은 몸통이 안쪽으로 굽었는데 머리와 꼬리가 마주하여 'C'자를 이룬다. 머리가 크고 꼬리가 뾰족하며 눈이 커다랗고 입이 크다. 커다란 귀는 뒤로 젖혀졌고 수염은 굽었으며 몸에는 구연운문(鉤連雲紋)을 새겼다. 입에는 양면으로 뚫은 구멍이 있어 끈을 끼워 착용할 수 있다. 한쪽 면은 평평하고 한쪽 면은 둥글고 볼록한데 양쪽 무늬가 대응되어 부조(浮彫)한 듯한 입체감이 있다.

옥룡은 5천여 년 전의 홍산문화(紅山文化) 유적지에서 발견된 바 있으며 이후에도 옥으로 새긴 용 또는 용문(龍紋)으로 장식된 기물(器物)이 다수 출토되었다. 고증에 의하면 서주(西周) 옥룡의 조형은 초기에는 곧은 것이 대부분이고 굽은 것은 드물었으며 중기에 이르러 반대로 굽은 것이 대부분이고 곧은 것은 드물었다. 말기에 이르러서는 역시 굽은 것이 대부분을 차지하고 조각이 정교하고 아름다웠다. 또한 초기에는 풍격이 고졸하고 선이 대범하였고, 중기에는 풍격이 성숙하고 비율이 알맞으며 조형이 생동하고 선이 유창하였으며, 말기에는 조형과 풍격이 점차 추상화·도안화되었다.

기룡형패(夔龍形佩)

청백옥(靑白玉) | 전국(戰國)
길이 8.5cm 너비 7.8cm 두께 0.4cm
서안시 안탑구(西安市 雁塔區) 오가분(吳家墳) 출토

Jade Pendant with Kui Dragon Motif

Green and white jade | Warring States Period
L 8.5cm W 7.8cm T 0.4cm
Excavated from Wujiafen in Yanta District, Xi'an

누공(鏤空)으로 조각한 납작한 기룡 모양이다. 기룡은 머리를 숙이고 입을 벌렸으며 입술은 위로 말렸고 눈은 둥글며 머리에는 뿔 두 개가 나 있고 목과 등에는 갈기가 있다. 몸은 굽었으며 꼬리는 늘어뜨리고 발은 엎드린 모양이다. 전체적으로 살짝 두드러진 곡문(穀紋)이 있으며 갈기, 꼬리, 발에는 호선(弧線)을 새기고 가장자리는 편사도(偏斜刀)로 안쪽을 향해 경사지게 깎아내어 곽(廓)을 이루었다. 복부에는 끈을 끼워 착용할 수 있게 마주하여 뚫은 작은 구멍이 나 있다.

기룡문황형패(夔龍紋璜形佩)

청백옥(靑白玉) | 전국(戰國)
길이 11cm 너비 2.4cm 두께 0.4cm
서안시 장안현(西安市 長安縣) 풍서(灃西)부품공장 출토

Jade Plaque with Kui Dragon Motif

Green and white jade | Warring States Period
L 11cm W 2.4cm T 0.4cm
Excavated from Fengxi Fittings Factory in Chang'an County, Xi'an

납작한 황(璜) 모양 패식(佩飾)으로 한쪽은 기룡 머리이고 다른 한쪽은 물고기 꼬리 모양이다. 용머리에는 능형(菱形) 눈, 잎 모양 귀, 위로 말린 입술을 음각(陰刻)하였고 입 부분에는 구멍이 있다. 몸통은 머리나 꼬리보다 좁은 편인데 감지법(減地法)으로 곡문(穀紋) 두 줄을 새겼고 배와 등은 비교적 두꺼운 곽(廓)을 이루었다. 꼬리 부분에는 평행선 여러 줄을 음각하였다.

043

용형패(龍形佩)

백옥(白玉) | 동한(東漢)
지름 2.6cm 두께 0.7cm
1972년 서안시 장안현(西安市 長安縣) 풍서(灃西)부품공장 출토

Dragon-shaped Jade Pendant

White jade | East Han Dynasty
D 2.6cm T 0.7cm
Excavated from Fengxi Fittings Factory in Chang'an County, Xi'an in 1972

전체적으로 납작한 원형(圓形)인데 굽은 용 모양으로 누공(鏤空)하였으며 몸통 세부는 대응되게 양면 조각하였다. 용은 머리와 꼬리가 맞닿았고 물방울 모양 눈, 커다란 코, 벌어진 커다란 입을 가졌으며 정수리에는 뿔이 나 있다. 몸통은 말렸고 하나뿐인 발은 튼실하며 몸과 다리 부분은 권운문(卷雲紋)으로 장식하고 목에서 꼬리까지는 모양에 따라 음각선 두 줄이 있다. 용의 복부, 머리, 등의 가장자리는 감지법(減地法)으로 연마하여 곽(廓)을 이루었다. 이 패식의 용 조형은 알맞은 원형을 취해 몸통이 굽고 꼬리가 들린 모양인데 동태감(動態感)이 짙고 형태가 자연스러우며 조형이 생동한 것이 살아 움직이는 듯하다. 옥으로 조각한 용 모양 패식은 재부, 등급, 신권(神權)의 상징으로 심오함이 내포되어 존귀함을 나타낸다.

044

용형패(龍形佩)

비취(翡翠) | 청(淸)
길이 6.8cm 너비 4.3cm 두께 0.7cm
1983년 서안시(西安市) 수집

Jade Pendant with Dragon Pattern

Emerald | Qing Dynasty
L 6.8cm W 4.3cm T 0.7cm
Collected in Xi'an in 1983

반원 모양으로 용문(龍紋)을 누공(鏤空)하였다. 용은 커다란 눈, 기다란 입, 뒤로 말린 기다란 뿔을 가졌다. 몸통은 융기되어 활 모양을 이루었고 머리는 배 아래쪽으로 되돌려 말린 꼬리 위에 얹었다.

용은 중국 역대 왕조에서 모두 최고 통치자인 황제 및 그 가족의 상징으로 용무늬는 황가(皇家)만의 장식이었다. 사회가 발전함에 따라 청대 건륭(乾隆)황제 시기, 용의 형상은 더욱더 세속화되어 위엄 있고 권위적인 이미지를 잃고 평민들이 사용하는 장식제재가 되었다. 이 패식은 바로 이 시기 장식특징의 구체적인 구현이다.

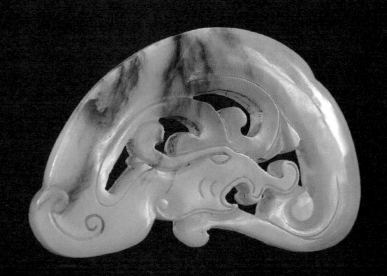

옥륵(玉瓅)

대롱 모양의 옥패식(玉佩飾)으로 신석기시대부터 명·청대(明·淸代)까지 제작되었다. 선진(先秦)시대에는 현문(弦紋) 또는 승문(繩紋)을 주로 조각하였고 한대(漢代) 이후부터 운룡(雲龍), 동물 및 화조 등 도안을 첨가하여 옥잡패(玉雜佩)에 사용하였다.

Jade Le is tubular jade pendant. It originated from the Neolithic Period and continued to be manufactured until Ming and Qing Dynasty. The Jade Le in the early Qin Dynasty were mainly carved with chord patterns of string patterns. After Han Dyansty, patterns of cloud and dragon, animals, as well as flowers and birds were added for decoration. Jade Le was used as appendix on group pendants.

045

선문륵(蟬紋瓅)
청백옥(靑白玉) | 서주(西周)
① 높이 4.3cm 지름 1.6cm
② 높이 3.1cm 지름 1.8cm
1984년 서안시 호현(西安市 戶縣) 출토

Jade Le with Cicada Pattern
Green and white jade | West Zhou Dynasty
① H 4.3cm D 1.6cm
② H 3.1cm D 1.8cm
Excavated from Huxian County, Xi'an in 1984

륵(瓅)은 둥근기둥 모양으로 표면에는 세로로 간소화된 선문(蟬紋) 두 개를 새겼다. 윗부분은 두드러진 각(角) 모양 돌기 네 개로 매미의 눈을 나타내고 아랫부분은 음각선으로 현문(弦紋)을 새겨 몸통을 나타냄으로써 간단하면서도 고졸하다. 구멍 안쪽과 양쪽 끝에는 끈을 꿰었던 흔적이 뚜렷하다.

①

②

046

운뢰문륵(雲雷紋璑)

청백옥(靑白玉) | 서주(西周)
큰 것: 높이 4.3cm 지름 2.4cm
작은 것: 높이 3.1cm 지름 1.9cm
1984년 서안시 호현(西安市 戶縣) 출토

Jade Le with Cloud and Thunder Patterns

Green and white jade | West Zhou Dynasty
Big piece: H 4.3cm D 2.4cm
Small piece: H 3.1cm D 1.9cm
Excavated from Huxian County, Xi'an in 1984

륵(璑)은 타원형 기둥 모양으로 가운데는 구멍이 있다. 표면 아래위 둘레에는
운뢰문(雲雷紋) 두 개를 음각(陰刻)하였는데 선이 단단하고 힘 있으며 곡선처리
가 자연스럽고 유창하다.

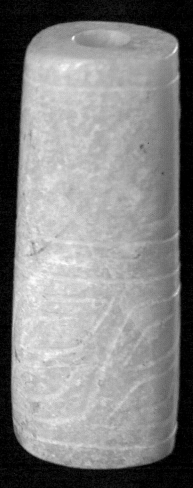

큰 것

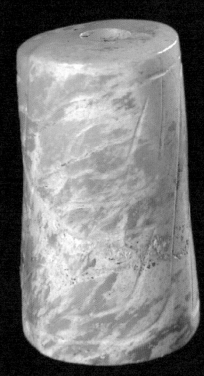

작은 것

작은 것

옥대구(玉帶鉤)

대구는 가죽 띠를 매는 데 사용하는 도구이다. 춘추(春秋)시대 북방으로부터 중원(中原)의 각 제후국에 전해졌고, 전국(戰國)시대부터 진·한대(秦·漢代)까지 성행했으며, 명·청대(明·淸代)까지 이어졌다. 옥대구는 보통 긴 막대기 모양으로 한쪽 끝은 안으로 굽어 있으며 용, 새, 사마귀 등 짐승이나 곤충 머리 모양을 조각했다. 나머지 한 끝은 비교적 넓은 구(鉤)의 꼬리이다. 전체적으로 활 모양으로 휘었으며 아래쪽에는 원형의 고정쇠가 있다. 옥대구 양식은 아래와 같이 여섯 가지로 나눌 수 있다. (1) 금조형(禽鳥形): 머리는 새 머리 또는 오리 머리 모양이고 몸체는 새 몸뚱이 모양이며 한 쌍의 날개도 보인다. 권운문(卷雲紋)을 음각한 것도 있다. (2) 비파형(琵琶形): 마치 비파의 뒷면과 같고 크기가 다양하며 대부분 용머리이다. (3) 장조형(長條形, 긴 막대기 모양): 몸체는 직사각형 혹은 네 각이 둥글거나 오목한 모양의 직사각형이다. (4) 곡봉형(曲棒形): 속칭 '니추배(泥鰍背, 미꾸라지 등)'라 한다. 몸체는 균형감 있는 몽둥이 모양으로 활처럼 굽은 형태이다. (5) 수면형(獸面形): 몸체는 넓고 짧으며 수면무늬를 새긴 것이 특징이다. (6) 당랑두형(螳螂肚形, 사마귀 배 모양): 몸체는 보통 하얗게 빛나고 민무늬이며 중간 부위가 융기되어 호형(弧形)을 이루었고 꼬리 끝은 꺼진 편이다.

고대 고분의 발굴상황을 보면 옥대구는 일반적으로 죽은 자의 허리춤에 가로로 놓여 있었다. 이로부터 대구는 옛날 사람들이 허리를 매거나, 옷깃에 걸거나 장신구 혹은 패식과 함께 사용하였음을 알 수 있다. 연대가 가장 이른 옥대구는 양저문화(良渚文化) 고분에서 발견되었고 상해시(上海市) 복천산(福泉山), 절강성(浙江省) 여항구(余杭區) 반산(反山), 요산(瑤山) 제단(祭壇) 등 양저문화 유적지에서도 모두 옥대구가 출토되었다.

춘추전국시대에 옥대구는 큰 발전이 있었다. 구(鉤)의 머리는 말, 오리, 새의 머리 모양과 비슷한데 윤곽만 있고 오관(五官)을 따로 조각하지 않았으며 민무늬였고 구의 몸체 가장자리는 비탈과 같이 매끌매끌하고 평평하였다. 전국 말기에 이르러 대구는 수가 늘어나고 질적으로 발전하였으며 분포범위, 형식, 제작기법이 전에 없이 크게 발전하였다. 한대(漢代)에 대구가 보편화되어 점차 복식의 중요한 장신구가 되었다. 위·진·남북조(魏·晉·南北朝)시대의 옥대구는 수량이 뚜렷하게 줄었는데 이는 옥대구가 쇠퇴단계에 들어섰음을 말해준다. 송대(宋代) 사람들은 옛것을 좋아했기에 전국 및 한대 시기 대구를 모방하여 만든 작품들이 간혹 나타난다. 명·청대(明·淸代)에 이르러 대구의 제작은 다시 활기를 띠어 수량이 늘어나기 시작하였는데 당시 크게 유행한 용머리 대구가 바로 후세 사람들이 용구(龍鉤)라 부르는 대구이다. 그러나 당시 옥대구는 이미 실용성을 상실하고 관리, 귀족, 문인, 아사(雅士)의 완상품(玩賞品)이 되었다.

Belt Buckle was used to hook The girdle which was coiled on the waist. It was first Passed from the north to different leud states during Spring and Autumn Period and became quite popular by Warring States and Qin, Dynasties. The prevalence continued to Ming and Qing Dynasties. The jade belt buckles were bar-shaped One end of buckle was the inward-coiled buckle head, carved in the shape of the head of dragon, beast, bird, mantis of other insects, and the other wider end is the buckle tail. The body of the buckle arched upward with a round pedunculated belly button on the lower side of the buckle. The pattern of the buckles could be divided into six types: 1. bird shape. The buckle head is in the shape of the bird head or duck head, and the body of the buckle takes on the shape of the bird body, with two wings recognizable. Some buckles were also engrave with winding cloud patterns on the bodies. 2. lute shape. The buckle takes on the shape of an inversed lute. It comes in different sizes and the buckle head is usually dragon head shaped. 3. bar shape. The body of the buckle is rectangular shaped or rectangle with rounded or reentrant angles. It usually has elongated form. 4. cooked stick shape: It is commonly called "eel's back". The body of the buckle is the arch-backed stick shape that is relatively even in width. 5. animal face shape. The body of the buckle is wide and short and is characterized by animal face patterns. 6 mantis belly shape. The body of the buckle is usually plain without carvings. The middle part hunches up ward and bends like an arc while the buckle tail slopes downward.

According to what have been excavated from the ancient tombs, jade belt buckles are usually placed transversely on the waist of the dead. This shows that belt buckle was used to attach the girdle, hook the collar, of served as small ornaments to be carried along. It can also be used together with other pendants in groups. The earliest jade buckles appeared in Liangzhu Culture tomb burials and were excavated in the Liangzhu Cultural Relics such as Fuquanshan in Shanghai, Fanshan in Yuhang, Zhejiang, as well as Jitan in Yaoshan, etc.

During the Spring and Autumn Period, jade buckle became very popular. Buckle head resembles the head of horse, duck, bird and so on. But it was only the resemblance in contour, and was without facial features. The surface is plain; the body of the buckle is like a slope, smooth and glossy. By the late Warring States Period, jade buckle was greatly improved both in quality and in quantity with unprecedented distribution range, number and variety, as well as exquisiteness in craft work. Belt buckles were popularized in Han Dynasty, and became important costume ornaments for people in Han Dynasty. By Wei, Jin, South and north Dynasties, the excavation of jade belt buckles distinctively reduced in number, and it is at the ebbing stage. Because people in Song Dynasty were in favor of the ancients, articles that imitated belt buckets in Warring States and Han Dynasty were occasionally discovered. By Ming and Qing Dynasties, the manufacture of belt buckets was revived, and the amount of belt buckles multiplied greatly. Dragon head shaped belt buckle prevailed and was commonly called "dragon" buckle by the later generations. But at that time, jade belt buckles had lost their practical usage and became playthings for the nobilities, literators and scholars.

047

용수현문대구(龍首弦紋帶鉤)

청백옥(靑白玉) | 전국(戰國)
길이 20cm 너비 3cm
1981년 서안시 미앙구 육촌보(西安市 未央區 六村堡)
서쪽 양과촌(梁果村) 한(漢) 건장궁(建章宮) 유적지 출토

Jade Belt Buckle with Dragon Head Motif and String Patterns

Green and white jade | Warring States Period
L 20cm W 3cm
Excavated from Zhanggong Relic from Han Dynasty in Liangguo
Village to the west of Liucunbu in Weiyang District, Xi'an in 1981

구멍이 나 있는 일곱 개 옥 기물을 철심(鐵芯)에 꿰어 만든 커다란 대구이다. 구수(鉤首)는 용머리 모양인데 입은 굳게 다물고 입꼬리 부분 수염은 아래에서 앞 위쪽으로 뻗었으며 콧구멍은 와문(渦紋) 두 개로 나타내었다. 눈은 능형(菱形)이고 눈꼬리는 길며 귀는 뒤로 젖혀졌고 쌍뿔은 소뿔 모양이며 목 갈기는 높고 굽었다. 단면(斷面)이 둥근 사각형 모양인 목 양측에는 가는 선으로 변형된 구연운문(鉤連雲紋)을 음각(陰刻)하였으며 운문 사이는 세밀한 망문(網紋)으로 장식하였다. 뒷목에는 구멍 한 쌍이 있는데 안쪽에서 가는 철사로 용수와 목 안에 있는 철심을 고정시켰다. 구신(鉤身)은 둥근 방망이 형태로 약간 굽었으며 앞뒤로 각각 밀접하게 배열된 요현문(凹弦紋) 10여 줄이 있다. 요현문 앞뒤와 한가운데는 각각 높은 철현문(凸弦紋)이 있으며 가운데 철현문에는 마주 보는 토끼 한 쌍을 대칭되게 원조(圓彫)하였는데 둘 사이에는 방형(方形) 2층 대(臺) 두 개가 있다. 뒷부분에는 둥근 손잡이가 달린 배꼽 고정쇠가 있다. 이 옥대구는 최고급 화전(和闐) 청백옥을 다듬어 만든 것으로 조형과 기법이 독특하고 선이 유창하며 연마기법 또한 뛰어나다. 출토된 지점이 한대(漢代) 유적지이나 용머리의 눈과 코, 운문(雲紋)의 특징으로 보아 전국(戰國)시대 유물로 추정된다.

048

용문대구(龍紋帶鉤)

백옥(白玉) | 원(元)
길이 14cm 너비 4.9cm 높이 4.2cm
서안시 안탑구 와호동(西安市 雁塔區 瓦胡同) 원묘(元墓) 출토

Jade Belt Buckle with Dragon Pattern

White jade | Yuan Dynasty
L 14cm W 4.9cm H 4.2cm
Excavated from Yuan Tomb in Wahutong in Yanta District, Xi'an

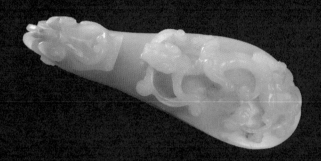

비파형(琵琶形) 대구이며 구수(鉤首)는 용머리 모양인데 넓고 납작하다. 돼지주둥이 모양 입은 살짝 벌어졌고 아래위 문치(門齒)는 가지런하고 양쪽 입꼬리에는 각각 작은 구멍이 나 있다. 코는 납작하며 베틀 북 모양 눈은 도드라졌으며 기다란 눈썹은 위로 말렸고 쌍뿔은 굽었다. 'U'자 모양 정수리 앞쪽은 세로로 음각(陰刻)하였고 수염과 갈기 세 가닥은 뒤로 젖혀졌다. 눈썹, 눈, 코, 입 모두 앞부분에 몰려 있어 전체 면부(面部)의 3분의 1밖에 차지하지 않는다. 구신(鉤身)에는 영지(靈芝)를 입에 문 이룡(螭龍)을 고부조하였고 그 주위는 구름으로 장식하였다. 이룡은 머리와 이마가 넓고 목은 오목하게 들어갔으며 갈기는 가로로 휘날리고 몸통은 둥글고 실팍하다. 사지는 기어 다니는 듯하고 관절과 양 어깨에는 운문(雲紋)을 장식하였으며 등 한가운데는 음각 쌍선(雙線)을 새겨 척추를 표현하고 그 양쪽에 가로 쌍선 세 쌍을 그어 늑골을 표현하였다. 아랫다리에는 세로 음각선 한 줄과 짧은 가로 사선 몇 줄로 근육과 골격을 나타내 힘을 표현했고 꼬리는 양측으로 갈라져 말렸다. 구신 뒷면은 호형(弧形)을 이루고 꼬리 쪽에는 곱자 다리 모양의 고정쇠 흔적이 남아 있다. 대구 가장자리 측면은 홈을 파고 모서리를 둥글게 다듬었다. 대구 위 크고 작은 용 한 쌍은 속칭 '창룡교자(蒼龍敎子)'로 위 세대가 아래 세대에 대한 교육의 중요성을 뜻한다.

049

용문대구(龍紋帶鉤)

청옥(靑玉) | 원(元)
길이 12.3cm 너비 3cm 높이 4cm
1999년 서안시 고신구(西安市 高新區) 원 지정(至正) 15년 묘지 출토

Jade Belt Buckle with Dragon Pattern

Green jade | Yuan Dynasty
L 12.3cm W 3cm H 4cm
Excavated from the Yuan Tomb in Gaoxin District, Xi'an in 1999

대구는 비파(琵琶) 모양이며 구수(鉤首)가 용머리 모양으로 넓고 납작하다. 돼지주둥이 모양 입에 아래위 문치(門齒)는 가지런하며 문치와 입꼬리 사이에 가로로 구멍이 나 있다. 도드라진 볼에는 음각(陰刻)한 짧은 사선과 권운문(卷雲紋)으로 수염을 나타냈다. 코는 납작하고 눈이 면부(面部)의 절반 가까이 차지하며 오목하게 들어갔다. 기다란 눈썹은 갈라져 위로 말렸고 구름 모양 두 귀는 정수리 앞에서 만나 'U'자를 이루었으며 갈기는 두 갈래로 나뉘어 목 좌우를 덮었다. 구신(鉤身)에는 이룡(螭龍)을 고부조하고 머리 아래와 몸 주위에 구름을 새겼다. 이룡은 넓은 머리와 이마, 휘날리는 갈기, 둥글고 튼실한 몸통에 사지는 기어 다니는 듯하고 관절과 양 어깨에는 운문(雲紋)을 장식하였다. 등 한가운데 음각된 쌍선(雙線)은 척추를, 그 양쪽에 있는 음각된 삼각문(三角紋)은 늑골을 나타낸다. 아랫다리에는 짧은 사선을 새겼으며 꼬리는 양쪽으로 갈라져 말렸다. 운문은 아래위 두 층으로 나뉘는데 위층은 둥근 구름 위에 여의운두문(如意雲頭紋)을 음각하였고 아래층은 양 뿔 모양 운두 여러 개로 이루어졌다. 아래층 운문의 옆 가장자리와 아래쪽은 거친데 섬세한 연마를 거치지 않았다. 구신은 두꺼운 편이고 가장자리는 둥글고 매끄럽다. 뒷면은 호형(弧形)을 이루는데 뒤쪽으로 치우친 위치에 둥근 손잡이가 달린 고정쇠가 있으며 고정쇠 머리는 둥글고 볼록하다. 이 옥대구는 원대(元代) 기년묘(紀年墓)에서 출토되었으며 형태, 문양이 전형적이어서 가치가 높다.

050

용수대구(龍首帶鉤)

백옥(白玉) | 원(元)
길이 9.6cm 너비 3cm 높이 2.5cm
1983년 서안시 수집

Jade Belt Buckle in the shape of a Dragon Head

White jade | Yuan Dynasty
L 9.6cm W 3cm H 2.5cm
Collected in Xi'an in 1983

대구는 당랑두형(螳螂肚形, 사마귀 배 모양)이다. 구수(鉤首)는 용머리를 원조(圓彫)하였는데 돼지주둥이 모양 입은 납작하고 넓으며 입꼬리가 눈을 넘어가고 납작한 코, 밖으로 뒤집힌 콧구멍에 두 눈은 볼록하고 둥글다. 'S'자 모양의 기다란 눈썹은 가로로 굽었고 두 귀는 뒤로 젖혀졌으며 기다란 뿔은 말렸다. 용의 눈은 대롱 모양 도구로, 콧구멍은 막대기 모양 도구로 뚫었으며 선은 모두 일면(一面) 파도법(坡刀法)으로 새겼다. 단면(斷面)이 반원 모양인 구신(鉤身)은 등이 안으로 오목하게 들어갔는데 뒤쪽으로 치우친 부분에 직사각형 곱자 모양 고정쇠가 있다. 이 대구는 조형이 소박하고 옹골차며 선이 힘 있고 유창하며 색상이 희고 재질이 섬세하다. 장식은 간단하지만 기품 있다.

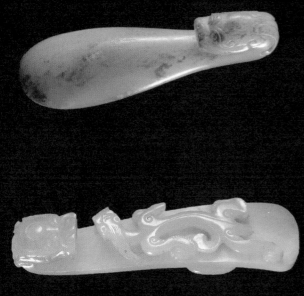

051

용수대구(龍首帶鉤)

청옥(靑玉) | 명(明)
길이 12.5cm 너비 2.9cm 높이 2.4cm
서안시(西安市) 수집

Jade Belt Buckle in the shape of a Dragon Head

Green jade | Ming Dynasty
L 12.5cm W 2.9cm H 2.4cm
Collected in Xi'an

막대기 모양으로 구수(鉤首)에는 용머리를 원조(圓彫)하였고 구신(鉤身)은 이룡(螭龍)을 누공(鏤空)·부조(浮彫)하였다. 용머리는 약간 네모지고 입은 넓고 평평하며 코는 여의운두(如意雲頭) 모양이다. 굵다란 눈썹은 위로 굽었고 이마에는 둥근 돌기가 있으며 두 귀는 뒤로 젖혀졌고 뿔은 말렸다. 구불구불한 이룡은 털을 휘날린다. 어깨와 허벅지에는 음각(陰刻)한 권운문(卷雲紋)이 있고 척추에는 용의 형태에 따라 새긴 구불구불한 음각선이 있다. 아랫다리에는 짧은 사선을 빼곡하게 새겼다. 구신 뒷면에는 둥근 손잡이가 있는 고정쇠가 있는데 지름이 구신 너비와 같다. 측면으로 보면 구신은 호형(弧形)이지만 호도(弧度)가 원대(元代), 청대(淸代)보다는 훨씬 작다. 가장자리는 모서리를 없애지 않았다.

052

용수대구(龍首帶鉤)

백옥(白玉) | 청(淸)
길이 11cm 너비 2.8cm 높이 2.9cm
1983년 서안시(西安市) 수집

Jade Belt Buckle in the shape of a Dragon Head

White jade | Qing Dynasty
L 11cm W 2.8cm H 2.9cm
Collected in Xi'an in 1983

대구는 비파(琵琶) 모양이며 구수(鉤首)는 용머리 모양인데 넓은 입을 살짝 벌리고 혀로 윗입술을 핥고 있다. 입안은 누공(鏤空)하였고 입술 가장자리는 음각선으로 그렸다. 여의(如意) 모양 코, 불거져 나온 눈, 굵은 눈썹에 두 귀는 뒤로 젖혀졌으며 쌍뿔은 양뿔 모양이다. 구신(鉤身)은 당랑두형(螳螂肚形)인데 감지법(減地法)으로 두드러진 구운문(鉤雲紋)과 여의문(如意紋)으로 이루어진 기하도안을 새겼으며 측면은 윤곽이 선명하다. 구신 뒷면은 호형(弧形)으로 굽었으며 가운데는 둥근 손잡이가 달린 고정쇠가 있다. 측면에서 보면 구수, 고정쇠, 구미(鉤尾)가 동일한 평면에 놓인다. 이 대구는 용의 머리와 오관(五官), 구신 도안의 특징 그리고 모서리 처리방식, 고정쇠의 높낮이가 모두 전형적인 청대(淸代) 대구의 특징을 띠었다.

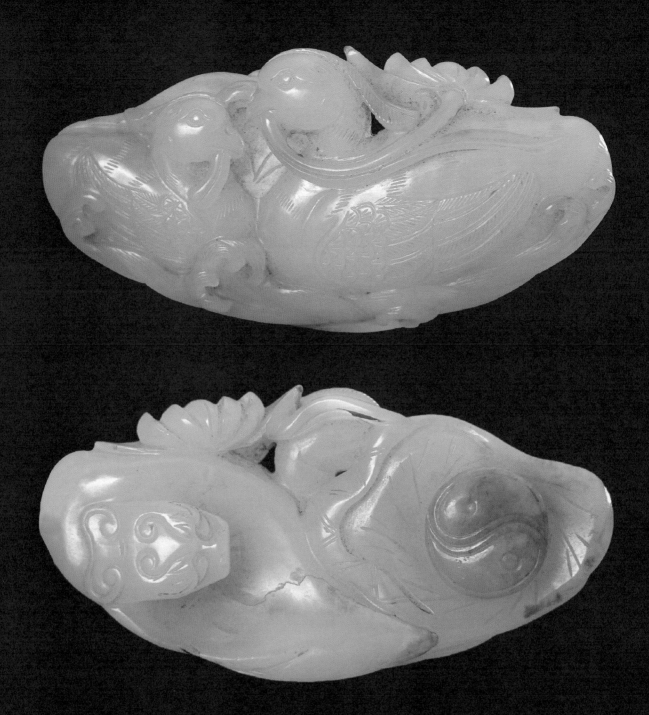

053

원앙문대구(鴛鴦紋帶鉤)

백옥(白玉) | 청(淸)
길이 8cm 너비 4.1cm 두께 1.9cm
1980년 서안시(西安市) 수집

Jade Belt Buckle with Mandarin Duck Patterns

White jade | Qing Dynasty
L 8cm W 4.1cm T 1.9cm
Collected in Xi'an in 1980

타원형이며 호숫가에서 노니는 원앙 한 쌍을 조각하였다. 앞면에는 원앙 한 쌍이 물 위에서 마주 하여 노니는데 배 아래쪽에는 파도가 일고 등에는 연잎이 떠 있으며 함께 줄기를 입에 물고 있다. 눈은 대롱 모양 도구로 조각하였고 눈꼬리는 살짝 긴 편이다. 전체적으로 저부조기법과 음각선으로 조각하였는데 원앙이 푸른 물결이 일렁이는 호수에서 노니는 모습을 생동감 있게 표현하였다. 뒷면에는 수면에 떠 있는 연잎과 용머리가 있는데 용머리를 갈고리로, 연밥을 고정쇠로 하였다. 용머리는 네모진 편이며 주먹코, 화염 모양 눈썹, 음각한 안으로 말린 쌍뿔, 운두(雲頭) 모양 갈기가 있다. 연잎의 엽맥(葉脈)은 '小(소)'자 모양 음각선을 둘러 나타냈고 연밥 위에는 태극(太極) 도안을 부조하였다. 이 대구는 무늬가 화려하고 구도가 독창적이며 도법(刀法)이 세련되고 완숙하며 연마가 정세(精細)한 것이 청대(淸代) 옥기 가운데 수작이다.

옥휴(玉觿)

상고(上古)시대 짐승 이빨을 패용하던 풍습에서 발전한 것으로 매듭을 푸는 데 쓰였다. 『설문(說文)』에서는 "패각(佩角)의 예리한 끝부분은 매듭을 풀 수 있다"고 하였다. 옥휴는 옥으로 만든 뿔 모양 기물로 원래는 몸에 지니고 다니는 실용적인 물품이었으나 춘추전국(春秋戰國)시대에 이르러 장신구로 변하였다. 옥휴의 용도는 두 가지로 나뉘는데 하나는 단독으로 사용하는 것이고 다른 하나는 다른 장신구와 함께 사용하는 것이다. 다른 장신구와 함께 사용할 때는 끝부분에 다는데 걸을 때면 다른 옥기와 부딪쳐 맑은 소리를 내므로 충아(沖牙)라고도 불렸다. 가장 이른 옥휴는 양저문화(良渚文化) 초기 고분에서 출토되었고 그 후 상·주대(商·周代)부터 한대(漢代)까지 줄곧 유행하였다. 시대가 변하면서 제작기법 또한 정교해져 아름다운 작품이 다수 나타났다. 옥휴는 조형이 다양하고 구도가 참신할 뿐 아니라 조각기술 또한 정교하였다.

Xi was originated from the custom of wearing beast teeth in the primeval times. The beast teeth were then used to unfasten knots on the ropes. According to the explanation on the book shuo wen (book of explanations) "the reason for wearing sharp-pointed horn is to unfasten the knots" Jade Xi is modeled on the horn shaped articles. It was originally worn by people for utility. By the Spring and Autumn Period and Warring State Period, jade Xi changed from an object of utility to ornament. It can be used in two ways: one is to be used alone, and the other is to be used together with other pendants in groups, mainly tied in the lowest so that ringing sounds could be heard when Xi strikes on other jade pendants during walking. Thus jade Xi got another name "Chong Ya" (clashing teeth). The earliest jade Xi was discovered in the early tombs in Liangzhu Culture, and was also found to be popular later in Shang an Zhou Dynasties. By the Spring and Autumn Period and Warring States Period and even to Han Dynasty, jade Xi were not only popular, but also finely crafted, with lot of delicate craft works appeared. The jade used at that time was of choice material, and was of various shapes and patterns. The design was both ingenious and novel, and jade was elaborately crafted.

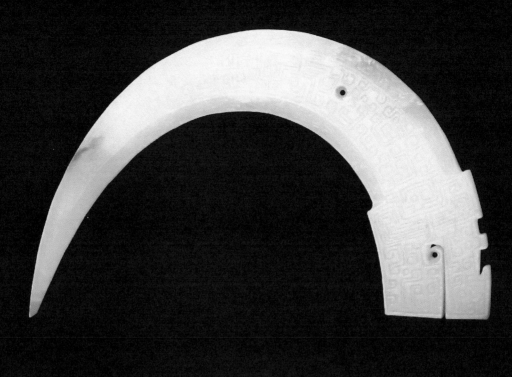

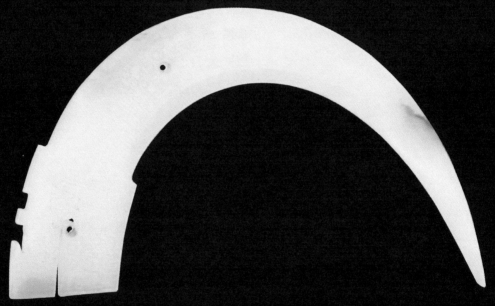

054

기룡문휴(夔龍紋觿)

백옥(白玉) | 춘추(春秋) 말기
길이 11cm 너비 2.4cm 두께 0.7cm
2002년 서안시 장안현 모파촌(西安市 長安縣 茅坡村) 출토

Jade Xi(horny pendants) with Kui Dragon Pattern

White jade | Spring and Autumn Period
L 11cm W 2.4cm T 0.7cm
Excavated from Maopo Village in Chang'an County, Xi'an in 2002

휴는 납작한 소뿔 모양으로 한쪽 끝이 뾰족하고 예리하며 다른 한쪽 끝은 방형(方形) 기룡 머리이다. 기룡은 입 부분을 누공(鏤空)하고 머리 위쪽 비아(扉牙)로 코와 뿔을 나타냈으며 전체적으로 구운문(鉤雲紋)을 음각(陰刻)하였다. 기룡 머리 부분은 윤곽이 뚜렷하고 몸통 아래위 양쪽은 양면을 경사지게 깎아내어 능(稜)을 이루었으며 입꼬리와 상반신 한가운데는 구멍을 뚫어 끈을 끼워 착용할 수 있게 하였다. 이 휴는 윤곽이 굽은 호형(弧形)이며 무늬가 세밀하며 연마가 정세(精細)하다.

055

옥휴(玉觿)

청옥(青玉) | 진(秦)
길이 11cm 너비 1cm 두께 0.7cm
1971년 서안시 미앙구 대명궁공사 연지촌(西安市 未央區 大明宮公社 聯志村) 출토

Jade Xi(horny pendants)

Green jade | Qin Dynasty
L 11cm W 1cm T 0.7cm
Excavated from Lianzhi Village at Daminggong Community in Weiyang District, Xi'an in 1971

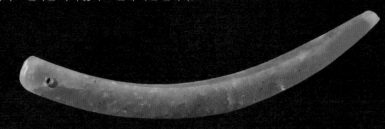

휴는 호형(弧形)을 이루며 머리가 크고 꼬리가 뾰족하며 단면(斷面)은 직사각형이다. 머리와 가까운 부분에는 마주하여 뚫은 구멍이 있는데 가운데가 좁고 양쪽 입구가 크며 타원형이다. 민무늬이고 연마를 하지 않아 표면이 거친 편이다.

056

누공조문휴(鏤空鳥紋觿)

백옥(白玉) | 한(漢)
길이 10.3cm 너비 1.7cm 두께 0.8cm
1978년 서안시 연호구(西安市 蓮湖區) 홍묘파(紅廟坡) 한묘(漢墓) 출토

Jade Xi with Hollow-carved Bird Patterns

White jade | Han Dynasty
L 10.3cm W 1.7cm T 0.8cm
Excavated from Han Tomb at Hongmiaopo in Lianhu District, Xi'an in 1978

납작한 봉조(鳳鳥) 모양의 누공(鏤空)한 휴이다. 봉조는 부리가 뾰족하고 볏이 높으며 고개를 돌려 깃을 입에 문 모습이다. 뾰족한 꼬리는 휴 머리로 하였다. 양면에는 입, 눈, 날개, 꼬리, 발 등 부위와 깃털을 가는 선으로 대응되게 음각(陰刻)하였다. 표면 및 측면 모서리는 매우 정세(精細)하게 연마하였으며 모서리는 각지고 단단하다.

057

옥충아(玉冲牙)

연옥(軟玉) | 한(漢)
길이 5.5cm 너비 1.9cm 두께 0.2cm
2001년 8월 서안시 신성구(西安市 新城區) 동물원 출토

Jade Chongya(clashing teeth)

Soft jade | Han Dynasty
L 5.5cm W 1.9cm T 0.2cm
Excavated from the zoo in Xincheng District, Xi'an in August 2001

민무늬 편(片)으로 송곳니 모양이며 둥근 부분에 작은 구멍이 나 있다. 표면은 평평하고 반질반질하게 연마하였고 가장자리는 각지고 단단하다. 이 충아는 머리 부분이 진갈색을 띠고 꼬리 부분은 연두색을 띤 것으로 보아 청해(青海) 곤륜산(崑崙山)에서 나는 연옥(軟玉)으로 만들었음을 알 수 있다.

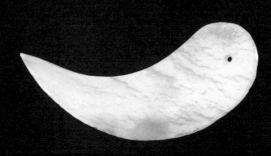

옥조패(玉組佩)

조패는 잡패(雜佩)라고도 한다. 상・주대(商・周代) 패식을 기초로 하여 발전해 온 것으로 일반적으로 몇 개에서 십여 개의 다양한 옥패식을 일정한 방식으로 조합하였으며 패용하는 부위 또한 다양하다.

춘추전국(春秋戰國)시대에는 허리의 좌우 양쪽에 7개 이상의 패식용 옥과 구슬로 구성된 장관옥패(長串玉佩)를 착용하는 것이 유행하였다. 윗부분은 가로로 놓인 마름모꼴 패옥으로 형(珩)이라고 한다. 형 아랫부분의 세 구멍에는 각각 연황(連璜), 정사각형 거(琚), 우(瑀)를 달아매었으며 그 아래에는 마주 보는 형태의 충아(沖牙) 한 쌍을 달아맸다. 충아는 납작한 형태의 짐승 이빨 모양으로 일반적으로 3가지 양식으로 나뉜다. 첫 번째는 용 모양 충아로 용의 꼬리는 긴 이빨과 비슷하고 용머리는 입을 벌린 모양이다. 두 번째는 기봉형(夔鳳形) 충아로 기봉의 몸체는 활처럼 휜 모양으로 입을 벌렸으며 발 하나가 꼬리를 밟고 있는데 꼬리 끝부분이 긴 이빨 모양이다. 세 번째는 옥황(玉璜)과 비슷한데 한 끝은 길고 뾰족하며 바깥쪽에는 정교한 문양이 조각되었다.

한대(漢代)에 이르러 옥조패는 전국시대보다 줄었지만 여전히 귀족의 장신구로 사용되었다. 예컨대『후한서(後漢書)』「여복제(輿服制)」에는 "효명(孝明)황제 시기까지 대패(大佩), 충아, 쌍우(雙瑀), 황(璜)으로 이루어졌으며 모두 백옥으로 만들어졌다"고 기록되어 있다.

Group Pendants, also called sundry pendants, were developed on the basis of the pendant ornaments in Shang and Zhou Dynasties. It is assembled by several or even over ten different jade pendants according to certain manners. The place for attachment of the pendants was not fixed.

During Spring and Autumn Period and Warring States Period, it was popular to wear on either side of the waist long strand of jade pendants consisted of more than seven pieces of jade articles and beads. The top sidelong one is a lozenge-shaped jade called Heng. There are three holes on the lower edge of Heng, each tied with a jade plaque(Huang) or square-shaped jade Ju, under which is the third tier of Chong Ya(clashing teeth) that comes in pairs. Chong Ya is the thin flake in the shape of beast teeth. Chong Ya usually take on three shapes: one is the dragon shaped Chong Ya, the tail of which resembles a long tooth, the mouth of which yawns open. The second type is Kui phoenix shaped Chong Ya, the body of which arched upward, with opened mouth. One claw of the phoenix tread on its tail, and the tail resembles a long tooth. The third type looks like Jade Plaque with a long pointed end, the outboard of which has finely carved decorations.

Jade group pendants were no longer popular during Han Dynasty, but still belonged to extravagant ornaments possessed by the upper nobilities. According to Book of Late Han Dynasty "Until Xiaoming Emperor, Chong Ya, double jade Yu, as well as jade Plaque are great pendants and are all made of white jade"

옥조패(玉組佩) (1)

백옥(白玉) | 서한(西漢)
서안시 미앙구 삼교진(西安市 未央區 三橋鎭) 한묘(漢墓) 출토

Jade Group Pendants (1)

White jade | West Han Dynasty
Excavated from Han Tomb in Sanqiao Town, Weiyang District, Xi'an

1. 옥기봉벽(玉夔鳳璧)
지름 7cm

Jade Disk with Kui Phoenix Patterns
D 7cm

척지법(剔地法)으로 조각한 것으로 안팎 가장자리에는 각기 철현문(凸弦紋)이 있다. 안쪽에 마주하여 뒤돌아보며 서 있는 기봉 한 쌍을 새겼다. 기봉은 볏이 높다랗고 양 날개가 위로 말렸으며 기다란 꽁지 일곱 가닥이 밖으로 말려 전체 벽면(璧面)을 가득 채웠다. 세부의 깃털은 가는 음각선으로 표현하여 생동감이 있다. 이 옥벽은 착용용으로 대롱 모양 옥 등과 함께 조패(組佩)를 이룬다.

2. 옥기봉형(玉夔鳳珩)
길이 9.9cm 너비 4cm

Jade Heng with Kui Phoenix Patterns
L 9.9cm W 4cm

편(片)으로 기봉이 날개를 펴고 날면서 머리 돌려 둘러보는 모습이다. 날개는 활짝 펴 호형(弧形)을 이루며 아래로 굽었고 꼬리는 양쪽으로 나뉘어 펼쳐졌는데 가는 선으로 음각(陰刻)하였다. 기다란 날개는 편사도(偏斜刀)로 조각하여 형상이 생동하고 커다란 날개, 뾰족한 부리, 커다란 눈은 흉악해 보인다. 전체적으로 황(璜) 모양이며 몸통 가운데와 양 날개 끝에는 각기 구멍이 하나씩 있어 끈을 끼워 착용하거나 걸어 놓을 수 있다.

3. 옥무녀(玉舞女)
길이 4.4cm 너비 2.2cm

Jade Dancers
L 4.4cm W 2.2cm

옥편(玉片) 한 쌍으로 인물은 동작이 같고 자태가 상반된 것이 대칭되게 춤추는 모습이다. 무녀는 교령(交領)의 소매가 넓은 장포(長袍)를 입고 허리에 띠를 매었으며 너울너울 춤추고 있다. 한 팔은 머리 위로 높이 들어 기다란 소매를 뿌리고 다른 한 팔은 내려 몸 쪽으로 굽혔는데 기다란 소매는 무릎 아래까지 드리웠다. 자태가 빼어나며 살짝 'S'자 모양을 이룬다. 무녀는 둥근 얼굴에 긴 눈썹, 가느다란 눈, 위로 올라간 입꼬리를 가졌으며 천진난만한 미소를 띠고 있다. 세부는 모두 가는 선으로 그렸으며 아래위로 구

멍이 있어 끈을 끼워 착용할 수 있다.

한대(漢代)에는 악무(樂舞)가 성행하였는데 황제, 귀족은 무녀를 노리개로 삼았다. 수준이 높은 궁정악인(宮廷樂人), 이를테면 병강(丙强), 경무(景武) 등은 황제의 총애를 받아 한때 떠받들어졌다. 옥무인은 바로 이러한 밤마다 노래와 춤으로 지새던 모습을 진실하게 반영한 것이다.

차림새와 춤 자태로 보아 무녀는 장수무(長袖舞)를 추고 있다. 이 춤은 중국 고대의 전통춤으로 전국(戰國)시대에 이미 유행하였다. 시문(詩文) 중에는 이에 대한 묘사가 다수 있다. 예를 들어『한비자(韓非子)』「오두(五蠹)」에서는 "소매가 길면 춤을 잘 추고, 돈이 많으면 장사를 잘 한다"고 하였고, 장형(張衡)은『관무부(觀舞賦)』에서 "수수(修袖)로 얼굴을 가리고, 청아한 목소리로 노래 부른다"고 하였는데 여기서 수수(修袖)는 긴 소매를 가리킨다. 또한『서경잡기(西京雜記)』에는 유방(劉邦)의 척(戚) 부인이 "교수(翹袖)하고 허리 꺾는 춤을 잘 춘다"는 기록이 있는데 여기서 교수(翹袖) 역시 장수무를 묘사한 것이다. 장수무는 두 소매를 돌리거나 일렁이게 하거나 휘날리게 함으로써 자태가 더욱 아름다워 보인다. 한대 장수무는 화상석(畵像石), 화상전(畵像甎), 옥공예, 칠기(漆器) 등에서도 많이 보인다.

4. 옥기봉충아(玉夔鳳沖牙)
길이 10cm 너비 2.3cm

Jade Chongya(clashing teeth) with Kui Phoenix Patterns
L 10cm W 2.3cm

두 점은 같은 모양으로 납작한 편(片)이다. 뒤돌아보는 기봉 부리가 뾰족하고 길며 정수리가 뾰족하고 높은 볏은 말렸으며 원형(圓形) 눈은 형형하게 빛난다. 몸통과 꼬리는 하나로 이어졌고 끝부분은 뾰족한데 세부는 음각선으로 그렸으며 깃털은 와문(渦紋)으로 나타냈다. 조형성과 장식성이 어우러진 작품으로 이런 모양의 옥기는 원래 실용적인 패식(佩飾) 휴(觿)로 훗날 충아(沖牙)로 발전하였는데 원래의 조형을 보존하고 봉조(鳳鳥)로 장식함으로써 예술성을 갖춘 조패(組佩) 장신구이다.

충아는 대부분 쌍을 이루는데 조형, 무늬가 비슷하고 대응되며 조패 하단에 달아매었다. 몸에 착용하면 걸을 때 다른 옥기와 부딪쳐 맑은 소리를 낸다.

5. 옥해치(玉獬豸)
길이 4.5cm 높이 3.7cm 두께 1.6cm

Jade Xie-Zhi(a legendary beast)
L 4.5cm H 3.7cm T 1.6cm

원조(圓彫)한 해치이다. 앞쪽 한 다리를 꿇고 다른 세 다리를 굽혀 엎디었다. 고개를 들고 가슴을 폈으며 정수리에는 뾰족한 뿔이 나 있다. 눈은 둥그렇고 입은 길며 두 귀는 곧추세웠으며 꼬리는 짧다. 양 날개 세부와 깃털은 가는 선으로 음각(陰刻)하였다. 해치는 상상 속 동물로 해록(解鹿), 굉호(䰠虎), 굴일(屈軼) 이라고도 부른다.

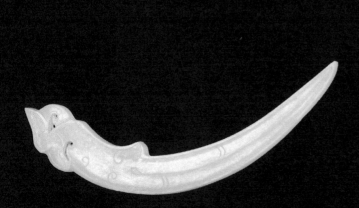

059

옥조패(玉組佩) (2)

백옥(白玉) | 서한(西漢)
2001년 8월 서안시 신성구(西安市 新城區) 동물원 출토

Jade Group Pendants (2)

White jade | West Han Dynasty
Excavated from the zoo in Xincheng District, Xi'an in August 2001

1. 옥벽(玉璧)

지름 6.2cm 구멍지름 4cm 두께 0.2cm

Jade Disk

D 6.2cm Bore D 4cm T 0.2cm

　석회화되어 흰색으로 변하였다. 안팎 가장자리
에는 윤(輪)이 있고 면은 오목하게 들어갔으며 윤
사이에는 봉조(鳳鳥) 네 마리를 투조(透彫)하였다.
뒤돌아보는 봉조는 목이 굽고 뾰족한 부리는 갈고
리 같고 높은 볏은 구름 같은데 날개를 펴고 날아오
르려는 듯하다. 넓고 오목한 선 세 줄로 날개를 나타
내었는데 봉조 두 마리가 날개 하나를 같이 한다. 가
는 선으로 봉조의 세부를 그렸다.

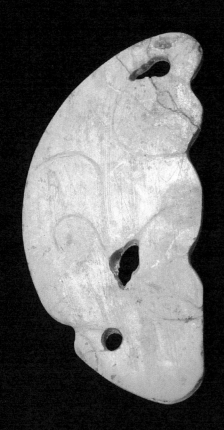

2. 옥무인(玉舞人)

길이 3.2cm 너비 1.6cm 두께 0.2cm

Jade Dancer

L 3.2cm W 1.6cm T 0.2cm

　청옥이지만 석회화되어 흰색으로 변하였다. 반
원 모양 편(片)으로 양면에는 옥무인을 선각(線刻)
하였다. 옥인은 둥근 얼굴에 가는 눈썹, 삼각형 모양
눈, 동그란 코, 작은 입을 가졌으며 머리를 오른쪽으
로 기울였다. 오른팔은 올리고 왼팔은 내렸으며 허
리선이 아름답다. 세부는 가는 선으로 그렸다.

3. 옥형(玉珩)

길이 8.2cm 너비 1.5cm 두께 0.3cm

Jade Heng

L 8.2cm W 1.5cm T 0.3cm

양쪽 끝의 용머리는 뒤돌아보는 모습이다. 위로 말린 입, 기다란 눈주름이 있는 둥근 눈에 뒤로 말린 긴 뿔에는 쌍호선(雙弧線) 2조가 있다. 용의 몸통도 기다란데 꼬리가 서로 맞닿았고 윗부분은 평평하고 가지런하며 한가운데는 구멍이 있다. 양측에는 쌍선(雙線) 권운문(卷雲紋)을 대칭되게 장식하였고 아래쪽에는 능형(菱形) 장식이 매달렸는데 가는 선 또는 쌍선 운문(雲紋)으로 세부를 그렸다.

4. 좌측옥무인(左側玉舞人)

길이 3.8cm 너비 1~1.6cm 두께 0.1~0.3cm

Left Jade Dancer

L 3.8cm W 1~1.6cm T 0.1~0.3cm

편(片)으로 한쪽은 평평하고 곧으며 양면에 무인을 선각(線刻)하였다. 무인은 얼굴을 앞으로 향하였으며 가는 눈썹에 능형(菱形) 눈, 작은 삼각형 코, 작은 '一(일)'자 입을 가지고 있다. 오른팔은 올리고 왼팔은 내렸는데 긴 소매를 몸 앞에 늘어뜨렸다. 세부는 가는 선으로 꾸몄으며 발에 작은 구멍이 나 있고 민무늬에 주사(朱砂)가 칠해졌다.

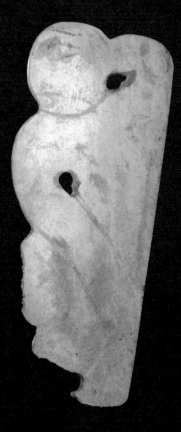

5. 우측옥무인(右側玉舞人)

길이 4cm 너비 1~1.7cm 두께 0.1~0.2cm

Right Jade Dancer

L 4cm W 1~1.7cm T 0.1~0.2cm

무인은 몸을 돌려 오른쪽을 향하였으므로 얼굴에는 가늘고 둥근 눈썹과 눈을 하나씩만 선각(線刻)하였다. 오른팔은 위로 올리고 왼팔은 내렸으며 긴 소매는 등 뒤에 늘어뜨렸다.

6. 옥형(玉珩)
길이 9.6cm 너비 2.2cm 두께 0.15cm

Jade Heng
L 9.6cm W 2.2cm T 0.15cm

양쪽 끝의 용머리는 뒤돌아보는 모습이고 꼬리가 서로 이어졌다. 입은 위로 말렸고 눈은 둥글며 기다란 눈주름이 있고 수염은 뒤로 넘겼으며 귀는 뒤로 하여 머리에 붙였다. 기다란 뿔은 아래로 말렸고 기다란 몸통은 위로 굽었으며 꼬리가 만나는 곳의 한가운데는 둥근 구멍이 나 있다. 용의 몸통 표면은 윤곽을 선각(線刻)하였는데 쌍호선(雙弧線) 6조로 꾸몄다. 아래쪽에는 권운(卷雲)을 투조(透彫)하고 세부를 가는 선 운문(雲紋)으로 꾸몄으며 겉에는 주사(朱砂)를 칠하였다.

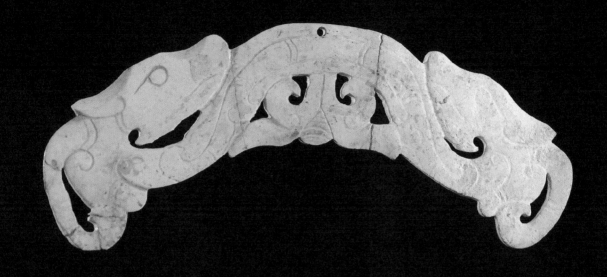

7. 운문옥패(雲紋玉佩)
변(邊)길이 각 4.2, 4.2, 4.8cm 두께 0.2cm

Jade Pendants with Cloud Patterns
side L 4.2, 4.2, 4.8cm T 0.2cm

투조(透彫)하였으며 삼각형에 가깝다. 세 변은 권운(卷雲) 모양이고 양면에는 운문(雲紋)을 선각(線刻)하였다. 한쪽 모서리에 작은 구멍이 나 있고 한쪽 면은 가공이 거친데 파손된 옥패를 가공하여 만든 듯하다.

8. 옥휴(玉觿)

길이 11cm 너비 2.7cm 두께 0.2cm

Jade Xi(horny pendants)

L 11cm W 2.7cm T 0.2cm

2점은 기룡(夔龍) 모양으로 모양. 크기가 같다. 기룡은 입을 벌리고 이를 드러냈으며 아랫입술은 뒤로 말렸다. 눈은 둥글고 기다란 눈주름이 있으며 코 부분에는 반원 모양 구멍을 누공(鏤空)하였다. 구름 모양 귀는 뒤로 젖혀졌고 기다란 뿔은 굽었다. 사지는 움츠렸으며 꼬리는 길고 뾰족하다. 가는 쌍선(雙線)으로 세부를 꾸몄다.

060

옥조패(玉組佩) (3)

백옥(白玉) | 서한(西漢)
2001년 8월 서안시 신성구(西安市 新城區) 동물원 출토

Jade Group Pendants (3)

White jade | West Han Dynasty
Excavated from the zoo in Xincheng District, Xi'an in August 2001

1. 옥원(玉瑗)

지름 8.8cm 구멍지름 4.8cm 두께 0.3cm

Jade Yuan

D 8.8cm Bore D 4.8cm T 0.3cm

안쪽 양면에 원숭이와 곰 각각 두 마리를 투조(透彫)하였다. 매 동물 바깥쪽 및 두 동물 사이 안팎에는 권운문(卷雲紋)을 선각(線刻)하였고 두 동물 사이 한가운데는 권운문을 투조하였다. 시계 반대 방향으로 첫 번째는 반쯤 주저앉은 원숭이인데 몸은 안쪽을 향하였고 고개를 돌려 쳐다보고 있다. 오른팔은 올려 물건을 든 듯하고 왼팔은 등 뒤로 내렸으며 무릎을 꿇고 다리를 뒤로 뻗었다. 가는 선으로 눈·코·입 등 세부를 새겼다. 두 번째는 앉은 모습의 원숭이로 두 팔을 올려 물건을 들었으며 얼굴은 안쪽을 향하여 오관(五官)이 분명하지 않다. 등은 굽고 두 다리는 가슴 앞에서 굽혔으며 꼬리는 위로 쳐들렸다. 가는 선으로 오관과 다른 세부를 새겼다. 세 번째는 주저앉은 곰이다. 짧고 뾰족한 귀는 위로 세워졌고 호형(弧形) 눈썹은 안으로 기울었으며 능형(菱形) 눈은 거꾸로 세워졌고 코는 길며 입은 뾰족하다. 앞다리는 곧게 세웠는데 발이 밖으로 뒤집혔다. 네 번째는 달리는 듯한 곰인데 머리는 삼각형 모양이고 뾰족한 귀는 뒤로 붙었으며 능형 눈은 거꾸로 세워졌고 코는 길고 입은 뾰족하다. 앞다리는 엎드렸고 엉덩이에는 가는 선으로 권운문을 새겼다.

2. 옥무인(玉舞人)

길이 4.5cm 너비 2.1cm 두께 0.1cm

Jade Dancer

L 4.5cm W 2.1cm T 0.1cm

몸은 'S'자형을 이룬다. 머리는 오른쪽으로 기울였고 오른팔은 머리 위를 지나 왼쪽 어깨에 닿았고 왼팔은 살짝 굽혀 허리를 잡았으며 다리는 굽어 반원 모양을 이루었다. 가는 쌍선(雙線)으로 눈썹, 눈, 입 등 세부를 새겼다.

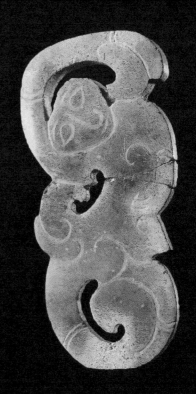

3. 옥형(玉珩)
길이 10cm 너비 2.1cm 두께 0.2cm

Jade Heng

L 10cm W 2.1cm T 0.2cm

양쪽 끝의 용머리는 뒤돌아보는 모습이다. 입은 위로 말렸고 눈은 둥글며 기다란 눈주름이 나 있다. 구름 모양 귀는 뒤로 젖혀졌고 튼실한 뒷다리는 굽혀 배에 붙었다. 꼬리는 서로 이어졌으며 윗부분 한가운데는 둥근 구멍이 나 있다. 아래쪽에는 마주 향한 권운문(卷雲紋) 두 개를 투조(透彫)하였고 세부는 가는 선으로 음각(陰刻)하였다.

4. 옥휴(玉觿)
길이 10cm 너비 1.2cm 두께 0.2cm

Jade Xi(horny pendants)

L 10cm W 1.2cm T 0.2cm

2점은 모양과 크기가 같은 봉조(鳳鳥)인데 그중 1점은 머리가 파손되었다. 봉조는 목이 굽고 뒤돌아보고 있다. 뾰족한 입은 갈고리 같으며 눈은 둥그렇고 볏은 구름 모양이다. 한쪽 날개는 앞으로 펼쳐 볏과 이어졌고 다른 한쪽 날개는 등에 붙였으며 다리는 구부렸고 꼬리는 길고 뾰족하다. 가는 선으로 눈, 날개, 꼬리 부분의 윤곽을 선각(線刻)하였다. 가운데 가는 선이 봉조를 아래위로 나누며 부분마다 두 개 내지 세 개의 쌍곡선(雙曲線)으로 꾸몄다.

5. 봉조옥패(鳳鳥玉佩)
길이 4.5cm 너비 1.8~3.5cm 두께 0.1~0.2cm

Jade Pendants with Phoenix and Bird Patterns
L 4.5cm W 1.8~3.5cm T 0.1~0.2cm

투조(透彫)한 것으로 2점은 모양과 크기가 똑같다. 뾰족한 입은 갈고리 같고 높은 볏은 구름 같다. 기다란 목은 뒤로 젖혀졌고 날개는 활짝 펼쳤으며 꼬리는 'S'자 모양을 이루고 다리는 곧게 세웠다. 가는 쌍선(雙線)으로 세부를 꾸몄다.

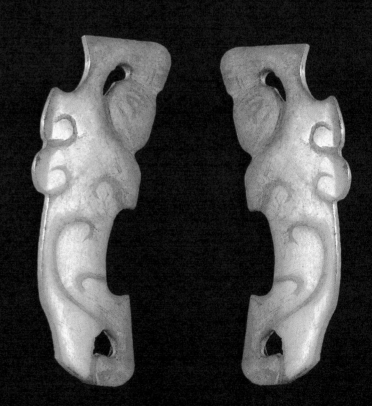

6. 옥무인(玉舞人)
길이 4cm 너비 1~1.3cm 두께 0.2cm

Jade Dancer
L 4cm W 1~1.3cm T 0.2cm

얼굴은 오른쪽 아래를 향하고 왼팔은 얼굴을 에돌아 왼쪽 위로 들었으며 오른팔은 뒤로 하여 왼쪽 가슴에 얹었는데 짐승 발 같다. 세부는 가는 선으로 꾸몄으며 오관(五官)은 분명치 않다.

7. 옥형(玉珩)
길이 7cm 너비 1.8cm 두께 0.3cm

Jade Heng(top jade in group pendants)
L 7cm W 1.8cm T 0.3cm

양쪽 끝은 모두 용머리이다. 용은 기다란 입을 살짝 벌리고 눈이 둥글며 기다란 눈주름이 나 있다. 이마가 높고 구름 모양의 귀 윗부분은 평평하고 가지런하다. 머리와 몸 사이에는 쌍호선(雙弧線)을 새기고 그 사이에 짧은 사선을 그었다. 두 마리의 몸통이 이어지는 곳 위쪽 한가운데는 둥근 구멍이 나 있고 몸통에는 운문(雲紋)을 선각하였다.

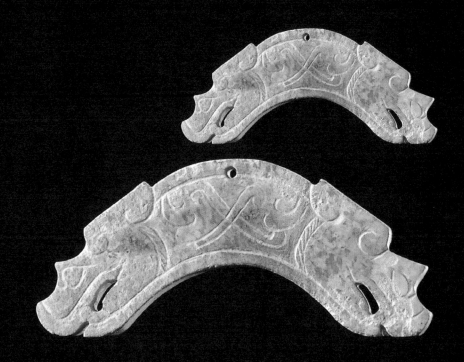

8. 옥무인(玉舞人)
길이 5cm 너비 1.5~1.6cm 두께 0.3cm

Jade Dancer
L 5cm W 1.5~1.6cm T 0.3cm

2점은 형태와 크기가 같고 자세가 상반된다. 낮은 관(冠)을 썼는데 위에는 첨각(尖角)이 있고 풀어헤친 머리는 선각(線刻)하였다. 무인은 풍만한 얼굴에 둥근 눈썹, 커다란 눈, 가느다란 코, 작은 입을 가졌다. 두 손은 가슴 앞에서 모았고 상반신은 기울었는데 등 뒤로 하나는 왼쪽으로, 다른 하나는 오른쪽으로 구름 모양 장신구를 늘어뜨렸다. 가는 쌍선(雙線)으로 세부를 꾸몄다.

섭형옥패(韘形玉佩)

섭(韘)은 활시위를 당길 때 손가락을 보호하는 고리로 청대(清代)에는 반지(扳指)라고 칭했다. 원래 기물은 대롱 모양이고 윗부분은 비스듬하며, 대롱 벽에는 활시위를 당길 때 고정 작용을 하는 홈과, 끈을 매는 구멍 두 개가 있으며, 표면에는 수면문(獸面紋)이 조각되어 있다. 전국(戰國)시대에 이르러, 전체적으로 납작하게 변했는데 중심부의 드리운 부분은 비스듬한 윗부분에서 변한 것이다. 그리고 윗부분에 비스듬한 구멍을 팠는데 납작한 깔때기 모양과 비슷하고 바깥 윤곽은 방패 모양이다. 윗부분의 한쪽에는 귀가 있는데 그 위에 작은 구멍을 뚫어 매달 수 있게 하였다. 이러한 형태 변화로 인해 활시위를 당기는 데 사용할 수 없게 되고 오직 패식으로만 사용하게 되었다. 한대(漢代)에 이르러, 이미 누조(鏤彫)로 조각한 방패 모양 패식으로 발전하였는데 윗부분은 뾰족하고 아랫부분은 둥글며 좌우 양측에는 출곽운문(出廓雲紋)을 이어 새겼다. 이런 종류의 패식은 한대 이후부터 청대 시기까지 줄곧 성행하였다.

Shè is the ring to protect the finger during arrow shooting when the finger draws the bowstring. It is also called Banzhi in Qing Dynasty. It is originally tubular shaped, slightly slanted on the top. On the wall of the tube is the groove for drawing the bowstring and the two bores for tying and attachment. The surface of the tube is also decorated with the drooping part evolved form the formerly slanting top. A tilted bore was made on the top, resembling the loop of a flat funnel. The outline is in the shape of a shield. An ear-like protrusion is on the top, with tiny bore for attachment. With such a change in shape, it could no longer be used to draw the bowstring. Rather, it has become pendant ornament. By Han Dynasty, it has developed in the shield shaped through-carved flake pendant; sharp on top and round at bottom with cloud pattern carvings on right and left side. Such pendant remained popular from Han Dynasty till Qing Dynasty.

061

이호섭형옥패(螭虎韘形玉佩)

백옥(白玉) | 서한(西漢)
길이 7.1cm 너비 4.6cm 두께 0.8cm
2001년 8월 서안시 신성구(西安市 新城區) 동물원 출토

Shè(finger ring) Shaped Jade Pendant with Chi Tiger Patterns

White jade | West Han Dynasty
L 7.1cm W 4.6cm T 0.8cm
Excavated from the zoo in Xincheng District, Xi'an in August 2001

납작한 계심(雞心) 모양으로 앞면은 살짝 볼록하고 뒷면은 약간 오목하며 윗부분은 뾰족하고 아랫부분은 호형(弧形)으로 굽었다. 둥근 두 눈, 높은 코, 넓은 입, 평평하고 가지런한 입술을 가진 이호(螭虎)가 등으로 담을 넘고 있다. 이마에서 꼬리까지 선을 음각(陰刻)하여 척추를 나타내고 허리에서는 호선(弧線)으로 늑골을 나타냈으며 경부(脛部) 뒤쪽은 짧고 세밀한 음각선으로 꾸몄다. 패의 오른편 위쪽에는 기좌(踑坐)한 우인(羽人)이 있고 왼편 위쪽에는 봉조(鳳鳥)가 날개를 펴고 뒤돌아보고 있다. 아래쪽 양측에는 출곽운문(出廓雲紋)을 새겼다.

누조섭형패(鏤彫鞢形佩)

청옥(青玉) | 서한(西漢)
① 높이 7.1cm 너비 4cm 두께 0.4cm
② 높이 4.4cm 너비 2.8cm 두께 0.3cm
1992년 서안시 미앙구 범남촌(西安市 未央區 範南村) 진청사묘(陳請士墓) 출토

Shè(finger ring) Shaped Jade Pendant with Hollow–carving

Green jade | West Han Dynasty
① L 7.1cm W 4cm T 0.4cm
② L 4.4cm W 2.8cm T 0.3cm
Excavated from Chenqingshi Tomb in Fannan Village Weiyang District, Xi'an in 1992

① 방패 모양 편(片)으로 위가 뾰족하고 아래가 둥근데 속칭 계심(鷄心)이라고도 한다. 가운데 둥근 구멍이 나 있다.
② 방패 모양 편(片)으로 형태는 ①과 같다.
2점 모두 섭형(鞢形) 권운문(卷雲紋) 패식으로 윤곽 밖에는 복잡한 권운문을 누조(鏤彫)하였다. 주체 표면은 변형된 운문(雲紋)을 음각(陰刻)하고 출곽문(出廓紋)으로 꾸몄다. 조형 구상이 교묘하고 기법이 정교하며 무늬가 복잡하고 재질이 온윤(溫潤)하고 섬세하다. 이 패식을 사용한 피장자(被葬者) 진청사(陳請士)는 당시 9급 5대부 이상 귀족이다.

063

쌍후섭형패(雙猴韘形佩)

백옥(白玉) | 서한(西漢)
길이 4cm 너비 4.1cm 두께 0.1~0.3cm
2001년 8월 서안시 신성구(西安市 新城區) 동물원 출토

Shè(finger ring) Shaped Jade Pendant with Double Monkey Patterns

White jade | West Han Dynasty
L 4cm W 4.1cm T 0.1~0.3cm
Excavated from the zoo in Xincheng District, Xi'an in August 2001

납작한 계심(鷄心) 모양으로 한가운데 둥근 구멍
이 있고 위부분이 뾰족하고 아랫부분이 둥글다. 가
운데 양측에는 가로로 평행 호선(弧線) 세 줄을 각
각 그었다. 주체 양측에는 출곽(出廓)한 원숭이를
누조(鏤彫)하였다. 두 원숭이는 형체, 자태가 똑같
은데 모두 가장자리에 매달린 모습이다. 얼굴, 관절,
손발은 모두 음각(陰刻)하였다.

064

이문섭형패(螭紋韘形佩)

백옥(白玉) | 청(淸)
지름 5cm 구멍지름 1.8cm 두께 0.7cm
1965년 서안시 안탑구 하가촌(西安市 雁塔區 何家村) 출토

Shè(finger ring) Shaped Jade Pendant with Chi Patterns

White jade | Qing Dynasty
D 5cm Bore D 1.8cm T 0.7cm
Excavated from Hejia Village in Yanta District, Xi'an in 1965

패는 원형에 가깝고 가운데 구멍이 나 있으며 이룡
(螭龍) 한 쌍을 조각하였다. 자욱한 구름 사이에서 보
일 듯 말 듯한 용은 마치 구름을 타고 노니는 것 같다.
섭형패는 '계심패(鷄心佩)'라고도 하는데 상대(商
代)에 나타났다. 원래는 실용품으로 대롱 모양이며 활
시위를 당길 때 엄지에 꼈다. 전국(戰國)시대에 점차
장식품으로 변하였고 한대(漢代)에 이르러서는 누조
(鏤彫)한 방패 모양 패식으로 발전하였다. 송대(宋代)
이후 모두 한대의 계심패를 본떠 만들었으나 모양만
비슷할 뿐 한대의 강건함은 보이지 않는다. 이 계심패
는 이룡 한 쌍이 구름 사이를 노니는 것이 신화(神話)
적 의경(意境)이 있을뿐더러 형상이 사실적이고 생동
하며 활발하다.

옥대판(玉帶板)

옥대판은 고대에 허리띠에 상감했던 옥 조각이다. 납작한 모양으로 만들어 허리띠에 달아 장식하므로 옥대식(玉帶飾), 옥대식편(玉帶飾片)이라고도 한다. 옥대는 착용한 사람의 품계와 부귀를 나타내는 상징이며 역대 제왕과 고관들만 착용하던 전용 장신구이다. 옥대판은 남북조(南北朝)시대에 최초로 나타났고 당대(唐代)에 이르러 사용 및 제작기법이 더욱 완숙해졌다. 당시 이미 명확한 옥대판 사용제도가 있었는데 "천자로부터 제후(諸侯), 왕, 공(公), 경(卿), 장(將), 상(相) 등 2품 이상의 관원에 한해 옥대의 사용을 허락한다"는 기록이 있다. 허리띠 하나에 일반적으로 9개, 10여 개 심지어 20여 개의 백옥(白玉)으로 만든 패식 조각을 달아 장식하고 어떤 것은 가장자리에 금을 둘렀다. 옥대판의 모양과 허리띠에 매단 부위에 따라 명칭도 달랐다. 예컨대 납작한 모양의 옥대판 중에서 직사각형, 정사각형, 타원형, 복숭아형은 모두 '과(銙)'라 부르고, 세 변이 편평하고 나머지 한 변이 원호형(圓弧形)인 허리띠 끝부분에 장식한 큰 옥대판을 '타미(鉈尾)'라고 부른다. 보통 옥대판은 재료 선정이 엄격한 편인데 대부분 고급 백옥을 많이 사용하였다. 허리띠에 닿는 옥대판 뒷면의 가공 기술은 간단하다. 표면은 거칠고 광택이 있고 하얀 민무늬인데 그 위에 작은 구멍 몇 개만 뚫어 실이나 금은 줄로 허리띠에 고정시킨다. 옥대판의 앞면은 다양한 문양을 조각하기도 하고 표면을 연마하여 민무늬로 된 것도 있다. 옥대판은 시대마다 문양이 달랐다.

옥대판은 남북조시대부터 명대(明代) 말기까지 천여 년 동안 사용되었다. 다양한 풍격의 수많은 옥대판은 중국 고대 옥 공예품 중에서도 독특한 유형으로 각 시대 옥공예의 특징을 보여준다.

Jade Belt Plate is the jade flake embedded in the girdle of the ancient people. It is made in the shape of a board, and is decorated on the girdle. Therefore, it is also called jade belt ornament, or jade belt ornament piece. Jade belt symbolize the official rank and wealth of the owners. It is the decorations used exclusively by emperors and high officials. Its symbolizing function can be seen in as early as South and North Dynasties. During Tang Dynasty, the usage and manufacture of jade belt plate were perfected. At that times, definite stipulations were already made on the usage of Jade belt plates: "emperors, leuds, princes, dukes, ministers, generals and prime ministers that are above second rank are allowed to wear jade belts". A girdle could be decorated with nine, over ten, or even over twenty belt plates that are made in white jade, some of which are even bordered with gold. Different forms of jade belt plates have different names, and their locations on the belt are also different. The jade belt plates that are rectangular, square, oval, and heart shaped are called "Kua", whereas the plate that is embedded on the ends of the girdle is called "Cha tail". It is bigger and has three straight and one arc-shaped sideline. Generally, during the manufacture of jade belt plates that is close to the girdle, i. e. the backside of the plate, the workmanship is quite simple. The surface is rough and plain without any patterns, only a few bore were drilled to enable the plate to be fixed on the girdle by threads or gold and silver threads. On the obverse side, various patterns were carved. There are also some plates whose obverse side only polished into smooth plain surface. Jade belt plates in different times show different features in the carving styles.

The wearing of jade belt plates has lasted more than one thousand years from South and North Dynasty to the end of Ming Dynasty. Large amount of jade belt plates in different styles have been found. They have become a unique category in the ancient jade art wares and have been a profile reflecting the jade carving style in different periods.

065

호선무문타미(胡旋舞紋銙尾)

백옥(白玉) │ 당(唐)
길이 10.1cm 너비 5.2cm 두께 1cm
1981년 섬서성 예천현(陝西省 禮泉縣) 당(唐) 소릉(昭陵) 출토

Jade Cha Tail(belt plate embedded
on the ends of girdle) with Dancing Pattern

White jade │ Tang Dynasty
L 10.1cm W 5.2cm T 1cm
Excavated from Zhaoling Tomb(Tang Dynasty) in Liquan County, Shaan'xi Province in 1981

　머리 부분이 둥근 사각형으로 앞면에는 호선무(서역의 민간무용)를 추
는 남자를 부조(浮彫)하였다. 남자는 구불구불한 긴 머리에 높다란 코,
우묵한 눈을 가졌으며 얼굴에 미소를 띠었다. 둥근 옷깃의 소매가 길고
몸에 붙는 옷과 하단 가장자리에 무늬를 장식한 기다란 치마를 입고 어
깨에 표대(飄帶)를 걸쳤으며 허리에는 띠를 매고 목이 높은 신을 신었
다. 팔꿈치를 굽혀 오른손을 올리고 왼손은 엉덩이에 얹었는데 두 손 모
두 소매에 가려졌다. 오른쪽 다리는 들고 왼쪽 다리는 살짝 굽혀 둥그런
양탄자 위에서 춤추고 있다. 양탄자 가장자리는 밧줄무늬로 장식하고
안쪽에는 '田(전)'자를 음각(陰刻)하였다. 이런 양탄자가 바로 당대(唐
代) 문헌에서 자주 언급되는 '무연(舞筵)'이다. 무늬는 회전 숫돌로 조각
하여 선이 유창하고 깔끔하며 또한 척지법(剔地法)을 사용함으로써 인
물 형상에 기복이 있어 저부조효과가 있다. 뒷면에서 방형(方形) 부분을
평면이 둥근 손잡이 모양과 직사각형 모양이 되게 깎아내고 그 위에 가
죽띠 머리를 못으로 고정시킬 수 있는 구멍 다섯 쌍을 뚫었다. 화전(和
闐) 백옥으로 된 이 타미(銙尾)는 척지·부조법을 사용하여 입체효과가
두드러지며 인물 형상을 새긴 음각선이 자연스럽다. 양면의 가장자리는
모두 모서리를 깎아내었고 정세(精細)하게 연마하였다. 사치함과 존귀
함을 드러내는 이 타미는 귀중한 재료, 뛰어난 기법에 완벽한 실용성까
지 갖추었다.

호인취횡적문방과(胡人吹橫笛紋方錡)

백옥(白玉) | 당(唐)
길이 5.1cm 너비 4.7cm 두께 0.9cm
1990년 서안시 미앙구(西安市 未央區) 관묘(關廟)초등학교 공사장 출토

Jade Kua(belt plate) with Foreign Musicians Playing Flute

White jade | Tang Dynasty
L 5.1cm W 4.7cm T 0.9cm
Excavated from construction building site of Guanmiao elementary school
in Weiyang District, Xi'an in 1990

앞면과 뒷면 크기가 같다. 앞면에는 네모난 양탄자 위에 가부좌를 하고 앉아 두 손으로 피리를 들고 부는 호인을 조각하였다. 호인은 밖으로 말린 기다란 머리에 높은 코와 우묵한 눈을 가졌다. 소매가 좁고 몸에 붙는 호복(胡服)을 입고 목이 높은 신을 신었으며 어깨에는 표대(飄帶)를 걸쳤다. 앞면 가장자리는 안쪽으로 경사졌으며 회전 숫돌로 인물의 윤곽과 세부를 조각하였다. 뒷면 네 모서리에는 각각 직각을 이루는 구멍 세 개를 뚫었는데 구멍 안에는 은정(銀釘)이 남아 있으며 뒷면 역시 연마하였다.

호인격박판문방과(胡人擊拍板紋方錡)

백옥(白玉) | 당(唐)
길이 4.2cm 너비 4cm 두께 0.7cm
1990년 서안시 미앙구(西安市 未央區) 관묘(關廟)초등학교 공사장 출토

Jade Kua(belt plate) with Foreign Musicians Playing Clappers

White jade | Tang Dynasty
L 4.2cm W 4cm T 0.7cm
Excavated from construction building site of Guanmiao elementary
school in Weiyang District, Xi'an in 1990

재질이 영롱하고 온윤(溫潤)하며 부드럽고 단단하다. 뒷면이 조금 크고 측면은 모두 비탈 모양을 이루며 모서리는 안쪽으로 경사졌다. 앞면에는 네모난 양탄자 위에 쭈그리고 앉아 가슴 앞에서 두 손으로 박판(拍板)을 들고 두드리는 호인을 조각하였다. 호인은 코가 높고 눈이 우묵하며 긴 머리가 밖으로 말렸고 수염이 정갈하다. 상반신을 드러내고 팔목에는 팔찌를 꼈으며 아래에는 긴 바지를 입고 허리에는 치마끈을 매었다. 뒷면은 연마하지 않았으며 네 모서리에는 각기 구멍 한 쌍씩을 뚫었다.

호인취필률문방과(胡人吹篳篥紋方銙)

백옥(白玉) | 당(唐)
길이 5.1cm 너비 4.7cm 두께 0.9cm
1990년 서안시 미앙구(西安市 未央區) 관묘(關廟)초등학교 공사장 출토

Jade Kua(belt plate) with the Motif of Foreign Musicians Playing Bili(shawm)

White jade | Tang Dynasty
L 5.1cm W 4.7cm T 0.9cm
Excavated from construction building site of Guanmiao elementary
school in Weiyang District, Xi'an in 1990

과(銙)는 앞뒤 면이 같다. 앞면에는 네모난 양탄자 위에서 가부좌 자세로 앉아 두 손으로 필률(고대 관악기의 하나)의 구멍을 눌러 연주하고 있는 호인을 조각하였다. 호인은 밖으로 말린 긴 머리, 구레나룻, 높은 코, 우묵한 눈을 가졌다. 소매가 좁고 몸에 붙는 호복(胡服)을 입고 목이 높은 신을 신었으며 어깨에는 표대(飄帶)를 걸쳤다. 필률은 가관(笳管)이라고도 부르는데 갈대로 만든 호루라기이다. 큰 것은 구멍이 앞에 7개, 뒤에 2개 도합 9개로 활음(滑音), 전음(顫音), 타음(打音), 쇄음(涮音), 치음(齒音)을 낼 수 있는데 당대(唐代) 십부악(十部樂)에서 중요한 악기이다. 조각 특징 및 뒷면 구멍은 모두 앞의 호인격박판문방과(胡人擊拍板紋方銙)와 같다.

호인장계루고파도뢰문방과 (胡人杖雞婁鼓播鞉牢紋方銙)

백옥(白玉) | 당(唐)
길이 5.1cm 너비 4.7cm 두께 0.9cm
1990년 서안시 미앙구(西安市 未央區) 관묘(關廟)초등학교 공사장 출토

Jade Kua(belt plate) with the Motif of Foreign Musicians Playing Drums

White jade | Tang Dynasty
L 5.1cm W 4.7cm T 0.9cm
Excavated from construction building site of Guanmiao elementary
school in Weiyang District, Xi'an in 1990

앞뒤 면이 같은 과(銙)로 앞면에는 네모난 양탄자 위에 쭈그리고 앉아 연주하는 호인을 조각하였다. 호인은 높은 코, 오목한 눈에 곱슬머리, 짧은 수염을 하고 소매가 좁고 몸에 붙는 호복(胡服)을 입고 어깨에 표대(飄帶)를 걸쳤으며 목이 높은 신을 신었다. 왼쪽 팔을 굽혀 팔꿈치로 무릎에 놓인 계루고(雞婁鼓, 북, 악기의 일종)를 누르고 손에는 도뢰[鞉牢, 노도(路鼗)와 비슷한 긴 손잡이의 작은 요고(搖鼓)]를 들었으며 오른손으로는 북채를 잡고 계루고를 두드리려는 듯하다. 호인의 머리 부분과 도뢰의 표면에는 심색(沁色, 옥기가 장시간 토양이나 물 및 기타 물질과 접촉하면서 자연적으로 생성된 물이나 광물질에 침식되어 일부 또는 전체 색상이 변하는 현상)현상이 있다. 앞면 가장자리는 안쪽으로 경사지고 뒷면은 앞의 호인격박판문방과(胡人擊拍板紋方銙)와 같다.

호인음주문방과(胡人飮酒紋方銙)

백옥(白玉) | 당(唐)
길이 5.1cm 너비 4.7cm 두께 0.9cm
1990년 서안시 미앙구(西安市 未央區) 관묘(關廟)초등학교 공사장 출토

Jade Kua(belt plate) with the Motif of Drinking Foreign Musician

White jade | Tang Dynasty
L 5.1cm W 4.7cm T 0.9cm
Excavated from construction building site of Guanmiao elementary
school in Weiyang District, Xi'an in 1990

　앞면은 네 변이 안쪽으로 경사지고 가운데에는 네모난 양
탄자 위에서 가부좌를 틀고 앉아 음주하는 호인을 조각하였
다. 호인은 코가 높고 눈이 우묵하며 곱슬머리에 구레나룻이
있다. 소매가 좁고 몸에 붙는 호복(胡服)을 입었으며 맨발이
다. 왼손은 무릎에 얹고 오른손은 가슴 앞에서 잔을 들었는데
투실투실한 얼굴은 즐거운 표정을 띠고 있다. 뒷면 네 모서리
에는 각기 직각 모양 구멍을 뚫었다.

호인격갈고문방과(胡人擊羯鼓紋方銙)

백옥(白玉) | 당(唐)
길이 5cm 너비 4.5cm 두께 0.9cm
1990년 서안시 미앙구(西安市 未央區) 관묘(關廟)초등학교 공사장 출토

Jade Kua(belt plate) with the Motif of Foreign Musicians Playing Jiegu Drum

White jade | Tang Dynasty
L 5cm W 4.5cm T 0.9cm
Excavated from construction building site of Guanmiao elementary school
in Weiyang District, Xi'an in 1990

　앞뒤 면이 같은 과(銙)로 왼쪽 하단이 떨어져나갔으며
뒷면은 연마하지 않았다. 가장자리는 안쪽으로 경사지며
가운데에는 네모난 양탄자 위에 앉아 양손으로 북채를 들
고 왼쪽에 둔 갈고(羯鼓)를 두드리는 호인을 조각하였다.
호인은 높은 코, 오목한 눈에 곱슬머리와 구레나룻을 가졌
다. 소매가 좁고 몸에 붙는 옷에 긴 바지를 입었는데 윗옷
가슴 쪽에 있는 단추가 뚜렷하게 보이며 어깨에는 표대(飄
帶)를 걸쳤다. 좌우 양측에는 실타래 모양 여의운문(如意
雲紋)을 새겼다. 호인 얼굴에는 심색(沁色) 현상이 있다. 뒷
면 네 모서리에는 각기 구멍 한 쌍을 뚫었다.

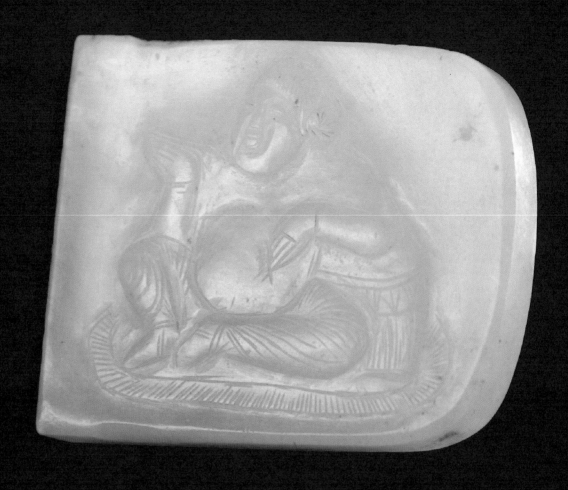

072

호인음주문원수구형과
(胡人飮酒紋圓首矩形銙)

백옥(白玉) ｜ 당(唐)
길이 5.1cm 너비 4.7cm 두께 0.9cm
1990년 서안시 미앙구(西安市 未央區) 관묘(關廟)초등학교 공사장 출토

Jade Kua(belt plate) with a Rounded End and the Motif of Foreign Musicians Drinking Wine

White jade ｜ Tang Dynasty
L 5.1cm W 4.7cm T 0.9cm
Excavated from construction building site of Guanmiao elementary school
in Weiyang District, Xi'an in 1990

앞뒤 면이 같다. 앞면 가장자리는 안쪽으로 경사졌으며 가운데에는 둥그런 양탄자 위에 앉아 있는 호인을 조각하였다. 배를 드러낸 호인은 왼팔을 굽혀 팔꿈치를 높은 깔개 위에 고이고 오른손에 잔을 들고 음주하며 주위를 둘러보고 있다. 호인은 높은 코에 우묵한 눈 그리고 곱슬머리를 가지고 만면에 웃음을 띠었으며 긴 바지를 입고 신을 신었다. 인물 주위를 모두 척지(剔地)하여 인물 형상이 더 두드러져 보인다. 뒷면은 연마하지 않았으며 둥근 머리 한가운데와 각진 모서리 양측에는 각기 구멍 한 쌍을 뚫었다.

073

옥대과(玉帶銙)

청옥(靑玉) | 당(唐)
길이 5.2cm 너비 5cm 두께 0.9cm
서안시 신성구 한삼채(西安市 新城區 韓森寨) 당묘(唐墓) 출토

Jade Belt Kua(belt plate embedded in the middle of the girdle)

Green jade | Tang Dynasty
L 5.2cm W 5cm T 0.9cm
Excavated from Tang Tomb in Hansenzhai in Xincheng District, Xi'an

대과는 정사각형으로 주제문양이 가장자리보다 높다. 앞면에는 반부조(半浮彫)기법으로 양탄자 위에 가부좌를 하고 앉아 비파를 타는 호인(胡人)을 조각하였다. 호인은 둥근 옷깃의 소매가 좁은 포(袍)를 입고 묶은 머리를 어깨에 늘어뜨렸으며 피백(披帛)은 어깨에서 양쪽 겨드랑이로 흘러내렸다가 다시 양측 위로 날린다. 앞면 가장자리는 밖에서 안으로 점차 낮아져 비탈을 이루는 동시에 사면에 테를 이루었다. 인물문(人物紋)은 돌기되어 가장자리보다 조금 높은 저부조 형태를 이루었다. 뒷면은 매끈하고 민무늬이며 네 모서리에는 작은 구멍 두 개를 뚫어 허리띠에 매달 수 있게 하였다. 서역(西域) 호인 형상을 조각한 인물문은 당대(唐代) 대과에서 만 볼 수 있는 특별한 문양이다.

074

소면옥대판(素面玉帶板)

묵옥(墨玉) | 당(唐)
장방형대판(長方形帶板): 길이 4.1cm 너비 3.5cm 두께 0.8cm
원수호대판(圓首弧帶板): 길이 3.9cm 최대너비 2.6cm 두께 1cm
타미(鉈尾): 길이 6.1cm 너비 3.7cm 두께 1cm
서안시 미앙구(西安市 未央區) 한성(漢城)에서 출토

Jade Belt Plate with Plain Surface

Celadon jade | Tang Dynasty
Quadrate belt plate: L 4.1cm W 3.5cm T 0.8cm
Arc shaped belt plate with a round head:
L 3.9cm Max W 2.6cm T 1cm
Cha tail(final belt plate): L 6.1cm W 3.7cm T 1cm
Excavated from Han Tomb in Weiyang District, Xi'an

옥대판은 세 가지 유형으로 나뉜다.

장방형대판(長方形帶板) 4점: 직사각형으로 한쪽에는 좁은 직사각형 투공(透孔)이 있고 뒷면 네 모서리에는 각기 구멍 하나가 있다.

원수호대판(圓首弧帶板) 5점: 세 변이 곧고 나머지 한 변은 호형(弧形)이다. 곧은 변 쪽에 직사각형 투공이 있고 뒷면에는 구멍 세 쌍이 있다.

타미(鉈尾) 1점: 둥근 머리의 직사각형으로 한쪽 변이 호형이며 표면은 광택이 나고 민무늬이다. 뒷면에는 쌍공(雙孔) 네 쌍이 있다.

이 옥대판은 조각이 정교하고 형태가 가지런하며 표면은 정세(精細)하게 연마되었다. 뒷면에서 직사각형 구멍을 살펴보면, 구멍 양쪽에 각각 병렬된 초승달 흔적 두 개와 그 사이 돌기된 끊긴 흔적을 볼 수 있다. 이는 가공할 때 먼저 회전 숫돌로 긴 두 변을 뚫은 후 사이 연결된 부분을 끊어버려 생긴 흔적이다. 뒷면은 구멍이 나 있어 동사(銅絲)로 허리띠와 연결할 수 있다. 이와 같이 구멍이 나 있는 옥대판은 칼, 해결추(解結錐, 고대에 뼈로 만든 매듭 푸는 도구) 등 생활도구를 매달 수 있다.

옥대과(玉帶銙)

백옥(白玉) | 당(唐)
길이 5cm 너비 4.7cm 두께 0.9cm
서안시(西安市) 교외 당묘(唐墓) 출토

Jade Belt Kua(belt plate embedded in the middle of the girdle)

White jade | Tang Dynasty
L 5cm W 4.7cm T 0.9cm
Excavated from Tang Tomb in the outskirt of Xi'an

가로로 넓은 방형(方形)이며 척지법(剔地法)으로 가부좌를 틀고 둥그런 양탄자 위에 앉아 두 손에 생황을 들고 연주하는 호인(胡人)을 조각하였다. 주제문양의 높은 부분은 가장자리와 높낮이가 같다. 호인은 긴 머리를 가르마하여 양쪽으로 계(髻)를 하였고 눈이 크고 코가 높다. 둥근 옷깃에 소매가 좁은 장포(長袍) 차림에 허리띠를 매었으며 코가 뾰족하고 목이 높은 신을 신었다. 어깨에 걸친 피백(披帛)은 정수리 위로 올렸다가 양쪽 겨드랑이로 흘러내렸으며 전체 모습이 생동하고 자연스럽다. 뒷면은 매끈하고 민무늬이며 네 모서리에는 각기 구멍을 뚫어 허리띠에 매달 수 있게 하였다. 전체 형상은 직선과 가는 곡선을 결합시킨 음각선으로 표현하였다. 옷 주름은 얕고도 가는 곡선으로 표현하였는데 선이 길고도 빽빽하지만 번잡하지 않은 것이 전형적인 당대(唐代) 풍격이다.

복수문대구(福壽紋帶扣)

백옥(白玉) | 원(元)
전체길이 9.5cm 너비 4.4cm 두께 1.7cm
1978년 서안시 미앙구 한성향(西安市 未央區 漢城鄉) 출토

Jade Belt Buckle with Fushou(symbolizing good fortune and longevity) Pattern

White jade | Yuan Dynasty
Total L 9.5cm W 4.4cm T 1.7cm
Excavated from Hancheng Village in Weiyang District, Xi'an in 1978

대구는 방형(方形) 대판(帶板) 두 개로 구성되었다. 하나는 얇고 네모진 갈고리가 있는데 위에는 수면문(獸面紋)을 조각하였고 다른 하나에는 대응되는 갈고리 구멍이 있다. 둘 다 복숭아와 박쥐로 이루어진 '복수길상(福壽吉祥)' 도안이 누조(鏤彫)되었는데 조각기법과 문양은 똑같고 방향만 상반된다. 대판 위 누조장식과 대판 사이 네 모서리는 각기 복숭아 나뭇잎으로 이어졌다. 측면에서 살펴보면 대판은 두께가 균일하고 살짝 'S'형을 이룬다. 대판 뒷면에는 둥그런 손잡이가 달린 고정쇠가 있으며 고정쇠 등은 평평하다. 대판 표면은 깔끔하고 반질반질하지만 도안에는 조각할 때 뚫은 원형(圓形) 구멍이 다듬지 않은 채로 남아 있어 기법이 투박하다.

원대(元代) 옥대판에는 용문(龍紋)과 사문(獅紋)이 많아지고 인물은 모두 몽고 귀족의 복식을 착용하였다. 끝이 뾰족한 원첨모(圓檐帽)를 쓰고 소매가 좁은 옷에 짧은 치마를 입고 허리띠를 매고 목이 높은 신을 신었는데 정적 또는 동적으로 형태가 다양하다. 조각기법에서는 부조(浮彫) 외에 다층(多層) 누공조각이 나타났다. 원대 옥대판은 대부분 테가 있는데 테 가운데를 오목하게 하거나 음각선 두 줄과 음각한 삼각형으로 장식하였고 이 외에 '亞(아)'자형 테와 커다란 연주문(聯珠紋) 테가 있다. 조각한 옥대판에는 늘 가공할 때 생긴 자그마한 원형 구멍이 남아 있다.

077

이문대구(螭紋帶扣)

청백옥(靑白玉) | 명(明)
길이 5.9cm 너비 5cm 두께 1.7cm
서안시 연호구(西安市 蓮湖區) 토문(土門) 출토

Jade Belt Buckle with Chi Pattern

Green and white jade | Ming Dynasty
L 5.9cm W 5cm T 1.7cm
Excavated from Tumen in Lianhu District, Xi'an

　　대구는 모서리가 둥근 직사각형으로 앞면이 두드러지고 뒷면이 오목하다. 앞면에는 크고 작은 이룡(螭龍) 한 쌍을 부조(浮彫)하고 주변 가장자리에는 가는 선 한 둘레를 음각(陰刻)하였다. 큰 이룡은 입에 영지를 물고 뒤돌아보는 모습이다. 사지는 기어오르는 듯하고 몸통은 굽었으며 꼬리를 흔드는 것이 구름을 타고 노니는 듯하다. 뒤따르는 작은 이룡은 영지 빼앗는 놀이를 즐기는 듯하다. 원대(元代)의 이룡과 비교할 때, 머리는 보다 짧고 뒷다리는 자태가 비슷하나 굽은 부분을 직각으로 처리하여 명대의 특징을 드러낸다. 뒷면은 외곽(外廓)과 같은 직사각형으로 누공(鏤空)하였는데 한쪽 가장자리 안쪽에는 납작한 네모 단추를 조각하고 대응되는 맞은편 가장자리에는 가로로 기다란 구멍을 누공하였다. 구멍은 바깥쪽이 크고 안쪽이 작다. 무늬와 가장자리는 비교적 세밀하게 연마하였으나 안쪽과 바닥은 그다지 평평하지도 광택이 나지도 않는다. 이는 명대 옥기에서 흔히 볼 수 있는 단점으로 형태만 추구하고 정교함을 추구하지 않았다.

078

옥대판(玉帶板)

백옥(白玉) | 명(明)
구형대과(矩形帶銙): 길이 4.7cm 너비 3.3cm 두께 0.6cm
장방형대과(長方形帶銙): 길이 3.2cm 너비 1.6cm 두께 0.6cm
도형대과(桃形帶銙): 길이 3.5cm 최대너비 3.3cm 두께 0.6cm
타미(銙尾): 길이 8.6cm 너비 3.3cm 두께 0.6cm
1982년 서안시 비림구(西安市 碑林區) 남곽문(南廓門) 출토

Jade Belt Buckle

White jade | Ming Dynasty
Rectangular belt Kua: L 4.7cm W 3.3cm T 0.6cm
Quadrate belt Kua: L 3.2cm W 1.6cm T 0.6cm
Heart shaped belt Kua: L 3.5cm W 3.3cm T 0.6cm
Cha tail(belt plate embedded on the ends of girdle):
L 8.6cm W 3.3cm T 0.6cm
Excavated from Nanguomen in Beilin District, Xi'an in 1982

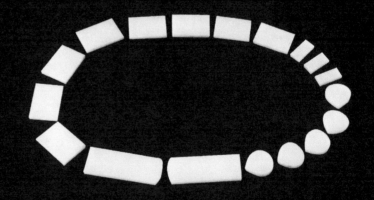

　　구형대과(矩形帶銙) 8점, 장방형대과(長方形帶銙) 3점, 도형대과(桃形帶銙) 5점, 타미(銙尾) 2점으로 이루어진 옥대판이다. 모두 납작한 편(片)으로 희고 광택이 나며 민무늬이다. 구형대과는 각각 구멍 세 개가 있고 장방형과 도형 대과에는 각기 구멍 두 개가 있다. 사미는 네 모서리에 모두 구멍이 있는데 그중 한 사미에는 방형(方形) 부분 양쪽에 각기 구멍 세 개가 있으며 안쪽에서 두 개씩 서로 통한다. 앞면과 측면은 정세(精細)하게 연마되었고 뒷면은 거친 편이며 앞면 가장자리는 모두 경사지게 깎아내었다.

　　명대(明代) 초기에는 원대(元代) 옥대판의 풍격을 답습하였으나 무늬 사용에는 엄격한 제도가 있었다. 홍무(洪武) 26년에는 무릇 1품 이상 관리만이 옥대(玉帶)를 사용할 수 있으며 대판은 민무늬도 가능하고 무늬를 장식할 수도 있다고 규정하였다. 명대 제도에서는 오직 제왕 및 제왕이 특별히 하사한 관리만이 용문(龍紋)이 새겨진 옥대를 사용할 수 있다고 규정지었다. 옥대판의 수량도 증가하여 명대 중·후기에 이르러서는 상대적으로 1세트에 20개로 고정되었으며 각각의 형태 및 허리띠에서의 배열위치도 모두 규정이 있었다. 명대 옥대판의 무늬는 용문(龍紋), 기린문(麒麟紋), 봉조학록(鳳鳥鶴鹿), 영지(靈芝), 백자문(百子紋), 영희도(嬰戲圖), 희사(戱獅), 쌍어(雙魚) 등으로 더욱 풍부해졌다. 조각 기법상에서는 평면 부조(浮彫) 외에도 다층(多層) 누조(鏤彫)·투조(透彫)기법을 사용하였다. 즉, 주제문양 아래에 한 층을 더 조각하여 주제 문양을 돋보이게 하였다.

용문대과(龍紋帶銙)

백옥(白玉) | 명(明)
길이 7.1cm 너비 5.6cm 두께 0.8cm
서안시 비림구(西安市 碑林區) 서안교통대학 동쪽 출토

Jade Belt Kua with Dragon Pattern

White jade | Ming Dynasty
L 7.1cm W 5.6cm T 0.8cm
Excavated at the east of Xi'an Jiaotong University in Beilin District, Xi'an

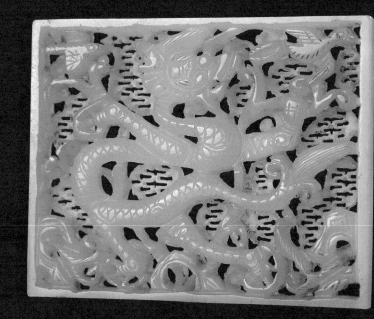

대과는 직사각형으로 네모난 테 안에 2층으로 투조(透彫)하였다. 위층 한가운데는 'S'자형으로 굽은 용을 조각하였는데 뒷다리는 앞뒤로 놓여 걸어 다니는 듯하고 앞다리는 좌우로 뻗었다. 위쪽에는 나는 새가 있고 아래쪽에는 바위와 초목이 있다. 전체 화면은 용이 산림 속에서 위풍당당한 모습을 표현하였다. 아래층은 비교적 얇은데 위층 무늬 사이에 바위를 누조(鏤彫)하였다. 뒷면에서 보면 위층 용의 몸통 가운데는 모두 누공하였고 네 모서리에는 각각 구멍이 있다. 구멍은 누공한 부위에서 막대기 모양 도구로 사선으로 뚫었기에 쉽게 보이지 않는다. 무늬 표면은 정세하게 연마되었으나 측면, 안쪽, 바닥은 평평하지도 매끄럽지도 않다.

080

용문대과(龍紋帶銙)

백옥(白玉) | 명(明)
변(邊)길이 6.3cm 두께 1cm
1983년 서안시(西安市) 수집

Jade Belt Kua with Dragon Pattern

White jade | Ming Dynasty
Side L 6.3cm T 1cm
Collected in Xi'an in 1983

대과는 정사각형으로 네모 테 안에 두 층으로 투조(透彫)하였다. 위층 가운데는 용을 조각하고 주위는 화훼로 꾸몄다. 둥근 눈에 기다란 뿔을 가진 용은 휘돌며 솟구치는 모습으로 털은 위로 뻗고 네 발톱은 풍차 모양을 이룬다. 목에서 꼬리까지 음각선을 그어 몸통의 구불구불함을 표현하였고 그 위쪽에 비아(扉牙) 모양 척추를 조각하였다. 용의 몸통과 사지에 그은 짧은 직선, 가느다란 아랫다리, 풍차 모양의 네 발톱은 모두 명대(明代) 말기 풍격에 속한다. 아래층에는 당초문(唐草紋)을 누조(鏤彫)하였다. 뒷면 네 모서리에는 각각 구멍 뚫린 꽃잎이 있는데 금속 줄로 허리띠를 고정시키는 데 사용되며 양쪽 모두 누공(鏤空)하여 쉽게 보이지 않는다. 무늬 표면은 정세(精細)하게 연마되었으나 측면, 안쪽, 바닥은 거칠다.

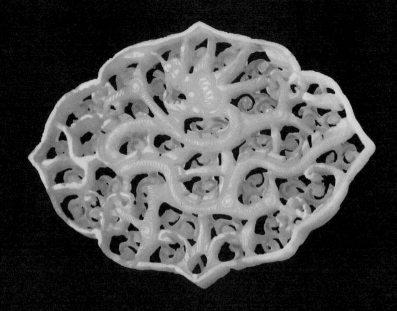

081

능화형용문과(菱花形龍紋銙)

백옥(白玉) | 명(明)
지름길이 6.7cm 너비 5.3cm 두께 0.7cm
1983년 서안시(西安市) 수집

Jade Kua with Diamond Shaped Dragon Pattern

White jade | Ming Dynasty
Caliber L 6.7cm W 5.3cm T 0.7cm
Collected in Xi'an in 1983

능화형으로 무늬는 두 층으로 투조(透彫)하였다. 위층은 구름에 휩싸인 용을 누조(鏤彫)하였는데 용머리는 짧고 굵으며 돼지코를 닮은 커다란 코는 위로 쳐들렸는데 끝부분에 수염이 있다. 올려다보는 모습으로 대롱 모양 도구를 사용하여 조각한 두 눈은 사선으로 놓였다. 털은 위로 뻗었고 꼬리는 뱀 꼬리 같다. 몸통과 사지가 가늘고 길며 경부(脛部)의 발끝까지 짧은 선을 빼곡하게 음각한 것은 명대(明代) 옥룡(玉龍)의 뚜렷한 특징이다. 아래층에는 당초문(唐草紋)을 누조하였다. 뒷면 능형의 네 모서리에는 모두 구멍을 뚫지 않았으나 그중 세 모서리의 가지와 잎이 끊어진 것으로 보아 이 옥대과(玉帶銙)는 아래층 네 모서리의 가지와 잎 사이를 금속 줄로 꿰어 허리띠에 고정시킨 것으로 추정된다.

082

천아천화타원형대과(天鵝穿花橢圓形帶銙)

백옥(白玉) | 명(明)
긴지름 5.9cm 짧은지름 4.9cm 두께 0.5cm
1978년 서안시(西安市) 수집

Oval Shaped Jade Kua with the Motif of Swan in the Flowers

White jade | Ming Dynasty
Long D 5.9cm Short D 4.9cm T 0.5cm
Collected in Xi'an in 1978

옥패(玉牌)는 타원형에 가까운데 무늬 세 층을 투조(透彫)하였다. 물, 연꽃, 화훼를 배경으로 하여 백조 한 마리가 입을 벌린 채 날개를 펴고 수중 꽃밭으로 날아들고 있다. 꽃잎 가운데는 안쪽으로 오목하게 들어갔고 꽃술에는 씨가 맺힌 원형 연밥이 있다. 수초는 얼기설기 자연스레 엉켜 입체감이 강하다. 백조의 아래위 입술은 거치(鋸齒) 모양으로 조각하였고 복부와 날개 깃털은 쌍선(雙線)으로 음각하였으며 양측에는 짧은 사선을 음각하였다. 뒷면은 희고 민무늬이며 깊고 얕은 송곳 및 맷돌 흔적이 남아 있으며 허리띠를 고정시킬 수 있는 구멍 세 개가 나 있다.

이 옥패의 구도는 금·원대(金·元代) '춘수옥(春水玉)'과 비슷한데 완벽한 도안은 백조 머리 위쪽에 해동청(海東靑) 한 마리가 더 있어야 한다. 해동청은 응골(鷹鶻) 또는 토골응(吐鶻鷹)이라고도 부르는데 주요한 서식지는 흑룡강(黑龍江) 유역이다. 용맹하여 기러기 또는 백조를 사냥하는 사냥매로 훈련시킬 수 있다. 이 옥패는 구도가 안정적이고 줄기와 가지가 가는 선 같고 잎·꽃잎·모서리가 예리한 것이 조각기법상 명대(明代) 중·후기 풍격에 속한다.

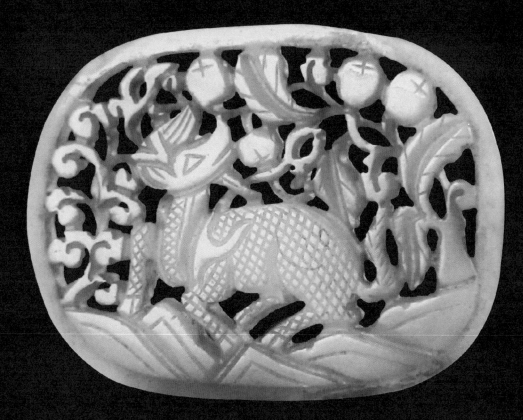

083

기린문대식(麒麟紋帶飾)

백옥(白玉) | 명(明)
타원형: 지름 4,5∼6cm 두께 0,5cm
도형(桃形): 길이 3,8cm 너비 3,2cm 두께 0,5cm
1982년 서안시 안탑구 삼효촌(西安市 雁塔區 三爻村) 출토

Ornaments with Qilin(a kind of dragon) Pattern

White jade | Ming Dynasty
Oval shape: D 4,5∼6cm T 0,5cm
Heart shape: L 3,8cm W 3,2cm T 0,5cm
Excavated from Sanyao Village in Yanta District, Xi'an in 1982

　같은 명대(明代) 무덤에서 출토된 2점은 무늬 제재가 같은데 하나
는 타원형이고 다른 하나는 도형(桃形)이다. 앞면은 가장자리를 낮게
연마하여 좁은 테를 만들고 가운데는 바위 사이를 거니는 기린을 투
조(透彫)하였으며 주위에는 꽃과 잎을 누공(鏤空)하였다. 기린은 머리
를 돌려 올려다보는데 삼각 눈, 위로 쳐들린 코, 살짝 벌어진 입, 비스
듬히 세운 귀를 가지고 있다. 턱에는 수염이 나 있고 정수리에는 뿔이
있으며 머리는 앞으로 뻗었고 어깨에는 화염문(火焰紋)이 있으며 꼬
리는 위로 쳐들렸다. 몸통에는 능형(菱形) 격자무늬를 새겨 비늘을 표
현했다. 뒷면은 희고 민무늬이며 조금 거칠고 구멍 여러 개가 있어 끈
을 꿰어 허리띠에 고정할 수 있다.
　기린은 중국 신화에 나오는 서수(瑞獸)로 사슴의 뿔과 발굽에, 온몸
에는 비늘이 있으며 형태가 뚜렷한 초식성 동물의 특징을 띠었다. 한
대(漢代)부터 기린은 청룡(靑龍), 백호(白虎), 현무(玄武), 주작(朱雀)과
함께 '중앙(中央)' 방위와 '토(土)' 행을 나타내는 신수(神獸)가 되었다.

용문도형대식(龍紋桃形帶飾)

백옥(白玉) | 명(明)
길이 6.7cm 너비 6.3cm 두께 2.1cm
1983년 서안시 비림구(西安市 碑林區) 남곽문(南廓門) 출토

Heart Shaped Jade Belt Ornament with Dragon Pattern

White jade | Ming Dynasty
L 6.7cm W 6.3cm T 2.1cm
Excavated from Nanguomen in Beilin District, Xi'an in 1983

도형(桃形)이며 틀 안에 무늬 두 층을 투조(透彫)하였다. 위층은 구름 속에서 노니는 용을 누조(鏤彫)하였는데 용머리는 짧은 편이고 올려다보는 자세이며 중도(重刀)로 조각하였다. 여의(如意) 모양 코는 위로 처들려 돼지코 같으며 끝부분에는 수염이 나 있다. 벌어진 입 사이로 이빨이 보이며 아래턱이 짧고 이마가 도드라졌다. 둥그런 두 눈은 볼록하게 튀어나왔고 뒤통수에는 곧은 쌍뿔이 나 있으며 머리카락은 위로 뻗었다. 몸통은 뱀과 같이 가늘고도 긴데 위에는 세밀한 망(網) 모양 인문(鱗紋)을 음각하였고 양측에는 촬모문(撮毛紋)을, 관절에는 권운문(卷雲紋)을 새겼다. 아랫다리는 가늘고 약하며 발가락이 네 개 달린 발은 풍차(風車) 모양이다. 아래층에는 당초문(唐草紋)을 누조하였다. 옥대식은 구리판에 상감되었으며 구리판 뒷면에는 고리와 갈고리로 이루어진 구리 단추가 있다. 고리는 구리판에 용접되었는데 가운데는 당초문을 누공(鏤空)하였고 가장자리에는 못으로 갈고리를 고정시킬 수 있는 구멍 세 개가 있고 한쪽에는 다리 모양 고정쇠가 있어 허리띠를 꿸 수 있다. 갈고리는 '丁(정)'자 모양이며 위에 판식(板式) 스프링이 있어 고리에 끼울 수 있다. 단추를 풀 때 둥근 구멍 위 장치(일실되었음)를 누르면 고리에서 뺄 수 있다. 갈고리의 우산 모양 부분에 다리 모양 고정쇠가 있고 그 위편 바깥쪽에 패식(佩飾)을 매달 수 있는 또 다른 다리 모양 고정쇠가 가로놓였다.

옥대식(玉帶飾)

백옥(白玉) | 청(淸)
길이 5cm 너비 3cm 두께 0.7cm
1982년 서안시(西安市) 수집

Jade Belt Ornament

White jade | Qing Dynasty
L 5cm W 3cm T 0.7cm
Collected in Xi'an in 1982

　납작한 직방체 모양으로 앞면에는 파도가 일렁이는 강 옆 산비탈에서 거닐고 있는 행인을 조각하였다. 교령(交領)의 소매가 넓은 장포(長袍)를 입고 허리띠를 맨 행인은 작은 다리 쪽으로 향했는데 길옆에는 나무들이 늘어섰고 건너편 기슭으로 운무(雲霧) 속 궁전과 누각이 보인다. 뒷면은 가운데가 오목하게 들어갔고 양쪽에는 구멍이 있어 허리띠에 매달 수 있다.

　이 대식은 압지은기법(壓地隱起法)으로 조각하여 양각한 무늬의 선을 도드라지게 한 것이 백묘화(白描畵)와 비슷하다. 일반적인 산수화가 근경(近景)에는 수림, 원경(遠景)에는 옅은 색의 산들을 배치한 후 기타 경물을 추가하여 그리는 것과 달리 이 대식은 '화면'이 작아 구상과 설계에서 제한을 받았다. 그러나 조각가는 자그마한 대식에 교묘한 구상과 배치로 행인, 산비탈, 다리, 나무 등을 하나로 녹여냈고 강 건너 보이는 궁전과 누각은 마치 신기루 같다. 이는 예술가의 산수화 구도에 대한 투철한 이해와 조각기법에 대한 자신감에 기인한 것으로 짙은 호소력이 있다.

　옥으로 조각된 이 '그림'은 중국 산수화와 마찬가지로 허와 실의 어우러짐을 강조하여 경계를 넓히고 화의(畵意)를 풍부히 하였다. 나무와 강기슭, 파도가 일렁이는 강, 운무 속에 싸인 누각이 하나로 어우러져 웅대한 기상과 심원(深遠)한 의경(意境)이 느껴진다. 주목할 만한 것은 중심부에 칼을 사용하지 않고서도 넓은 강을 표현해내어 보는 이로 하여금 가슴이 확 트이게 한다. 근경의 바위, 비탈길, 나무, 다리에는 극히 적게 칼을 사용하여 간단하면서도 가지런하게 표현함으로써 강을 넓어 보이게 하였다. 건너편의 누각은 보일 듯 말 듯한 것이 자연계의 변화에 부합되며 운무까지 더하여 '신경(神景)'처럼 보이고 가까운 곳에 있지만 닿을 수 없는 느낌을 준다. 특히 그 속에 행인이 있어 짙은 생활의 정취를 더해준다.

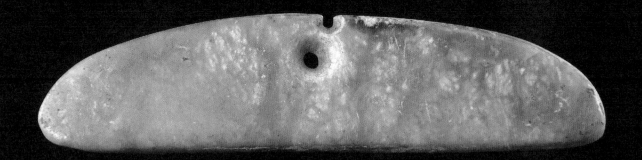

086

옥식(玉飾)

밀옥(密玉) | 양소문화(仰韶文化)
길이 6.4cm 너비 1.4cm 두께 0.4cm
2004년 서안시 안탑구 어화채(西安市 雁塔區 魚化寨) 출토

Jade Ornament

Mi jade | YangShao Culture
D 6.4cm W 1.4cm T 0.4cm
Excavated from Yuhuazhai Village in Yanta District, Xi'an in 2004

청옥에 흰색 반점이 있으며 납작한 모양인데 평면은 반원(半圓)에 가깝다. 가운데 위쪽에는 양면으로 뚫은 구멍이 있으며 그 옆 가장자리에는 손상된 구멍이 있다. 전체적으로 연마하였으며 민무늬이다.

087

옥악(玉鸎)

청백옥(青白玉) | 상(商)
길이 5.3cm 너비 2.5cm 두께 1cm
1981년 서안시 파교구 모서공사(西安市 灞橋區 毛西公社) 출토

Jade Fish Hawk

Green and white jade | Shang Dynasty
L 5.3cm W 2.5cm T 1cm
Excavated from Maoxi Village in Baqiao District, Xi'an in 1981

원조(圓彫)한 악(鸎)은 서 있는 모습으로 눈이 동그랗고 부리가 굽었으며 볏은 높고 말렸으며 양 날개에는 운문(雲紋)을 그려 깃털을 나타내었는데 이는 물수리의 특징을 반영한 것이다. 부리 가운데는 구멍이 있는데 한쪽이 크고 다른 한쪽이 작은 것이 양면으로 뚫은 것이며 끈을 꿰어 착용할 수 있다. 머리 부분은 양면을 대응되게 조각하였고 목 아래는 단면(單面)만 조각하였다. 깃털과 다리 윤곽은 쌍선(雙線)과 단선(單線)을 결합해 음각(陰刻)하였는데 선이 대범하고 굽은 곳에는 칼자국이 많으며 가장자리는 모두 경사지게 깎아내었고 전체적으로 정세(精細)하게 연마하였다. 청록색 가운데 옅은 노란색이 서려 있으며 흙이 침투된 흔적이 있다. 이 옥악의 출토지점은 노우파(老牛坡) 상대(商代) 유적지와 파수(灞水)의 사이에 위치해 있는데 출토지점과 특징으로 보아 상대 유물로 추정된다.

악은 '어응(魚鷹)'이라고도 부르는데 훈련시켜 어획활동에 사용할 수 있다. 상ㆍ주대(商ㆍ周代)에는 생산, 생활과 연관 있는 많은 동물 형상, 이를테면 옥어(玉魚), 옥잠(玉蠶) 등이 장식품으로 조각되었다. 악은 어획활동에 사용되는 도구로써 옥악의 출현은 어획이 당시 이미 중요한 생산활동이었음을 말해준다.

옥연(玉燕)

청백옥(青白玉) ┃ 서주(西周)
길이 3.8cm 너비 2.2cm 두께 0.4cm
1975년 서안시 장안현(西安市 長安縣) 장가파(張家坡) 출토

Jade Swallow

Green and white jade ┃ West Zhou Dynasty
L 3.8cm W 2.2cm T 0.4cm
Excavated from Zhangjiapo in Chang'an County, Xi'an in 1975

제비는 납작한 모양으로 날개를 펴고 나는 모습이다. 부리는 뾰족하고 눈은 둥글며 양 날개는 펼쳤고 짧은 꼬리는 둘로 나뉘었다. 두 눈, 날개와 꼬리의 깃털은 편사도법(偏斜刀法)으로 새겼고 조형은 간단한데 과장되고 도안화된 기법으로 세부를 묘사하였다. 눈은 큰 동그라미 두 개로, 양 날개는 와문(渦紋)으로 새겨 형상이 고졸하지만 생동감이 넘쳐난다.

제비는 철새로 제비가 돌아온다는 것은 만물이 소생하는 봄이 다가왔음을 말해준다. 고대 사회에서 제비는 기후변화의 상징이자 만물이 엄동설한을 지나 소생하는 구세주로서 사람들은 제비를 새로운 생명을 싹틔우는 원천으로, 생명의 지속을 주재하는 징조로 여겼다.

옥곤충(玉昆蟲)

청백옥(青白玉) ┃ 서주(西周)
길이 3cm 너비 1.5cm 두께 0.3cm
1978년 서안시 호현(西安市 戶縣) 출토

Jade Insect

Green and white jade ┃ West Zhou Dynasty
L 3cm W 1.5cm T 0.3cm
Excavated from Huxian County, Xi'an in 1978

납작한 편(片) 모양 청옥으로 양면에 조각하였다. 곤충은 작고 가벼우며 머리가 좁고 꼬리가 넓다. 머리는 '山(산)'자 모양이고 입은 길고 뾰족하며 양옆 둥근 눈은 볼록하게 튀어나왔다. 목에는 음각(陰刻)한 쌍선(雙線)으로 이루어진 관현문(寬弦紋)이 있고 등에는 가운데로 모은 양 날개가 있다. 꼬리는 좁아지면서 오목한 것이 길고도 넓으며 끝부분은 둘로 나뉘었다. 입부분에는 구멍이 가로로 나 있어 끈을 꿰어 매달 수 있다. 이 옥곤충은 납작한 옥으로 조각하여 조형이 간단하고 선이 대범하다. 표면은 연마상태가 그다지 정세(精細)하지 않고 형체가 자그마하며 표현기법이 질박하다.

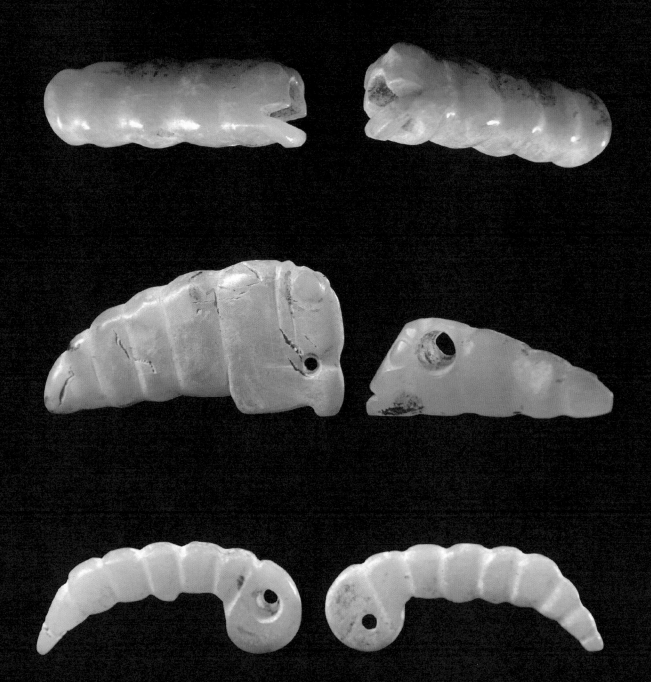

090

옥잠(玉蠶)

청백옥(青白玉) | 서주(西周)
방관형(方管形): 길이 3cm 너비 0.9cm 높이 1cm
편체삼각형(扁體三角形): 길이 2.4~3.2cm 너비 0.8~1.5cm 두께 0.5cm
편체호형(扁體弧形): 길이 2.6cm 너비 0.8cm 두께 0.3cm
1981년 서안시 호현(西安市 戶縣) 출토

Jade Silkworm

Green and white jade | West Zhou Dynasty
Quadrate tube shape: L 3cm W 0.9cm H 1cm
Flat triangular shape: L 2.4~3.2cm W 0.8~1.5cm T 0.5cm
Flat arc shape: L 2.6cm W 0.8cm T 0.3cm
Excavated from Huxian County, Xi'an in 1981

누에는 네모 관형(管形), 납작한 삼각형, 납작한 호형(弧形) 세 가지로 몸통은 모두 참대 마디 모양이다. 네모 관형 누에는 이마가 들어가고 턱이 돌출되었으며 압지은기법(壓地隱起法)으로 둥그런 두 눈을 도드라지게 하였다. 입구가 넓고 안쪽이 좁은 오목한 홈으로 살짝 벌어진 입을 표현하였는데 입속에는 아래를 향한 구멍이 있다. 그 외 머리부터 꼬리까지 양쪽으로 뚫은 구멍이 있어 실을 꿰어 매달 수 있다. 납작한 삼각형 누에는 머리가 비탈 모양으로 경사지고 평평하다. 눈은 음각선으로 그렸고 머리 부분에 양쪽에서 뚫은 구멍이 있다. 납작한 호형 누에는 머리 부분이 동글납작한데 나팔 모양 구멍이 가로로 나 있으며 몸은 굵고 꼬리는 뾰족하다.

옥잠은 상·주대(商·周代) 유적지와 무덤에서 많이 발견되었고 이 시기 일부 청동기(青銅器)에도 잠문(蠶紋)이 있는데 이는 당시 양잠업이 상당히 발전했음을 말해준다.

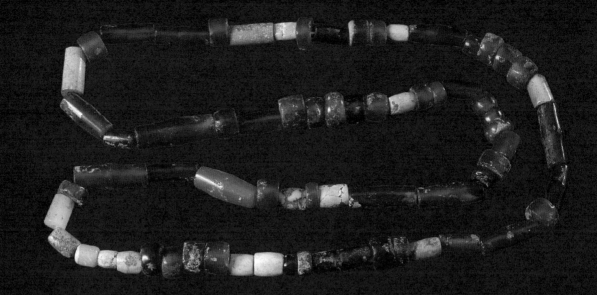

091

옥수(玉髓), 송석관주(松石串珠)

옥수, 송석 | 서주(西周)
옥수최대지름 2.8cm 송석최대지름 1.5cm
1978년 서안시 호현(西安市 戶縣) 출토

Jade Bead String

Chalcedony, Turquoise | West Zhou Dynasty
Chalcedony max D 2.8cm Turquoise max D 1.5cm
Excavated from Huxian County, Xi'an in 1978

모두 429개로 구성되었다. 옥수관식(玉髓串飾)은 둥근 환형(環形)과 둥근 관형(管形)으로 나뉘는데 모두 주황색이며 반투명하다. 환형은 가장자리가 약간 호형(弧形)이고 관형은 가운데가 볼록하며 가운데 있는 구멍은 크기가 서로 다르다. 송석관식은 모두 관(管) 모양이며 표면이 볼록하게 융기되고 색상은 청록색에 가까우며 일부는 형태가 가지런하지 못하다.

092

수면문진식착형옥식(獸面紋秦式鑿形玉飾)

백옥(白玉) | 전국(戰國)
길이 9.7cm 너비 2cm 두께 0.4cm
1976년 서안시 안탑구(西安市 雁塔區) 사파(沙坡) 한묘(漢墓) 출토

Chisel-shaped Jade Pendant with Beast Face Patterns

White jade | Warring States Period
L 9.7cm W 2cm T 0.4cm
Excavated from Han Tomb at Shapo in Yanta District, Xi'an in 1976

　납작한 기룡(夔龍) 모양으로 머리가 크고 꼬리가 뾰족하며 단면(單面) 조각하였다. 기룡은 엎드려 기는 모양으로 앞으로 뺄은 입, 커다란 눈, 기다란 눈썹을 가지고 있으며 이마에는 능형(菱形) 망문(網紋)이 있다. 머리와 몸 사이에는 좁은 홈이 있는데 홈의 양쪽 끝은 누공(鏤空)하여 매달 수 있게 하였다. 몸통은 아래위로 반대방향의 대칭되는 동그란 와문(渦紋)과 누공된 직각선에 의해 S자형을 이루고 양쪽에 돌출된 비아(扉牙)는 사지를 나타낸다. 꼬리 부분은 얇은 편(片)으로 가운데가 살짝 융기되었으며 양측과 끝부분은 경사지게 깎아내어 날을 이루었다. 몸통과 꼬리 부분에는 여러 조의 진식(秦式) 용문(龍紋)이 음각되어 있는데 분포가 적절하여 가득 차게 보이면서도 난잡하지 않으며 선이 강건하면서도 유창하다. 기룡은 형태가 생동하고도 과장되었으며 전체적으로 연마가 잘 되어 표면이 반질반질하고 윤이 난다. 이 휴(觿)는 한대(漢代) 무덤에서 출토되었으나 기하형 기룡 및 운뢰문(雲雷紋) 등 특징으로 보아 전국(戰國)시대 진(秦)나라 유물로 추정된다.

용문진식공자형관함환옥식
(龍紋秦式工字形管銜環玉飾)

투섬석옥(透閃石玉) | 전국(戰國)
길이 5.2cm 너비 3.1cm 두께 1.2cm
1982년 서안시 장안현(西安市 長安縣) 위곡(韋曲) 전국묘(戰國墓) 출토

I-shaped Tubular Jade Pendant with Dragon Pattern in Qin Style

Tremolite | Warring States Period
L 5.2cm W 3.1cm T 1.2cm
Excavated from Warring States Tomb in the South of Weiqu in Chang'an County, Xi'an in 1982

관(管) 두 개가 병렬되었는데 중심부가 이어졌고 한쪽 관 측면에는 방형(方形) 다리 모양 꼭지가 두드러져 나왔으며 꼭지에는 작은 고리가 달려 있다. 둘 다 속이 비었는데 마주하여 뚫은 것이라 입구가 크고 가지런하지 못하며 가운데가 작다. 두 관 및 연결부분에는 여러 조의 진식(秦式) 용문(龍紋)을 새겼는데 배치가 적절하여 복잡하지만 정연하다.

옥패(玉佩) 위 문양은 수직도(垂直刀)와 편사도(偏斜刀)를 결합하는 기법을 사용하여 양각선(陽刻線)으로 된 구운문(鉤雲紋)을 새겼다. 이 옥식(玉飾)은 먼저 필요한 형태와 개수에 따라 재료를 서로 다른 방향에서 끊이지 않고 연결된 여러 조각으로 톱질한 후 이어진 부분에 고리를 연결하였다. 만약 더 많은 옥식을 연결하려면 고리가 없이 이어진 부분을 끊어버림으로써 이 기물과 마찬가지로 조각마다 고리로 연결하여 펼칠 수도, 접칠 수도 있게 한다. 마지막으로 각 마디와 고리에 무늬를 새기거나 누공(鏤空)한다. 제작과정은 자르기, 구멍 뚫기, 누조(鏤彫), 무늬 새기기 등으로 나눌 수 있다. 이런 연환(連環) 옥식은 전에는 볼 수 없던 형태로 춘추전국(春秋戰國)시대 중국의 옥공예가 전에 없이 발전하였음을 말해주며 중국 옥기발전사에서 중요한 의의가 있다. 섬서(陝西)역사박물관에 구리 재질의 같은 유형 기물이 소장되어 있다. 이 옥식의 고리 안쪽 가장자리 일부는 끈에 의해 마모되었는데 이로 보아 패식으로 추정된다.

마노환(瑪瑙環)

마노 | 전국(戰國)
지름 7.5cm 두께 1cm
1983년 서안시 파교구 파교공사(西安市 灞橋區 灞橋公社) 한묘(漢墓) 출토

Agate Ring

Agate | Warring States Period
D 7.5cm T 1cm
Excavated from Han Tomb at Baqiao Community in Baqiao District, Xi'an in 1983

원형(圓形)이며 단면(斷面)은 불규칙한 다변형으로 바깥쪽은 예각이등변삼각형을, 아래위와 안쪽은 오각형을 이룬다. 형태가 가지런하고 연마가 정세(精細)하며 광택이 난다. 한묘(漢墓)에서 출토되었으나 형태가 똑같은 마노환이 춘추(春秋) 말기 무덤에서 발견된 바 있고 전국(戰國) 초기 초묘(楚墓)에서 똑같은 모양의 옥환(玉環)이 출토된 바 있으므로 춘추전국시대 유물로 추정된다. 이 환은 마노로 조각되었는데 엷은 유백색에 붉은색이 살짝 서려 있고 유리성질이 강하며 투명하고 윤이 난다.

환은 벽옥(璧玉)류 패옥으로 구멍[호(好)] 지름과 옥[육(肉)] 지름은 거의 비슷하고 벽 구멍보다 큰 편인데 옷, 물건을 매거나 또는 조패(組佩)에도 사용된다. 춘추전국시대 무덤에서 출토된 것이 많으며 보편적으로 납작한 환형(環形)이다. 단면(單面) 또는 양면으로 조각하며 단면(斷面)은 6각형, 8각형, 타원형, 능형(菱形), 원형을 이룬다. 한대(漢代)에는 반룡환(蟠龍環)이 유행하였고 당대(唐代)에는 조형이 참신하고 조각이 정교한 각종 환이 유행하였는데 누조(鏤彫) 문양이 새롭게 나타났으며 송·원대(宋·元代) 옥환은 이를 기반으로 발전하였다.

095

마노패(瑪瑙佩)

마노 | 한(漢)
길이 5.6cm~7.5cm 너비 3.3cm~4.4cm 두께 0.4cm~0.5cm
서안시(西安市) 수집

Agate Pendant

Agate | Han Dynasty
L 5.6cm~7.5cm W 3.3cm~4.4cm T 0.4cm~0.5cm
Collected in Xi'an

　3점 모두 불규칙한 편(片) 모양 오각형이며 가운데는 막대기 모양 도구를 이용하여 뚫은 구멍이 가로로 나 있어 패용할 수 있다. 전부 매끄럽고 민무늬이며 광택처리가 섬세하게 되었고 색감이 뛰어나다. 장신구는 암홍색과 짙은 갈색을 바탕으로 하여 흰색, 황색이 섞여 있으며 색 덩어리 가운데는 흰색, 황색 가는 선이 조밀하고 규칙적으로 배열되어 있다. 색상이 아름답고 무늬와 결이 자연스러우며 층차(層次)가 분명하여 고급스럽고 화려해 보인다.

　이와 같은 자연적인 결의 무늬는 인위적으로 조각한 것보다 훨씬 아름답다. 전하는 바에 의하면 이런 마노는 중원(中原)이 아닌 서역(西域)에서 나는 것으로 상인과 사절들에 의해 '비단길'을 거쳐 중원으로 들어왔다. 삼국(三國) 시대 위문제(魏文帝)는 "마노는 서역에서 나는데 무늬가 아롱지다"고 말한 바 있다.

096

옥해치(玉獬豸)

백옥(白玉) | 한(漢)
높이 3.5cm 너비 2.3cm 두께 1.1cm
서안시 안탑구(西安市 雁塔區) 사파(沙坡) 서한묘(西漢墓) 출토

Jade Xie-Zhi(a legendary beast)

White jade | Han Dynasty
H 3.5cm W 2.3cm T 1.1cm
Excavated from West Han Tomb in Shapo in Yanta District, Xi'an

　백옥을 원조(圓彫)한 것으로 일부는 진한 갈색을 띠었다. 해치는 방형(方形) 받침 위에서 기는 모습인데 머리는 좌측을 향하였다. 커다란 눈, 높은 코, 큰 입, 뒤로 젖힌 두 귀를 가지고 머리에는 외뿔이 나 있으며 짧은 꼬리는 엉덩이에 붙었다.

　해치는 고대 신화 중의 신수(神獸)이다. 『후한서(後漢書)』권40에 "해치는 신령스러운 양(羊)으로 시비곡절을 분별할 수 있다. 초왕(楚王)이 얻은 후 관(冠)장식으로 하였다."라고 하였고, 주석에서는 『이물지(異物志)』를 인용하여 "동북쪽 황무지에는 해치라는 짐승이 있는데 외뿔에 성격이 곧다. 싸움을 보면 바르지 않은 사람을 찌르니 이를 들은 사람은 논하기를 나쁜 사람만 문다고 하였다"고 적고 있다. 고로 '해치가 판결한다'라는 설이 있어 해치의 형상은 역대 법관의 별칭으로 사용되었다.

　이 옥해치는 비록 작지만 조각에 있어서 시대적 풍격이 뚜렷하다. 대체적인 윤곽을 조각한 다음 가는 선으로 눈, 코, 입 및 세부를 음각(陰刻)하였는데 정적인 모습이다. 머리를 측면으로 돌리고 '臣(신)'자 모양 눈을 커다랗게 뜬 모습은 마치 주위의 움직임을 경계하고 수시로 공격할 준비를 하는 듯하다. 정적인 가운데 동적인 면이 있어 고요함 속의 '풍파' 또는 '위험'을 느끼게 하며 신수의 길들이지 않은 야성적인 기세를 드러낸다. 구상이 활발하고 형식에 얽매이지 않았으며 동감(動感)에 치중하여 표현하였다. 각종 조각기법을 결합하여 사용함으로써 형태가 생동감 있고 사실적이며 조형이 참신하고 조각기법이 절묘한 경지에 이르러 찬탄을 금치 못하게 한다. 해치의 목 가운데 있는 작은 구멍 입구 양쪽에 마흔(磨痕)이 있는 것으로 보아 장신구임을 알 수 있다.

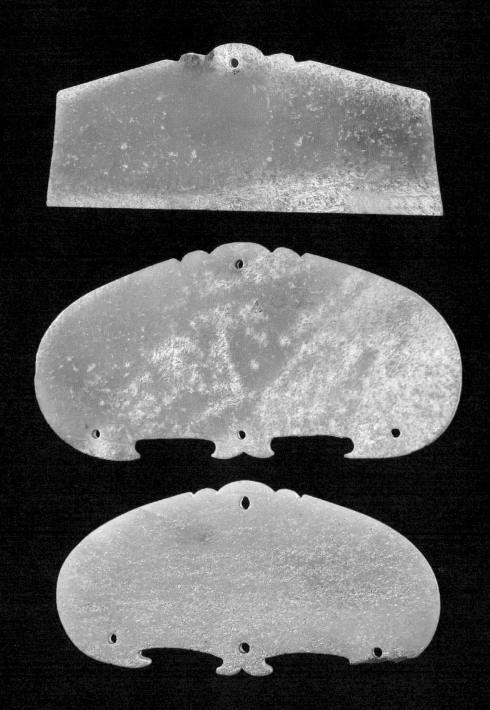

097

편복형형(蝙蝠形珩)

청백옥(青白玉) | 북주(北周)
길이 12.8cm~13.3cm 너비 5.5cm~6.2cm 두께 0.5cm~0.6cm
1981년 서안시 안탑구(西安市 雁塔區) 소채(小寨) 북주묘(北周墓) 출토

**Jade Heng(top jade in group pendants)
In the shape of a Bat**

Green and white jade | North Zhou Dynasty
L 12.8cm~13.3cm W 5.5cm~6.2cm T 0.5cm~0.6cm
Excavated from North Zhou Tomb in Xiaozhai, Yanta District, Xi'an in 1981

3점 모두 납작하며 그중 2점은 박쥐 모양이고 나머지 1점은 간소화된 박쥐 모양 형(珩)이다. 박쥐 모양은 머리가 3연호(連弧) 모양이고 날개는 뾰족하고 안쪽으로 굽었으며 꼬리는 '人(인)'자 모양이다. 머리, 꼬리, 양쪽 날개에 각각 구멍이 나 있다. 박쥐 모양 형은 머리 부분은 앞에 2점과 같고 일부분이 비탈 모양이며 몸통, 날개, 꼬리는 계단 모양으로 간소화되었다. 3점 모두 민무늬이며 희고 매끄러우나 연마는 일반 수준이다.

남북조(南北朝)시대, 옥기 발전은 저조기에 들어섰으며 예옥(禮玉)과 장옥(葬玉)은 기본적으로 역사무대에서 사라졌고 장식예술품이 점차 주도적 위치를 차지하게 되었다. 따라서 옥기 또한 애초의 정치화, 계급화에서 세속화에로 나아갔다.

098

금양옥패(金鑲玉佩)

백옥(白玉) ｜ 당(唐)
높이 4.2cm 최대너비 5cm 두께 0.4cm
1976년 서안시 미앙구 손가만(西安市 未央區 孫家灣) 당 대명궁(大明宮) 유적지 출토

Jade Pendants Bordered with Gold

White jade ｜ Tang Dynasty
H 4.2cm Max W 5cm T 0.4cm
Excavated from Tang Daminggong Relic in SunjiaWan in Weiyang District, Xi'an in 1976

삼각형으로 윗부분이 뾰족하고 아래쪽이 평평하며 양 변은 3연호(三連弧) 모양이고 단면(單面) 조각하였다. 앞면은 금을 상감한 변형된 쌍봉문(雙鳳紋)으로 장식하였는데 새의 몸통은 둥그런 곡선으로 표현하였다. 새는 머리와 목을 곧게 폈으며 뾰족한 부리, 기다란 볏에 날개, 꼬리, 발은 '人(인)'자형을 이룬다. 주요 부위에는 모두 권운문(卷雲紋)을 새기고 무늬 부분에는 모두 금을 상감하였다. 끝부분에 실을 꿰어 매달 수 있는 꿀벌 허리 모양 구멍이 나 있다.

옥 금은입사(金銀入絲)공예는 춘추(春秋)시대에 나타나 전국(戰國)에서 당대(唐代)까지 가장 유행하였다. 이 옥패로 볼 때, 무늬 부분은 음각선의 밑부분과 측면에 금박을 붙였는데 긴밀도가 높고 금박 표면도 평평하다. 투명하고 온윤(溫潤)한 흰색의 옥 장신구에 금입사한 무늬는 더욱 기품 있고 화려해 보인다.

이 옥패의 조형은 짙은 서역(西域) 풍격을 띠었는데 금입사와 운문(雲紋)은 전통적인 공예이자 문양으로 전통공예 및 문화예술을 기반으로 하고 외래문화를 받아들여 발전한 것이다. 따라서 한대(漢代)의 예술풍격에서 완전히 벗어나 한층 성숙된 새로운 예술풍격으로 거듭났으며 호매(豪邁)하고 낭만적이며 화려한 시대적 특징을 띠어 당대 금은입사공예가 이미 높은 수준에 이르렀음을 말해준다.

①

②

099

옥화잠두(玉花簪頭)

백옥(白玉) ㅣ 당(唐)
①②③ 길이 10~11,5cm 너비 2,8~4cm 두께 0,2cm
1981년 서안(西安)교통대학원 내 흥경궁(興慶宮) 유적지 출토

Jade Hairpin with Flower Pattern

White jade ㅣ Tang Dynasty
①②③ L 10~11,5cm W 2,8~4cm T 0,2cm
Excavated from Xingqing Palace Relic in Xi'an Jiaotong University in 1981

① 옥봉문잠두(玉鳳紋簪頭) 1점: 납작한 잎 모양으로 앞부분 꽃잎에 봉조(鳳鳥) 한 마리를 조각하였다. 봉조는 나는 모습으로 양 날개를 펼치고 꼬리가 위로 쳐들렸다. 봉조 아래쪽 꽃잎은 구름과 같아 봉조의 나는 모습과 하나로 어우러진다. 봉조문은 조문(鳥紋)에서 발전한 것으로 자연계 각종 아름다운 조류 형상의 결정체라고 할 수 있는데 봉조가 날아옐 때는 온갖 새가 뒤따르므로 새 중의 왕이라 불리기도 한다.

② 옥원앙잠두(玉鴛鴦簪頭) 1점: 납작한 잎 모양으로 꽃 네 송이가 흐드러지게 피어 있는데 그중 가장 큰 꽃송이 위에 물에서 노니는 원앙 한 쌍을 새겼다. 원앙은 자고로 사랑의 새로 불리며 암수가 항상 붙어 있어 부부간의 금슬이 좋음을 나타낸다.

③

③ 옥석류화잠두(玉石榴花簪頭) 4점: 납작한 잎 모양으로 꽃잎 앞
부분에 석류 하나가 있고 아래쪽에는 활짝 핀 석류꽃 몇 송이가 있다.
조밀한 격자무늬는 석류 씨를 나타낸다.
　　납작한 잎 모양의 옥화잠두 6점이다. 모두 간단한 호선(孤線)으로
윤곽을 그리고 규칙적인 음각선으로 세부를 새겼는데 선의 밀도가
적당하여 층차감(層次感)이 있다. 잠두의 한쪽 끝은 뒤집힌 사다리꼴
돌기가 있는데 은 재질의 몸통 끝부분과 못으로 잇는 데 사용된다.

100

"희보춘선"패(喜報春先佩)

백옥(白玉) | 송(宋)
길이 4.2cm 너비 3.8cm 두께 0.8cm
1980년 서안시 안탑구(西安市 雁塔區) 출토

Jade Pendant with "the Forecast of Coming of the Spring"

White jade | Song Dynasty
L 4.2cm W 3.8cm T 0.8cm
Excavated from Yanta District, Xi'an in 1980

납작한 옥패(玉佩)로 단면(單面) 누공(鏤空)하였다. 까치 한 마리가 날개를 펼쳐 날고 있는데 긴 꼬리는 위로 휘날린다. 입에는 매화가지를 물었는데 마침 꽃이 머리 위에서 활짝 피었다. 윤곽을 누공한 기초 위에서 오목하게 새기는 기법과 음각선으로 새의 몸통, 꽃가지, 깃털, 잎맥을 뚜렷하게 조각하였다. 꽃잎, 잎, 가지는 안에서 밖으로 비스듬히 뻗고 꽃잎과 잎 가운데는 오목하고 깊게 조각하여 층차가 분명하고 입체감이 있다.

이 옥패의 조형은 송대(宋代)에 나타난 길상(吉祥)도안으로 '희보춘선(喜報春先)'이라 부른다. '희(喜)'자는 까치의 중국 이름 첫 글자이고 매화는 추위를 이겨내고 피어나는 꽃으로 희보춘선은 봄소식을 남 먼저 알린다는 뜻인 동시에 새로운 희망을 나타내기도 한다.

101

누조구녹학문패(鏤彫龜鹿鶴紋牌)

백옥(白玉) | 송(宋)
높이 6.2cm 너비 5.4cm 두께 0.7cm
1982년 서안시 비림구(西安市 碑林區) 서안(西安)교통대학 동쪽 출토

Jade Board with Hollow-carved Tortoise, Deer and Crane Patterns

White jade | Song Dynasty
H 6.2cm W 5.4cm T 0.7cm
Excavated at the east of Xi'an Jiaotong University in Beilin District, Xi'an in 1982

옥패는 세워 놓은 알 모양으로 밑부분은 평평하며 누공(鏤空)하였다. 바위 사이로 소나무, 대나무, 영지가 있으며 거북 한 마리가 그 사이를 기어가고 있는데 거북이 토해낸 입김은 뭉게뭉게 상운(祥雲)이 되었다. 그리고 사슴 한 마리가 하늘 위의 학을 뒤돌아 올려다보고 있다. 거북은 사령(四靈) 중 하나로 길흉을 점치고 장수하여 신수(神獸)로 여겨지며 승천(昇天) 시 탈것이기도 하다. 사슴과 학은 장수를 뜻하고 사시장철 푸른 소나무와 대나무는 곧은 절개를 나타낸다. 영지 또한 고목에서 피어나므로 고목에 꽃이 핌을 뜻한다. 이 문양은 많은 길상(吉祥)의 뜻을 포함하고 있는데 사슴과 학은 '녹학동춘(鹿鶴同春)', 거북과 학은 '귀학연년(龜鶴延年)', 사슴과 영지는 '복록의(福祿意)'로 평안, 장수, 풍족함 등을 나타낸다.

옥패 뒷면은 연마하였으며 도안의 밑부분에는 끈을 끼워 매달 수 있는 구멍 두 개가 있다.

102

옥마(玉馬)

백옥(白玉) | 송(宋)
길이 2.7cm 너비 1.1cm 높이 2cm
1979년 서안시(西安市) 수집

Jade Horse

White jade | Song Dynasty
L 2.7cm W 1.1cm H 2cm
Collected in Xi'an in 1979

말은 다리를 구부리고 엎드려 있으며 고개를 살짝 숙였다. 머리가 큰 편이고 두 눈은 대칭되는 호선(弧線)을 편도(偏刀)로 새겨 표현하였는데 앞뒤 눈꼬리가 이어 지지 않았다. 콧방울, 입술은 몇 획만으로 표현하고 두 귀는 곧추세웠으며 음각(陰刻)된 목 갈기는 좌우로 나뉘었다. 말은 표정이 돈후하고 온순하며 자그마한 것이 사랑스럽다. 몸통 가운데는 위를 향한 구멍이 있어 끈을 끼워 매달 수 있다.

103

이룡천화패(螭龍穿花牌)

백옥(白玉) | 원(元)
긴지름 7.6cm 짧은지름 6.1cm 두께 1.3cm
1983년 서안시 안탑구 전가만촌(西安市 雁塔區 田家灣村) 출토

Jade Board with Chi Dragon and Flower Patterns

White jade | Yuan Dynasty
Long D 7.6cm Short D 6.1cm T 1.3cm
Excavated from Tianjiawan Village in Yanta District, Xi'an in 1983

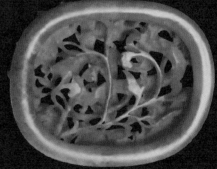

둥글넓적한 환(環) 위에 관지화엽(串枝花葉)과 그 속에서 노니는 이룡(螭龍)을 누조(鏤彫)하였다. 얽히고설킨 꽃가지는 안에서 밖으로 비스듬히 뻗고 꽃잎은 말렸으며 잎맥이 뚜렷하다. 이룡은 머리가 둥근 편이고 동그란 눈, 굵은 눈썹, 비스듬히 세운 두 귀를 가지고 있는데 목 갈기가 흩날리고 가는 목이 오목하게 들어갔다. 앞다리는 엎드리고 뒷다리는 앞뒤로 놓였으며 몸통은 옆으로 굽혀 'U'자형을 이루고 긴 꼬리는 말려 몸을 돌려 엎드린 모양새이다. 척추는 음각(陰刻) 쌍선(雙線)으로 새기고 가로로 음각선 몇 줄을 더해 대나무 마디 모양을 이루었다. 어깨 관절은 권운문(卷雲紋)으로 장식하고 사지와 허리는 꽃가지에 가려졌다.

옥패(玉佩)는 누조기법으로 조각하였는데 먼저 표면의 꽃과 잎을 조각한 후 사이사이를 오목하게 하고 얽히고설킨 줄기와 가지 그리고 이룡을 누조하였다. 사이는 먼저 막대기 모양 도구를 사용하여 구멍을 뚫은 후 다시 실톱으로 잘라내었다. 뒷면 가운데는 누공(鏤空)하였고 환의 가장자리는 모두 둥글게 연마하였다. 이룡의 허리와 환 사이에는 납작하고 기다란 구멍이 나 있어 끈을 끼워 매달 수 있다. 이런 고부조(高浮彫) · 누조기법은 원대(元代) 옥공예에서 흔히 볼 수 있는 입체조각기법이며 잎 모양과 이룡의 특징 역시 원대 특징을 띠었다.

하엽어추(荷葉魚墜)

골(骨) | 금(金)
길이 3.7cm 너비 2.7cm 두께 1.6cm
1981년 서안시 미앙구 범가채(西安市 未央區 範家寨) 출토

Jade Pendant with Lotus Leaf and Fish Patterns

Bone | Jin Dynasty
L 3.7cm W 2.7cm T 1.6cm
Excavated from Fanjiazhai Village in Weiyang District, Xi'an in 1981

추는 납작한 네모 모양으로 물고기 한 마리가 연잎 위에서 입에 수초를 물고 있다. 연잎은 아치형으로 양옆은 안쪽으로 말리고 앞뒤 잎맥은 가는 선으로 조각하였다. 물고기 입에 물린 풀잎 두 잎이 연잎 아래위로 떠 있다. 물고기 몸통은 곧은 편이고 입 부분에는 내민 입술을 음각선으로 그렸다. 동그란 눈은 대롱 모양 도구로 뚫어 만든 것이다. 아가미는 구철법(鉤徹法)으로 새겼고 비늘은 세밀한 격자무늬로 표현하였다. 등지느러미 가장자리에는 거치(鋸齒)를 새기고 배지느러미는 배와 평행되게 꼬리까지 새겼으며 둘로 나뉜 꼬리는 한쪽으로 흔들었다. 전체적인 형상은 물고기가 헤엄쳐 수초로 향하는 순간을 표현한 것으로 물고기 몸통이 굵지 않았으나 힘이 느껴진다. 물고기 조형은 둥글고 통통한데 선이 부드러운 가운데 힘이 있어 물고기가 먹이를 덮칠 때의 동적인 미를 잘 보여준다. 물고기 각 부위의 선이 뚜렷하고 분명하며 배열이 정연하여 사실감을 더해주었다. 추의 윗부분에는 나팔모양의 막대기 모양 도구로 뚫은 구멍이 있는데 실을 꿰어 매달 수 있다.

연잎과 물고기는 전통적인 길상(吉祥)문양으로 상서로움을 뜻한다. 중문(中文)에서 '魚(어)'와 '餘(여)'는 같은 발음으로 여분의 재물을 뜻하고 연잎은 연꽃이 만발함을 뜻하며 '蓮(연)'과 '連(연)'도 같은 발음이다. 물고기와 연잎을 제재로 한 옥추패(玉墜佩)를 몸에 착용하면 '연년유여(連年有餘, 해마다 여유가 있다)'의 뜻으로 기복(祈福)을 의미한다.

목우추(牧牛墜)

청백옥(靑白玉) | 원(元)
길이 4cm 너비 3.5cm 높이 2cm
1968년 서안시 안탑구 하가촌(西安市 雁塔區 何家村) 출토

Jade Pendants in the shape of an Ox

Green and white jade | Yuan Dynasty
L 4cm W 3.5cm H 2cm
Excavated from Hejia Village in Yanta District, Xi'an in 1968

소 세 마리가 다리를 굽히고 나란히 엎드려 있는데 가운데 소는 양옆 소와 반대방향이다. 한쪽 옆의 소는 머리를 숙인 채 휴식하고 있고 가운데 소는 머리를 들어 멀리 바라보며 다른 한쪽에는 송아지가 늙은 소 몸에 기대어 있다. 목동은 왼쪽 다리를 올리고 가운데 있는 늙은 소의 등 뒤쪽에 기대어 양손으로 피리를 불고 있다. 전체적으로 간단하게 조각하였는데 소의 눈, 코, 입은 작은 구멍만으로 나타냈으며 도법(刀法)은 대범하고 힘 있다. 가운데 소의 허리 부분 양측에는 각각 구멍이 있어 끈을 꿰어 매달 수 있다.

이 작품의 제재는 '동자가 방목하다'에서 따온 것이다. 당시 농촌에서 소를 방목하던 정경을 반영한 이런 제재는 원대(元代) 이후 유행하였는데 회화, 죽목아각(竹木牙刻), 동기(銅器), 옥공예에서 모두 사용되었으며 시사(詩詞)와 희극(戱劇)에서도 나타났다. 이 작품은 일상생활 속 소를 생동감 있게 표현함으로써 특별한 의경(意境)을 만들어내었다. 늙은 소 두 마리가 등을 맞대고 조용히 엎드려 있고 옆에는 송아지가 어미 소 곁에 기대어 있다. 소 등 뒤에 기대어 피리를 부는 목동의 표정을 보면 마치 '목동의 노래'가 들리는 듯하다.

원앙학하추(鴛鴦鶴荷墜)

백옥(白玉) | 명(明)
길이 4.6cm 너비 4.2cm 두께 1.5cm
1978년 서안시(西安市) 수집

White Jade Pendant with Mandarin Ducks, Crane and Lotus Patterns

White jade | Ming Dynasty
L 4.6cm W 4.2cm T 1.5cm
Collected in Xi'an in 1978

추(墜)는 원조(圓彫)하였는데 앞면은 살짝 볼록하고 뒷면은 평평한 편이다. 앞면에는 연꽃과 연잎이 가득한데 그 위에서 원앙 한 쌍이 입에 연밥을 문 채 노닐고 있다. 뒷면에는 학 한 마리가 연잎 위에 서서 뒤돌아보는데 목이 굽고 입에는 연꽃 줄기를 물었으며 학 옆에는 연밥이 있다. 학과 원앙은 형태가 자연스럽고 생동감이 있으며 깃털은 권운문(卷雲紋), 호선(弧線), 평행(平行) 음각선으로 구성되었다. 연꽃 꽃잎과 연잎은 두껍고 활짝 펼쳐졌으며 잎맥은 뚜렷하다.

옥추(玉墜)의 문양은 두 가지 내용을 포함한다. 원앙과 연꽃으로 구성된 도안은 '원앙희하(鴛鴦戲荷)'이다. 고대에는 "원앙을 부러워하지 신선을 부러워하지 않는다"라는 속담이 있었는데 이는 부부간 금슬이 좋은 것이 신선이 되는 것보다 낫다는 뜻이다. 학과 연꽃은 '학명구고(鶴鳴九皐)'를 이르며 장수와 상서로움을 뜻한다. 옛사람들은 학을 하늘의 서조(瑞鳥)로 여겼다. 그리하여 『시경(詩經)』「소아(小雅)」에서는 "깊은 늪 가운데서 울어대는 학 소리 하늘까지 울려 퍼지네"라고 읊고, 『회남자(淮南子)』「설임훈(說林訓)」에서는 "학은 천년을 살면서 천하를 노닌다"라고 적고 있다. 당대(唐代) 왕건(王建)은 시에서 "복숭아꽃 백 송이로 봄이 되지 않고, 학은 천년을 장수해도 신선이 되지 못하네"라고 읊고, 『구탄(九嘆)』「원유(遠游)」에서는 "학이 무리 지어 요광(瑤光, 고대 중국 사람들이 북두칠성 가운데 마지막 별을 이르는 말)으로 날아가네"라고 읊고 있다.

107

마노조형추(瑪瑙棗形墜)

옥수(玉髓) | 청(淸)
길이 5.2cm 너비 3.2cm 두께 2.2cm
1978년 서안시(西安市) 수집

Agate Pendant in the shape of Jujube

Chalcedony | Qing Dynasty
L 5.2cm W 3.2cm T 2.2cm
Collected in Xi'an in 1978

붉은색 마노로 대추 세 알을 조각하였는데 두 알은 위에 있고 나머지 한 알은 아래에 놓았다. 대추에는 가는 선을 가로로 여러 줄 그어 무르익었음을 나타내었다. 또한 마노의 색상과 특성을 교묘하게 이용하여 대추씨 다섯 개를 조각하였는데 대추씨에는 불규칙한 작은 홈을 점각(點刻)하였다. 전체적으로 간단하면서도 생동감 있게 조각하였다.

108

"희상미초"잠(喜上眉梢簪)

백옥(白玉) | 명(明)
전체길이 23cm 높이 2.7cm 두께 0.3cm
서안시(西安市) 수집

Jade Hairpin

White jade | Ming Dynasty
Total L 23cm H 2.7cm T 0.3cm
Collected in Xi'an

은으로 된 몸체와 옥잠두(玉簪頭)로 이루어졌다. 잠두는 납작한 모양으로 매화가지에 앉아 있는 까치 한 마리를 양면 조각하였다. 까치는 몸을 기울이고 머리를 쳐들었으며 뾰족한 부리를 벌려 희소식을 알리는 듯하다. 날개는 등에 모이고 긴 꽁지는 살짝 펼쳤으며 몸통 세부는 모두 음각(陰刻)하였다. 까치 아래쪽 가지에는 매화가 활짝 피어 있고 뒤쪽에는 잎들이 나 있다. 매화 윤곽은 5연호(連弧) 모양이고 가운데 꽃술은 격자무늬로 표현하였으며 꽃잎과 잎은 오목하게 새겼다. 까치 몸통과 꽃가지 사이는 막대기 모양 도구로 누공(鏤空)하였는데 표면은 정세(精細)하게 연마하였으나 측면 가장자리와 누공한 부분의 안쪽은 거칠고 뚫은 흔적이 뚜렷하다.

잠두 도안은 전통적인 길상(吉祥)문양이다. 까치는 희소식을 알리는 새이고 '梅(매)'자는 '眉(미)'자와 같은 발음이므로 "까치가 매화가지에 앉아 있다", 즉 기뻐서 눈썹 꼬리가 올라간다는 뜻이다.

옥잠은 여성용 머리장신구로 일반적으로 금속장신구의 부품이다. 당대(唐代) 이후 옥으로 만든 잠이 성행하였다.

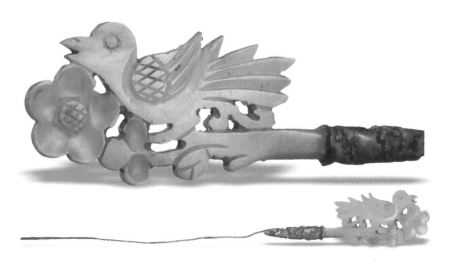

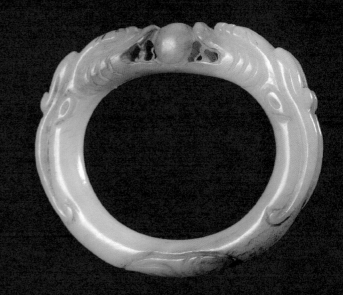

109

"이룡희주"탁(二龍戲珠鐲)

백옥(白玉) | 청(淸)
긴지름 7.3cm 짧은지름 6.1cm 두께 1.1cm
1983년 서안시(西安市) 섬서(陝西)사범대학 출토

Jade Bracelet with the Motif of "Two dragons playing with a ball"

White jade | Qing Dynasty
Long D 7.3cm Short D 6.1cm T 1.1cm
Excavated from Shaan'xi Normal University in Xi'an in 1983

타원형 고리 모양이며 '이룡희주도(二龍戲珠圖)'를 조각하였다. 용은 머리를 마주하고 함께 둥근 구슬을 입에 물어 원형(圓形)을 이루었다. 용 두 마리는 모두 머리 부분만 조각하였는데 조형이 같다. 입은 길고 코는 넓으며 굵고 긴 눈썹은 치켜세웠다. 쌍뿔과 갈기 두 가닥은 용 형태에 따라 굽었으며 서로 이어진 몸통 가운데는 운문(雲紋)을 새겼다. 용머리와 운문은 섬세하게 조각하고 오관(五官)과 수염, 머리카락은 정세(精細)하게 연마하였으나 막대기 모양 도구로 누공(鏤空)한 용의 입 안쪽은 정밀하게 연마하지 않았다.

이룡희주는 명·청대(明·淸代) 옥팔찌에서 흔히 볼 수 있는 제재이다. 중국 고대 전설에서 용주(龍珠)는 용의 원기가 담긴 결정체로 용 두 마리가 용주를 서로 빼앗는 모습을 예술적으로 표현하여 아름다운 생활에 대한 추구를 나타내었다.

옥탁(玉鐲)은 팔찌의 일종으로 신석기시대 양저문화(良渚文化)에서 최초로 나타났다. 선진(先秦)시대 옥탁 조형은 양저문화의 영향을 받아 높은 통형(筒形)에 탁벽(鐲壁)은 납작하고 구연(口沿)은 평평하고 곧다. 그 후 점차 두껍고 낮게 발전하다가 당·송대(唐·宋代)에 이르러 원기둥 모양 옥탁이 나타났다. 명대(明代) 옥탁은 내벽이 평평하고 곧으며 외벽이 둥글고 볼록한 부죽식(剖竹式) 또는 교사식(絞絲式)이다. 청대(淸代)에는 이룡희주식이 성행하였고 이외 외벽에 도안 또는 길상어(吉祥語)를 조각하였다.

110

쌍수추(雙獸墜)

백옥(白玉) | 청(淸)
길이 5.4cm 너비 4.4cm 두께 1cm
1978년 서안시(西安市) 수집

Jade Double Beast Pendants

White jade | Qing Dynasty
L 5.4cm W 4.4cm T 1cm
Collected in Xi'an in 1978

타원형이며 원조(圓彫)하였다. 짐승 두 마리가 엎드려 있는데 입은 기다랗고 눈은 크며 큰 귀는 뒤로 젖혀졌고 긴 꼬리는 서로의 머리 밑에 깔려 있다. 서로 마주 보면서 함께 기다란 수대(綬帶)를 입에 물고 있는데 전체적으로 구상이 교묘하고 공예가 뛰어나다.

조각가는 음각(陰刻), 부조(浮彫), 원조, 누조(鏤彫) 등 기법을 사용하여 빼어난 기예로 둥근 몸통, 건장한 사지, 커다란 콧구멍을 조각해내었다. 짐승은 오소리로 성질이 거칠고 사나운데 전체적인 조형은 되레 온순하고 사랑스러워 보이며 가만히 엎드려 마주 보는 모습은 서로 사랑을 나누는 듯하다.

오소리 '환(獾)'과 기쁠 '환(歡)'은 동음이의어이고 긴 수대의 장수(長綬)와 장수(長壽)는 같은 발음으로 함께 장수하고 영원토록 금슬이 좋다는 의미이다.

111

쌍어추(雙魚墜)

백옥(白玉) | 청(淸)
길이 5.9cm 너비 5.5cm 두께 1.1cm
1978년 서안시(西安市) 수집

Jade Double Fish Pendants

White jade | Qing Dynasty
L 5.9cm W 5.5cm T 1.1cm
Collected in Xi'an in 1978

물고기 한 쌍을 조각하였다. 둘 다 같은 방향으로 놓였으며 몸통은 하나가 곧고 하나는 굽었으며 입에는 각각 수초(水草)를 물고 있다. 동그란 눈은 대롱 모양 도구로 뚫었으며 등지느러미는 짧은 호선(弧線)을 세로로 새겨 표현하고 가슴지느러미, 배지느러미는 연속된 기다란 삼각무늬로 표현하였다. 몸통 가운데는 형태에 따른 곡선이 있으며 양측에는 '米(미)'자를 드문드문 음각(陰刻)하였다. 꼬리는 활 모양으로 펼쳤는데 윤곽은 연호형(連弧形)이고 양면에는 방사상(放射狀) 호선을 새겼다. 물고기가 물속에서 헤엄치다가 먹이를 먹는 순간을 포착하여 표현한 것으로 생활의 정취가 짙다.

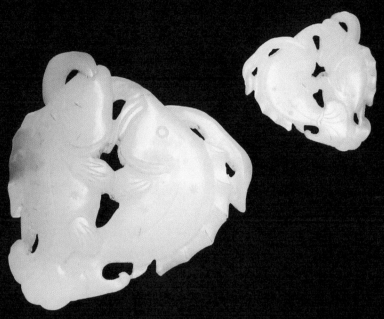

112

"유해희금섬"추(劉海戲金蟾墜)

백옥(白玉) | 청(淸)
높이 4.7cm 최대지름 3.6cm 두께 1.7cm
1982년 서안시 안탑구 삼효촌(西安市 雁塔區 三爻村) 출토

**Jade Pendant with the Motif of Liuhai
(a god in the Chinese legend) Playing with Toad**

White jade | Qing Dynasty
H 4.7cm Max D 3.6cm T 1.7cm
Excavated from Sanyao Village in Yanta District, Xi'an in 1982

동자(童子)가 조롱박 위에 기어올라 한 손으로는 덩굴을 잡고 다른 한 손으로는 돈을 꿴 끈을 들고 조롱박 아래에 있는 금섬(金蟾)을 희롱하는 모습을 조각하였다. 동자는 무릎을 꿇고 등을 구부렸으며 머리를 돌려 장난스럽게 웃고 있는데 형상이 우스꽝스럽다. 등에는 박쥐 한 마리가 앉아 있다. 이 도안 이름은 '유해희섬(劉海戲蟾)'인데 도교(道敎) 전설 중 피곡(辟穀)하여 몸을 가볍게 한 인물에서 견강부회(牽强附會)하여 만들어낸 것이다. 금섬은 세발청개구리로 고대에는 이것을 얻으면 부유해진다고 여겨 넘쳐나는 재물과 행복을 뜻하게 되었다. 박쥐는 날 수 있는 포유동물이고 '蝠(복)'자가 행복 '복(福)'자와 같은 발음이기에 행복이 날아듦을 의미한다. 팔보(八寶) 중 하나인 조롱박은 도교 팔선(八仙) 중 철괴리(鐵拐李)가 지닌 보물로 철괴리는 조롱박 속 단약(丹藥)으로 사람을 구함으로써 행복을 가져다주었다. 이 옥추는 유해희금섬, 박쥐, 조롱박 등을 유기적으로 결합시켜 길상(吉祥)도안을 이루었다.

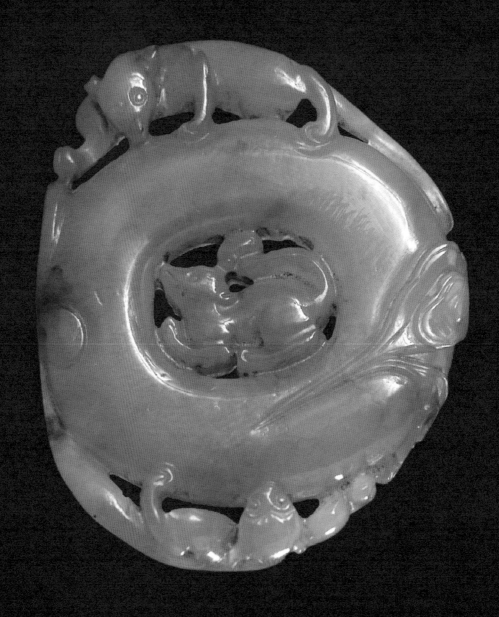

113

이룡운문추(螭龍雲紋墜)

비취(翡翠) | 청(淸)
긴지름 3,9cm 짧은지름 3.1cm 두께 0.7cm
1983년 서안시(西安市) 수집

Green Jade Board with Chi Dragon and Cloud Patterns

Emerald | Qing Dynasty
Long D 3,9cm Short D 3.1cm T 0,7cm
Collected in Xi'an 1983

환형(環形)으로 가운데 구멍이 나 있으며 이룡(螭龍) 한 마리가 구멍 안에 엎드려 있다. 머리를 높이 처든 이룡은 두 눈을 둥그렇게 떴고 사지를 굽혔으며 기다란 꼬리는 위로 말려 등에 놓았다. 원환(圓環) 밖에는 아래위로 이룡이 있는데 고개를 기웃하고 구멍 안을 들여다보고 있으며 사지는 걷는 듯하고 기다란 꼬리는 뒤에 끌렸다. 옆에는 구름 세 송이가 있어 이룡들이 구름 속에서 노닒을 뜻한다. 세 마리 모두 형태가 상이한데 구멍 안 이룡은 몸을 굽혀 조용히 엎드리고 있으며 머리를 높이 쳐들고 가만히 있는 모습이 숨어 있는 듯하다. 바깥쪽 두 마리는 구름 속에서 거닐며 마주하여 구멍 안을 들여다보는 것이 마치 구멍 속 친구를 찾는 듯하다.

셋 다 몸통이 굵고 건장하며 사지가 힘 있는 것이 위풍당당한 모습이다. 구멍 속 이룡은 기민하고 총명해 보이고 바깥쪽 두 마리는 눈빛으로 보아 끝내 친구를 찾아낸 듯하다. 사나운 동물이 아이들처럼 숨바꼭질을 하는 모습에서 풍부한 상상력과 짙은 생활의 정취를 느낄 수 있다.

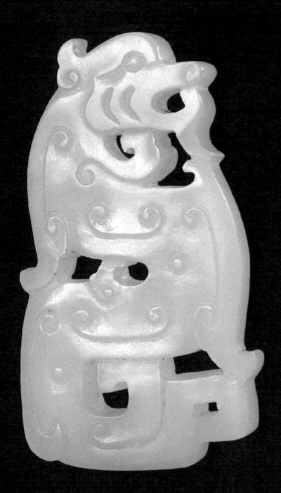

114
기룡형패(夔龍形牌)

백옥(白玉) | 청(淸)
길이 6.7cm 너비 3.9cm 두께 0.8cm
1981년 서안시(西安市) 수집

Jade Board with Kui Dragon Pattern

White jade | Qing Dynasty
L 6.7cm W 3.9cm T 0.8cm
Collected in Xi'an in 1981

기룡은 머리를 돌려 뒤돌아보고 있는데 두 눈은 둥그렇게 뜨고 코는 넓고 입은 크며 머리카락은 뒤로 말렸다. 몸통은 'S'자 모양이고 꼬리가 위로 쳐들렸는데 위로 말린 꼬리 끝에 주저앉았으며 온몸에는 구연운문(鉤連雲紋)을 새겼다. 전체적으로 원조(圓彫), 음각(陰刻), 누공(鏤空) 등 기법을 사용하여 전설 속 동물을 생동감 있게 표현하였다.

상·주대(商·周代)에 기룡은 기물(器物)의 장식도안으로 사용되었는데 신비하고 공포스러운 분위기가 있어 권력과 지위의 상징이 되었다. 청대(淸代) 통치계급은 골동품을 좋아하였는데 특히 건륭(乾隆)시기에 성행하였다. 윗사람이 즐기면 아랫사람은 더욱 좋아하기 마련이어서 민간에서도 방고(倣古)가 유행하였고 이 패식이 곧 그 사례이다.

115
앵무문패(鸚鵡紋牌)

백옥(白玉) | 청(淸)
지름 5.5cm 두께 0.8cm
1978년 서안시(西安市) 수집

Jade Board with Parrot Pattern

White jade | Qing Dynasty
D 5.5cm T 0.8cm
Collected in Xi'an in 1978

연주문(聯珠紋) 환(環) 안에 앵무새 한 마리를 조각하였다. 앵무새는 동그란 눈, 갈고리 모양 부리를 가졌으며 긴 꼬리를 내려뜨리고 뒤돌아보며 날갯짓하고 있다. 한쪽 발은 횡목(橫木)을 딛고 다른 한쪽 발에는 기다란 끈이 매어져 있는데 끈은 횡목에 감겨 있다. 연주 환과 횡목은 앵무새를 가두는 데 쓰였다. 놀란 앵무새가 날아오르려다가 끈 때문에 어찌할 수 없이 고개를 돌려 뒤돌아보고는 횡목에서 오가며 불의의 습격을 방지하는 것 같은 모습이 매우 사실적이다. 연주는 알알이 정교하고 기다란 끈이 횡목에 감긴 것 역시 정묘(精妙)하기 그지없으며 앵무새 온몸의 깃털 또한 티 없이 깨끗하고 희다. 전체적으로 조각가의 뛰어난 표현력과 빼어난 기예를 엿볼 수 있다.

앵무새 옥패식(玉牌飾)은 몸에 착용하는 것으로 민간에서 유행하였으며 이는 당시 옥 제조 수준과 풍속을 보여준다. 이 패식은 특징과 조각도법(刀法)으로 보아 청대(淸代) 건륭(乾隆) 이후 작품이다.

116

복수방형패(福壽方形牌)

백옥(白玉) | 명(明)
길이 5.7cm 너비 4.6cm 두께 0.4cm
1983년 서안시(西安市) 수집

Jade Square Board Symbolizing Happiness and Longevity

White jade | Ming Dynasty
L 5.7cm W 4.6cm T 0.4cm
Collected in Xi'an in 1983

직사각형이며 여러 층으로 투조(透彫)하였다. 테는 참대 마디 모양이고 가운데는 '壽(수)'자를 전서체(篆書體)로 누조(鏤彫)하고 주위를 관지(串枝) 매화와 댓잎으로 장식하였으며 오른편 아래쪽에는 박쥐를 새겼다. '壽(수)'는 글자체가 반듯하고 꽃가지는 안에서 밖으로 비스듬히 뻗었으며 가지와 잎은 서로 얽혔으며 박쥐는 날개를 펴고 날아엔다. 글자의 필획, 꽃잎, 댓잎의 표면은 오목하게 새겼고 참대 마디가 이어지는 부분은 살짝 튀어나왔는데 그 위에 음각선을 그렸다. 앞면은 정세(精細)하게 연마하였고 뒷면은 평평하고 빛난다.

'수(壽)'는 장수를 뜻하고 박쥐 '복(蝠)'과 행복 '복(福)'은 같은 발음이며, 매화와 참대는 추위를 이겨내므로 이 옥패의 문양은 장수, 행복과 지조를 의미한다.

117

옥마책(玉螞蚱)

백옥(白玉) | 청(淸)
길이 4cm 너비 0.7cm 높이 1.3cm
서안시(西安市) 수집

Jade Grasshopper

White jade | Qing Dynasty
L 4cm W 0.7cm H 1.3cm
Collected in Xi'an

메뚜기는 몸통이 기다랗고 날씬하다. 두 눈은 볼록하게 튀어나왔고 긴 날개는 몸에 붙였으며 두 뒷다리는 배 옆에 모으고 날아오르려는 듯하다. 조각기법이 간단하고 세부는 음각선으로 그렸다. 선이 유창하고 조형이 사실적이며 전체적으로 생동하면서도 자연스럽다. 메뚜기는 가을에 활동하는 곤충으로 가을의 상징이기도 하다. 황량한 늦가을 들판에서 차가운 바람이 불고 벌거벗은 나무들이 추위에 떨 때 메뚜기의 울음까지 들리면 그야말로 처량하기 그지없는 가을 진풍경인 것이다.

청대(淸代) 강희(康熙) · 옹정(雍正) · 건륭(乾隆) 시기는 중국 전통사회의 절정기로 사회가 안정되고 경제가 발전하여 '강건성세(康乾盛世)'를 이루었다. 그러나 통치계급의 '문자옥(文字獄)'은 뜻 있는 이들을 실망시켰고 그들은 자신의 감정을 자연에 기탁하여 표현할 수밖에 없었다. 이 옥메뚜기는 바로 이러한 처량하고 실망스러운 심경을 반영한 것이다.

118

옥와구(玉臥狗)

백옥(白玉) | 청(淸)
길이 3.7cm 너비 1.4cm 높이 1.3cm
서안시(西安市) 수집

Jade Reclining Dog

White jade | Qing Dynasty
L 3.7cm W 1.4cm H 1.3cm
Collected in Xi'an

개는 엎드린 모습으로 고개를 들고 입을 처들었으며 두 눈을 동그랗게 뜨고 커다란 귀를 아래로 늘어뜨렸다. 사지는 앞으로 굽혔고 편도(偏刀)로 뒷다리 관절을 새겼으며 꼬리는 위로 말려 둔부에 붙였다. 앞다리 사이에 구멍이 있어 실을 꿰어 매달 수 있다. 작고 정교한데 몇 획 사용하지 않고서도 눈, 코, 입, 사지를 그려내었으며 비율이 알맞고 형태가 정확하다. 개의 기민한 자태를 형상적으로 표현하였다.

이 작품은 실용 장식품으로 선추(扇墜), 검추(劍墜), 여의추(如意墜), 불진추(拂塵墜) 및 기타 추식(墜飾)으로 사용할 수 있다. 기법과 개의 특징으로 보아 건륭조(乾隆朝) 이후 작품으로 추정된다.

상감옥기

象嵌玉器

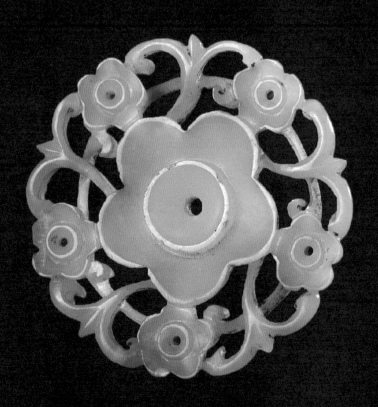

상감옥기(象嵌玉器)는 부분품으로 다른 기구(器具)에 상감된 옥장식품이며 보통 단독으로 사용하지 않는다. 고대 중국에서는 흔히 기구 위에 옥장식을 상감하였는데 이는 첫째, 미를 추구하고 가치를 높이기 위해서이고, 둘째, 신통함으로 복을 얻기 위해서였다. 중국은 상고(上古) 시대 이미 녹송석(綠松石)이 상감된 기구가 나타났고 주대(周代)에 이르러 유행처럼 번졌으며 옥을 상감한 기구의 품종도 다양해졌다. 그중 제도로 규정된 품종에는 식기(食器)류에 속하는 옥작(玉爵, 청동으로 만든 다리가 세 개 달린 술잔), 옥두(玉豆), 옥잔(玉琖, 술잔의 일종), 가구류에 속하는 옥궤(玉几), 여복(輿服)류에 속하는 옥로(玉輅)와 관리복식, 제기(祭器)에 속하는 옥찬(玉瓚), 나규(裸圭, 종묘를 제사할 때 쓰는 옥기) 등이 있다. 이 밖에, 제도적 규정은 없지만 군용(軍用) 기구로는 옥석으로 장식한 칼, 활, 지팡이, 창 및 보검에 상감된 수(首), 심(鐔), 체(璏), 필(珌) 등이 있다. 상감옥기는 중국 옥 문화의 고유한 특징으로 후세에 많은 영향을 끼쳤으며 선진(先秦)시대부터 수천 년을 이어 오며 수많은 작품을 남겼다.

Embedded jade articles are fittings that are inlayed in other objects and are not used alone. Many utensils in ancient times are embedded with jade articles for decoration to raise the aesthetic value for one reason, and to seek auspiciousness as well as turquoise had existed. By Zhou Dynasty, jade embedment had become very popular. The variety of the implements that was embedded with jade is abundant. The implements that had been listed into the institution are jade wine vessel, jade food utensil, jade cup, jade tea table, jade Ge and official trappings, as well as articles used for sacrifice such as jade Zen(ceremonial ladel), and jade Gui(tablet). Beside that, there are military implements that were not listed in the institutions, which also had jade embedment for decoration such as knife, bow, staff, spear as well as Shou(head), Xin, Zhi and Bi fitting on the sword. Embedded jade pendant is an important feature in Chinese jade culture, which influence the later generations greatly. Ever after early Qin Dynasty, jade embedded articles emerged in endlessly for thousands of years.

옥검구(玉劍具)

춘추전국(春秋戰國)시대부터 한대(漢代)까지 유행하였던 칼자루나 칼집 위에 상감된 옥장식을 일러 옥검구(玉劍具)라고 하였다. 검은 당시 제후(諸侯), 대부(大夫)들이 패용하던 것으로 위에 옥을 상감함으로써 신분과 지위를 나타냈다. 춘추전국시대부터 한대까지 옥으로 된 검장식이 대량으로 출현하였는데 이는 추측건대 "군자는 반드시 옥을 달아야 한다", "군자는 이유 없이 옥을 몸에서 떼지 않으며 군자의 덕은 옥과 같이 티가 없어야 한다"라는 패옥(佩玉)의 개념과 밀접한 관계가 있는 듯하다.

옥검구는 수(首), 심(鐔), 체(璏), 필(珌) 등 네 가지로 이루어졌다. 칼자루 끝부분의 장식품이 '수(首)', 자루와 칼날 경계선 부분이 '심(鐔)', 즉 보편적으로 '검격(劍格)'이라고 부르는 부위이다. 칼집 중간의 검대(劍帶)를 연결하는 단추가 '체(璏)' 또는 '수(璲)', 칼집 끝부분의 장식품이 '필(珌)' 또는 '표(摽)'이다. 필은 원래 구리로 만들었지만 옥검구에서는 옥으로 대체하였다.

From Spring and Autumn Period and Warring States Period till Han Dynasty, it is popular to embed jade ornaments in the handle and sheath of the word. Such jade ornaments are called Jade Sword Pieces. At that time, sword is a must to the leuds and senior officials, and using jade to decorate sword indicates the identity and status of the owners. The emergence of large number of jade sword ornaments at that time has much to do with the influences of the sayings such as "A man of honor in the ancient times must wear jade" and "jade don't leave a gentleman for no reason and the morality of a gentleman can be compared jade" and so on.

A complete set of jade sword pieces have four parts, namely Shou(head), Xin, Zhi and Bi. The sword finial in called Shou, the junction between the handle and body of the sword is called Xin, the button that decorats the middle part of the sheath to tie the sword strap on is called Zhi, also known as Sui. The pendant decorating the lower end of the sheath is called Bi, also known as Biao, which was originally made in copper, but was replaced by jade in the jade sword decorations.

119

곡문검수(谷紋劍首)

청백옥(靑白玉) | 전국(戰國)
① 지름 4.1cm 두께 1cm
② 지름 5.7cm 두께 1.7cm
1976년 서안시 미앙구(西安市 未央區) 한묘(漢墓) 출토

Jade Sword Finial with Grain Patterns

Green and white jade | Warring States Period
① D 4.1cm T 1cm
② D 5.7cm T 1.7cm
Excavated from Han Tomb in Weiyang District, Xi'an in 1976

2점 모두 둥근 떡 모양으로 단면(斷面)은 사다리꼴이다. 앞면 문양은 안팎으로 나뉘는데 안팎 모두 가장자리는 현문(弦紋) 1둘레를 음각(陰刻)하여 내외곽(廓)을 이룬다. 안쪽에는 유창한 구운문(鉤雲紋)을 선각(線刻)하였고 가운데는 마름모꼴 망문(網紋)이 있는데 평면은 검수의 가장자리와 동일선상에 놓인다. 바깥쪽은 감지법(減地法)으로 곡문(穀紋)을 새겼는데 돌기된 곡문의 크기와 꼬리 선 길이가 일치한 것이 도법(刀法)이 매우 예리하다. 뒷면 가운데는 둥그런 대(臺)가 도드라져 나왔으며 주변은 비탈 모양이다. 대 가운데는 칼자루를 꽂는 홈이 있다. 큰 검수의 홈 바깥쪽에는 구멍 세 개가 사선으로 홈과 통하였는데 못으로 칼자루를 고정하는 데 쓰인다.

120

누공이문검수(鏤空螭紋劍首)

백옥(白玉) | 한(漢)
길이 8.3cm 높이 6cm 두께 2.6cm
1976년 서안시 미앙구(西安市 未央區) 홍기(紅旗)기계공장 출토

Jade Sword Finial with Hollow-carved Chi Pattern

White jade | Han Dynasty
L 8.3cm H 6cm T 2.6cm
Excavated from Hongqi Machinery Factory in Weiyang District, Xi'an in 1976

검수의 밑부분은 평평하며 칼자루를 고정시킬 수 있는 둥그런 구멍 두 개가 있다. 앞뒤 면 및 양 측면에는 구름 속에서 노니는 각양각색의 이룡(螭龍)과 괴수(怪獸)를 입체조각·부조(浮彫)·누공(鏤空) 등 기법을 사용하여 생동감 있게 조각하였다. 윗부분에 있는 이룡은 눈을 동그랗게 뜨고 입을 살짝 벌린 채 구름 위에 기어올라 머리를 기울여 내려다보고 있다. 단단하고 힘 있는 앞발로 구름을 밟고 있는데 융기된 다리 근육, 둥근 몸통, 울퉁불퉁한 배에는 마치 수시로 분출될 수 있는 힘이 숨겨져 있는 것 같다. 또 한 마리는 구름을 타고 넘어가고 있는데 머리 위 실타래 같은 기다란 수염은 구름 따라 흩날리고 예리하고 뾰족한 발은 구름을 잡고 뛰어오르려는 것 같다. 다른 이룡들도 고개를 들고 눈을 부릅뜨고 내달리는 것이 마치 상대와 맞붙어 싸우려는 것 같다. 작은 괴수는 이룡이 무서워 멀리 몸을 숨겼는데 떨어질까 봐 뒤돌아 내려다보며 구름자락을 꼭 잡았다. 전체적으로 이룡이 떼 지어 하늘에서 소란 피우는 모습을 표현한 듯하다. 이룡은 모두 구조가 'S'자형으로 곡선미가 있어 리듬감, 율동감을 드러낸다. 뭉게뭉게 피어 오른 구름은 이룡을 더욱 도드라져 보이게 하는데 이러한 대비적·과장적인 기법으로 이룡이 박투(搏鬪)하려는 듯한 장면을 나타내었다.

121

곡문검심(谷紋劍鐔)

백옥(白玉) | 한(漢)
길이 5.4cm 너비 2.7cm 두께 2.7cm
1975년 서안시 안탑구 어화채(西安市 雁塔區 魚化寨) 한묘(漢墓) 출토

Jade Xin(a sword ornament) with Grain Pattern

White jade | Han Dynasty
L 5.4cm W 2.7cm T 2.7cm
Excavated from Han Tomb in Yuhua Village in Yanta District, Xi'an in 1975

'山(산)'자 모양으로 윗부분이 뾰족하게 돌기되고 아랫부분이 오목하게 들어갔다. 측면으로 보면 마름모 모양이며 가운데 부분 아래위는 비대칭으로 누공(鏤空)하였다. 윗부분은 둥글넓적하게 누공하여 칼자루가 지나갈 수 있게 하고 아랫부분은 마름모로 누공하여 칼날 어깨 부분이 끼이게 하였다. 면(面)에는 곡문(穀紋)을 가득 새겼다. 검심은 속칭 검격(劍格)이라고도 부르는데 칼날과 칼자루 사이 옥 장식이다.

122

이룡문체(螭龍紋璏)

청백옥(青白玉) | 한(漢)
길이 4.2cm 너비 2.2cm 두께 1.1cm
1972년 서안시 장안현 아방궁공사 북가촌대대(西安市 長安縣 阿房宮公社 北可村大隊) 출토

Jade Zhi(a sword ornament) with Chi Dragon Pattern

Green and white jade | Han Dynasty
L 4.2cm W 2.2cm T 1.1cm
Excavated from Beike Village in Efang'gong Community Chang'an County, Xi'an in 1972

내려다보면 직사각형으로 앞뒤 양쪽 끝은 안쪽으로 말렸다. 뒷면에는 가죽띠를 꿸 수 있는 직사각형 구멍이 나 있다. 앞면에는 몸을 구름 속에 감춘 이룡(螭龍) 한 마리를 부조(浮彫)하였다. 이룡은 몸을 돌려 머리를 허리 위에 두었으며 사지 관절과 둘로 나뉜 꼬리 부분은 호선(弧線)으로 꾸며졌다. 등과 주위에는 가는 음각선으로 운문(雲紋)을 새겨 이룡이 구름 속에서 용틀임하는 용맹스러운 모습을 나타내었다. 이룡 몸통을 가는 선으로 새기는 기법은 동한(東漢) 이룡에서 볼 수 있는 주요한 특징이다.

123

이룡문체(螭龍紋璏)

청백옥(青白玉) | 한(漢)
길이 6.3cm 너비 3cm 두께 1.4cm
1972년 서안시 장안현 아방궁공사(西安市 長安縣 阿房宮公社) 출토

Jade Zhi(a sword ornament) with Chi Dragon Pattern

Green and white jade | Han Dynasty
L 6.3cm W 3cm T 1.4cm
Excavated from Efang'gong Community Chang'an County, Xi'an in 19722

내려다보면 직사각형이며 앞뒤 끝부분은 안쪽으로 말렸다. 뒷면에는 가죽띠를 꿸 수 있는 직사각형 구멍이 나 있다. 앞면에는 구름 속 이룡(螭龍)을 부조(浮彫)하였는데 머리와 엉덩이 부분은 가장자리 밖으로 돌출되었다. 이룡은 몸통이 'S'자형으로 굽었고 사지는 걷는 자세를 취하였으며 체면(璏面)은 감지법(減地法)으로 운문(雲紋)을 음각하였다. 조형이 시원하고 힘 있으며 문양 구도가 체면에 제한받지 않고 구름 속에서 노니는 이룡의 웅위한 자세를 생동감 있게 표현하였다.

124

자모이룡문체(子母螭龍紋璏)

청백옥(靑白玉) | 한(漢)
길이 10.2cm 너비 2.5cm 높이 2cm
1983년 서안시 초탄향 장천호촌(西安市 草灘鄕 張千戶村) 출토

Jade Zhi with Son Dragon and Mother Dragon Patterns

Green and white jade | Han Dynasty
L 10.2cm W 2.5cm H 2cm
Excavated from Zhangqianhu Village in Caotan area, Xi'an in 1983

내려다보면 직사각형이고 앞뒤 양쪽 끝은 안쪽으로 말렸으며 뒷면에는 가죽띠를 꿸 수 있는 직사각형 구멍이 있다. 앞면에는 이룡(螭龍) 모자(母子)를 고부조(高浮彫)하였는데 조형, 자태가 기본적으로 같고 머리를 기울여 마주 보며 뛰노는 모습이다. 입은 모두 누공(鏤空)하였고 입꼬리도 구멍을 뚫어 표현하였으며 눈알은 살짝 처졌고 눈썹은 곧추 섰는데 안쪽으로 굽었다. 콧마루에는 평행 호선(弧線) 두 줄이 음각(陰刻)되었고 귀는 애완견 귀처럼 늘어뜨려졌으며 꼬리는 구름을 뚫고 뻗었다. 머리, 어깨, 허벅지, 꼬리 윗부분은 평평하게 연마하고 가장자리는 '유사모조[游絲毛彫, 한대(漢代) 옥공예 기법으로 가늘고 얕지만 법도가 엄정하다]'식 가는 음각선으로 새겼다. 옥 재료 일부분에 진한 갈색이 섞여 있는데 조각가는 '초색(俏色, 옥공예 가운데서 옥석의 천연색을 그대로 이용하는 기법)'기법으로 이룡모(螭龍母)의 머리와 어깨를 진한 갈색으로 함으로써 생동감을 더해주었다.

125

수면운문체(獸面雲紋璏)

청백옥(靑白玉) | 한(漢)
길이 7.9cm 너비 2.1cm 두께 1.1cm
1981년 서안시 파교구 신축공사 북요대대(西安市 灞橋區 新築公社 北窯大隊) 출토

Jade Zhi with Animal Face and Cloud Patterns

Green and white jade | Han Dynasty
L 7.9cm W 2.1cm T 1.1cm
Excavated from Beiyao Village in Xinzhu Community Baqiao District, Xi'an in 1981

내려다보면 네모 모양으로 앞뒤 양쪽 끝은 안쪽으로 말렸으며 뒷면에는 가죽띠를 꿸 수 있는 직사각형 구멍이 나 있다. 앞면 문양은 압지은 기법(壓地隱起法)으로 새겼다. 한쪽에 수면(獸面)을 새겼는데 쌍뿔, 커다란 눈, 코, 입이 있다. 수면의 윗부분에는 중심선을 따라 좌우로 대칭되는 이방연속(二方連續) 구운문(鉤雲紋)이 있고 사이사이를 망문(網紋) 또는 평행 절곡선(折曲線)으로 꾸몄으며 양쪽 가장자리에는 각각 음각선으로 곽(廓)을 새겼다. 다른 한쪽에는 절곡기하문(折曲幾何紋)을 음각하였는데 아래위로 음각선 하나를 사이 두었다. 체(璏)의 양쪽 끝과 가운데 문양은 보건대 독립적이지만, 사실은 수면을 머리로, 중심선을 척추로, 운문을 몸통 무늬로, 기하문을 꼬리로 한 완벽한 수문(獸紋)이다.

126

수면운문체(獸面雲紋璏)

청백옥(靑白玉) | 한(漢)
길이 12cm 너비 2.4cm 두께 1.7cm
1983년 서안시 파교구 수류향(西安市 灞橋區 水流鄕) 출토

Jade Zhi with Animal Face and Cloud Patterns

Green and white jade | Han Dynasty
L 12cm W 2.4cm T 1.7cm
Excavated from Shuiliu Village Baqiao District, Xi'an in 1983

내려다보면 네모 모양이고 측면에서 보면 아치형 다리 모양이다. 뒷면에는 가죽띠를 꿸 수 있는 직사각형 구멍이 있다. 앞면 문양은 압지은 기법(壓地隱起法)으로 조각하였다. 한쪽 끝에는 거꾸로 된 수면(獸面)이 있는데 눈썹, 눈, 코가 뚜렷하다. 수면 뒤 척추를 나타내는 중심선을 사이에 두고 좌우에는 구운문(鉤雲紋)이 대칭되게 있다. 다른 한쪽 가운데는 삼각형 망문(網紋)을 새겨 둘로 나뉜 꼬리를 나타냈다.

이문필(螭紋珌)

백옥(白玉) | 한(漢)
높이 5.6cm 위길이 5.2cm 아래길이 7.3cm 두께 2.6cm
1983년 서안시 미앙구(西安市 未央區) 홍기(紅旗)기계공장 공사장 출토

Jade Bi(a sword ornament) with Chi Patterns

White jade | Han Dynasty
H 5.6cm Upper L 5.2cm Lower L 7.3cm T 2.6cm
Excavated from Hongqi Machinery Factory in Weiyang District, Xi'an in 1983

사다리꼴 모양이고 단면(斷面)은 기다란 올리브 모양이며 양면 모두 이문(螭紋)을 부조(浮彫)하였다. 한쪽 면에는 구름 속 이룡(螭龍)을 저부조하였는데 이룡 몸통은 가로로 'S'자형을 이루고 구름이 허리를 가로지른다. 이룡은 고개를 처들고 눈썹을 곧추 세웠는데 안쪽으로 굽었으며 눈알은 살짝 처졌고 콧마루에는 쌍호선(雙弧線)이 음각되었다. 짧은 귀는 곧추 세웠고 긴 갈기는 굽었다. 척추는 목에서 꼬리까지 음각선으로 나타내고 어깨와 허벅지는 권운문(卷雲紋)으로 꾸몄으며 꼬리는 실타래 모양이다. 이룡 주위에는 운문(雲紋) 몇 개를 부조·음각(陰刻)하였으며 필면(珌面) 가장자리는 비교적 두껍다. 다른 한쪽 면에는 크고 작은 이룡 두 마리를 고부조하였는데 형태는 앞면 이룡과 기본적으로 같으며 몸통 역시 'S'자형을 이룬다. 두 마리는 함께 수대(綬帶)를 물었는데 수대가 작은 이룡의 몸 아래 구름을 가로지나 이룡이 솟구치는 모습과 수대의 흩날림이 강렬해 보인다. 이 면의 세 모서리 가장자리 부근에는 음각선이 있는데 곽(廓)을 나타낸다. 필의 윗부분에는 쐐기 못으로 칼집과 연결시키는 홈이 나 있다.

이룡봉문검수(螭龍鳳紋劍首)

백옥(白玉) | 청(淸)
길이 4.8cm 위너비 3.3cm 아래너비 2.6cm 두께 1.5cm
1983년 서안시(西安市) 수집

Jade Sword Finial with Chi Dragon and Bird Patterns

White jade | Qing Dynasty
L 4.8cm Upper W 3.3cm Lower W 2.6cm T 1.5cm
Collected in Xi'an in 1983

사다리꼴로 아래위 모서리에는 비아(扉牙) 세 개가 있으며 비아 가운데는 홈이 나 있다. 앞뒤 면에는 각각 이룡문(螭龍紋)과 봉조문(鳳鳥紋)을 부조(浮彫)하고 주위에는 음각선을 둘러 사다리꼴 테를 이루었다. 이룡은 머리가 타원형인데 눈은 동그랗고 눈섭은 굵었으며 귀는 늘어뜨렸다. 둥근 가슴은 쭉 폈고 몸통은 곧은 편이며 꼬리는 굽었다. 앞다리는 모두 앞으로 뺐었고 뒷다리는 앞뒤로 놓였다. 다른 한 면에는 봉조가 측면으로 서 있는데 부리가 뾰족하고 살짝 굽었으며 눈꼬리가 비교적 길고 긴 볏이 뒤로 젖혀졌으며 날개를 펴고 꽁지를 쳐들었다. 몸통에는 권운문(卷雲紋)과 절곡문(折曲紋)으로 깃털을 나타냈다. 이 검수(劍首)의 이룡문과 봉조문은 모두 진·한대(秦·漢代)의 같은 문양을 모방하였지만 윤곽선을 볼 때 꺾이는 부분이 예리하고 굽은 부분의 호(弧)가 둥글고 알찬 것으로 보아 전형적인 청대(淸代) 옥공예 기법이다.

수문체(獸紋璲)

백옥(白玉) | 청(淸)
길이 6.8cm 너비 2.5cm 높이 1.3cm
1983년 서안시(西安市) 수집

Jade Zhi with Animal Patterns

White jade | Qing Dynasty
L 6.8cm W 2.5cm H 1.3cm
Collected in Xi'an in 1983

내려다보면 네모 모양으로 앞뒤 양쪽 끝은 안쪽으로 말렸으며 뒷면에는 허리띠를 꿸 수 있는 직사각형 구멍이 나 있다. 앞면에는 크고 작은 수문(獸紋) 두 쌍을 부조(浮彫)하였는데 큰 것은 가운데에 있고 작은 것은 양쪽 끝에 있으며 둘씩 서로 꼬리를 물고 에워쌌다. 네 마리 모두 머리가 크고 몸통이 'U'자형을 이루는데 작으며 사지가 없다. 주위에는 파도무늬가 있어 수중에서 노니는 것 같다. 두 쌍의 수문은 조형이 비슷한데 약간의 구별점이 있다. 왼쪽 한 쌍에서 큰 것은 머리가 새머리 측면 같고 눈은 타원형이며 눈꼬리가 길고 부리가 뾰족하다. 작은 것은 머리가 약간 네모나고 얼굴, 이마, 뿔이 3층 계단을 이룬다. 사다리꼴 얼굴에 소용돌이 두 개로 눈을 나타냈고 이마는 평평한데 목과 너비가 같으며 'U'자형 뿔 두 개는 곧게 섰다. 오른쪽 한 쌍에서 큰 것은 머리가 오리머리 측면 같고 동그란 눈에, 기다란 입을 가졌다. 작은 것의 모양은 왼쪽 것과 비슷한데 얼굴이 삼각형이다. 전체 화면은 구도가 대칭되고 동적이며 도법(刀法)이 힘 있고 유창하며 연마가 정세(精細)하게 되어 예술성과 실용성을 모두 구비한 흔치 않은 수작이다.

130

수면필(獸面珌)

사문석(蛇紋石) 대리암(大理岩) | 청(淸)
길이 5.1cm 너비 4.2cm 두께 2cm
서안시(西安市) 수집

Jade Bi(a sword ornament) with Animal Patterns

Serpentine marble | Qing Dynasty
L 5.1cm W 4.2cm T 2cm
Collected in Xi'an

　사다리꼴로 단면(斷面)은 올리브 모양이며 양면 모두 수면(獸面)으로 장식하였다. 수면은 약간 네모지고 눈은 크며 위 눈꺼풀은 평평하고 눈꼬리는 얼굴을 벗어났으며 눈썹은 모나고 꺾인 것이 네모에 가까우며 코는 주먹코이다. 이마 양측, 이마 한가운데 그리고 볼에는 각각 돌기가 있으며 벌린 입으로 이빨을 드러낸 것이 흉측스러워 보인다. 수면 윤곽 주위는 오목하게 연마하였고 압지은기법(壓地隱起法)으로 조각한 코 가장자리는 음각선으로 윤곽을 그렸으며 눈구멍, 입술은 편도(偏刀)로 경사지게 깎아내어 흉악한 눈빛과 벌어진 입을 부각시켜 수면의 공포감을 강화하였다. 필(珌)의 윗부분은 양면으로 경사지게 깎아내었고 맨 위쪽과 사다리꼴의 양쪽 사변은 평평하게 연마하였다. 필 아랫부분의 평면은 올리브 모양으로 가운데는 둥그런 홈이 나 있다. 홈 양쪽에는 각각 사선으로 홈의 중간까지 구멍을 뚫어 칼집을 고정시키게 하였다.

131

홍안타원형옥편(鴻雁橢圓形玉片)

백옥(白玉) | 송(宋)
길이 3.5cm 너비 2.5cm 두께 0.5cm
1981년 서안시 장안현(西安市 長安縣) 위곡(韋曲) 수집

Oval Shaped Jade Ornament with Wild Goose Pattern

White jade | Song Dynasty
L 3.5cm W 2.5cm T 0.5cm
Collected in Weiqu in Chang'an County, Xi'an in 1981

옥패(玉牌)는 타원형으로 나는 기러기를 단면(單面) 부조(浮彫)하였다. 기러기는 목을 빼고 날개를 펼쳤으며 기다란 부리, 동그란 눈, 긴 목을 가졌는데 몸과 날개의 깃털이 뚜렷하게 보인다. 주위에는 운문(雲紋) 몇 개가 있다. 기러기 윤곽은 압지은기법(壓地隱起法)으로 조각하였고 깃털은 사도(斜刀)와 음각선으로 표현하였으며 구름은 편사도(偏斜刀)로 새겼다.

기러기는 철새로 계절의 변화에 따라 남북으로 이동하는데 종래로 이를 어기지 않는다. 이 특징은 인간이 추구하는 감정과 맞아떨어지면서 기러기는 먼 곳에 있는 가족이나 고향에 대한 그리움으로 상징되었다.

뒷면은 민무늬로 깔끔하며 오른쪽에는 구리못이 남아 있는 구멍 하나가 있고 왼쪽에는 사선으로 누공(鏤空)한 호형(弧形) 구멍이 있는데 상감하거나 고정하는 데 사용된다.

132

이룡문옥편(螭龍紋玉片)

백옥(白玉) | 원(元)
지름 4.1cm 두께 0.6cm
1976년 서안시 안탑구(西安市 雁塔區) 동쪽 하가촌(何家村) 출토

Round Jade Flake with Chi Dragon Pattern

White jade | Yuan Dynasty
D 4.1cm T 0.6cm
Excavated from East Hejia Village in Yanta District, Xi'an in 1976

한 쌍으로 두 점의 모양과 문양은 똑같다. 동글납작한 모양으로 앞면에는 이룡(螭龍)을 부조(浮彫)하였다. 이룡은 머리가 네모나고 입이 평평하며 눈, 코는 얼굴의 앞부분에 모여 있고 귀는 고양이 귀 같다. 목은 오목하고 몸통은 옆으로 돌렸으며 사지는 힘이 있고 꼬리는 둘로 나뉘고 굽었다. 등에는 깊은 음각선으로 새긴 척추가 있고 뒤쪽 아랫다리 뒤편에는 짧은 음각 사선(斜線) 몇 줄이 있다. 조형은 한대(漢代)의 것과 비슷하나 도법(刀法), 머리, 목 등 부위의 특징은 모두 원대(元代)의 것이다. 패(牌)의 뒷면은 평평하지 않고 막대기 모양 도구를 사용하여 남긴 얕고 둥글며 오목한 흔적이 남아 있다. 가장자리와 가까운 곳에는 사선으로 누조(鏤彫)한 크고 작은 호형(弧形) 구멍 두 개가 대응되게 있는데 못으로 상감하는 데 쓰인다.

133

옥홍안(玉鴻雁)

백옥(白玉) | 원(元)
길이 2.8~4.5cm 높이 2.7~3.4cm 두께 0.6cm
1971년 서안시 안탑구 하가촌(西安市 雁塔區 何家村) 출토

Jade Wild Goose

White jade | Yuan Dynasty
L 2.8~4.5cm H 2.7~3.4cm T 0.6cm
Excavated from Hejia Village in Yanta District, Xi'an in 1971

기러기 네 마리는 자태가 상이한데 각각 날갯짓하거나 날개를 펴고 날거나 날개를 모으고 착지하거나 서서 바라보는 모습이다. 이는 기러기 비행과정 중 네 가지 동작으로 마치 기러기가 날아오르는 순간에서 착지하는 순간을 묘사한 듯하다. 기러기는 기본특징이 일치한데 오리 부리, 동그란 눈, 긴 목, 짧은 꽁지를 가졌으며 각 부위 깃털은 가는 음각선으로 그렸다. 조각기법이 완숙하고 형태가 사실적이고 생동감이 있으며 연마기술 또한 빼어나다. 옥은 희고 윤이 나는데 흙 침투 흔적이 있다. 이 기러기 세트는 단면(單面) 부조(浮彫)하였는데 다른 한 면은 민무늬이다. 구멍이 없는 것으로 보아 목제(木製) 기물(器物)의 장식품인 듯하다.

134

봉문옥편(鳳紋玉片)

백옥(白玉) | 청(淸)
길이 4.5cm 높이 2cm 두께 3cm
1970년 서안시(西安市) 수집

Jade Board with Phoenix Pattern

White jade | Qing Dynasty
L 4.5cm H 2cm T 3cm
Collected in Xi'an in 1970

옥봉(玉鳳) 한 쌍으로 납작한 모양에 형태는 같으며 방향이 상반되고 단면(單面) 조각하였다. 봉조(鳳鳥)는 날개를 펴고 고개를 돌렸으며 부리는 갈고리 모양이고 눈은 길며 볏은 높고 정수리 깃털은 뒤로 젖혀져 위로 말렸다. 목 깃털은 드리워져 흩날리고 긴 다리는 굽혔으며 기다란 꼬리는 바람에 나부낀다. 날개 앞에 구름 한 송이를 조각하여 구름 속에서 날고 있음을 나타냈다. 봉조의 조형 및 세부 모두 정교하다.

봉조는 옛사람들이 당시 심미관에 따라 자연계 각종 새의 형태를 종합하여 만들어낸 장식 문양이다. 초기 봉문은 사실상 일반적인 조류 도안이었으며 한대(漢代) 이후 형상과 특징이 점차 뚜렷해졌다. 봉문은 신비한 색채를 띤 동시에 형태가 아름다워 역대로 사람들이 좋아하는 장식 문양이다.

135

이문타원형옥편(螭紋橢圓形玉片)

백옥(白玉) | 명(明)
긴지름 5.5cm 짧은지름 4.9cm 두께 1.5cm
1983년 서안시(西安市) 수집

Oval-shaped Board with Chi Pattern

White jade | Ming Dynasty
Long D 5.5cm Short D 4.9cm T 1.5cm
Collected in Xi'an in 1983

타원형이고 2층으로 투조(透彫)하였으며 가장자리는 연주문(聯珠紋)이고 안쪽에는 타원형을 이룬 이룡(螭龍)이 엎드려 있다. 고개를 쳐든 이룡은 평평한 입, 처들린 코, 둥그런 눈, 곧추 세운 눈썹, 권운문(卷雲紋) 귀를 가졌으며 정수리 머리털과 수염은 뒤로 나부낀다. 몸통은 가늘고 길며 앞다리는 유연하게 굽혔고 뒷다리 중 하나는 굽히고 하나는 곧게 폈다. 다리 관절은 모두 권운문으로 장식하고 척추는 굽은 몸통에 선을 그어 나타냈다. 발목 가장자리부터 발바닥까지는 짧고 가는 음각선을 새겼고 꼬리는 위로 굽었는데 사이에는 관지화(串枝花)가 있다.

136

매화단형옥편(梅花團形玉片)

백옥(白玉) | 명(明)
지름 5.1cm 두께 0.7cm
1978년 서안시(西安市) 수집

Roundish Jade Board with Plum Blossom Patterns

White jade | Ming Dynasty
D 5.1cm T 0.7cm
Collected in Xi'an in 1978

　동글납작한 옥패(玉牌)로 여러 층으로 투조(透彫)하였으며 측면에서 보면 접시 모양이다. 한가운데는 오판매화(五瓣梅花)가 있고 바깥쪽 원환형(圓環形) 꽃가지에는 작은 매화 다섯 송이가 안쪽 꽃잎과 대응되게 있다. 매화 사이로 관지화(串枝花)가 안쪽에서 밖으로 비스듬히 뻗어 나왔는데 양쪽으로 갈라진 꽃잎은 인접한 작은 매화와 연결되었다. 매화 꽃술은 모두 나팔 모양이며 가운데는 보석을 상감할 구멍이 있다.

137

남옥인(男玉人)

청옥(靑玉) | 송(宋)
높이 3.4cm 너비 2cm 두께 0.6cm
1989년 서안시 미앙구 육촌보향 서가채(西安市 未央區 六村堡鄉 徐家寨) 출토

Jade Man

Green jade | Song Dynasty
H 3.4cm W 2cm T 0.6cm
Excavated from Xujiazhai Village in Liucunbu, Weiyang District, Xi'an in 1989

　옥인은 몸통이 납작하고 부조(浮彫)하였다. 관을 쓰고 교령(交領)의 소매가 넓은 장포(長袍)를 입고 띠를 매었다. 두 손을 가슴 앞에서 포개어 넓은 소매가 배 앞으로 흘러내렸고 가부좌를 하고 앉아 있다. 초승달 같은 눈썹, 가느다란 눈, 파 줄기 모양의 작은 코, 앵두 입을 가지고 있는데 오관(五官)은 모두 음각(陰刻)하였다. 가늘고 짧은 직선 또는 곡선으로 표현한 옷주름은 자연스럽고 유창하다. 옷차림새와 관모는 송대(宋代)에 유행한 것으로 송대 장택단(張擇端)의 〈청명상하도(淸明上河圖)〉와 조길(趙佶)의 〈청금도(聽琴圖)〉에서 모두 이러한 차림새를 찾아볼 수 있다. 등이 평평한 것으로 보아 다른 기물에 상감했던 장식품으로 보인다. 파묻혔던 관계로 앞면 대부분은 석회화되었다.

138

옥응수(玉鷹首)

청옥(青玉) | 당(唐)
길이 11cm 너비 6cm 두께 5cm
1979년 서안시(西安市) 당 대명궁(大明宮) 유적지 출토

Jade Hawk Head

Green jade | Tang Dynasty
L 11cm W 6cm T 5cm
Excavated from Daminggong Relic(Tang Dynasty), Xi'an in 1979

원조(圓彫)한 매 머리로 굵은 눈썹을 찌푸리고 두 눈은 멀리 바라보며 콧방울은 살짝 볼록하고 입은 크며 부리는 갈고리 같다. 입 양쪽에는 대롱 모양 도구로 뚫은 구멍과 쐐기 모양 홈이 대응되게 있어 마치 부리를 조금 벌린 듯하다. 볼은 편사도(偏斜刀)로 새기고 그 뒤로 음각(陰刻) 직선과 권운문(卷雲紋)으로 목의 깃털을 나타냈다. 머리 뒷부분은 방형(方形)으로 위쪽에는 동그란 구멍 다섯 개가 나 있고 뒤쪽에는 대롱 모양 도구로 뚫은 큰 구멍이 있다. 위쪽 뒷부분의 구멍 하나와 뒤쪽 큰 구멍은 서로 통하는데 이 구멍들은 옥응수를 끈채 또는 기타 기물에 고정시키는 데 사용된 것으로 추정된다. 이 옥응수는 직육면체 옥을 간단하게 가공하여 윤곽을 만든 다음 다시 음각선으로 눈, 부리, 깃털 등 세부를 새긴 것으로 선이 대범하고 힘 있다. 회전 숫돌을 깊게 사용하여 가운데가 굵고 곧으며 끝부분이 비교적 가늘다. 도법(刀法)이 힘차고 표현기법이 간단하고 생동감이 있다.

139

옥룡수(玉龍首)

청옥(青玉) | 당(唐)
길이 18cm 너비 7.4cm 높이 10cm
1980년 서안시 안탑구(西安市 雁塔區) 곡강지(曲江池) 당 부용원(芙蓉園) 유적지 출토

Jade Dragon Head

Green jade | Tang Dynasty
L 18cm W 7.4cm H 10cm
Excavated from Furongyuan Relic in Qujiangchi, Yanta District, Xi'an in 1980

용머리는 직육면체에 가깝다. 두 눈은 '臣(신)'자 모양이고 긴 눈썹은 꼬리가 위로 말렸으며 코는 넓고 이빨은 넓은 입 밖에 드러났으며 뒤집힌 윗입술은 쳐들렸고 커다란 귀는 뒤로 젖혀졌다. 정수리는 평평한데 위에는 뒤로 젖혀진 기다란 뿔을 누조(鏤彫)하였다. 용머리 뒷부분과 밑부분은 가지런한데 가운데에 직사각형에 가까운 홈이 있다. 홈 아래쪽과 안쪽 한 면은 반원 모양이고 다른 두 면은 가지런하다. 홈 안쪽 톱자국과 채 파내지 않은 속이 있는 것으로 보아 먼저 가로세로 양 방향에서 대롱 모양 도구로 구멍을 뚫은 후 다시 가운데 부분을 잘라낸 듯하다. 용머리 쌍뿔 사이에 있는 구멍은 홈과 서로 통한다. 용머리에서 입, 이빨, 눈썹, 입술 등 부위는 비교적 굵은 음각선으로, 수염, 눈썹 털 등은 가는 음각선으로 새겼다. 회전 숫돌로 연마한 특징이 뚜렷한데 도법(刀法)이 강건하고 힘 있으며 조형이 사실적이고 형상이 용맹스러워 조각성이 뛰어나다. 이 옥룡수는 당대(唐代) 부용원(芙蓉園) 유적지에서 출토된 것으로 홈 형태와 구멍 부위로 보아 어용(御用) 유람선의 상감 옥 장식이다. 이빨 사이, 입술 가장자리, 눈구멍, 귓바퀴 등에 주사(朱砂)가 남아 있는데 원래 이런 부위를 주사로 장식하였음을 알 수 있다.

장옥

葬玉

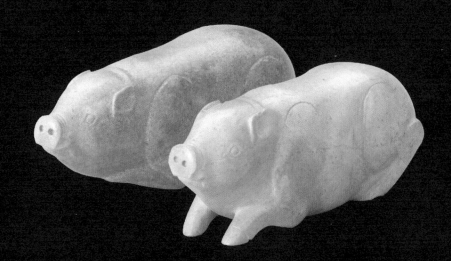

장옥(葬玉)은 시신을 납관할 때 쓰는 옥으로 죽은 자의 몸이나 관 안에 놓아 시신과 함께 묻는 부장품이다. 함옥(琀玉), 반옥(飯玉), 명목(瞑目), 이(珥) 등 부장품이 모두 장옥에 속한다. 고대 장례에서 옥을 사용한 이유는 다음과 같다. 우선 옥기(玉器)가 현세에서 특권의 상징이므로 저승에서도 마찬가지일 것이라고 생각했다. 따라서 고인이 저승에서도 생전의 지위를 누릴 수 있도록 옥기를 무덤에 묻었다. 시신을 처리할 때 사용했던 진(瑱), 비색(鼻塞) 등 구규옥(九竅玉)이 모두 이에 속한다. 후세 사람들이 사용했던 악돈(握豚) 및 유명한 금루옥의(金縷玉衣)도 단순한 부장품에서 영혼불멸 사상의 출현과 함께 점차 장례의식으로 발전하였다. 그 후 통치자들은 이런 사상과 방법을 제도로 규정하였다. 다음으로 고대에는 죽은 자의 몸이나 관 안에 옥을 놓으면 시신의 부패를 방지할 수 있다고 여겼다. 옥석재료는 안정적인 화학성질로 인해 시간이 지나도 쉽게 부식되지 않는다. 고대 사람들은 옥이 부식되지 않기 때문에 시신도 부패하지 않을 것이라고 생각한 것이다. 『포박자(抱樸子)』에서도 "구규(九竅)에 금옥(金玉)을 넣으면 죽은 자가 부패하지 않는다"라는 기록이 있다. 이러한 이유로 장례에서 옥을 사용하는 기풍이 성행하였다. 중국 고대 고분에서 세계적으로 보기 드물게 수많은 옥기가 출토된 원인도 여기에 있다.

Burial jade are jade articles that are put on the body of the dead or inside the coffin, which is buried together with the corpse. The burial jade include orifice plug, etc. The ancient people use jade ware in burial ceremonies mainly for two reasons. Firstly, when ancient people buried the dead, they put on jade as stoppers in the nine apertures of the body, placed jade pigs in the hands of the dead, put on jade garment with gold thread for the dead. All this developed from the simply belief that the soul never dies to the later burial ceremony. The ancients believed that since jade served as the symbol of power and authority in the world, it would remain the same in the underworld. In order to make sure that the dead will remain their superior status after death, they did the best that they could bury the precious jade articles together with the dead people in the tomb. This belief and practice were later included into the institution systems. Secondly, the ancients believed that with jade articles placed on and in the body of the dead, as well as inside the coffin, the corpse would never decay. The chemical nature of jade is very stable, and will not easily molder even after thousands of years. This is natural attribute of jade. But people in the ancient times believed that if the jade does not decay, it would prevent the body from decaying as well. As is said in the book Bao-pu-zi "With gold and jade in the nine apertures in the body, the dead would never decay." Thus comes the prevalence of burial jade. This is a major reason for the uniquely large amount of jade articles excavated in the ancient tombs in China.

옥선(玉蟬)

옥선은 함옥(琀玉)의 일종이다. 죽은 자의 입에 물건을 물리는 풍습은 석기시대까지 거슬러 올라갈 수 있으며 상·주(商·周) 이래로 줄곧 유지되었다. 『주례』「천관(天官)」「천부(天府)」에는 "대상(大喪)에는 옥을 물린다"라는 기록이 있는데 이 중 대상은 황제의 장례를 가리킨다. 지체와 신분에 따라 물리는 물건도 서로 달랐는데 황제가 붕(崩)하면 옥을 물리고, 나머지 사람들의 경우 벽(璧), 구슬, 모(瑁), 쌀, 조개 등을 물렸다.

함옥을 매미 모양으로 만드는 풍습은 서주(西周)시기에 시작된 후 진·한(秦·漢)과 위·진·남북조(魏·晉·南北朝)시대에 유행하였다. 매미는 번데기로 변하여 땅 밑을 뚫고 들어갈 수 있을 뿐만 아니라 허물을 벗고 나무 위로 날아오를 수 있으므로 부활의 능력이 있다고 하여 고대에는 매미를 신충(神蟲)이라고 여겼다. 그리하여 사람들은 죽은 자의 입에 옥매미를 물려 매미처럼 부활하길 소망하였다.

Jade cicada is a kind of jade plug. The practice of placing things in the mouth of the dead can be traced back to the Stone Ages. Such a practice has been preserved from Shang and Zhou Dynasties. According to Zhou Rites "cicada jade was placed in the mouths of the demised emperors". If the emperor demised, jade was placed in his mouth, while people of other identities have Bi, pearls, Mao, rice, or shell put in their mouths after death. The objects that are placed in the mouths differ according to the identity and status of the dead.

The custom of making the jade plug in the shape of a cicada originated from West Zhou Dynasty, and prevailed in Qin, Han, Southern and Northern Dynasties. The ancient people believed cicada could transform into the ground, and the power of renascence after exuviations, cicada was regarded as a divine insect. People thus put jade cicada in the mouth of the dead, hoping they can revive just like cicadas do.

140

옥선(玉蟬)

청백옥(青白玉) | 진(秦)
길이 4.9cm 너비 2.3cm 두께 1cm
1969년 서안시 안탑구 북지두촌(西安市 雁塔區 北池頭村) 진묘(秦墓) 출토

Jade Cicada

Green and white jade | Qin Dynasty
L 4.9cm W 2.3cm T 1cm
Excavated from Qin Tomb at Beichitou Village in Yanta District, Xi'an in 1969

긴 타원형으로 머리와 꼬리가 모두 뾰족하다. 두 눈은 양측에 볼록하게 조각하였고 눈 사이에는 거치문(鋸齒紋)을 장식하여 목을 나타냈다. 등에는 편사도(偏斜刀)로 오목하게 새긴 삼각형이 있고 그 뒤로 곧은 철릉(凸稜)이 나 있다. 양옆의 경사지고 평평한 부분은 날개이고 그 위에 'S'형 연운문(連雲紋)을 음각하여 혈맥을 나타냈으며 배는 둥글고 볼록하다. 옥은 푸른색 가운데 노란빛이 서려 있으며 온윤(溫潤)하고도 섬세하다. 형상이 간단하고 조형이 생동한데 대체적으로 윤곽을 조각한 다음 목, 날개 위 혈맥을 가는 선으로 음각하여 매미의 몸통, 머리, 날개의 질감을 표현하였다.

141

옥선(玉蟬)

청백옥(靑白玉) | 한(漢)
길이 5.2cm 너비 2.7cm 두께 0.7cm
1995년 서안시(西安市) 수집

Jade Cicada

Green and white jade | Han Dynasty
L 5.2cm W 2.7cm T 0.7cm
Collected in Xi'an in 1995

　매미의 머리는 살짝 호형(弧形)을 이루며 볼록한 두 눈은 좌우 양쪽에 놓였다. 등에는 가운데로 모은 두 날개를 조각하였다. 배 양측에는 각각 비스듬한 곡선으로 배의 윤곽을, 윗배 가운데는 머리에 닿은 방사상(放射狀) 호선(弧線)으로 울림통을, 아랫배에는 호형 횡문(橫紋) 일곱 줄로 신축기능을 가진 마디를 나타내었다. 매미는 조형이 사실적이고 생동감이 있으며 칼 댄 곳마다 예리함이 엿보이며 선이 유창하고 힘 있는 것이 전형적인 서한(西漢) 말기 옥선 공예 특징을 띠었다. 또한 연마기술이 뛰어난데 특히 파형(坡形) 선이 매끈하고 균열이 없다. 몸통은 매우 깔끔하고 윤이 나며 유리질감이 강하다.

옥저(玉豬)

악옥(握玉)의 일종으로 옥돼지는 부장품에 속한다. 죽은 자의 손에 놓는 옥기로 상 · 주대(商 · 周代)에는 조개나 황형(璜形) 옥 조각 등이 있었다. 동한(東漢) 초기부터는 시신의 양손에 옥돼지를 놓는 풍습이 성행하였다. 돼지는 농업경제 발전을 상징하며 생활의 안정과 풍족함을 의미하기도 한다. 옥돼지를 악옥으로 쓰는 목적은 첫째, 재부를 상징하고, 둘째, 죽은 자에게 음식을 제공함을 뜻한다.

Jade pig is a kind of holding jade, which belong to burial articles. Jade Holdings are jade articles placed in the hands of the dead. During the Shang and Zhou Dynasties, jade holdings are in the form of shells and plaques. Since early East Han Dynasty, the practice of grasping two jade pigs, each in one hand, became popular. Pigs are the symbol of agricultural and economical development, representing the stability and richness of life. Using jade pigs as jade holdings have two significances: one is to symbolize wealth, another is to offer food to the deceased.

142
옥저(玉豬)

장석암(長石岩) | 서한(西漢)
길이 13.5cm 높이 5cm
1989년 서안시 안탑구 산문구촌(西安市 雁塔區 山門口村) 한묘(漢墓) 출토

Jade Pig

Feldspar | West Han Dynasty
L 13.5cm H 5cm
Excavated from the Han Tomb at Shanmenkou Village in Yanta District, Xi'an in 1989

원조(圓彫)한 옥돼지 한 쌍으로 조형이 같고 자태도 비슷하다. 코는 평평하고 콧구멍은 막대기 모양 도구로 작은 구멍을 뚫어 나타내었으며 콧마루에는 현문(弦紋) 세 줄을 새기고 코 아래에는 비스듬한 호선(弧線) 한 줄을 그어 미소를 띤 듯한 입을 표현했다. 눈은 올리브 모양인데 압지은기법(壓地隱起法)으로 조각하여 볼록하게 나옴으로써 특별히 생기 있어 보인다. 귀는 비대칭으로 교차된 호선 두 줄로 이루어졌고 볼록하게 튀어나온 짧은 꼬리는 엉덩이에 붙었다. 턱, 목, 어깨, 허벅지에는 간단한 호선 몇 줄을 그어 튼실한 몸을 표현하였다. 한 마리는 앞다리로 땅을 짚고 다른 한 마리는 앞다리를 하나는 앞으로 뻗고 하나는 굽혔으며 둘 다 뒷다리는 힘껏 박차고 일어나는 모습으로 먹이를 덮치려는 것 같다. 조각기법이 같고 형태가 사실적이며 몸통이 토실토실하고 생동감이 있으며 사랑스럽다. 돼지가 몸을 일으키려는 찰나의 동작을 세부적으로 묘사하였는데 표현기법이 빼어난 것이 보기 드문 한대(漢代) 예술 공예품이다.

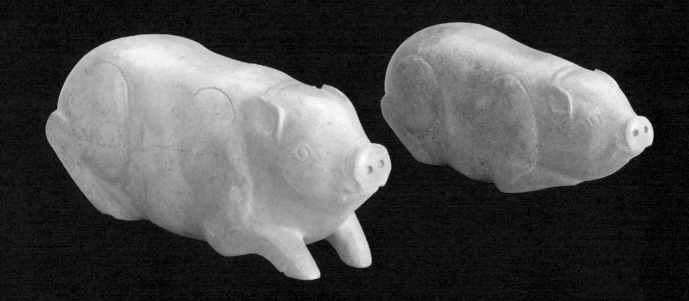

143

옥저(玉豬)

청옥(靑玉) | 한(漢)
길이 11.8cm 너비 2.6cm 높이 3cm
1987년 서안시 연호구(西安市 蓮湖區) 홍묘파(紅廟坡) 한묘(漢墓) 출토

Jade Pig

Green jade | Han Dynasty
L 11.8cm W 2.6cm H 3cm
Excavated from Han Tomb at Hongmiaopo in Lianhu District, Xi'an in 1987

　돼지는 엎드린 모양으로 눈, 귀, 사지 및 각 부위 윤곽은 모두 힘 있는 편사도법(偏斜刀法)으로 새겼으며 배 아래, 입 그리고 꼬리는 옥 모양에 따라 평면으로 조각하였다. 도법은 힘 있고 대범하며 재주를 남김없이 발휘하여 몇 안 되는 칼질로 돼지의 형상을 생동감 있게 표현하였다. 이런 기법을 '한팔도(漢八刀)'라 한다.

144

옥저(玉豬)

청옥(靑玉) | 한(漢)
길이 11.5cm 너비 4.4cm 두께 0.7cm
2002년 서안시 장안현 모파촌(西安市 長安縣 茅坡村) 출토

Jade Pig

Green jade | Han Dynasty
L 11.5cm W 4.4cm T 0.7cm
Excavated from Maopo Village in Chang'an County, Xi'an in 2002

　엎드린 돼지 모양으로 납작하며 양면(兩面) 조각하였다. 눈은 능형(菱形)이고 돌출된 주둥이에는 양쪽으로 각기 뾰족하고 기다란 이빨이 뻗어 나왔다. 가늘고 긴 두 귀는 뒤로 젖혀졌고 척추의 곧추선 갈기는 앞으로 뻗었으며 짧은 꼬리는 살짝 말렸다. 도법(刀法)이 간단한데 가는 선으로 돼지의 입, 눈, 털, 사지를 음각(陰刻)하였다. 휴식 중에도 기민하게 살피는 돼지의 형상을 생동감 있게 표현하였다.

　돼지는 인류가 가장 일찍 길들인 동물 가운데 하나이다. 선사 시대 전설 속 3황5제 시대부터 돼지는 재부의 상징으로 여겨졌다. 제사 제물과 무덤 속 부장품으로 다량 사용되었으며 옥기 제재로서의 돼지는 서주(西周)와 한대(漢代)에 비교적 많이 보인다. 상·주(商·周) 및 그전 시대 통치계급은 실제 돼지를 순장(殉葬)하였고 한대에는 일반적으로 옥돼지를 배장(陪葬)하였다. 제물로 쓰는 습속은 현재까지 지속되고 있다.

145

활석저(滑石豬)

활석 | 당(唐)
길이 5cm 너비 1.6cm 높이 1.8cm
1988년 서안시 장안현 모파촌(西安市 長安縣 茅坡村) 당묘(唐墓) 출토

Talcum Pig

Talcum | Tang Dynasty
L 5cm W 1.6cm H 1.8cm
Excavated from Tang Tomb at Maopo Village in Chang'an County, Xi'an in 1988

　돼지는 커다란 머리에 넓은 입, 처들린 코를 가졌다. 목과 등에는 이빨 모양 갈기가 있고 몸통은 살찌고 짧으며 다리는 굵고 긴데 땅을 박차고 뛰어오르는 듯하다. 조형이 과장되고 생동감이 있으며 독특하고 재밌는데 멧돼지가 달릴 때의 힘찬 자세를 형상적으로 묘사하였다.

기구 및 진열용 옥기

器具 玉器

실용성이 있는 옥제(玉製) 기구(器具)들은 상대(商代)에 최초로 나타났는데 주로 구(臼), 반(盤) 및 궤(簋) 등이며 이들은 대부분 사용했던 흔적이 남아 있다. 진 · 한(秦 · 漢) 이후부터 배(杯), 완(盌), 존(尊), 베개 등 실용성 및 장식성을 갖춘 옥제 기구들이 점차 많아졌다. 그중 진열용 예술품은 대부분 원조(圓彫)기법으로 제작한 인물, 동물, 화목(花木) 문양의 옥기이고 대부분 거의 모두 착용용 구멍이 없다. 상 · 주(商 · 周)에서 진 · 한까지 옥조(玉鳥), 옥복수(玉伏獸), 옥토(玉兎), 옥마(玉馬) 등이 이런 형태이다. 당대(唐代) 이후부터는 진열용 옥기가 점차 늘어났으며 조수화목(鳥獸花木) 형태의 작품들은 조형이 새롭고 독특하다. 기법으로는 최대한 교작[巧作=초색(俏色), 옥석의 각종 형태, 색상, 질적인 구조 등 변하지 않는 요소를 이용하여 마치 자연적으로 형태를 형성한 것처럼 옥기를 제작하는 작업] 기술을 사용함으로써 생동감이 있을 뿐만 아니라 색상이 화려하고 자연스러웠다.

Jade utensils for practical use appears early in Shang Dynasty, mainly mortars, plates, and Gui(food vessels), most of which show evidences of being used. Jade utensils multiplied after Qin and Han Dynasties. The common items are cups, bowls, wine vessels and pillows etc. They serve as both utility ware and extravagant artworks for inner decoration. The specified display ornaments are mainly of human characters, animals, flowers and trees motifs, most of which have mo bore for tying and fixation. The jade birds, jade crouching beasts, jade rabbits, jade horses and so on from the Shang, Zhou to Qin, Han Periods all belong to this. The number of jade displays gradually increased after Tang Dynasty. Many artworks with the motif of bird, beast, flowers and trees are not only novel and exquisite in design, but also adopt the Qiao technique, which made the work vivid and without factitiousness.

옥인(玉印)

옥은 중국 고대 도장재료 중의 하나이다. 옥인은 전국(戰國)시대부터 사용되기 시작하여 양한(兩漢)시대에 전성기를 맞았다. 중국의 관인(官印) 중 옥인은 제후(帝后)의 전용품이었다. 그중 진·한대(秦·漢代)의 제왕은 전부 백옥(白玉)인 이호뉴(螭虎鈕) 옥새 여섯 개를 사용하였다. 이(螭, 교룡)는 『설문(說文)』에서 '용과 비슷한 황색'의 신수(神獸)라고 해석하였는데 황제는 이의 용맹함으로 황제의 권위를 드러내었다. 백관들은 옥을 사용할 수 없었고 왕, 후(侯), 태자, 승상, 태위 및 중앙정부에 협력한 소수민족 수녀는 모두 구뉴(龜鈕), 타뉴(駝鈕) 등 금인(金印)을 사용하고, 이천석(二千石), 중이천석(中二千石) 고관들은 구뉴 은인(銀印), 천석(千石)부터 이백석(二百石)까지 관리는 비뉴(鼻鈕) 동인(銅印)을 사용했다. 이러한 구분은 위·진대(魏·晉代)부터 수·당대(隋·唐代)까지 큰 변화가 없었고 송대(宋代)에 이르러 백관들은 일률적으로 구리로 만든 도장을 사용하였다. 금·원대(金·元代)에 지속적으로 발전하였고 명대(明代)는 송·원(宋·元)의 제도를 본받아 제왕의 옥새를 대부분 옥으로 만들었고 용뉴(龍鈕)로 황제의 숭고한 지위를 나타냈다. 청대(淸代)도 이를 따랐다.

이와 비교해 민간의 사인(私印)은 수천 년간 재료나 손잡이 양식의 제한을 받지 않았고 품계의 구분 또한 없었다. 진·한대의 손잡이 양식에는 거북이, 코, 옛날 돈, 사슴, 개구리, 반룡(盤龍) 등이 있었다. 인문(印文)의 선은 대부분 가늘면서도 힘이 있는 버들잎 모양이며 필획구조는 방(方)과 원(圓)이 조화를 이루었다. 문자는 세로로 긴 직사각형 모양이며 동시에 조충서(鳥蟲書)와 초형인(肖形印)이 나타났다. 조충서는 한대 무전(繆篆)을 기초로 발전한 것으로 새, 곤충, 물고기, 용 등의 형상을 본떠 만들었다. 초형인은 형상을 도형화한 것으로 간결하고 소박하며 짙은 운치가 있다. 상서로운 동물을 도형화해 영생과 길함을 추구하는 한대 사람들의 바람을 반영하였다. 위·진·남북조(魏·晉·南北朝)시대에는 한대 풍격을 기초로 호방함과 무게감을 추구하였는데 손잡이인 거북이의 네 다리는 똑바로 선 자세를 취하고 있으며 전체적으로 더욱 두꺼워졌다. 수·당대 비뉴(鼻鈕)는 점차 높아지고 원형 구멍이 길어졌으며, 구멍이 없는 인뉴(印鈕)도 나타났다.

Jade is one of the materials used in ancient China to make royal and official seals. Jade seals started in the Warring States Period and reached the height of popularity in West and East Han Dynasties. In the system of ancient Chines official seals, jade seals could only be used by the emperors and queens. The emperors in the Qin and Han Dynasties each had six royal seals. All of the seals are in the shape of Chi tiger made in white jade. According to the book Shuo Wen, Chi is a divine animal that is yellow in color and resembles a dragon. Emperors using such seal hoped the valiancy of Chi can subdue all the liegemen in the court. The officials were not allowed to possess jade seals. Infantes, dukes, princes, prime ministers and Tai-wei(senior military officials) as well as the minority leaders that have subdued and pledged allegiance to the emperor could use gold seals with the knob in the shape of tortoise or camel. The owner of the seal had a monthly salary of two thousand Shi(unit of dry measure for grains). Other senior officials use silver seal with tortoise shaped knob. Officials with a salary of one thousand Shi and two hundred Shi use copper seal with nose shaped knob. Such a condition remained relatively unchanged in Wei, Jin and even to Sui, Tang Dynasties. During Song Dynasty, all the official seals were made of copper, and such practice continued in Jin and Yuan Dynasties. Government in the Ming Dynasty inherited the seal system used in Song and Yuan Dynasties, and emperors use jade seal with dragon knob, symbolizing prominent status. Qing Dynasty followed such practice.

However, during the past thousands of years, private seals were not restricted by the material of the seal, the pattern of the knob, and order of the ranks. The knob of the jade seal in Qin and Han Dynasty is in the shape of tortoise, nose, ancient coin, deer, frog, coiled dragon and so on. The strokes of the seal inscriptions usually resemble willow leaves, which are slender and yet not fragile. The seal is in the combination of square and round, with the round knob being contained in the square base. The Chinese characters in the seal are slender rectangular formed. At the men time, bird, insect, and animal patterns also appeared in the seal bottom to beatify the inscriptions of squiggled Chines characters. Adding animal patterns into the impression of the seal is both meaningful and appealing. Such image seal are mainly in the motif of rare birds and auspicious beasts, which reflect people's desire for good fortune and longevity. The seal in Wei, Jin, Southern and Northern Dynasties basically maintained the style in Han Dynasty, only with stronger and heavier inclinations. The tortoise shaped seal knob stood on four legs, the base of the seal got thicker. By Sui and Tang Dynasties, the seal knob gradually got taller, with bigger bores. Some seal knobs have no bores.

146

옥인(玉印)

백옥(白玉) | 진(秦)
변(邊)길이 1.8cm 높이 0.9cm
서안시(西安市) 수집

Jade Seal

White jade | Qin Dynasty
Side L 1.8cm H 0.9cm
Collected in Xi'an

단면(單面) 인으로 인배(印背)는 언덕을 이루고 복두뉴(覆斗鈕)에는 구멍이 있으며 인면(印面)에는 '戌日月(술일월)'이 전서체로 음각(陰刻)되어 있다.

147

옥인(玉印)

백옥(白玉) | 한(漢)
변(邊)길이 1.4cm 높이 1.3cm
서안시 미앙구 장천호촌(西安市 未央區 張千戶村) 출토

Jade Seal

White jade | Han Dynasty
Side L 1.4cm H 1.3cm
Excavated from Zhangqianhu Village in Weiyang District, Xi'an

단면(單面) 인으로 인배(印背)는 평평하다. 와형뉴(瓦形鈕)에는 구멍이 있고 정사각형 인면(印面)에는 '陳樂成(진락성)'이 전각(篆刻)되어 있다.

148

옥인(玉印)

청백옥(青白玉) | 한(漢)
변(邊)길이 1.5cm 높이 1.3cm
서안시(西安市) 수집

Jade Seal

Green and white jade | Han Dynasty
Side L 1.5cm H 1.3cm
Collected in Xi'an

단면(單面) 인으로 인배(印背)는 언덕을 이룬다. 단형뉴(壇形鈕)에는 마주하여 뚫은 구멍이 있고 정사각형 인면(印面)에는 '宋桁印(송항인)'이 전서체로 음각되어 있으며 사인(私印)이다.

149

옥인(玉印)

백옥(白玉) | 한(漢)
변(邊)길이 1.7cm 높이 1.4cm
서안시(西安市) 수집

Jade Seal

White jade | Han Dynasty
Side L 1.7cm H 1.4cm
Collected in Xi'an

단면(單面) 인으로 인배(印背)는 언덕을 이룬다. 단형뉴(壇形鈕)에는 마주하여 뚫은 구멍이 있고 벽에는 구연운문(鉤連雲紋)이 음각(陰刻)되어 있다. 정사각형 인면(印面)에는 '姚維(요유)'가 전서체로 음각되어 있으며 사인(私印)이다.

수정인(水晶印)

수정 | 서한(西漢)
변(邊)길이 2.1cm 높이 1.5cm
1992년 서안시 미앙구 범남촌(西安市 未央區 範南村) 출토

Crystal Seal

Crystal | West Han Dynasty
Side L 2.1cm H 1.5cm
Excavated from Fannan Village in Weiyang District, Xi'an in 1992

단면(單面) 인으로 인배(印背)는 언덕 모양이다. 복두형뉴(覆斗形鈕)에는 구멍이 있고 수정 속에는 운기문(雲氣紋)이 있으며 인면(印面)에는 '陳請士(진청사)'가 전각 (篆刻)되어 있다.

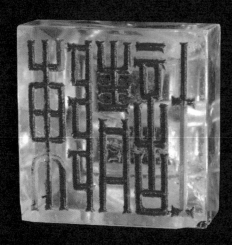

옥인(玉印)

청옥(靑玉) | 서한(西漢)
변(邊)길이 2.1cm 높이 1.3cm
1992년 서안시 미앙구 범남촌(西安市 未央區 範南村) 출토

Jade Seal

Green jade | West Han Dynasty
Side L 2.1cm H 1.3cm
Excavated from Fannan Village in Weiyang District, Xi'an in 1992

단면(單面) 인으로 인배(印背)는 언덕 모양이고 복두형뉴(覆斗形鈕)에는 구멍이 있으며 인면(印面)에는 '陳請士(진청사)'가 전각(篆刻)되어 있다.

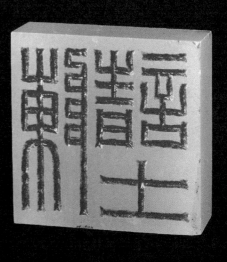

옥인(玉印)

녹송석(綠松石) | 진(晉)
변(邊)길이 1.5cm 높이 1.7cm
서안시(西安市) 수집

Jade Seal

Turquoise | Jin Dynasty
Side L 1.5cm H 1.7cm
Collected in Xi'an

단면(單面) 인으로 인배(印背)는 평평하며 수형뉴
(獸形鈕)이다. 짐승 머리는 살짝 기울었고 땅에 끌리
는 꼬리는 굽었으며 솟구쳐 오르는 자세를 취하였다.
인면(印面)에는 쌍봉문(雙鳳紋)을 음각(陰刻)하였다.
큰 봉황은 기다란 부리에 높은 관, 긴 꽁지가 있고 날
개를 펼쳤으며 작은 봉황은 뒤돌아보고 있으며 초형
인(肖形印)이다.

153

고족배(高足杯)

청옥(靑玉) | 진(秦)
높이 14.5cm 입지름 6.4cm 발지름 4.5cm
1976년 9월 서안시 장안현 차류촌(西安市 長安縣 車劉村) 진 아방궁(阿房宮) 유적지 출토

Jade Cup with High Stem

Green jade | Qin Dynasty
H 14.5cm Mouth D 6.4cm Bottom D 4.5cm
Excavated from Efang'gong Relic(Qin Dynasty) in Cheliu Village, Chang'an County, Xi'an in sep. 1976

옥배(玉杯)는 잔과 받침을 붙여 만든 것으로 잔은 입
이 크고 바닥이 작은 통(桶) 모양이고 받침은 옥두(玉豆)
모양이다. 잔의 구연(口沿) 가장자리는 감지법(減地法)
을 사용하여 곽(廓)을 이루었다. 잔은 쌍구현문(雙鉤弦
紋) 세 줄에 의해 네 층으로 나뉘는데 구연과 가까운 데
로부터 사체엽(四蒂葉)과 연운문(連雲紋), 곡정구운문
(穀丁鉤雲紋), 기하형 구운문(鉤雲紋), 변형된 운두문(雲
頭紋) 순이다. 받침 윗부분에는 네모 테 다섯 개가 음각
되었고 테 속에는 각각 'S'자 모양의 간소화된 봉문(鳳
紋)이 교차되어 있다. 입과 밑굽의 문양은 이방연속(二
方連續)이고 배 문양은 점산식(點散式) 사방연속(四方連
續)이다. 잔의 곡정구운문은 압지은기법(壓地隱起法)과
음각선을 결합한 기법으로 먼저 곡정문을 조각하여 곡
정이 도드라지게 한 다음 음각선으로 운문을 그려 상하
좌우로 이어진 유기적인 사방연속이 되게 하였다. 잔의
기타 문양은 저부조하여 알차고 질박하다. 이 옥배 조형
은 대범하면서도 우아한데 색상은 푸른색 가운데 노란
빛이 서려 있어 아름답고 윤이 나며 연마와 광택처리가
매우 정세(精細)하게 되었다. 진(秦) 아방궁(阿房宮) 유적
지에서 출토된 것으로 커다란 기형과 비범한 예술풍격
으로 보아 어용(御用) 제품으로 추정된다.

저형침(豬形枕)

청옥(青玉) | 한(漢)
길이 24.2cm 너비 11cm 높이 9cm
1982년 서안시 미앙구(西安市 未央區) 한성(漢城) 유적지 안 서석왕촌(西席王村) 출토

Pig-shaped Pillow

Green jade | Han Dynasty
L 24.2cm W 11cm H 9cm
Excavated from Han Relic at Xiwang Village in Weiyang District, Xi'an in 1982

돼지 모양으로 직육면체에 가깝다. 돼지는 주둥이가 평평한
데 'U'형 곡선으로 입과 입술을 나타냈다. 주둥이 위쪽 살짝 기
울어진 사면은 코이며 작은 구멍 두 개를 뚫어 콧구멍으로 하였
다. 두 눈은 가는 선으로 작은 동그라미를 그려 표현하고 그 위쪽
에 두 귀를 볼록하게 조각하였으며 귓등은 살짝 오목하게 하였
다. 엉덩이 가운데는 송곳 모양 꼬리를 볼록하게 조각하였고 사
지 윤곽은 간단한 곡선 몇 개로 나타냈다. 윗부분은 평평하여 베
개로 쓸 수 있다. 이 저형침은 조형이 대범하고 간단하며 구상적
(具象的)이지만 다듬지 않은 것이 '한팔도(漢八刀)'의 완숙한 저
력을 엿볼 수 있다.

155

옥방분합(玉方粉盒)

청옥(靑玉) | 당(唐)
길이 4.5cm 너비 3.5cm 높이 1.4cm
1976년 서안시(西安市) 당대(唐代) 궁성(宮城) 유적지 안 출토

Jade Square Powder Box

Green jade | Tang Dynasty
L 4.5cm W 3.5cm H 1.4cm
Excavated from Tang Dynasty Royal Palace Relic in Xi'an in 1976

합(盒)은 모서리가 둥근 방형(方形)이고 뚜껑과 몸통은 자모구(子母扣)이며 한쪽에는 아래위로 환형(環形) 금단추가 상감되어 있고 맞은편에는 손잡이가 있다. 뚜껑과 몸통은 대칭되며 문양도 같은데 앞면 가장자리에는 합 모양과 같은 곽(廓)이 있으며 안쪽에는 감지법(減地法)으로 조각한 활짝 핀 연꽃이 있고 주위에는 가지와 잎이 둘려져 있다. 잎맥은 음각(陰刻)하였으며 꽃잎과 잎이 굽은 부분은 방사상(放射狀) 음각선으로 나타내었다. 곽 바깥쪽 경사진 측면에는 당초문(唐草紋)을 음각하였다. 손잡이는 함께 노니는 원앙 한 쌍을 누조(鏤彫)하였는데 원앙의 눈, 부리, 날개, 꽁지 등은 음각선으로 새겼다. 옥합은 척지각화(剔地刻花), 세선음각(細線陰刻), 누공(鏤空), 투조(透彫) 등 여러 기법을 사용하였으며 당대(唐代) 옥 기물 가운데 수작이다.

156

마노구(瑪瑙臼)

마노 | 당(唐)
높이 7.5cm 입지름 13.5cm 가장자리두께 0.7cm
1968년 서안시 신성구 한삼채(西安市 新城區 韓森寨) 출토

Agate Mortar

Agate | Tang Dynasty
H 7.5cm Mouth D 13.5cm Fringe T 0.7cm
Excavated from Hansenzhai in Xincheng District, Xi'an in 1968

짙은 갈색에 유백색 띠무늬가 섞인 마노(瑪瑙)로 만들어진 절구이다. 긴 타원형 모양으로 배는 살짝 볼록하고 아래로 점차 좁아진다. 안바닥은 매끄럽고 바깥바닥에는 낮은 권족(圈足)이 달렸다. 전체적으로 문양이 없지만 마노 자체의 무늬가 자연스럽게 어우러져 광채가 난다. 절구와 공이는 함께 사용되며 약을 빻는 용기이다.

마노는 옥수(玉髓)의 일종으로 다양한 색상에 띠무늬가 분포되었다. 무늬와 색상에 따라 대상마노(帶狀瑪瑙), 태문마노(苔紋瑪瑙), 벽옥마노(碧玉瑪瑙), 산호마노(珊瑚瑪瑙), 수담마노(水膽瑪瑙) 등으로 나뉜다. 마노란 이름은 불경에서 온 것으로 불교가 중국에 전해진 다음에야 경옥(瓊玉) 또는 적옥(赤玉)을 '마노'라 바꿔 부르게 되었다. 중국 서북(西北), 화북(華北), 동북(東北), 서남(西南), 화남(華南) 등 여러 지역에서 모두 생산된다.

사형향훈(獅形香薰)

활석(滑石) | 당(唐)
전체높이 12.8cm 사자높이 9cm
밑받침입지름 4.8cm 밑지름 7cm
1999년 서안시 안탑구(西安市 雁塔區) 삼인창(三印廠) 출토

Lion-shaped Jade Incense Burner

Talcum | Tang Dynasty
Total H 12.8cm Lion H 9cm
Base Mouth D 4.8cm Bottom D 7cm
Excavated from Third Printery factory in Yanta District, Xi'an in 1999

순백의 한백옥(漢白玉)으로 제작되었다. 사자는
입을 벌리고 주저앉은 모습이며 아랫배에서 입까지
구멍이 나 있다. 향훈은 평평한 바닥, 깊은 배, 모인
입을 가진 합(盒) 모양으로 앞면에 구멍이 뚫려 있다.
전체적으로 연마하여 섬세하고 반질반질하다.

158

쌍동자(雙童子)

장석암(長石岩) | 원(元)
높이 4.5cm 너비 3.2cm 두께 2.1cm
1965년 서안시 안탑구 하가촌(西安市 雁塔區 何家村) 출토

Two Boys

Feldspar | Yuan Dynasty
H 4.5cm W 3.2cm T 2.1cm
Excavated from Hejia Village Yanta District, Xi'an in 1965

삼각기둥 모양으로 뛰놀고 있는 동자 둘을 조각한 옥추(玉墜)이다. 하나는 반쯤 꿇은 상태에서 양손으로 연꽃가지를 잡고 왼쪽으로 머리를 기울였다. 다른 하나는 두 다리에 힘을 주어 아래 동자의 등을 타고 있는데 왼손으로는 아래 동자의 이마를 짚고 오른손으로는 연꽃가지를 잡아당기며 머리는 역시 왼쪽으로 기울였다. 둘 다 작은 입을 살짝 벌리고 눈을 살포시 감고서 유쾌하게 웃는 모습이다. 동그란 머리에는 이마에만 머리카락을 남겼고 소매가 넓은 마고자를 입었는데 머리카락과 옷주름은 가는 선으로 음각(陰刻)하였다. 연꽃가지에는 구멍이 여러 개 나 있는데 끈을 꿰어 매다는 데 쓰인다. 원조(圓彫)·투조(透彫) 기법으로 조각되었는데 전체적으로 칼놀림이 거칠어 선이 투박하고 고졸하며 가공기술이 간단하다. 동자의 장난기 많고 귀여우며 움직이기 좋아하는 천진하고 활발한 형상을 생생하게 묘사하였다.

167

159

옥기린(玉麒麟)

석영암옥(石英岩玉) | 원(元)
길이 4cm 최대너비 1.5cm 높이 4.8cm
1972년 서안시 미앙구 육촌보 서가채(西安市 未央區 六村堡 徐家寨) 출토

Jade Qilin(a divine beast in Chinese legends)

Quartzite jade | Yuan Dynasty
L 4cm Max W 1.5cm H 4.8cm
Excavated from Xujiazhai in Liucunbu, Weiyang District, Xi'an in 1972

기린은 엎드린 자세로 가슴을 펴고 고개를 들었으며 살짝 벌린 입 사이로
는 뾰족한 이빨이 드러나고 턱밑 수염은 가슴에 드리웠다. 눈은 두드러지고
코는 크며 귀는 뒤로 젖혀졌고 쌍뿔 끝부분은 위로 말렸으며 커다란 꼬리는
아래로 드리웠다. 활짝 편 양 날개 사이에는 홈이 있다. 기린은 몸집이 탄탄
하고 표정이 위엄 있고 사나운데 날리는 수염과 펼친 양 날개는 더욱 위풍
당당해 보인다. 투조(透彫), 철조(凸彫), 음각(陰刻), 편사도(偏斜刀) 등 여러
기법을 사용하였는데 입은 막대기 모양 도구로 누공(鏤空)하고, 눈, 귀, 뿔은
압지은기법(壓地隱起法)으로 새겼으며 뿔, 날개, 사지, 꼬리는 철조하였다.
가슴 앞 가로로 난 평행 호선(弧線), 볼과 날개 끝의 권운문(卷雲紋)은 편사
도로 조각하였고 수염, 날개, 다리, 발은 가는 선으로 음각하였다. 기법이 정
교하고 연마기술이 뛰어나 아름답고 윤이 난다. 이 기린은 위가 좁고 아래
가 넓으며 무게중심이 비교적 낮은 것이 진열품에 속한다.

160

옥벽사(玉辟邪)

마노(瑪瑙) | 명(明)
길이 7.4cm 너비 2.5cm 높이 2.7cm
1979년 서안시(西安市) 수집

Jade Bixie(talisman)

Agate | Ming Dynasty
L 7.4cm W 2.5cm H 2.7cm
Collected in Xi'an in 1979

벽사(辟邪)는 엎드린 자세로 커다란 머리 부분은 둥글고 옹골지다. 눈썹은 굵고 눈은 둥글며 커다란 입
은 살짝 벌리고 두 귀는 뒤로 젖혀졌으며 쌍뿔은 길고 양 날개는 등에 모았다. 사지는 굵고 힘 있으며 꼬리
는 왼쪽 뒷다리를 지나 배 옆으로 말렸고 표정은 진지하고 신중하다. 날개, 귀, 뿔은 목과 등에 붙이고 어깨
가 융기되고 가슴과 배는 수축된 것이 기세등등해 보인다. 마노로 조각되어 재질이 섬세하고 노란색 가운
데 갈색이 섞여 있어 동물 가죽 질감이 짙다. 뚜렷한 자연적 예술 형태를 지니고 있다.

벽사는 고대 전설 속 신수(神獸)로 머리에는 짧은 뿔이 있으며 사자와 비슷한데 날개가 있다. 옛사람들은
"불상사를 없애므로 벽사라 한다", "사발(射魃), 벽사는 모두 악귀를 쫓는다", "벽사는 귀신을 쫓을 수 있다"
고 하였다. 전하는 바에 의하면 뿔로 불성실한 사람을 찌른다고 한다. 한대(漢代) 이후 옥공예에서 많이 보
이며 길상(吉祥)을 바라는 데 사용된다.

이 옥벽사의 형태와 조각기법은 뚜렷한 한대 풍격을 띠었다. 그러나 음각한 가는 선의 흔적과 사용한 도
구는 명대(明代) 특징을 지니고 있어 한대 작품을 모방한 것으로 보인다.

161

누조인물노정(鏤彫人物爐頂)

백옥(白玉) | 명(明)
높이 3.6cm 너비 3.2cm 두께 1.9cm
1980년 서안시(西安市) 수집

Jade Stove Roof with Hollow-carved Figure

White jade | Ming Dynasty
H 3.6cm W 3.2cm T 1.9cm
Collected in Xi'an in 1980

노정(爐頂)은 위가 경사진 원기둥 모양이며 누공(鏤空)·투조(透彫)하였다. 바위에는 소나무와 영지가 자라고 있고 앞쪽에는 노인과 학이 서 있다. 노인은 정수리가 볼록하게 나왔고 넓은 이마에 기다란 귀, 긴 눈썹에 넓은 코를 가지고 있으며 흰 머리에 기다란 수염이 있다. 교령(交領)의 소매가 넓은 장포(長袍)를 입고 허리에 띠를 매었다. 학은 뒤돌아 노인을 바라보고 있는데 기다란 부리, 동그란 눈을 가지고 날개를 모으고 꽁지를 드리웠으며 기다란 다리는 앞뒤로 놓인 것이 걷고 있는 것 같다. 밑바닥에는 직사각형 돌기가 있으며 양옆에는 뚜껑을 고정시키는 데 쓰이는 구멍이 나 있다.

이 노정은 전통적인 길상(吉祥)문양을 하나로 어우러지게 누조하여 유기적이고 완벽한 기구(器具)를 이루었다. 누조가 정교하고 도법(刀法)이 완숙하며 형상이 생동하고 사실적이어서 다채롭다. 백옥을 조각하여 만든 것으로 재질이 섬세하고 온윤(溫潤)하여 아름답다.

162

누조룡형노정(鏤彫龍形爐頂)

백옥(白玉) | 명(明)
길이 4.5cm 너비 4cm 높이 3.6cm
1983년 서안시(西安市) 수집

Jade Stove Roof with the Pattern of Hollow-carved Dragon

White jade | Ming Dynasty
L 4.5cm W 4cm H 3.6cm
Collected in Xi'an in 1983

노정(爐頂)은 조금 네모지고 밑바닥은 평평하며 용을 제재로 누공(鏤空)하였다. 용의 몸통은 방형(方形)을 취하여 구불구불하고 얼굴은 중도(重刀)로 조각하였다. 둥근 눈은 돌출되었고 코는 위로 쳐들렸으며 콧구멍은 하늘을 향하였다. 코 양옆에는 수염이 나 있고 두 귀는 뒤로 젖혀졌으며 기다란 뿔은 굵고 탄탄하며 턱밑에는 화구(火球)가 있다. 온몸에 격자무늬를 음각(陰刻)하여 비늘을 표현하였다. 사지는 곧게 세웠으며 아랫다리에는 세로로 된 음각 직선이 있다. 밑바닥 가운데는 타원형 구멍이 있고 주변은 오목하게 새겼다.

'노정'은 향로 상단을 말하는 것으로 명대(明代) 고렴(高濂)이 쓴 『준생팔전(遵生八箋)』에서 당·송(唐·宋) 이래 옥기에 이 명칭이 있음을 적고 있다.

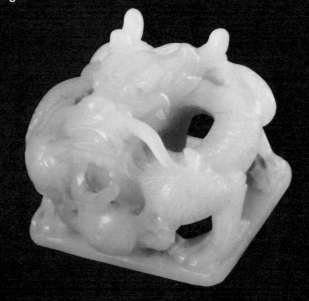

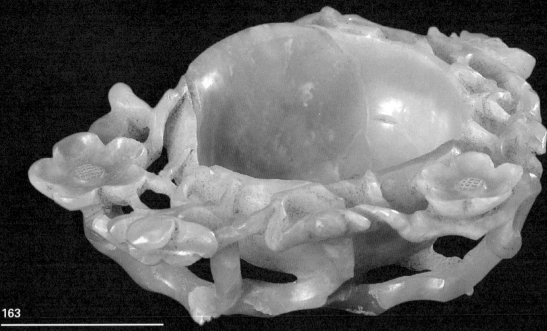

163

매화문배(梅花紋杯)

백옥(白玉) | 명(明)
길이 11cm 너비 8.5cm 높이 3.8cm 입지름 6cm
1980년 서안시(西安市) 수집

Jade Cup with Plum Blossoms

White jade | Ming Dynasty
L 11cm W 8.5cm H 3.8cm Mouth D 6cm
Collected in Xi'an in 1980

　낮고 둥그런 배(杯)로 구연(口沿)은 안쪽으로 모였으며
한쪽에 유(流)가 있다. 안바닥은 살짝 볼록한데 가운데는
음각(陰刻)한 호선(弧線) 세 개로 이루어진 삼각무늬가 있
고 주위에는 편사도(偏斜刀)로 조각한 꽃잎 네 개가 있다.
입 주위에는 매화 여섯 송이가 있는데 활짝 펼쳐진 꽃잎 가
운데에 망(網) 모양 꽃술이 있으며 금방 터질 것 같은 꽃망
울은 자연스럽게 말렸다. 누공(鏤空)한 꽃가지는 아래에서
위로 뻗어 배를 장식할뿐더러 받침과 손잡이 작용도 한다.
이 옥배는 매화를 제재로 하여 구상이 교묘하고 전체적인
구도가 합리적이며 꽃과 가지가 조화를 이루어 예술적·
실용적 가치가 모두 높다.

164

누공향낭(鏤空香囊)

백옥(白玉) | 청(淸)
높이 1.7cm 지름 6cm
1983년 서안시(西安市) 수집

Jade Incense Burner
with Hollow-carved Patterns

White jade | Qing Dynasty
H 1.7cm D 6cm
Collected in Xi'an in 1983

동글납작한 합(盒) 모양으로 누공(鏤空)·투조(透彫)하였고 아래위 조형과 문양은 똑같으며 자모구(子母扣)이다. 문양은 현문(弦紋)에 의해 안팎으로 나뉘는데 안쪽에는 연꽃 위에 놓인 보합(寶盒)이 있다. 보합 속에서는 영지(靈芝)가 뚜껑을 열고 뻗어 나왔으며 위쪽에는 봉황이 날고 있다. 봉황은 볏이 높고 기다란 입에 꽃을 물고서 날개를 펴고 뒤돌아보고 있다. 바깥쪽에는 관지화(串枝花)가 새겨져 있다.

향낭은 훈향(薰香) 옥기로 기형(器形)은 한대(漢代) 이전의 난방용 훈로(熏爐)에서 따온 것이다. 후에 옥으로 모방하였는데 난방용이 아닌 향료를 넣어두는 전문 용기로서 계화(桂花), 장미, 재스민 등 여러 가지 꽃을 꺾어 넣어두었다. 기형이 비교적 큰 것은 거실에 진열하거나 탁자에 놓아두고 비교적 작은 것은 허리에 매달 수 있다. 꽃향기가 자연스럽게 밖으로 퍼져 환경 및 심신 건강에도 유익하다. 훗날 인도의 전단향(旃檀香), 이란의 안식향(安息香), 베트남 북부의 용뇌향(龍腦香) 등 수입된 진귀한 향료로 향을 피우면 머리가 맑아지고 벽사하는 효능이 있었다. 이는 실용적이면서도 감상 가치가 있는 옥기 품종이다.

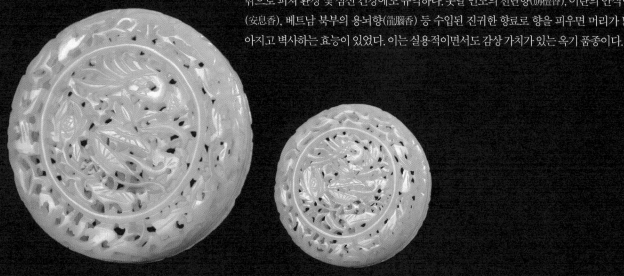

165

사련합(四聯盒)

청백옥(靑白玉) | 청(淸)
길이 7cm 너비 6cm 높이 4cm
1983년 서안시(西安市) 수집

Jade Quadripartite Boxes

Green and white jade | Qing Dynasty
L 7cm W 6cm H 4cm
Collected in Xi'an in 1983

합은 방형(方形)으로 네 모서리는 볼록하게 돌기되었으며 밑바닥에는 모양이 같은 권족(圈足)이 달려 있다. 덮개와 몸통으로 구성되었으며 자모구(子母扣)를 이룬다. 덮개 표면은 살짝 융기되고 네 모서리는 합 모양에 따라 여의문(如意紋)을 새긴 다음 직선으로 연결하였으며 안쪽에는 여의문과 변형된 여의권운문(如意卷雲紋)으로 채웠는데 양각(陽刻)함으로써 입체적 효과가 있다. 여의운문은 여의병단문(如意柄端紋)을 가리키는데 속칭 여의운두문(如意雲頭紋)으로 영지(靈芝) 또는 구름 모양이다. 여의는 법기(法器)의 일종으로 범어로 '아나률타'라 부른다. 송대(宋代) 오증(吳曾)이 쓴『능개재만록(能改齋漫錄)』「여의」,『석씨요람(釋氏要覽)』「도구(道具)」에 모두 기록되어 있다. 원래는 불교에서 강론할 때 쓰던 도구로 그 위에 경전을 기록하여 참고하였다. 근대에 이르러 여의는 길상(吉祥)을 뜻하게 되어 완상품(玩賞品)으로만 사용되고 여의문도 운문으로 변하여 여의운문이라 부르며 '여의고승(如意高升, 바라던 대로 높은 곳에 오름)'을 뜻하게 되었다.

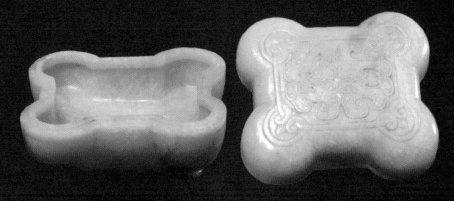

주금천연형비연호(酒金天然形鼻煙壺)

백옥(白玉) | 청(淸)
높이 7.1cm 최대배지름 4.5cm
1981년 서안시(西安市) 수집

Jade Snuff Box with Gold Inlaid

White jade | Qing Dynasty
H 7.1cm Max Ventral D 4.5cm
Collected in Xi'an in 1981

비연호(鼻煙壺, 코담배병)는 옥의 천연 형태에 따라 속을 모두 파내었다. 윗부분 작은 구멍을 입으로 하고 바닥에는 낮은 권족(圈足)이 달렸다. 표면에는 연이어진 산들을 부조(浮彫)하였는데 산 속에는 이호(螭虎), 표범, 승냥이가 있고 산 정상에는 영지(靈芝)가 있다. 비연호는 산봉우리마냥 주위 산들이 받쳐주는 가운데 우뚝 솟아 있다. 옥 재질은 섬세하고 온윤(溫潤)하며 색상은 희고 이 밖에 노란색 껍질이 있다. 옥의 천연 색상을 이용하여 조각하였는데 노란색 가운데 붉은색이 서리고 흰색 가운데 푸른색이 감도는, 즉 난색과 한색의 대비적인 효과를 통해 산의 기세를 두드러지게 표현한 것이 구상이 절묘하고 의경(意境)이 참신하다. 주위 산들의 푸른빛은 마치 가없이 펼쳐진 하늘의 가느다란 실구름 같고 주황빛은 아름다운 노을마냥 산천을 붉게 물들였으며 산에는 안개가 자욱하다. 산속 이호, 표범, 승냥이의 강건하고 사나우며 야생적인 특징 또한 정확하고 생동하게 조각하였다.

비연(鼻煙, 코담배)은 명대(明代) 말기에 중국에 전해졌는데 청(淸) 강희(康熙)연간에 처음으로 비연호가 나타났다. 그 후 궁정(宮廷) 조판처(造辦處)에서는 황제의 명에 따라 각 작방(作坊) 및 경덕진(景德鎭) 어요(御窯), 소주(蘇州)·양주(揚州)의 옥작(玉作)에 각종 재질의 여러 가지 비연호를 제작하게 하였다. 건륭조(乾隆朝)에 절정에 달하여 생산량이 많을뿐더러 품종이 다양하고 공에 또한 정교하였다. 가경조(嘉慶朝) 이후에는 생산량이 감소되어 일부 품종은 생산이 중단되었으나 일부 품종은 청왕조가 무너질 때까지 지속적으로 생산되었으니 바로 어제(御製) 또는 궁조(宮造) 비연호이다. 윗사람이 좋아하면 아랫사람들이 따른다고 청대에 백성들이 비연을 마시는 것은 풍기(風氣)가 되었으며 따라서 각지 민간 작방에서는 너도나도 비연호를 제작하였다. 이에 따라 생산량이 많고 품종이 다양했으며 모양이 신기한 것이 이루 헤아릴 수 없었다. 자그마한 비연호의 제작에는 각종 기법이 사용되는데 이는 역사적으로 전례 없던 것이다. 비연호의 종류는 대체적으로 법랑(琺瑯), 파리(玻璃), 도자기, 옥석(玉石), 칠기(漆器), 파리태화법랑(玻璃胎畵琺瑯), 죽목아각조각(竹木牙角彫刻), 상감(象嵌), 내화(內畵) 등 아홉 가지로 나눌 수 있다. 매 종류는 또다시 각종 기법이 사용되는데 세분하면 근 백여 가지 품종이 있다.

비연호는 신기한 예술적 매력으로 인해 황제에서 백성에 이르기까지 모두의 사랑을 받았으며 청대 및 그 이후로는 실용품에서 예술 감상품으로 변하여 다투어 소장하는 애장품이 되었다. 때문에 중화민국 시기에 이르러 비연을 하는 이는 거의 없었지만 비연호는 여전히 제작되었다.

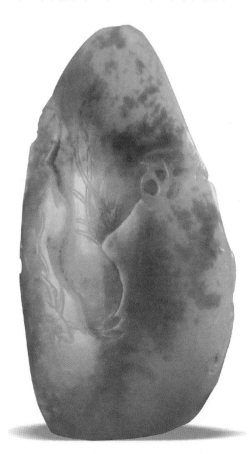

167

사련병(四聯瓶)

청옥(青玉) | 청(清)
높이 13cm 입길이 3cm 입너비 2.5cm
배길이 4.9cm 배너비 3.3cm
1980년 서안시(西安市) 수집

Jade Quadripartite Bottles

Green jade | Qing Dynasty
H 13cm Mouth L 3cm Mouth W 2.5cm
Ventral L 4.9cm Ventral W 3.3cm
Collected in Xi'an in 1980

　기신(器身)은 병 네 개가 서로 연결된 듯한데 입, 목, 배, 권족(圈足)의 평면은 모서리가 둥글고 돌기된 방형(方形)을 이룬다. 병 중심은 입에서 배까지 대롱 같은 도구로 아래위가 똑같이 둥글고 곧은 통(筒) 모양으로 뚫었다. 병은 둥근 입술, 긴 목, 접힌 어깨, 곧은 배에 높은 권족을 가졌다. 구연(口沿) 모서리에는 각기 권운문(卷雲紋)을 음각하고 목 아래에는 변형된 초엽문(蕉葉紋)을, 어깨에는 운뢰문(雲雷紋)을 새겼다. 윗배에는 교룡(蛟龍) 일곱 마리가 있고 아랫배에는 변형된 초엽문과 여의운두문(如意雲頭紋)이 있다. 색상은 진녹색이고 재질은 섬세하고 단단하다.

　사련병의 '사(四)'는 춘하추동을 뜻하고 병(瓶)은 평안하다는 '평(平)'과 같은 발음으로 한 해 동안 평안함을 뜻한다. 운문, 변형 초엽문 및 반룡문(盤龍紋)은 모두 서주(西周)시대 동기(銅器) 문양을 본뜬 것으로 조형이 참신하다. 또한 무게감이 있고 질박하고 기품 있으며 고풍스럽다.

168

이형배(匜形杯)

백옥(白玉) | 청(清)
높이 7.5cm 너비 7cm 두께 4.5cm
1981년 서안시(西安市) 수집

Jade Yi-shaped Cup

White jade | Qing Dynasty
H 7.5cm W 7cm T 4.5cm
Collected in Xi'an in 1981

　이(匜) 모양 배(杯)로 배는 깊고 납작하며 구연(口沿)은 살짝 밖으로 벌어졌고 한쪽에는 유(流)가 있으며 배벽은 곧은 편으로 아래로 내려가면서 좁아지고 바닥은 평평하다. 구연 외벽에는 세로 줄을 사이에 둔 운뢰문(雲雷紋)이 있다. 배 부분 문양은 3층으로 나뉜다. 위층은 유의 아래쪽에 변형된 초엽문(蕉葉紋)을, 양쪽에 기룡문(夔龍紋)을, 뒷면에 변형된 선문(蟬紋)을 새겼다. 가운데 층은 서로 대칭되는 도철문(饕餮紋) 한 쌍을 새기고 아래층은 바닥과 가까운 부분에 변형된 초엽문을 새겼다. 배 부분 문양은 감지법(減地法)으로 조각하였고 세부는 직도(直刀)와 사도(斜刀)로 새겼다.

　이(匜)는 서주(西周) 중기에서 서한(西漢)시대까지 유행했던 청동 대야인데 이 옥배(玉杯)는 초기 청동 이(匜) 조형을 본떠 만든 것이다. 문양은 상 · 주대(商 · 周代)에 흔히 볼 수 있는 것이지만 세부 특징 및 양문(陽紋) 기법은 뚜렷한 청대(清代) 옥기 특징을 띠었다.

초색복록수산자(俏色福祿壽山子)

백옥(白玉) | 청(淸)
높이 10.5cm 너비 8.1cm 두께 2.2cm
1982년 서안시(西安市) 수집

Jade Fu, Lu, Shou(the three gods in charge of good fortune, official career and longevity)

White jade | Qing Dynasty
H 10.5cm W 8.1cm T 2.2cm
Collected in Xi'an in 1982

산 모양으로 앞뒤 면에 문양을 부조(浮彫)하였다. 앞면은 옥의 황갈색 껍질을 이용하여 소나무와 뒤돌아보며 서 있는 학을 새겼다. 산비탈에는 사슴 한 마리가 있고 산 뒤로 커다란 나무 한 그루가 있으며 그 아래에는 참대와 영지(靈芝)가 있다.

학은 장수의 상징이다. 장생불로하는 신조(神鳥)로 학을 타고 하늘에 올라 신선과 만날 수 있다고 전해진다. 사슴 역시 장수의 상징으로 신선이 될 때 탈것이다. 소나무는 나무 중의 으뜸으로 사시장철 푸르며 대나무는 추운 겨울을 이겨내는 동시에 역시 사시장철 푸르다. 영지는 균류식물로 썩지 않으며 전하는 바에 의하면 복용하면 늙지 않고 죽은 사람도 살릴 수 있다고 한다. 이 몇 가지 동식물은 모두 길상(吉祥)과 장수를 뜻한다.

이 작품은 원조(圓彫)한 것이다. 수목(樹木)은 옥의 황갈색을 빌려 '바림질함으로써' 줄기의 웅건함과 힘 있음을 표현하여 아름답고 활기 넘치며 질감이 뛰어나다. 산비탈 쪽의 사슴과 참대와 바위 위에 서서 이를 뒤돌아보는 학은 서로 호응한다. 사슴은 몸통이 둥글고 학은 깃털이 하얀 것이 조형이 정확하고 형태에 생동감이 있다. 참대, 영지, 운문(雲紋)은 옥산(玉山)이 참대 숲에서 우뚝 솟게 받쳐준다. 황혼이 깃든 산속에 을씨년스러운 분위기가 감돈다면 사슴, 학, 소나무, 영지는 모두 영성(靈性)을 띠어 생명의 활력을 불어넣음으로써 늦가을의 산림 풍경을 아름답게 단장한다.

삼족섬(三足蟾)

청옥(靑玉) ｜ 청(淸)
높이 4.7cm 길이 11cm 너비 7.9cm
1980년 서안시(西安市) 수집

Jade Toad with Three Legs

Green jade ｜ Qing Dynasty
H 4.7cm L 11cm W 7.9cm
Collected in Xi'an in 1980

섬(蟾)은 발 세 개가 있는데 앞 두 발은 땅을 짚고 꼬리 가운데 나 있는 나머지 한 발은 땅을 박차고 있다. 머리는 살짝 쳐들었고 넓은 입은 꾹 다물었으며 콧구멍은 올리브 모양이고 둥그런 눈은 살짝 도드라졌으며 등에는 돌기된 척추가 있고 척추 양쪽은 납작하고 평평한 유정(乳釘)으로 장식되었다. 사지가 튼실하고 입은 음각선 한 줄로 나타내었는데 입꼬리가 올라가 미소를 띤 듯하다. 몸통은 둥글고 풍만하며 발에는 발톱이 세 개씩 있다. 눈은 대롱 모양 도구로 뚫었으며 눈구멍, 콧구멍, 척추, 유정은 모두 음기법(陰起法)으로 조각하여 윤곽이 뚜렷하고 입체감이 있다.

삼족섬은 신격화된 섬여(蟾蜍)로 나합마(癩蛤蟆), 개합마(疥蛤蟆)라고도 불린다. 양서동물로 회갈색을 띠며 피부 표면에는 돌기가 있다. 곤충과 도마뱀붙이를 잡아먹어 농작물에 유익하며 귀샘 및 피부의 분비물은 섬소(蟾酥)로 만들어 약으로 쓸 수 있다. 섬여는 원래 발이 네 개로 삼족섬은 존재하지 않는다. 삼족섬은 '유해(劉海)가 섬여를 희롱하다'라는 민간 전설에 의해 광범위하게 전해지게 되었다. 청대(淸代) 초기『견호집(堅瓠集)』5에서는 "유해가 섬여를 희롱한다는 이야기는 모르는 이가 없다. 오늘날 그림 속 더벅머리에 맨발로 만면에 웃음을 띤 자가 곧 유해로 삼족섬을 가지고 다니며 희롱한다"라고 적고 있다. 청대 맹뇌보(孟籟甫)는『풍가필담(豊暇筆談)』에서 더 생동하게 묘사하고 있다. "유해가 우물을 긷던 중 커다란 삼족섬을 얻게 되었다. 기다란 채색 끈으로 매어 어깨에 올려놓고 다니면서 사람들에게 '이놈이 도망가서 1년이 되어도 찾지 못했는데 오늘 드디어 찾게 되었소'라고 흐뭇하게 말하였다. 이 이야기가 마을에 퍼지게 되고……서로 보려고 너도나도 몰려들었다." 이렇게 삼족섬은 귀중한 길상물(吉祥物)이 되었고 훗날 연화(年畵), 조소(彫塑)에 '유해가 섬여를 희롱하다'뿐만 아니라 삼족섬 단독 형상도 나타나게 되었다.

이 삼족섬은 형태가 자연스럽고 생동감이 있다. 두 눈은 형형하게 빛나고 표정이 우스꽝스럽고 재미있다. 표면은 정세(精細)하게 연마되었고 색상은 비취색으로 투명하고 빛난다.

171

하엽원앙(荷葉鴛鴦)

석영암(石英岩) | 청(淸)
길이 9cm 너비 3.1cm 높이 6cm
서안시(西安市) 수집

Jade Pendants with the Motif of Mandarin Ducks and
Lotus Leaves Patterns

Quartzite | Qing Dynasty
L 9cm W 3.1cm H 6cm
Collected in Xi'an

　연잎 위에 떠 있는 원앙은 입에 연꽃가지를 물었는데 연꽃은 가슴 앞에 드리워졌다. 원조(圓彫)
한 것으로 원앙의 눈, 코, 입, 깃털, 꽁지 및 연잎의 입맥은 모두 음각(陰刻)하였다. 재료의 천연 무늬
에 따라 교묘하게 설계하고 조각함으로써 원앙의 윗입술, 정수리, 꽁지깃 그리고 연꽃잎과 줄기는
모두 진한 갈색을 띠었다. 조형, 재질, 색상이 혼연일체를 이룬 것이 빼어난 기예를 자랑한다.

옥동자(玉童子)

당옥(糖玉) | 청(淸)
높이 3.8cm 너비 2.9cm 두께 2.8cm
서안시 안탑구 삼효촌(西安市 雁塔區 三爻村) 출토

Jade Boy

Drown jade | Qing Dynasty
H 3.8cm W 2.9cm T 2.8cm
Excavated from Sanyao Village in Yanta District, Xi'an

포동포동한 동자는 둥근 옷깃에 소매가 좁은 포
(袍)를 입고 다리를 굽히고 앉아 머리를 기울이고 올
려다보고 있다. 두 손으로 연꽃가지를 잡았는데 커
다란 연꽃과 잎은 어깨에 닿았다. 동자는 정수리에
머리 한 움큼이 남아 있고 동글동글한 얼굴에 작은
눈썹, 눈, 입과 도드라진 코를 가졌는데 천진난만한
웃음을 지은 것이 사랑스러울뿐더러 복스럽기까지
하다. 오관(五官)은 모두 편도(偏刀)로 경사지게 깎
아내어 광대뼈, 콧마루가 비교적 높고 아래위 입술
이 도드라졌으며 눈썹 그리고 눈꼬리가 연결되지
않았는데 선이 매끄럽지 않으며 조각 흔적이 남아
있다. 재료의 색상을 교묘하게 이용한 초색(俏色)기
법을 사용하여 머리 부분은 흰색으로, 몸은 황갈색
으로 함으로써 예술적 효과를 높였다.

Jade Ritual Artifacts

1. Jade Disk

The Jade is flat and round, and there is a perforation in the center. The rim is not so smooth. And the rim is not so polished. The centered perforation is not in the center. The orifice is in the shape of trumpet, with one end big and the other end small. The two sides are quite flat with uneven thickness. The surface is not subjected to polishing treatment. The piece of jade disk is a little hairy, with little volume and irregular shape. The craft is natural and rough with the characteristic of classical early craft.

2. Jade Disk

The jade is flat and round and the taken round is not regular and smooth. The center perforation is molded by single-sided pipe drill, with one end big and the other end small. There are crack trails along the edge of the two ends. On the one side of the jade there is a straight and thick slopping line, which makes one side higher and the other side lower. The entire jade is plain without lines. The rim is badly damaged while the surface is polished and fine, smooth and bright. The jade contains more impurity, with rough nature. A part of it is cleanly and pervious to light, and other parts are brown. The entire jade shows original feature particularly.

3. Jade Disk with Cattail Patterns

The jade disk is flat and round, two sides of which are ornamented with cattail patterns separately. Around the hole is a thin protuberant line to form a thick internal outline. Along the rim of jade proper draws a circle inwardly with inclined cutting and forms a slope outline. When carving the cattail patterns, firstly draw the overlapping curve in the shape of diamond on the surface of the jade. After carving all the lines, chamfer the two acute angles of each diamond to mold ordered and sequential cattail patterns. The surface and the flank of the internal and outer rim of the jade disk are all subjected to polishing treatment. Part of the jade is bluish white with large sugar color.

Cattail pattern is kind of fine textured grain with hexagonal radioactive structure. Rituals of the Zhou Dynasty Chunguan Dazongbo says, "Jade is divided into six classes to grade people; the baron wares jade disc with cattail patterns." It can be seen that the jade disc with cattail pattern is a special ritual to mark the identity of the feudal dukes or princes who are in the rank of baron, one of the five ranks of nobilities(the other four ranks namely duke, marquis, earl and viscount). Cattail is a kind of water plants which can be used to weave the mat, thus, the so-called cattail pattern is actually a mat pattern. Rituals of the Zhou Dynasty Chunguan Dazongbo says, "recorded that the cattail is used as the mat with which to make the person settled down…" the mat can also be expounded as "land", and occupy a mat of land is considered as a good omen. The earliest unearthed object of jade disk with cattail pattern were found in the Spring and Autumn period, and continued to the Qin Dynasty and Han Dynasty.

4. Jade Disk with Grain Patterns

Engrave a shade line around the internal and outer rim separately to form an outline, within which is ornamented with basse-taille grain line. The grain lines are arranged in order and distributed evenly. Obviously, the surface of the jade is engraved to be cob webbing in diamond or square in advance, and then grind the grain lines in each of the gridding. The surface and the flank of the internal and outer rim of the jade disk are all subjected to polishing treatment.

According to Rituals of the Zhou Dynasty Chunguan Dazongbo says, Jade is divided into six classes to grade the people; the viscount wares jade disc with grain patterns. It can be seen that the jade disc with grain patterns is a special ritual to mark the identity of the feudal dukes or princes who are in the rank of viscount, one of the five ranks of nobilities(the other four ranks namely duke, marquis, earl and baron). Grain is the general term of all kinds of cereals and also it is also used to represent emolument. When grain is used for describing the jade, it then means "goodness". The earliest unearthed object of jade disk with grain pattern were found in the Spring and Autumn period, and continued to the Qin Dynasty and the Han Dynasty.

5. Jade Disk with Phoenix Patterns

The jade disk is flat and round. Engrave thin protuberant lines around the rim of hole and the jade proper separately to form a thicker internal and outer outline. The surface of the jade disk is divided into the internal section and the outer section by intaglio lines. The internal section is ornamented with cattail pattern which are orderly arranged. The outer section is ornamented with three phoenixes with curled tails which are leaning to one side and following one by one. They have long beak and curled phoenix coronet and are glancing back in a prostrate posture with curly wings and tails. The lines are compacted and meticulous, with sense of rhythm. It is a proper combination of arts and the engrave requirements.

The phoenix images on the jades of the Han Dynasty have identical characteristics. Origin of Chinese Characters completed in the Eastern Han Dynasty describes phoenix clearly, "phoenix is an omniscience bird." An old wise man said, "The image of phoenix is composed of the first part of Anser and the second part of Qilin(a kind of dragon), the snake' neck and the fish's tail, the stork's forehead and the mandarin duck's cheek, the dragon's pattern and the tortoise's back, the swallow's the lower jaw and the golden pheasant's beak, and the feather is in five colors". The phoenix images on the jades are variant, while the features of heads are nearly identical with that described in the book of Origin of Chinese Characters. The beaks are really like exaggerated ones of cocks', and most of them are with the mouths open and crowing.

6. Jade Disk with Dragon Patterns

The jade disk is flat and round. Engrave thin protuberant lines around the rim of the hole and jade proper separately to form a thicker internal and outer outline. The center part of the surface of the jade disk is divided into the internal section and the outer section by intaglio lines. The internal section is ornamented with cattail pattern which are orderly arranged. Engrave four double-body dragon patterns with the identical sizes and shapes with the techniques of combining protuberant lines with shallow groove shape and thin intaglio lines. The face of the dragon is ferocious, with open eyes, straight nose and wide mouth. And there are S shaped wave lines on the two sides of the face.

The two sides of the jade as well as the internal and outer edges are polished carefully. Observe the surface of the jade meticulously, one can find that there are signs of lines engraved by intaglio lines on the outer section of the dragon patterns. For these signs are engraved shallowly, they are difficult to be detected.

7. Jade Disk Cong(a long hollow piece of jade with rectangular sides)

The Cong is in the shape of straight tube. Perforation is realized by the technique of tube drilling added sand and drill thoroughly. The wall of perforation is thin. It protrudes three square shaped arc bases on the surface with the technique of reducing the base materials. The base surface is smooth and plain, without patterns. The surface of the jade and the internal wall of the perforation are polished by grinding, thus, they are smooth and mild. Observe the surface of the jade meticulously, one can find that the one side of the short perforation is higher and the other side is lower.

8. Plain Surfaced Cong(a long hollow piece of jade with rectangular sides)

The outline of the Cong is square but the internal part is in the shape of round. There are perforations on both ends. The four sides are smooth and plain, without patterns. The internal and outer surfaces are smooth and well-polished. Scrutinize the perforations, one can find that the center part of the perforation is a little bulging, which shows that the perforations are drilled from both sides of the jade to the opposite directions. After the perforation, the internal surface of the jade is subjected to fine grinding and polishing.

9. Short Square Cong(a long hollow piece of jade with rectangular sides)

The body of the Cong is pretty short. Its outline is square but the internal part is in the shape of round. There are short perforations on both ends. And the surface is smooth and plain, without patterns. The center part of the perforation is a little bulging, which shows that the perforations are drilled from both sides of the jade to the opposite directions. After the perforation, the internal surface of the jade is subjected to grinding to remove the trace and finally, polishing.

10. Jade Plaque with Double Dragon Patterns

The jade plaque is flat and arc-shaped. On the one side carves double dragon patterns, and the other side is smooth and plain. The two dragons are both have large heads and small bodies towards opposite directions, and the bodies are alternately arranged. Ornamentation lines are engraved with the techniques of combining thin intaglio lines and protuberant lines with shallow groove shape. The engrave technique is tough and smooth. Both ends of the jade plaque have raised edges and perforations. The perforation across one end is drilled into the shape of trumpet by one-sided rod drilling, and that on the other side is double-sided drilled. There are engraving marks on the center section of the perforation; the orificeis in the shape of a horse hoof. The whole jade plaque is well grinding and polishing, crystal clear and warm.

The jade plaque is more common in the tombs of Western Zhou Dynasty. They are placed mostly at the chest and abdomen of the tomb owner.

11. Jade Plaque with Bird Patterns

The jade plaque is flat and arc-shaped. Both sides are engraved with patterns of standing bird. The head and the front body of the bird are protruded to represent the beak, crown and feather. A variety of circle round lines in circular arc or zigzag shape namely Jade Le with cloud and thunder pattern in the technique of thin intaglio lines and the protuberant lines with shallow groove shape on the body represent beak, crown, wings, tails and claws. Edges are removed from the front and behind section of the bird body through oblique grinding, while the edge of crown is clear angular. The perforation of the middle part of the top of crown as well as the hook beak is drilled from single-sided.

This bird-shaped jade plaque is similar with that of the Shang Dynasty adjusted from the shape but the polishing process is significantly higher than this period. The ornamentation lines are tough and smooth. The turning of line is natural, without burrs. The more popular carving technique of protuberant lines with shallow groove shape of the Western Zhou Dynasty is adopted.

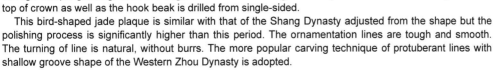

12. Jade Plaque with Bird Patterns

The jade plaque is flat and arc-shaped. Both sides are engraved with bird patterns symmetrically. The bird is in the posture of standing, with round eyes, hook beak and short tail. Crown, wing, and feather are presented by all kinds of rolling cloud patterns. The edges in the front of the bird body are all polished while the other edges are kept tough. The perforations of the two ends are made by drilling from two opposite directions. There are engraving marks in the center section of the perforations.

13. Jade Plaque with Animal Head Patterns

Engrave the thin intaglio to sketch the beast head on the two ends of the jade plaque, with two sides engraved. The appearance of the two beast heads are the same, with a long mouth open and showing the teeth. Diamond eyes and the ears are closed backwardly. The surface is grinded to be smooth, while the polishing is not so fine.

14. Jade Plaque with Plain Surface

The jade plaque is flat and arc-shaped, with plain surface and without patterns. In the middle part of the upper jade, there is a perforation drilled from two opposite directions, with engraving marks in the perforation. The orificeof the perforation is in the shape of horse shoe. The appearance is delicate, with meticulous grinding but not subjected to polishing.

15. Jade Yuan with Tao Patterns

The jade Yuan is flat and in the shape of ring, and the hole is two times as the Jade proper. The whole body of the jade is engraved with Tao patterns, and the slant arcs on the two sides engraved with the techniques of protuberant lines with shallow groove shape connected one after the other and stretched in spiral. Each arc is of the thickness and with uniform curvature. They are natural and smooth, with rhythm. The color is light yellow, crystal and shiny.

The jade Tao pattern, namely the roll pattern, is a kind of pattern made by imitating the multi-strand rolls. The earliest pattern appeared on the pottery of new Stone Age, and later on it is appeared on the bronze wares, porcelains, stone inscriptions and jade article as the auxiliary patterns. The Tao patterns for the ancient jade wares are mostly used for ornamentation of utensils or the edge of the graphic pattern. Sometimes it is used on the animals' body.

16. Jade Yuan with Grain Patterns

The jade Yuan is flat and round. Engrave thin protuberant lines around the rim of hole and the jade proper separately to form a thicker internal and outer outline. The two sides are ornamented with successive square grain patterns evenly. The protruding part of each grain is identical. The spiral patterns engraved in thin intaglio lines and the end of the lines are connected with the next grain patterns. The top of the grain patterns is spinous, thus, you will feel prick when you touch it. And this is a particular characteristic of the grain pattern on the jade of the period of Warring States.

17. Jade Yuan with Grain Patterns

The jade Yuan is flat and round. Engrave thin protuberant lines around the rim of the hole and the jade proper separately to form a thicker internal and outer outline. Both the two sides are ornamented with grain patterns, which are arranged orderly. The surface of the jade is engraved to be cob webbing in diamond or square in advance, and then grind the grain lines in each of the gridding. Comparatively speaking, the grain patterns on the Ai are plump and smooth-skinned. They are not like the spinous ones as those in the Warring States nor like the lower and flat patterns in the Han Dynasty. The appearance of the whole jade is well-polished and has refraction light.

18. Jade Zhang

The jade Zhang is flat and in the shape of acute angle. The upper end is acute angle and looks like half of the jade tablet. The whole jade is plain and without patterns. The appearance of the jade is grinded to be smooth, with meticulous polishing. The surface and the edge are all very lubricant. This kind of Zhang are mostly belongs in the period of the Spring and Autumn period.

19. Jade Tablet(Gui)

The two jade tablets are of the same appearance. The lower part of the jade tablet is in the shape of cuboid, and the upper end is in the shape of triangle. The thickness of the jade tablet is unevenness. The surface and the edge are all grinded but not subjected to polishing.

20. Jade Hu(Tiger-shaped jade)

The Jade Hu is a flat profile with the shape of tiger. The thin intaglio lines are used to sketch the mouth, the nose, the eyes, the limbs and the tail on the two sides. The mouth of the tiger is slightly open with olive-shaped eyes. The ears are closed backwardly, and the four limbs acts as the walking status. The strong tail rolls up to the back.

21. Jade Handle-shaped Article

It is in the shape of half-sword, and the handle is girdling. The end of the section was rectangular with a circular eye. The central part decorated with five raised broadband, and on the front there is a vertical concave broadband which runs through it. The spacing between the third and the fourth raised broadband is bigger, within which carves the beast eye pattern with the front lines, and engraves the ax-shaped pattern with side lines. The front part is a little girdling and is decorated with two convex edges and the front-end is more pointed.

According to the characteristic of the eyes of the beast, Mr. Yang Jianfang confirmed that the handle-shaped ware is the object of Erllitou period. If the view point is true, it shall be the earliest handle-shaped ware found in China at present.

22. Jade Handle-shaped Article

The handle-shaped ware is in the shape of half-sword, and is similar to the shape of rectangle, with the upper part wide and the lower part narrow. The two angles on the topare cut down to form a ladder shape. There is a short tenon at the lower end. And there is a perforation in the shape of the horn at the senter section of the base part. There are two thin intaglio lines at the front and the back of the handle separately, the center section of which is grinded to form two parallel embossment patterns with the technique of reducing the base materials and protuberant lines with shallow groove shape. One side of the ware is grinded to be round and other edges are all grinded. The lines on the appearance are arranged in order. The surface of the ware is well grinding and polishing, crystal clear and warm.

23. Jade Handle-shaped Article

The handle-shaped ware is in the shape of half-sword, and is similar to the shape of rectangle. The two angles on the top are cut down to form a ladder shape. There are two thin intaglio lines at the front and the back of the handle separately, the center section of which is grinded to form two parallel embossment patterns with the technique of reducing the base materials and protuberant lines with shallow groove shape. The front and back angles on the one side of the ware is chamfer to shape the blade. The jade contains much impurity and there are soil leaching marks.

24. Jade Axe

The axe body is nearly trapezoid, with narrow back and wide blade. The center section bulges out, and the profile is in the shape of olive. The blade is arc and curved and double-sided grinding. Near the top, there is a perforation in the shape of trumpet formed by one-sided rod drilling. The perforation is used to tie the rope to fasten the wooden handle. The craft of the jade axe is simple and plain, local part of which is in uneven thickness. The shape and the appearance is less regular, and the location of the perforation is not in the middle. The nature of the jade is coarse, with many vestiges as well as engraving marks, thus, the original characteristics is obvious.

25. Jade Axe

The axe body is flat trapezoid, with wide blade and narrow back. The blade is in the shape of arc and it is molded through double-sided grinding. The two broadsides are straight in upper part and a little outwardly at the lower part, with smooth edge and rim. The top is cut to flat, with coarse surface. Near the middle of the top, there is a perforation in the shape of trumpet formed by one-sided rod drilling which is used to tie the rope to fasten the wooden handle. The color of the jade is dark green, and the nature of the jade is fine and smooth and also it is meticulous polished. There is no damage occurred to the blade, nor binding marks to the perforation.

26. Jade Knife with Three Borings

The axe body is prolate trapezoid, with wide blade and narrow back. The blade is molded through single-sided inclined grinding with several breaks, which is caused by cutting. Near the back, there are three perforations in the shape of trumpet formed by one-sided rod drilling which are used to tie the rope to fasten the wooden handle. The edges of the front sides are chamfered, with top side grinded to be smooth. The process of blade, corner and perforation are all performed on the same side. The other side is subjected to the plane processing only. Observe the jade knife and one can find that though the knife face is grinded finely, the thickness of the knife body is slightly unevenness. The blade and the edges are not so regular, and the three perforations are not the same size, and the space between which is unequal and unsymmetric. In a word, it has the common characteristics of the neolith of the New Stone period.

27. Jade Spade

The axe body is flat trapezoid, with wide blade and narrow back. The blade is in the shape of arc and it is molded through single-sided grinding. One of the broadside edges on the front for the other three edges

is grinded to be round. The back is plain and smooth with clear edge. Near the middle of the top, there is a perforation in the shape of trumpet formed by one-sided rod drilling which is used to tie the rope to fasten the wooden handle. There are broken marks on the orifice of the drilling hole. The process of blade, edge and perforation are all performed on the same side. The other side is subjected to the plane polishing processing only. The color of the jade is dark green, and the nature of the jade is fine and smooth and also it is meticulous polished, with shining slice-shaped crystallizing objects on the surface. The whole jade is grinded to be smooth. There is no damage occurred to the blade, nor binding marks to the perforation, which implied that the spade is not a practical one. The spade is excavated from keshengzhuang Relic, which is in the west of Xi'an, where a lot of Longshan cultural relics were unearthed.

28. Jade Spade

The axe body is flat rectangle, the blade of which is a little wide and slightly arc and curve. It is molded by single-sided grinding. The top is grinded to be flat. The broadside edge on the positive side is chamfered. One of the broadside edges on the front for the two edges is grinded to be arc angle. The back is plain and smooth with clear edge. Near the middle of the top, there is a perforation drilled from opposite directions which is used to tie the rope to fasten the wooden handle. The process of blade and edge are all performed on the same side. The other side is subjected to the plane polishing processing only. The color of the jade is dark green, and the nature of the jade is fine and smooth. The whole jade is grinded to be smooth. There is no damage occurred to the blade, nor binding marks to the perforation, which implied that the spade is not a practical one.

29. Jade Spade

The axe body is flat and a little similar to the trapezoid, with wide blade and narrow back. The blade of the jade spade is arc and curve, which is molded by single-sided grinding. The top edge and one of the broadside edges on the front are grinded to be round. The other broadside edge is kept original. There is half concave perforation across the upper part, which shows that the width when it was made is one time of the present width. The other part of the perforation might be damaged in the process, thus, it is divided into two parts from the point of perforation. The back of the jade spade is plain and smooth with clear edge around. Near the middle of the top, there is a perforation drilled from opposite directions by rod drilling which is used to tie the rope to fasten the wooden handle. The orifice on the back is big while it is small on the front side. Mao xi Village in Baqiao District of Xi'an, where the jade spade was excavated from, is next to the Shan Dynasty Relic in Laoniupo. Jade wares are found here for many times. Identified from the craft of the jade, it is confirmed to be the object of the Shang Dynasty.

30. Jade Dagger-axe

The Yuan of jade dagger-axe is wide and slightly curved, in the center part of which there is a spine. The forwardly part is in the shape of triangle, and the both sides are blade, with one side being curve and the other side being straight. The Nei of the jade dagger-axe is in the shape of rectangle with perforation. At the junction place of the Nei and the Yuan, there are bears on both sides. Near the Yuan, there is trumpet-shaped perforation. The back part of the Yuan is decorated with four marks edge. This piece of jade dagger-axe is carved by the serpentine jade commonly seen in the place of Qinling. Most of the jade wares and baldrics of the Shang and Zhou Dynasty unearthed in Xi'an are processed with this kind of materials. The jade dagger-axe is smooth, bright and clean, with fine polishing. Even the space between the perforation and the Tooth is polished meticulously. In addition, there is no slightest injury occurred to whole body. Identified from the characteristics of Neizhi, Feileng(usually protruding strip), the long Yuan and the ridges, the jade dagger-axe s confirmed to be the object of the late Shang Dynasty.

31. Jade Man and Woman

The two jade human characters are similar in shape, and in the shape of rectangular sheet. The upper part is the outline of the head and the upper body. Thin intaglio lines sketches the contours of the hair, eyebrows, eyes, nose, mouth, etc. And a thin line is used to represent the waistband. The one that have beard carved on the upper lip is men, and another is women. The carving is plain with simple image. No perforation available for attaching the baldrics. For the jade human character is commonly used in worship during the Qin Dynasty, the right partner may be used as sacrifice. Such kinds of jades are appeared in the Qin Dynasty firstly, and the shapes are basically the same. Only men and women with distinctive characteristics of the times have a certain sense on the development of jade human character and their costumes of the times.

Jade Pendants

32. Jade Ji(Hairpin)

It is in the shape of cone, the profile of which is oval. The upper part is uncompleted, while the end part is sharp. The stick of the hairpin is straight. Its appearance is obviously marked by grinding. Jade hairpin is a kind of baldrics for ancient people to tie the hair up. In ancient times, the man ties up the hair on the top of the head, and they insert the hairpin into the hair to fix the hair for fear of scattering. The women in ancient

China used the hairpin to fix up the hair styles. It is also a kind of ornamentation.

33. Jade Ji(Hairpin)

The hairpin is in the shape of a long cone. The top is flat while the end is sharp but dull. The stick of the hairpin is straight, smooth and well-polished.

34. Jade Fish

The body of the fish is prolate and straight. The head is in the shape of triangle and the width of tail is reduced and bifurcate. An intaglio line with the end bend down to used to represent the closed mouth of the fish. Two concentric circles are sketched to represent the eyes of the fish. The body is ornamented with tile lines, which represent the scale. The upper fin and the tail are represented by intaglio lines. There are perforations with the same shape of Chinese character near the mouth and the tail separately. The upper fin is molded by double-sided chamfer to form a sharp edge. The head and the abdomen is grinded to be round. One side of the fish is stained with much zinnober.

35. Jade Fish

The body of the fish is prolate. The mouth is open and the body is straight and the tail is bifurcate. A triangle engraved by intaglio lines is used to represent the open mouth. The eyes, cheek and upper fin and lower fin are all represented by intaglio lines. There is a perforation in the place of mouth used for stringing. The dorsal fin and the tail are molded by double-sided chamfer to form the blade. The other edges are all subjected to grinding to remove the sharpness. The surface is well-polished, gentle and smooth.

36. Jade Fish

The body of the fish is oblate and strip-typed, double-sided engraving. The mouth is round and the tail is wide, with stout body. The eyes are little circles. Parallel short lines are carved between two parallel arc lines to form the cheek of the fish. A straight line is carved to form the tail, and at the end, there are several parallel lines carved horizontally. On the one side of the fish belly, there is a thick slope line remained for cutting materials. The edge is grinded smoothly.

37. Jade Fish

The body of the fish is flat. The head is narrow and the tail is wide. The big eyes are round and the cheek is in the shape of arc. There is a big fin on the back and two small fins on the belly, with a bifurcate tail. There is a perforation in the mouth. The eyes, cheek, and fins are all sketched with thin intaglio lines. The surface is well-polished. The edges around is chamfered double-sided to form the blade.

38. Jade Fish

The body of the fish is oblate and rectangle. The mouth is round and the tail is wide. The belly is bulged and the tail is bifurcate. It is double-sided engraving. Thin intaglio lines are used to draw the outline of the cheek and the fin. The bifurcate part of the tail is grinded and cut in the an acute triangle. The eye is represented by a perforation. The two perforations on the two sides are not corresponded, only thorough at the intersection place of the two perforations. The upper and lower body of the fish is chamfered and double-sided to form the blade.

39. Jade Cicada Pendant

The cicada is in the shape of cylinder. The top of the head is in and the lower jaw is outside. Both the two eyes are protruding, and the neck is ornamented with broad bind lines. Both wings are in the slope status. The U-shaped intaglio lines are used to sketch the outline of the abdomen. The two ends of the lines are curved into the shape of volute at the two sides of the upper abdomen to represent the tymapanum of the cicada. Several horizontal arc lines are curved at the lower abdomen to represent the uromere which can stretch out and draw back. A perforation goes through the center from the head to the end to stringing. Jade cicada can be used at funeral, namely Han cicada, and also can be used for ornamentation. This one is jade cicada for bearing.

40. Jade Dragon

The body of the dragon bent inwardly with its head looking forwardly to its tail, like the letter C. The dragon head is giant and the tail is reduced to be smaller. It has large eyes and big mouth, with big ears closed backwardly and curly beard. It is decorated with the clouding patterns. There is a perforation in the mouth, which is drilled from opposite directions for stringing. One side of the dragon body is flat and the other side is bulge. Both sides have the patterns corresponded with each other, thus it left us relief three-dimensional sense.

Jade dragon is found in the Hongshan culture relics 500years ago. Later, dragons carved with jade and wares ornamented by dragon patterns were excavated more and more. According to the textual research, most of the dragon patterns in the early stage in the Western Zhou Dynasty were dragons with straight body, while the dragons with curved bodies were a few. Then in the middle period, most of the jade

dragons were dragons with curved bodies, while the dragons with straight bodies were a few. When in the later period, the dragons with curved bodies were still occupied most of the techniques with exquisite engravings. The early jade dragons were characterized of primitive simplicity, with coarse lines. The jade dragons on the middle period were with mature techniques and coordinated proportions. Its appearances were vivid and the lines were smooth. The appearances and shapes of the jade dragons in the later period were transferred into abstract and patterning.

41. Jade Pendant with Kui Dragon Motif

The pendant is flat and in the form of dragon, with hollow out techniques to carve. The dragon nods and opens the mouth. The lips roll up and eyes are round. There are two horns on the head. Hairs are on the neck and the spine. The body is curved and the tail is drop, with the feet prone. The whole body is engraved with hidden grain patterns. And the arc lines are curved to sketch the hair, tail, and feet. Cut inwardly to form the perimeter outline with slant cutting way. There is a pair of small perforations at the abdomen for stringing.

42. Jade Plaque with Kui Dragon Motif

The pendant is flat and in the shape of plaque. One end is molded into the shape of the head of Kui dragon and the other end is molded into the shape of fish tail. The dragon head is outlined by one intaglio line, with diamond eyes, leaf ear, and rolled-up lips on it. There is a perforation at the palce of mouth. The body is a little narrower, compared with the head and the tail. Two rows of grain patterns is grinded with the technique of reducing the base materials to form thick outlines at the abdomen and back. There are several intaglio parallel lines engraved at the part of the tail.

43. Dragon-shaped Jade Pendant

The pendant is flat and round. Hollow-carved technique is employed to mold the curly dragon. The narrow part of the dragon body is curved correspondingly for both sides. The head is connected with its tail. It has water-drop eyes, big nose, big mouth, and horns on the top of the head. The body curves back, supported by a strong single foot. Both the body and the legs are ornamented with cloud patterns. There are double intaglio lines along the body from the neck to the tail. The abdomen and the rims of the head and the back are carved by the technique of reducing the base materials to form the outline. It is proper to take the roundness as the base materials for the shape of the dragon body. The body curves up and the tail raises. It seems that the dragon is galloping on the cloud and leaping on the water. It is dynamic, natural and vivid as though it were living. The jade pendant with dragon motif is a symbol of the fortune, rank, religious authority, and extreme dignity, which has deep significance.

44. Jade Pendant with Dragon Pattern

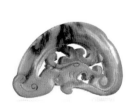

The pendant is approximate to a semi-circle. The dragon patterns on it are carved by employing the hollow-carved technique. The jade dragon has large eyes and long mouth, with the long horns curved backwardly. The body of the dragon rises archwise. The dragon head is backwardly and underneath the abdomen, which places on the curved tail.

Dragon is the symbol of the supreme imperator and his family in past dynasties of ancient Chinese. It is a particular symbol for the imperator family to employ dragon patterns as a decoration. With the development of the society, the image of dragon was secularized step by step, thus, the sacred and paramount characteristics of the dragon were lost and dragon became the decoration materials for the common people. This pendant is a reflection of the indea of this period.

45. Jade Le with Cicada Pattern

Le is a cylinder. The surface is decorated with two simplified cicada patterns vertically. The four hidden protruding corner-like objects on the upper part present a pair of eyes of the cicada. The protuberant lines carved by the intaglio lines at the lower part symbolize the body of the cicada, which is simple and unsophisticated. In the perforation and the two ends there are of clear trace of stringing.

46. Jade Le with Cloud and Thunder Patterns

Le is in the shape of and oblong cylinder, in the center of which there is a perforation. Two circumferences of cloud and thunder patterns around the surface of the jade body are carved through intaglio lines. The lines are powerful and vigorous, natural and smooth.

47. Jade Belt Buckle with Dragon Head Motif and String Patterns

The shape of the belt buckle is large. It is composed of seven jades with perforations, which are stringed together with one iron core. The buckle head is in the shape of dragon head. The mouth is closed and the underneath beard stretches forwardly. The two sting patterns represents the nostrils. The eyes are in the shape of diamond, and the canthuses are long. The ears are closed backwardly, and the two horns are in the shape of the ox horn. A strand of hair on the neck raised up highly. The neck profile is in the shape of square, and the two sides of the neck are engraved with clouding patterns of variant buckle through thin

intaglio lines. The space of the clouding patterns are decorated with close overlapping curve. There is a little perforation across the back of the neck, in which there is a thin iron wire used to fix up the dragon head and the iron core in the neck. The body of the buckle is in the shape of rod and is a little curve. There are ten closely arranged concave string patterns in the front and the back of the buckle separately. There are raised string patterns for a circle separately in the front and the back as well as the middle part of the buckle. Two rabbits are carved face to face on the middle raised string patterns, between which there are two square double stages. On the back, there is a round umbilical button. This jade belt buckle is engraved by adopting first-class Hetian green and white jade, with unique process and smooth lines and fine polishing. Though the exavated place is in the Han Dynasty relics, it shall be the object of the Warring Staes, identified from the characteristics of the eyes and nose on the dragon head and the clouding patterns.

48. Jade Belt Buckle with Dragon Pattern

The belt buckle is in the shape of Pipa(a plucked string instrument with a fretted fingerboard). The hook of the buckle is in the shape of dragon head, which is flat and wide. The mouth which is like a dog's is open, and two rows of teeth are arranged orderly. There is a small perforation across each of the corners of the mouth. The nose end is short and flat, and the diamond eyes are protruding. The long eyebrows roll up, and the horns curl. The U-shaped top is engraved with intaglio lines vertically, and three wisps of beard are closed backwardly. The eyebrows, eyes, nose, and mouth are collected in the front of the head, only takes up one third of the whole head. The embossment of a Chi Dragon with Lucid Ganoderma in the mouth in molded on the body of the buckle, with clouds around. The Chi Dragon is in the gesture of creeping. The forehead of the dragon is wide, and the neck is concave. The horsehair is dancing horizontally. The body is plump, and is crawling on the four limbs. The joint and the shoulders are decorated with cloud patterns. The double intaglio lines on the middle of the back represent the spinal column, three pairs of horizontal double lines beside which represent the rib. A vertical intaglio lines on the shanks and several horizontal short lines represent the sense of vigor. The tail is bifurcate and curves to the two sides. The back of the buckle is in the shape of arc, and near the end there is a remaining trace of button. The edge of the buckle is engraved by intaglio lines and the edges are polished smoothly. There is a large dragon on the head of the buckle and a small one on the body of the buckle, which are commonly called black dragon motherhood.

49. Jade Belt Buckle with Dragon Pattern

The belt buckle is in the shape of Pipa(a plucked string instrument with a fretted fingerboard). The hook of the buckle is in the shape of dragon head, which is flat and wide. The mouth is like a dog's and two rows of front tooth are arranged orderly. A perforation goes through from the front tooth and the corner of the mouth. The waist is protruding and short and slant intaglio lines as well as cloud patterns are adopted to represent the beard. The nose end is short and flat. The rim of the eye takes up half of the face. The eye holes are deep and the long eyebrows are bifurcate and rolls up. The cloud-shaped ears connect at the top to form a letter U. Two strands of hair on the neck lie on the two sides of the neck. The protruding carve method is adopted to decorate a Chi Dragon at the buckle body. Clouds are carved underneath the head and beside the body. The forehead of the dragon is wide, and the horsehair is dancing. The body is plump, and is crawling on the four limbs. The joint and the shoulders are decorated with cloud patterns. The double intaglio lines on the middle of the back represent the spinal column. Several intaglio triangle patterns represent the rib. Short and slant lines are carved to ornament the shanks. The tail is bifurcate and curves to the two sides. There are two levels of cloud patterns. The upper level is engraved with Auspicious cloud patterns, and the lower level is composed of several clouds like goat horns. The side edges and the base of the lower level are very coarse, without fine polishing. The buckle body is pretty thick, and the edges are smooth and evasive. The back is molded into arc. At the back place, there is a round handle navel button, with the button point being round and bulge. The jade belt buckle was excavated from the Jinian tomb of the Yuan Dynasty. The appearance and the shape of the jade are extremely classical, thus it is valuable.

50. Jade Belt Buckle in the shape of a Dragon Head

The belt buckle is in the shape of mantis belly. The cone at the buckle head is like the dragon head. The mouth is like a dog's, which is wide and flat. The corner of the mouth is over the eyes, and the nose is flat, with the holes outwardly. The two eyes are bulge, and the long eyebrows are curved horizontally as the letter "S". The two ears are closed backwardly, and the long horns are curved. The pupil is molded by tubular drill, while the holes are molded by rod drilling. The lines are all carved by one-sided slope cutting. The buckle body is in the shape of mantis belly, and the profile is half circle. The back is concave inwardly, the later part of which are a rectangle button. The shape of the buckle is simple, plain and plump. The lines are forceful, smooth and natural. The color is white, and the nature is fine. Though the decoration is simple, it has the character of dignity.

51. Jade Belt Buckle in the shape of a Dragon Head

The belt buckle is in the shape of strip. The cone at the buckle head is like the dragon head. The buckle body is used to emboss a Chi Dragon. The head of the dragon is a little square. The top of head is flat and broad. The nose is molded with auspicious cloud, and the threadiness thick eyebrows curve up. The forehead is decorated with a round convex, both the ears are closed backwardly, and the horns are curved. The Chi Dragon is zigzagging to form the buckle body. The hair is dancing, and cloud patterns are curved

with intaglio lines at the part of shoulder and the crotch. A intaglio line on the back goes along the ridge, and dense slant short lines are engraved on the shanks. At the back of the buckle body, there is a round handle navel button, with the diameter equal to the width of the buckle body. Observe from the side, the buckle is in the shape of arc, while the radian is much gentler than that of the Yuan Dynasty and the Qing Dynasty. The edges around is not subjected to treatment.

52. Jade Belt Buckle in the Shape of a Dragon Head

The belt buckle is in the shape of Pipa(a plucked string instrument with a fretted fingerboard). The hook of the buckle is in the shape of dragon head. The large mouth is slightly open, and the tongue licks the upper lip. The middle of the mouth is hollowed out. The lip rim is outlined by an intaglio line. The dragon has auspicious nose, bulge eyes and thick eyebrows, as well as double horns which are in the shape of goat horns. The buckle body is in the shape of mantis belly, which is to decorate the geometric pattern composed by hidden cloud patterns and auspicious patterns molded by reducing the base materials. Clear edges are kept at the side of the buckle body. The back of the buckle body is arc. In the middle of the backside, there is a round handle navel button. Observe from the side face, the three points underneath the buckle head, the button, and the buckle end are at the same plane. The five senses of the belt buckle in the shape of a dragon head and image characteristics of the buckle body, as well as the treatment of the edges and the height of the button shows typical characteristics of that of the Qing Dynasty.

53. Jade Belt Buckle with Mandarin Duck Patterns

The belt buckle is in the shape of oblong, which are the image of a pair of mandarin ducks. The two mandarin ducks at the front are swimming face to face. The waves are added under the abdomens for ornamentation, and lotus leaves are covered on the backs of the two mandarin ducks. They share one stalk together. The eyes are carved by tubular drill, with longer eye end. The whole pattern is molded by combining bas-reliefs and intaglio lines, which shows the situation vividly that the mandarin ducks are having fun on the lake with ripples. The back of the belt buckle is the image of lotus leaves which emerged from the lake water and dragon head. The dragon head is as the buckle and the lotus is as the button. The dragon head is similar to a square, the nose is like the head of garlic, and the eyebrows are like the flame. The intaglio two horns are curved inwardly. The hair on the neck is carved into clouds. The leaf veins come from a circle of intaglio Chinese character, one of the strokes of which is long and the other two strokes are short. On the lotus is the embossment of "Taichi" pattern. With rich ornamentation, meticulous image construction, sophisticated and fine cutting, as well as extremely polishing, the belt buckle is considered as the works of high quality.

54. Jade Xi(horny pendants) with Kui Dragon Pattern

Xi(horny pendants) is in the shape of ox horn. One end is sharp and the other end is carved into square head of the Kui dragon. The mouth of the Kui dragon is hollow-up, the teeth on the top of the head represents the nose and the horns. The whole body is carved intaglio cloud patterns. The edges on the head of the Kui dragon are clear. Both sides of the upper and lower body are subjected to double-sided chamfering to form edges. The mouth corner and the middle part of the upper body is perforated a hole for stinging. The outline of Xi(horny pendants) is arc and smooth, the ornamentation is fine and closely woven, and the polishing is meticulous.

55. Jade Xi(horny pendants)

Xi(horny pendants) is in the shape of arc. The head of the jade is big and the end is reduced to be small. The profile is rectangle. There is a perforation drilled from opposite directions near the head. The center part of the perforation is small and the two orifices are big and in the shape of oblong. The appearance of the jade is smooth and plain. It is a little unsmooth since it is not subjected to the polishing.

56. Jade Xi with Hollow-carved Bird Patterns

Xi is flat and in the shape of phoenix. It is carved by hollow out technique. The phoenix has sharp beak and high crown, and is turning round for his feather. The sharp end is as the Xi head. The beak, eyes, wing, tail, claw, etc and feather are outlined by thin intaglio lines correspondingly on both sides. The polishing of the plain and the side edges are very meticulous, and edges and corners are kept sharper.

57. Jade Chongya(clashing teeth)

It is plain and in the shape of slice, with the shape of tusk. There is a small perforation across the round end. The surface is polished to be smooth. The edges around are kept sharp. The head of the Chongya is in the color of sugar, while the end is like the color of apple. The materials of the jade are the soft jade produced in the Kunlun Mountain, in Qinghai.

58. Jade Group Pendants (1)

1. Jade Disk with Kui Phoenix Patterns

Tidi Carving (A kind of carving technique of removing the materials around the pattern itself and to highlight the pattern) is adopted. There is one raised string pattern on the external edges and the internal rims. The inner part is carved into a pair of Kui phoenixes, which is standing oppositely and turning back to look over. They have high crowns, and both the wings are rolling up. Seven long tails are curving back to cover the whole disk surface. The feathers on the narrow part are outlined with thin intaglio lines, lively and vivid. The jade disk belongs to the disk for wearing, and make up combination ornamentation with jade pipes.

2. Jade Heng with Kui Phoenix Patterns

It is in the shape of slice. The phoenix is in the posture of observing when it is flying. Its beak is sharp. Both the two swings are unfolding and bow down to form and arc. The tail is bifurcate into two parts and outlined by thin intaglio lines. The long wings are carved by techniques of deflection cutting to achieve a vivid image. The two wings are broad, the beak is sharp and the eyes are big, which is ferocious and frightened. The whole body is in the shape of plaque, with one perforation in it. There is a hole in the end of each wing for stringing and heng.

3. Jade Dancers

There is a pair of persons on the jade slice who have the same motions with opposite postures, which achieves a symmetrical dancing posture. The dancing girl wares a robe with cross-collar and wide sleeves, with a belt attached to the waist. She is happy and dancing, with one arm holds on around the head to throw off the long sleeves and the other arm drops down and bend inwardly. In addition, the long sleeve drooped down to the knee, which makes up and elegant figure that slightly similar to the shape of letter "S". The dancing girl is with round faces, long eyebrows, thin eyes as well as naive smile on the faces. The details are all outlined with lines. There are perforations separately on the upper end and the lower end for stringing.

The music and dancing prevailed very much in the Han Dynasty. The empire and the nobles usually enjoy the dances of the women. For example, the skillful court dancers Bingqiang, and Wujing are celebrated for satisfying the empire's favor. The jade dancing girl is and authentic representation of the song and dance scenery overnight.

It can be seen from the dancer's dress and posture that the performance is the long-sleeved dance. This dance is a traditional dance in ancient China, and it was popular in the period of Warring States. More than one poetry make descriptions on it. For instance, the book Hanfeizi describes "long sleeves are suitable for dancing, efficient capital are useful for trading". The monograph Lunheng by Wang Chong describes "raise slim sleeves for hiding the faces, spread the voice to sing freely", "slim sleeves" here refers to "long sleeves". Miscellaneous History of Xijing records that Mrs. Qi, Liu, Bang's wife "is good at the dance with raised-up sleeves". Here "raised-up sleeves" is also a description of long-sleeved dance. In the long-sleeved dance, one can makes the sleeves rotate, rippling and flowing effortlessly and naturally, which makes the dance more graceful. The long-sleeved dance in the Han Dynasty are commonly seen not only on the stone portraits and brick portraits, but also on the crafts like jades and lacquers.

4. Jade Chongya(clashing teeth) with Kui Phoenix Patterns

The two pieces are with the same styles and in the slice shape. The head turns back with sharp and long beak. The top head is sharp, with curved crown and vigorous round eyes. The body and the tails are connected together, with a sharp end. The details are outlined with intaglio lines and the swirls represent the feathers. The shaping technique and the ornamentation technique are combined together. The jade was supposed to be the Xi to ware, but later, it developed to be the Chongya for ornamentation and kept the original shape. With the phoenix as the ornamentation, this jade is a combination pendant with high artistic features.

Chongya usually appears by pairs. The shape and the emblazonry are correspondingly ornamented on the lower end of the pendant. With it attached to the body, it sounds comfortable when the person walks.

5. Jade Xie-Zhi(a legendary beast)

It is in the shape of cone. One front leg goes down on his knees, with other three legs twisted and crouched. It holds its head high and in a high spirit. On the head there stands a sharp horn, and the two ears erect. The eyes are round and the mouth is long. Its tail is short. The double wings and feathers on the detail part are outlined with intaglio thin lines. The Jade Xie-Zhi is an imagined animal, also named Xie-Lu, Gong-Hu and Qu-Yi.

59. Jade Group Pendants (2)

1. Jade Disk

It has been calcified into the white color. The internal and external cincture is concave, between which four phoenixes are molded by the technique of openwork carving. The phoenix turns back with the neck curved, the sharp beak of which bends inwardly. With the crown high and wings open, it seems to fly. The feathers are outlined by three intaglio lines. Every two phoenixes share one wing. The detail part is outlined by thin lines.

2. Jade Dancer

It was a green jade, but color has been calcified into white. It is half round and slice-shaped. Both sides are carved by lines to outline the dancer. The dancer has her head inclined to the front, with round faces, triangular eyes, thin eyebrows, round nose, and small mouth. The right arm raises up while the left arm drop down. The waist of the dancer is outlined by thin lines, which makes a graceful gesture.

3. Jade Heng

The two dragon heads on the two ends separately turn back and the mouths roll up. The eyes are round with long canthus lines. Both the two dragon horns are long and roll backwardly, ornamented with two groups of double arc lines. The tails are connected together, with the top being flat and leveled. In the middle there is a perforation across the Jade Heng, two sides of which are ornamented with rolling cloud patterns in double lines symmetrically. Under the cloud patterns are the diamond pendants, the details of which are sketched with thin lines or double cloud patterns.

4. Left Jade Dancer

It is slice-shaped. One part of the jade is flat. Two sides of the jade are curved with lines to mold the dancer. The dancer turn her faces ahead, with thin eyebrows, diamond eyes, triangular nose and small mouth. Her right arm rises up, with the long sleeve fluttering before the chest. The chest is patterned with thin lines. On the foot there is a tiny perforation. And the face is coated with zinnober.

5. Right Jade Dancer

The dancer leans to the front, thus only one curved and thin eyebrow and one eye are on the face. The right arm raises up while the left one drop down, with the long sleeve fluttering to the back.

6. Jade Heng

The two dragon heads on the two ends separately turn back and the tails are connected together. The mouth roll up and the eyes are round with long canthus lines. The beard goes backwardly and the ears attached to the head backwardly. The long horns roll down and the body are long and curved up. There is a perforation in the center of the place where the tails connected together. The outline of the dragon body is curved on the surface, within which added six groups of double arc lines. Under the dragon body, cloud-shaped pendants are molded by the technique of openwork carving. The detail parts are ornamented with cloud patterns in thin lines. The external is painted with zinnober.

7. Jade Pendant with Cloud Patterns

It is molded by the technique of openwork carving and in the shape of similar triangle. The three edges are in the shapes of rolling clouds. Both the two sides are curved with lines. There is a tiny perforation in one of the edges. One of the edges is processed coarsely. It seems that it is processed from an incomplete jade pendant.

8. Jade Xi(horny pendants)

The shapes and appearances of the two pieces are the same. Both are in the shapes of dragon Kui. The dragon Kui is opening the mouth and baring the teeth, with the lower lip rolled backwardly. The eyes are round with long canthus lines. On the nose, a hole is curved by the technique of openwork carving. The cloudlike ears go backwardly and the long horns retreat from rolling up. The four limbs curl up, and the tails are sharp and slim. The details are sketched with double thin lines.

60. Jade Group Pendants(3)

1. Jade Yuan

It is molded by the technique of openwork curving. Four animal images including two monkeys and two bears are engraved on the internal double sides. The outside of each animal and the place between the two animals are curved with rolling cloud patterns. In the center of two animals, a rolling cloud pattern is also engraved by the technique of openwork curving. The four animal images in anticlockwise order are as below. One of the monkeys is in the posture of half squat, with the body inclined inwardly. It looks over shoulder and looks at the front horizontally, with the right arm lifting up. It seems that he holds some objects with his hand. The left arm drops to the back of the body. The legs curl down and push back. The details of the eyes, the nose, and the mouth are sketched with the thin lines. Another monkey is in the posture of sitting, with the upper limb lifting up. It seems that he holds an object with his hand. The faces incline inwardly, the five senses on which are ambiguous. The monkey's back is arc, with the hind legs curling before the bosom and the tail rising up. The detail on the face and other parts are curved by thin lines. One of the bears is in the shape of squat, with the sharp and short ears standing uprightly, the arc eyebrows declining inwardly and he diamond eyes reverse vertically. Its nose is long and the mouth is sharp. The front legs are standing uprightly while the feet go outwardly. The other bear is in the posture of running. The bear's head is similar to a triangle, and the sharp ears are attached the body backwardly. The diamond eyes reverse vertically. Its nose is long and the mouth is sharp. The front legs bend over and the buttock is engraved with rolling cloud patterns by thin lines.

2. Jade Dancer

The body is in the shape of the letter "S". The dancer leans her head to the front and lifts up her right arm over the head and to the left shoulder. The left arm of the dancer curves slightly, the hand of whom touches the waist. The lower limbs curves to be a semicircle. The details on the places of eyebrows, eyes and mouth are sketched with double thin lines.

3. Jade Heng

The two dragons' heads on the two ends separately turn back. The mouths roll up and the eyes are round with long canthus lines. The cloudlike ears go backwardly. Its hind legs are strong and curly attached to the abdomen. The tails are connected with each other. There is a round perforation in the upper center of the tail. The lower part of the jade is engraved with two pairs of rolling cloud patterns which rolls toward each other. The detail parts are ornamented by thin intaglio lines.

4. Jade Xi(horny pendants)

The shapes and appearances of the two pieces are the same. Both are in the shape of phoenix. One of them is uncompleted in the head. The phoenix twists its neck to looks back with round eyes, with the sharp beak hook-shaped. One of the wings spread forward and connected with the cloudlike crown, and the other wing attaches to the back. The legs twist, and the tails are sharp and slim. The eyes and the feather are engraved with thin lines. And the tails are outlined with lines, with a thin line in the middle divided the tail into the upper part and the lower part. And every part is decorated with two or three groups of double curve lines.

5. Jade Pendants with Phoenix and Bird Patterns

The shapes and appearances of the two pieces are the same. It is molded by the technique of openwork curving. The sharp beak retreats, the cloudlike crown is upright, the long neck stretches backwardly and the wings are unfolded. The tail is in the shape of the letter "S" and the legs stand erectly. The details are carved with double thin lines.

6. Jade Dancer

The dancer turns his face to bottom right. The left arm rises up round the left face. The right arm touches on the left side of the chest from the back. It seems that it is the paw. The detail part is decorated with the thin lines and the five senses are ambiguous.

7. Jade Heng(top jade in group pendants)

The two ends are in the shape of dragon head. The dragon head are long, with the mouth open slightly. The eyes are round with long canthus lines. The forehead is high, and the cloudlike ears are top flat and leveled. The double arc lines are curved between the head and the body. Among them, short and oblique lines are ornamented. The bodies of the two dragons are connected with each other. There is a round perforation at the upper middle part of the connecting place. There are cloud patterns carved on the bodies.

8. Jade Dancer

The shapes and appearances of the two pieces are the same, while the postures are opposite. The crowns are short, and there are sharp horns on the tops. The hairs are curved by lines, and the facial features are plump. The eyebrows are curve and the eyes are big. The noses are thin and the mouths are small. Both the two hands are humped up before the chest. The upper bodies incline and behind the bodies there are two cloudlike drooping pendants separately on the left behind(right behind). The details are outlined by double thin lines.

61. Shè(finger ring) Shaped Jade Pendant with Chi Tiger Patterns

The pendant is flat heart-shaped. The front is slightly bulging, while the reverse side is a little concave. The top is sharp while the bottom is arc. A Chi Tiger crosses the wall forward from its back. Its two eyes are round, and the top of head are flat. Its nose is protruding, and the mouth is broad. There is an intaglio line outlined the back ridge form the forehead to the tail. The ribs at the waist are presented by arc lines. The

back of the shin is decorated with detailed short intaglio lines. There is a person kneeling on his legs on the right upper corner while on the left upper corner, there is a phoenix spreading feather and turn round its head. The two sides at the lower part is decorated with cloud patterns.

62. Shè(finger ring) Shaped Jade Pendant with Hollow-carving

① It is flat and peltate, with the upper part sharp and the lower part round. It is namely heart-shaped pendant, with one perforation at the center.

② It is flat and peltate, with the same shape and appearance.

There are rolling cloud patterns with complicated hollow-carved technique at the outline of the two Xie-typed pendants with rolling cloud patterns. The sufaces of the bodies are outline the variant cloud patterns with intaglio lines and ornamented with the contour patterns. The shape is ingenious, the craft is meticulous, and the patterns vary completely. The jade nature is mild and fine. The tomb owner Chen, Qingshi who adopted the pendant should be the noble at that time, above the level of Wudafu of ninth rank.

63. Shè(finger ring) Shaped Jade Pendant with Double Monkey Patterns

The pendant is flat heart-shaped, with one perforation at the center. The upper part is sharp and the lower part is round. Two sides of the middle part are carved separately whin three parallel arc lines. Two sides of the two bodies are hollow-carved outline monkeys with the same shape and posture. They are all climbing. The faces, joints, heads and feet are all carved by intaglio lines.

64. Shè(finger ring) Shaped Jade Pendant with Chi Patterns

The pendant is similar to the circle, the center which is a perforation. A pair of Chi dragons are engraved, with clouds and frost together. The dragons crawl among them. Sometimes then are hidden and sometimes they can be seen. It seeme that the dragons are walking across the clouds.

Chi type pendant is also called heart-shaped pendant. It appeared at the Shang Dynasty. At the beginning, it is a practical ware. It is cylindrical and can be put on the thumb to pull the bow and shoot. In the period of Warring States, it evolved into a piece of ornament. Until the Han Dynasty, it developed into the slice-shaped hollow-carved pendant in the shape of shield. The imitations are commonly seen based on the heart-shaped pendant of the Han Dynasty every dynasty after Song. They have the shape of the pendant of the Han Dynasty, but not the vigorous spirit of the pendant. With the floating clouds, the two Chi is playing together in a fairy artistic circumstance. The image is lively and vivid.

65. Jade Cha Tail(belt plate embedded on the ends of girdle) with Dancing Pattern

Cha tail is with a round head and in the shape of rectangle. On the front engraves a man having the Huteng dance. The dancer has the long curve hair and upright nose and deepset eyes, with smile on his face. He wears tights with a round collar and half sleeve, with a longuette tied to the waist. The lower hem of the longuette is decorated with laceworks. He wears the long knee boots and has his elbow curved and raises the right head. The left hand of the dancer presses on the buttocks. Both the hands are hidden in the sleeves. The right leg is springing up, while the left leg is slightly curved. The belt is over the shoulder of the dancer. The edge of the round blanket is decorated with dropping strings, the internal of which is carved with a Chinese character by intaglio lines. The round blanket is the very "bamboo mat spread on the floor for people to sit". The patterns are curved and grinded by stone roller, with smooth and clear lines. The technique of removing the ambient materials excluded the patterns is employed to make an embossment effect with concaves and convexes. One end of the square materials on the reverse side is cut into a lower level, which is in the shape of round handle and rectangle. Five holes are drilled on the level and nailed together with the leather belt. This Cha tail is engraved with Hetian white jade, by adopting the technique of demirelief to realize the three-dimensional effect. The intaglio lines which outline the person image is soft and natural. The two edges on both sides are cut into smooth, with fine polishing. With valuable materials. luxury and dignity are achieved by combining perfectly the excellent techniques and the practical applicability together.

66. Jade Kua(belt plate) with Foreign Musicians Playing Flute

The front and the reverse side are equal in size. On the front engraves a Northern People sitting on the square blanket with a flute. He has upright nose and deepset eyes, with long hair curled outward. He wears a Hu costume tights with narrow sleeves. He wears the long knee boots and has the ribbon on his shoulder. He is in the posture of playing, with both his hands holding the flute. The front edge of the Jade Kua slants inwardly, the outline and every detail of which are grinded and carved with stone roller. Three holes are drilled separately on the four corners of the reverse side. And there are still silver nails remained in the perforations. The back is also polished.

67. Jade kua(belt plate) with Foreign Musicians Playing Clappers

The nature of the jade is glittering and translucent, fine and smooth, with the base a little bigger. Both the flanks are in slope, and the edges incline inwardly. The front is grinded and engraved to be the Northern People with upright nose and deepset eyes, crouching on the square blanket and striking the clappers. His long hair curled outward, and the curly beard is combed well. The upper body is bare, while the lower body is in the long trousers. A bracelet is worn the wrist, and a skirt is attached at the waist. Both the two hands hold the clappers before the chest to play clappers. The reverse side is not subjected to polishing, the four corners of which are separately drilled one hole.

68. Jade Kua(belt plate) with the Motif of Foreign Musicians Playing Bili(shawm)

The front and the reverse side of the jade Kua are of the same size. The northern person who is hunkering on the square blanket and playing Bili is grinded and engraved on the front of the jade. His long hair curled outward, and the curly beard is combed well. He has upright nose and deepset eyes. He wears a Hu costume tights with narrow sleeves. He wears the long knee boots and has the ribbon on his shoulder. He presses both his hands on the pipe orifices to keep a posture of playing. Bili is also called Qieguan pipe. Qieguan pipe is reed whistle. Big one has nine holes, seven of them are at the front of the pipe and the other two one s are at the back. It can play portamento, trill, Dayin, Shuanyin, and Chiyin(techniques in playing music with Bili). It is an important musical instrument in the ten kinds of instruments of the Tang Dynasty. The feature of grinding and engraving of the jade Kua and the perforations are the same with the former one. The reverse side is not subjected to polishing, neither.

69. Jade Kua(belt plate) with the Motif of Foreign Musicians Playing Drums

The front and the reverse side of the jade Kua are of the same size. The northern person who is playing music by crouching on the square blanket is grinded and engraved on the front of the jade. He has upright nose and deepset eyes, curved hair and short beard. He wears a Hu costume tights with narrow sleeves. He wears the long knee boots and has the ribbon on his shoulder. The left arm curves to hold the Jilougu drum onto the left knee, with the left hand hold the Taolao drum(small rattle drum with long handle), while the right hand with a stick would like to strike the Jilougu drum. Impregnation has occurred to the color of head of the Northern People and the Taolao drum. The front edge slants inward. The perforations are the same with the former one. The reverse side was not subjected to polishing, neither.

70. Jade Kua(belt plate) with the Motif of Drinking Foreign Musician

The four edges of the front slant inwardly. And on the square Kua grinds a Northern people sitting on the square blanket and drinking the wine. He has upright nose and deepset eyes, curved hair and curly beard. He wears a Hu costume tights with narrow sleeves, with the bared foot, The left hand is on the knee, while the right hand holds a cup before the chest. With plump faces, he is drinking the wine. It seems that he is happy and pleased with himself. Holes in right angle are drilled on the four corners of the reverse side.

71. Jade Kua(belt plate) with the Motif of Foreign Musicians Playing Jiegu Drum

The left bottom corner is lost. Both sides are of the same size. The reverse side is not polishing, with the edges slanted inwardly. And on the square Kua grinds a Northern People sitting on the square blanket and striking the Jiegu Drum. He has upright nose and deepset eyes, curved hair and curly beard. He wears a Hu costume tights with narrow sleeves and a pair of long trousers. There is a row of buttons clearly on the upper outer garment. The shoulder is decorated with ribbons. Both the left and the right sides are grinded with twisted auspicious cloud patterns. The Jiegu Drum is placed on the left side. Both the hands of the Northern people hold the stick in the posture of striking. Impregnation has occurred to the color of faces of the Northern People. In addition, holes in right angle are drilled on the four corners of the reverse side.

72. Jade Kua(belt plate) with a Rounded End and the Motif of Foreign Musicians Drinking Wine

Both sides are of the same size. The front edges slant inwardly. And in the middle of the square Kua grinds a Northern People, who are sitting on the round blanket, with beard abdomen. The left arm is curved and leans to the high cushion. The right hand of the person holds a cup and is going to drink He has upright nose, deepset eyes and curved hair, with bare upper body. He wears a pair of long trousers, and his feet are in the shoes. He is in smile, with two eyes looking around. The technique of removing the materials around the image of the figure is employed to make an embossment effect. The reverse side was not subjected into polishing. A pair of holes is drilled separately in the middle of the round head and both sides of the square corner.

73. Jade Belt Kua(belt plate embedded in the middle of the girdle)

The belt is in the shape of square. The theme patterns are higher than the rim's. On the front engraves the image of a Northern People who is sitting on the carpet by cross his legs and playing pipa (a plucked string instrument with a fretted figure board) by employing the technique of demirelief. The Northern People wears the robe with round collar and narrow sleeves. The hair is tied up and hung down to the shoulder. The silk belts droop from the two axillas and then flutter up on the left side and the right side. The belt surface slants in the shape of slope inwardly to form a fovea and also form naturally a round rim. The figure pattern is in bas-relief in the middle of the belt Kua, which is a little higher than the rim. The reverse side of the belf Kua is smooth without patterns. Two small perforations are drilled in the four corners in order to convenient people to tie it to the belt. The carved image patterns based on the people in the Western Regions in ancient China is a characteristic pattern in Kua patterns of the Tang Dynasty.

74. Jade Belt Plate with Plain Surface

This batch of jade belt plates are divided into three types:

There are 4 belt plates which are in the rectangle shape: it is in the shape of rectangle. There is a perforation in the shape of rectangle on one side and three pairs of holes on the four corners in the reverse side.

There are 5 arc shaped belt plates with round heads. The three sides are straight. And the only one side is in the shape of arc. On the straight side there is a rectangle perforation and on the reverse side there are three holes.

Cha tail is for one piece: it is in the shape of rectangle with a round head. One side is in the shape of arc. The surface is smooth and plain. On the reverse side there are four pairs of perforations.

This batch of jade belt plate is meticulously engraved, with regular shape and well polished surface. Observed the rectangle from the reverse side, it can be seen that there are two paralleled traces in the shape of crescent moon separately on the two perforation ends. And there are protruding broken stubbles, It shows that the perforation process is to getting through the two sides of the rectangle with stone roller firstly and then carving the joint part, thereby, the protruding broken stubbles are left at the two ends of the rectangles. The holes on the reverse side are connected through copper thread and leather belt. This type of jade belt plate can be used to hang the knife, Jiezhui(a tool to remove the knot in ancient China), etc.

75. Jade Belt Kua(belt plate embedded in the middle of the girdle)

The belt Kua is in the shape of square and horizontally broad. A Northern People playing music is carved by the hidden technique of removing the materials around the image itself. The top point of the theme patterns are leveled with the edges. the long hair of the figure is divided into two strands. He has big eyes and upright nose. The Northern People wears the robe with round collar and narrow sleeves, with belt tide to the waist. On the shoulder there is a silk belt from the top of head down to the two axillas. He wears a boot with sharp head, and twists to sit on his foot on the round blanket, with two hands holding a Sheng(a reed pipe wind instrument). The whole image is molded by the intaglio lines, combined straight lines and curved thin lines together. The folding lines of the clothes are represented by curved shallow thin lines. Those lines are long and close but not complicated, which is the classical characteristics of the Tang Dynasty.

76. Jade Belt Buckle with Fushou(symbolizing good fortune and longevity) Pattern

The belt buckle is composed of two square belt plates. On one part there is thin slice hook, with patterns of beast image grinded on it, while on the other part there are corresponding holes to the hook. On both the belt plates, the image "longevous and auspicious" composed by peaches and bats are molded by hollow-carved technique, with the same techniques but different directions. The place between the decorations hollow-carved on the belt plate and the belt plate shall be hollow-carved. The four corners top and bottom are connected with a piece of leave of the peach tree. Observe from the flank of the belt plate, the thinness of the plate is well-distributed and similar to the shape of the letter "S". On the back, there is a round umbilical button. The back, there is a round umbilical button. The back of the button is pretty flat. The surface of the belt plate is bright and well-lubricated, while the round drillings in the process of engraving is remained on the image without polishing. The technique of carving is coarse.

The patterns of dragon and lion on the jade plate of the Yuan Dynasty became more and more. Most of the figures have the dress and personal adornment with the style of the Mongolia noble's. Usually they have narrow sleeves and short skirts and wear the hat with pointed top and round brim. They bind up the waist and tie the belt, with long boot on the feet. Some of them are quiet and others are seemed to be dynamic, with different shapes. Besides of the technique of relief, there was multi-leveled hollow-carved technique. Most of the jade plates of the Yuan Dynasty were with rims, and the middle part of the rims were made to be low-lying areas, or two intaglio lines and triangular intaglios were as the rim decoration. There are rims in the shape of the chinese character "亚" and the rims with patterns of big joint-circles in the yuan Dynasty. Often there remain the round holes on the engraved jade plates when drilling the perforations.

77. Jade Belt Buckle with Chi Pattern

The belt buckle is octangle-shaped, with the front side convex and the reverse side concave. There are two Chi Dragons embossed on the positive side with one big and the other small. The rim around the embossment is curved by intaglio thin lines. The big Chi Dragon is looking back, with a lucid ganoderma in the mouth. It is curving the body and climbing with the four limbs, with the tail swaying. It seems that the dragon is walking across the clouds. The small dragon is following after the big one to grab the lucid ganoderma. The head of the dragon is smaller than that of the Yuan Dynasty. The gestures of the hind legs are similar with that of the Yuan Dynasty, while the corner pieces are processed by square angle which shows the feature of the dragon in the Ming Dynasty. The reverse side is hollowed out to be octangle with the same size of the outline. The internal of the edge on one side is engraved with a flat and square buckle tongue, and the corresponding edge is hollowed horizontally a hole in the strip form. The outside orifice is big while the inside orifice is small. The patterns and the polishing around is pretty fine, while the inner cavity and the base are not so smooth, which have the jade defection of the Ming Dynasty of seeking after the excellent shape but not the meticulous craft.

78. Jade Belt Buckle

This set of round belt plate is composed of 8 rectangle belt Kuas, 3 oblong belt Kuas, 5 belt Kuas in the shape of heartand 2 Cha tails. All of them are flat shape, without patterns on the surface. There are 3 holes on each rectangle belt Kuas, and 2 on oblong belt Kuas and belt Kuas in the shape of peach. There are holes on each corner of the Cha tails. There are 3 holes on each of the end for one of the Cha tail square Kuas, and the bottom of the 3 holes are crossed with each other. The positive side and the flank are polished meticulously, while the reverse side is coarse. the edges on the positive side are all slightly slanted.

The jade belt plate of the early Ming Dynasty still stuck to the style of that of the Yuan Dynasty, while there were strict regulations on the employment of the jade plate. In the 26th year of the Hongwu reign, the regulation was that the officials who ranked in the first level and above could use the jade belt, and the belt plate could be plain without patterns and also it could be decorated with patterns and images. The systems in the Ming Dynasty regulated that only the empire and officials who were authorized by the empire could use the jade belt number was also increased. In the middle or later period of the Ming Dynasty the number was relatively fixed that 20 jade belt plates were composed of a complete set. In addition, the shape of each one and the arrangement on the waistband were regulated clearly. The patterns on the jade belt plate were richer. There were patterns about dragon, Qilin(a kind of dragon), phoenix, bird, crane, and deer, lucid ganoderma, hundreds of sons, playing offspring image, playing lion, double fish, etc. As far as the carving technique was concerned, multi-layer hollow-carved technique and openwork carving were employed in a wide range, besides the embossment technique. It means that carving a layer of image under the theme patterns to set off the whole effect of the image.

79. Jade Belt Kua with Dragon Pattern

The Belt Kua is in the shape of rectangle, and double layers of openwork carving were decorated in the pane. A dragon with S-shaped body is curved in the middle part of the upper layer. The two hind legs are in the posture of walking with one leg before the other one, while the forelegs stretch to left and right separately. There are birds at the upper part and hills and grasses at the bottom part. The entire picture represents a majestic appearance that the dragon is walking in the forest. The lower layer is thinner. Hills and stones are pierced in the space of the upper patterns. Seen from the reverse side, the center part of the dragon body on the upper patterns is entirely pierced, with four holes on each of the corner. The holes are subjected into inclined pipe drilling from the pierced part, thus, it is pretty hidden. The surface of the pattern is polished meticulously, while the side wall, internal cavity and the base are not so smooth.

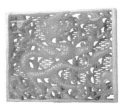

80. Jade Belt Kua with Dragon Pattern

The Belt Kua is in the shape of rectangle, and double layers of openwork carving were decorated in the pane. A dragon is pierced in the middle part of the upper layer, with flowers and plants decorated around. The dragon is in the posture of spinning and flying swiftly upward, with the hair upward. The eyes are round, the horns are long, and the four paws are in the shape of windmill. There is one intaglio line along the body from the neck to the tail to outline the curved posture of the dragon, the upper part of which is decorated with ridges in the shape of tooth. The dragon body and the four limbs are decorated with short straight lines. with the shanks thin and lean and the paws in the shape of windmill, which are belong to the style of the late Ming Dynasty. The lower layer is pierced with twisted flowers and grasses on the branches. There are perforations across the images of one flower with leave on the four corners of the reverse side, used to fix the cortical belt. For the two sides are pierced it seemed to be much hidden. The surface of the pattern is polished meticulously, while the side wall, internal cavity and the base are not so smooth.

81. Jade Kua with Diamond Shaped Dragon Pattern

The Belt Kua is in the shape of diamond, and double layers of openwork carving were decorated. A dragon is pierced in the upper layer, winding round in the clouds. The dragon head is tubbiness, with the big mose upright, which is like a pig's mose. There is beard at the end. The head is upward, and the eyes are molded by inclined lines and carved with pipe drilling tools. The hair is upright, and the tail is like that of a snake. The body and the four limbs are thin and long. There are close intaglio short lines from neck to paws, which is a distinguishing feature of jade dragon of the Ming Dynasty. The lower layer is pierced with twisted flowers and grasses on the branches. The four corners of the diamond on the reverse side are not drilled, but the pierced branches and leaves on three corners are damaged. It can be deducted from this that the jade belt Kua is fixed to the Cortical belt with the metal wire getting through directly the lower layer of branches and leaves on the four corners.

82. Oval Shaped Jade Kua with the Motif of Swan in the Flowers

The jade plate is similar to an oval. Three layers of patterns is pierced and hollowed out, and the backgrounds are water, lotus, as well as flowers and plants. A swan is tweeting, with the mouth opening, and stretching wings to hide into the flowers and grasses in water. The lotus petals are convex and is about to fold. There are round lotus seedpods in the center of the flowers, with lotus seeds. The waterweeds are curved naturally, turned over and crossed with each other, which realizes a sense of stereoscopic

impression. The upper lip and the lower lip are crossed into the shape of zigzag. The hair on the abdomen and the feathers are outlined with double intaglio lines, the two sides of which are carved with short intaglio lines. The reverse side is smooth and plain, with deep or shallow drilling trace and X trace, as well as three holes to fixing the Cortical belt.

The composition of the picture is similar to "Spring Water Jade". A falco rusticolus obsoletus shall be added to the top of the swan head to compose a compete pattern. Falco rusticolus obsoletus is also called Yinggu, Tuguying in Chinese, and mainly lives in Heilongjiang watershed. It is brave, and can be trained to be falcon to hunt the wild goose and the swan. The picture of the plate are supposed to take the theme from this, and the composition of the picture is symmetrical. The branches and peduncles are like thin lines, and the leaves and petals are with sharp edges. The engraving technique belongs to that of the middle and later Ming Dynasty.

83. Ornaments with Qilin(a kind of dragon) Pattern

The two pieces are excavated from the same tomb of the Ming Dynasty, with the same subjects. One is oval square shaped, and the other is heart shaped. The rim of the positive side is molded to be a narrow side by the technique of reducing the base materials. A Qilin(a kind of Dragon) is hollowed out in th certer part, truning its head back and walking in the hills. It has triangualr eyes, with mouth open, beard on the chin, horns on the top of head, and flame patterns on the shoulder. The nose is upright, ears inclined, hair are forward and tail is rise. The inclined girds on the body are flakes. The back is flat, plain and a little coarse. There are more holes for stringing and fixing to the Cortical belt.

With deer's horns, Qilin is one of the auspicious legendary animals in China. With deer's hoof and flakes all over the body, the pattern of the body has an obvious phytophagous feature. From the Han Dynasty on, listed with the four spiritual animals namely Green Dragon, White Tiger, Black Tortoise and Rosefinch, Qilin(a kind of dragon) became the spiritual animal represented the center position and "Tu"(one of the five elements).

84. Heart Shaped Jade Belt Ornament with Dragon Pattern

The belt ornament is heart shaped. Double layers of openwork carving were decorated in the pane. A dragon which twists in the clouds is pierced on the upper layer, which is carved deeply. The head of the dragon is short, and is in a posture of looking upward. The auspicious nose is in an cocking-up posture as a pig's nose, with beard on the end. The mouth is open, the lower chin is short and the forehead is prominence. The two eyes are round and protruding, two straight horns are at the back of the head, and the hair is upward. The dragon body is like a snake, thin and long. Intaglio lines are carved to form the close mesh ripples. There is a strand of hair at the flank of the body, and the joint is decorated with rolling cloud patterns. The shanks are thin and lean, and the paws are in the shape of windmill. The lower layer is pierced with patterns of twisted flowers and grasses on the branches. The jade belt ornament is imbedded into the copper shell. At the reverse side of the copper shell a copper buckle is welded. The copper buckle is composed of two parts, namely buckle body and buckle tongue. The buckle body is welded onto the copper shell, and the center part is pierced with patterns of twisted flowers and grasses on the branches. There are three holes which are used to pass through the rivet and fix the buckle body. There is bridge form button on one side to get through the cortical belt. The buckle tongue is in shape of the letter T. On the tongue there is plate-typed spring. Insert the buckle body and spring up, it will be locked at the edge. When clearing the buckle, press down the device on the round hole, extraction can be realized. There is a bridge form button on the umbrella-shaped back of the buckle tongue. On the upper out flank of the button, there is another bridge form button horizontally used for hanging.

85. Jade Belt Ornament

The belt is in the shape of flat rectangle. The positive side is carved with rivers and waves. There is a person walking along the hillside which is beside the bank. She wears robe with cross collar and wide sleeves, with a belt tied to the waist. She walks slowly to the small bridge. The trees make a pleasant shade. On the other side of the river bank, there are palaces and pavilions hidden in the clouds. The center part of the reverse side is concave, and there are perforations on two side, which are used to tie the ornament to the belt.

This belt ornament is grinded by the technique of removing the ambient materials excluded the patterns to make the protruding lines prominent. As a picture of line drawing in traditional ink and brush style, this picture is a small one, thus, the content of the picture could not be arranged well, not along the presentation of hills behind hills. The general waterscape is that the forest is as close shot, while the hills in light color are as the distant view. After the main structure is determined, other sceneries are produced step by step to finish the art of composition. The artist makes wonderful layout for the "image" of the little jade belt ornament. All the images, such as walking persons, hillside, small bridge and big trees, intricate with each other. Seen from the river, the palaces and the pavilions are like the sight of mirage. The artist's comprehension on the layout of the landscape painting and confidence on the caving produces so magnificent and intense scenery, which deepens the infection to the appreciator. This piece of jade "picture" engraved is identical with the Chinese landscape painting, which strives for the intermingled deficiency and excess, development of the artistic conception and enrichment of the connotation. It integrates the sparse trees, slope, bank, waves and floating clouds, thus, it produces a magnificent atmosphere and deep artistic conception. The more especial point is that there is no cutting in the center of the picture, which expresses the vast river and makes people relaxed and happy. Less curving is also abided by in the carving of close hill stones and slope, as well as the image of the two trees and one bridge, which strives to express a regular simple arrangement and achieve the scenery of vast river water. The palaces and pavilions on the other side are hidden and set off by forest and clouds and rasults in a broken and misty image immediately, which is named "spirit scenery" and conform to the natural regulations. The picture expresses a broad sight within a limited space, especially the walking person, who added strong living temperament and interest to the "picture."

86. Jade Ornament

It is flat, and the white sports are mingled with the green jade. The flat surface is similar to a semi-circle. There is a perforation in the upper center part, which is molded by double-sided drilling in opposite directions, next to which, there is a perforation on the edge. The entire jade is polished and plain without patterns.

87. Jade Fish Hawk

It is three-dimensional and full relief. The fish hawk has round eyes and hook-shaped beak. Both the wings are decorated with cloud patterns, which show the feathers. With the high rolling crown, the fish-hawk is in a posture of standing. The features of the fish-hawk are presented by the eyes, beak, crown and feathers. There is a perforation in the center of the hook-shaped beak. One orifice is large and the other orifice is small. They are drilled from the counter directions for stringing. The head is curved symmetrically and double-sided. It is curvrd single-sided bellow the neck. The head is curved symmetrically and double-sided. It is curved single-sided bellow the neck. The feathers on the body and the outline of shanks are sketched by combination of double intaglio lines and single intaglio lines. The lines are course and there are burrs at the nooks, with the edges around evenly chamfered. The entire jade is polished well. The nature of the jade is dark green with shining light yellow and soil leaching sports. The excavation place of the jade fish-hawk is on the other bank of Bashui River, opposite to the place where the Laoniupo Shang Dynasty Relic is found. Seen from the excavation place and the features of the jade, it sould be the relic of the Shang Dynasty.

Fish-hawk is also named "osprey." It can be used for hunting fish after being trained. In the Shang Dynasty, many images about the animal were adopted in the carving of pendants, for instance, the jade fish, jade silk-warm, etc. Fish-hawk is a tool for people to hunt the fish. The appearance of the jade fish-hawk shows that fishing had been an important activity at that time.

88. Jade Swallow

The jade is flat and in the posture of flying. It has sharp beak and round eyes, with both wings unfolded and short tail bifurcate. The feathers on the eyes, wings and tails are sketched with inclined cutting, which makes a simplified shape. The faces are carved with the skills of exaggeration and patterning. The eyes are represented by only two big circles, while the two feathers are represented by carving swirl grains. Though it is a primitive image, but it is vivid. The swallow belongs to migratory bird. The arrival of the swallows predicts the arrival of the spring. Everything becomes green in the spring, thus, swallow in ancient China was a sign that the weather was warmer or colder. Swallow is the savior of everything in the severe winter. Therefore, people considered swallow as the life-spring and the omen that dominate the reproduce of the life.

89. Jade Insect

The insect is carved with flat green jade and with two sides engraved. The volume is small, with narrow head and wide tail. the mouth is sharp and long, and the eyes are bulging and round. A wide protuberant line is carved by double intaglio lines to mold the neck. Two folded wings are carved on the back. The width of tail is reduced and molded by the technique of removing the materials around the patterns. It is long but wide, and is bifurcate at the end. There is a perforation horizontally at the place of the mouth for stringing. This piece of jade is carved with slice-shaped materials, with simple shape and coarse lines. The surface is not so polishing, the size is small and the representation is natural and primitive.

90. Jade Silkworm

There are three kinds for the body shape of the silk-warm, namely square tube shaped, flat triangular shaped and flat arc-shaped silkworm. All the bodies are in the shape of bamboo joint. For square tube shaped silkworm, the forehead is short and the chin is protruding. The technique of removing the materials around the patterns and intaglio lines are adopted to mold the round eyes. A concave groove with wide orifice and narrow base is used to represent the slightly opened mouth. There is a perforation downward across the center of the mouth. In addition, there is another perforation from the head to the tail for stringing, which is drilled from opposite directions meanwhile. For the flat triangular silkworm, the head is in the shape of slope, and the eyes are sketched with intaglio lines. The perforation is drilled from two sides of the head. For the flat arc-shaped silkworm, the head is flat and round, and there is a trumpet shaped perforation horizontally. The body is curved and the tail is pointed. Most of the jade silkworms were found in the relics and tombs of the Shang Dynasty. Some bronze wares of this period were decorated with the silkworm patterns, which show that the textile industry by silkworm was quite prosperous.

91. Jade Bead String

There are in all 429. Chalcedony is divided into two kinds, namely circular ring and circular tube. Both are in the color of orange and are semi-crystal. The outer rim of the circular ring is similar to arc. The middle part of the circular tube is bulging, and the size of the perforation in the middle is not the same. The jade bead strings are all tubular shaped. The surface is bulging, and the color is close to the pine green. Parts are not so regular in the shape.

92. Chisel-shaped Jade Pendant with Beast Face Patterns

It is flat and in the shape of Kui Dragon. the head is big and the tail is small. And it is engraved single-sided. The Kui Dragon is in a posture of creeping, with the mouth stretched forward. The eyes are large and the eyebrows are long. the forehead is decorated with diamond cob webbing. The head and the body are separated with a narrow groove, and the two ends of the groove are hollowed out for stringing. The body is made to the shape of letter "S" through the upper and lower circular vortexes which are symmetrical in counter direction and hollow out right angel line. The tooth protruding on two sides represent the hint legs. The tails are thin and the center part is a little bulging. Two sides of the point of tail are chamfered to be blade. Several groups of Qin-style dragon patterns are curved with intaglio lines on the body and the tail. The spacing of pattern distribution is proper, thus it is not disordered. The lines are smooth but with force. The shape of the Kui Dragon is vivid and exaggerated. The entire body is well-polished, with smooth and moist surface. Though the X jade was excavated from the tomb of the Han Dynasty, it should belong to the relic of the Qin People of the period of the Warring States, seen from the geometry shape of the Kui Dragon and the style of the cloud patterns.

93. I-shaped Tubular Jade Pendant with Dragon Pattern in Qin Style

There is an embossing square bridge button at the side of the pipe, and among the button there is a little mobilizable ring. The double-barreled pipe is hollowed in the center and is molded by drilling from counter directions. The orifice is big, while the center part of the perforating is narrow with regular orifice. The double-barreled pipe and the joint place are decorated with groups of Qin-style dragon patterns. The spacing of pattern layout is proper, miscellaneous but not disordered. The patterns on the jade pendant are molded by techniques of combining hammer and inclined cutting, to sketch the cloud patterns with protruding lines. The fabrication of the jade is that first cut the base materials from different directions into small uncut jade in slice according to the number required and then connect a mobilizable loop at each uncut place. If connecting more jade pendants, break the uncut jade without the connected mobiliable loop, As the ware, each uncut jade is connected with mobiliable loop, which facilitates the folding and unfolding. At last, carve or pierce patterns. The process is divided into cutting, perforation, piercing and carving patterns. The jade pendant with connected loops had never seen before. It shows that the jade craft of China had developed into an unprecedented period in the period of the Spring and Autumn the Warring States, which have an important significance on the jade development history. In Shaanxi History Museum, the same ware in copper is collected. Part of the internal rim of the mobiliable loop on the jade ware polished, due to stringing obviously. Therefore, it can be inferred that the jade ware should be a pendant.

94. Agate Ring

The ring is round, and the cross section is in the irregular shape. The outside is in the shape of isosceles acute triangle. The upper and the inner side are in the shape of pentagon. The shape and appearance is regular and smooth, with fine grinding and polishing. Though this ring was excavated from the Han Dynasty, the agate ring of the same shape and appearance had been found in the tombs of the late Spring and Autumn period, and also in Chu tombs in the early Warring States which might be the relics of the Spring and Autumn period and the period of the Warring States. The ring is carved with agate, with light cream color but close to light red. It is crystal and has refraction light.

The ring is disk-shaped pendant. The diameter of hole and the diameter of jade proper are similar. And the hole is larger, compared with cinclides. It is used to tie the clothes or to form a pendant. Many were excavated from the tombs of the Spring and Autumn period and the period of Warring States. Usually it is slice-shaped ring with single angle or dihedral angle carving. The sections are hexagon, octagon, oval, diamond or round. Curled-up dragon was popular in the Han Dynasty. All kinds of ring-shaped novelty, exquisite piercings in the Tang Dynasty became new styles of piercing patterns. The jade ring of the Song Dynasty and the Yuan Dynasty had great improvement based on the former ones.

95. Agate Pendant

Three agates are all in the shape of irregular pentagon. A straight perforation is drilled horizontally at the center part by rod drilling for stringing. The entire body of three agate pendants are bright and plain, well-polished and with excellent color. The base color decorated by agate slice is deep red and deep brown, mingled with white and yellow. There are white and yellow thin lines arranged closely and orderly in the white and yellow color lumps, which are colorful. The patterns are at ease, with clear layers. The nature and color appears to be noble and magnificent.

The skin texture patterns from nature surpass the intentional carving by humanity. It is said that this kind of agate is not grown in Central China, but in the Western Regions. It was brought in the Central China by the merchants and diplomatic envoys through the Silk Road. Empire Cao Pi in the period of Three Kingdoms hod ever said, "Agate is from the Western Regions with patterns interlaced".

96. Jade Xie-Zhi(a legendary beast)

It is a piece of white jade and carved by the technique of circular engravure. Xie-Zhi, a kind of therion in ancient China, is in the posture of creeping on the square stage. It has big eyes, upright nose and big mouth, with the only horn on the head. The head turns to left, the ears are closed backward, and the short tail ties to the side of buttock.

Jade Xie-Zhi is a kind of therion in ancient times. The 14th volume of Book of the Later Han records, "Xie-Zhi is a spirit goat. It can distinguish right and wrong. King of Chu had ever captured one and used it as a crown", Notice referred from "Record of Foreign Matter" said, "in the barren of northeastern area, there is a kind of beast named Xie-Zhi. It has one horn and is loyal. It will fight with person who is not loyal. It will bite the person who is not upright." People spoke "Xie-Zhi Litigation" in ancient times, thus, the image of Xie-Zhi became the pronoun of judiciary officers in the history.

Though the body of the jade Xie-Zhi is small, the style for a certain period is distinct. Based on the outline, the intaglio thin lines are employed to sketch the eyes, nose, mouth and detail. The style is quiet. The head turns to one side, the eyes open as the shape of Chinese character "臣". It seems that it is watching out for the sound around and gets ready to attack immediately. It is an act in motionless and silence, which makes people feel danger and disturbance in calm. It represents the wild spirit of the beast. The design is vivacious, not limited to the layout. Combined with many carving techniques, it focuses on the dynamic skillfully. the image is intensely alive and lifelike, which achieves an excellent masterpiece. there is one small perforation in the middle of the neck. Two ends of the orifice are rubbed, which shows that it is a pendant ornament.

97. Jade Heng(top jade in group pendants) in the shape of a Bat

There are three pieces in all, all of which are flat. Two pieces are bat-shaped. There are three arcs connected with each other to form the head. The wing tips hook back. There are four perforations separately in head, tail and two wings. the other piece is a Jade Heng in the shape of simplified Bat. The head is the same with the former ones. part of the image is in the shape of slope. The body, wing, and tail are simplified as trapezoid. All the three Jade Hengs are plain and without patterns. The surface is smooth, but the polishing effect is common.

In the Northern and Southern Dynasties, the development of jade ware decayed. The ritual jade and the jade for burial withdraw from the historical stage. The decoration craft became the mainstream day by day. A conversion from the politics-focused and grade-focused orientation to secularization occurs to the jade ware.

98. Jade Pendants Bordered with Gold

The jade pendant is in the shape of triangular, with point top and flat base. The tow waists are three connected arcs and single-sided carved. The positive side is decorated with double phoenix patterns bordered with gold. The bird body is carved into circular arc. The head and the neck stretch out. Sharp beak, long crown. Each of the main parts is decorated with rolling cloud patterns. All the ornamented parts are bordered with gold. Close to the top, there are wasp waist hole for stringing.

The craft of jade pendants bordered with gold was started from the Spring and Autumn period, and got popular from the period of Warring Sates. Seen from this piece of jade pendants, the ornamentation are achieved by attaching gold foil to the groove bottom and side wall of intaglio lines and then make the two combined closely and the surface of gold foil flat. Ornamentation bordered with gold are decorated on the crystal and smooth jade, which appears to be noble and magnificent.

The shape of this jade pendant is rich of style of the Western Regions. The bordered gold and cloud patterns are traditional craft and patterns. It develops based on the traditional craft and cultural art and taken in the foreign culture. It is free from the art style of the Han Dynasty and form a more mature art style. It is bold, generous and magnificent, which shows that the craft that pendants are bordered with gold.

99. Jade Hairpin with Flower Pattern

① There is one jade hairpin with phoenix pattern. It is slice shaped and looks like a leave. A phoenix is carved on the flower leaf of the front end. It is in the posture of flying with two wings unfolded and tail cocking-up. The flower leaf under the phoenix is as the cloud in the air, harmonious with flying of the bird. Phoenix pattern came from the bird pattern, and it is also the combination of many bird images in the nature. When flying, hundreds of birds follow after, therefore, it is called the king of the bird.

② There is one jade hairpin with mandarin pattern. It is slice shaped and looks like a leave. Four flowers bloom luxuriantly. A pair of mandarins playing with water is decorated on the biggest flower. Mandarin has been praised to be love bird to present the happiness between the husband and the wife.

③ There are 4 jade hairpins with pomegranate flower pattern. A pomegranate is carved on the flower leaf of the front end, under which there are several blooming pomegranate. The close inclined grid is used to present the seeds of pomegranate.

There are six jade hairpins with flower patterns. All of them are slice shaped and look like leaves. The outlines are sketched with simple arc, and the details are decorated with intaglio lines. The space between the lines are proper, thus it is not disordered. In addition, the sense of layering is strong. There is a rabbit in the shape of reversed trapezoid on one end of the hairpin. Meanwhile, it is connected with the end of silver hairpin by rivet.

100. Jade Pendant with "the Forecast of Coming of the Spring"

The jade pendant is flat, and is carved by single face. A magpie is flying with wings unfolded and a plum blossom in the mouth. Its long tail flutters in the wind. On the top of head, there are flowers in full bloom. Based on the outline curved by piercing, the technique of removing the ambient materials excluded the patterns, hollowing carving to make low-lying areas and adding intaglio lines are adopted to carve the body of bird and flowers and branches. The feather and leaf vein are clear and petals and branches are oblique outward. The petals and the center part of leaves are engraved with intaglio lines, which are intervened with clear stereo perception.

The image of this jade pendant is an auspicious pattern appeared in the Song Dynasty named the Forecast of Coming of the Spring. Happiness is the first Chinese character of the name of magpie. The plum blossom is cold-resistant and blooms in the early spring. The Forecast of Coming of the Spring means that magpie takes the lead in forecasting the coming of the spring and symbolize the hope.

101. Jade Board with Hollow-carved Tortoise, Deer and Crane Patterns

The jade board is vertical type and in the shape of ovoid. The bottom is flat slightly and is hollowed out. Among the stones there are pine trees, bamboos and Lucid Ganoderma. There is a tortoise crawled between the stones. The tortoise sprays out pieces of auspicious cloud. A deer turns back to looking up the crane in the sky. Tortoise is one of the four spirit animals. It can predict good or ill luck and is considered to be an omniscience beast. When person goes west, he usually rides on its back. Deer and crane are immortal beast and immortal bird, and they suggest longevity. Pine trees and bamboos live through four seasons. Bamboos have joints, which means upright. Lucid Ganoderma live together with the ancient trees or rotten woods, which means that the rotten woods come with spring. This group of lucid Ganoderma is "good fortune and emolument", which means the peace, longevity, and abundance.

The reverse side is polished. On the bottom part of the image there are two perforations for stringing.

102. Jade Horse

The jade horse twists the legs and crouches, nodding the head. The head is a little bigger. The eyes are curved with offset tool and double arc lines, with canthuses not connected. the nose and the mouth are molded by a few of lines. The two ears are upright. The intaglio beard is combed to left and right separately. The expression of the horse is honest and tolerant. Its body is small and lovely. There is a perforation across the center part of the horse for stringing.

103. Jade Board with Chi Dragon and Flower Patterns

Flowering branch are pierced in the oval square ring, among which there is a curled-up dragon passing through. Closely flowering branches are criss-cross and stretches outwardly. Floral leaves are curled up with clear leave veins. Head of the curled-up dragon is slightly round. The eyes are round, eyebrows are thick, ears are upright, hair on the neck is swinging, and the narrow neck is concave. The front limbs are creeping, while the two hind legs are with one in front of the other. The body turns to one side to form a "U" shape. The long tail curls back in the posture of creeping. The backbone is carved with double intaglio lines horizontally to make it to be the shape of bamboo joint. The joint of shoulder is decorated with rolling cloud patterns. Four limbs and the waist are covered with flowering branches.

This piece of jade is carved with three-dimensional piercing technique. The lines are used to engrave the flowers and leaves on surface layer. the space between the flowers and leaves are molded with the technique of removing the materials around the pattern itself. And then the interveined branches and Pan Dragon are pierced. In the spaces drilled piercing holes and then cut with a fretsaw. The center part of the reverse side is hollowed out and the edges of the oval square ring are polished. There is a flat through hole between the dragon waist and the ring for stringing. The technique of high relief and piercing is the deep layer three-dimensional jade carving method commonly used in the Yuan Dynasty.

104. Jade Pendant with Lotus Leaf and Fish Patterns

The pendant is slightly flat. There is a fish floating on the lotus leaf with waterweeds in the mouth. The lotus leave is arc-shaped. The leave flank curls inwardly, and the leave vein of both sides are carved with thin lines. There is a fish floating on the lotus, with the stem of waterweed in the mouth. Two leaves are floating around the lotus leave. The body of the fish is straight. There is an intaglio line represented the lip of fish. The lip stretches forwardly and is open. The round eyes are pipe-drilled. The branches are sketched with protuberant lines wing shallow groove shape. The scales on the surface are represented with closely-arranged grid patterns. The rims of dorsal fin are engraved with saw tooth. The pelvic fin is extended to tail and leveled with abdomen. The bifurcate tail sways to one side. The entire image is to represent the situation of the swimming fish rushing at the waterweeds. Though the fish body is not curved, the image is quite forceful. The shape of fish body is round and strong. The soft lines and straight lines are mingled together, which expresses the dynamic beauty when the fish is preying. The lines on the whole body are clear and bright, well-arranged. The lines in perfect order strengthen the sense of reality. On the upper part there is a pipe-drilled perforation in the shape of trumpet for stringing.

The lotus and swimming fish is a traditional auspicious pattern with propitious omen. In Chinese, the word "fish" means that people have enough and spare property. The lotus leave represents the blooming lotus. It is a blessing to wear the jade pendant with pattern of lotus and swimming fish, which suggests enough and spare properties in successive year.

105. Jade Pendants in the shape of an Ox

Three oxen twist the limbs and crouch in parallel. The ox in the middle faces to the opposite directions. The ox on the side is bowing its head and having rest. The ox in the middle is looking up in he sky. There is a small calf lean close to the ox. The cowboy curls his left leg and leans o the back of the ox, tow hands holding a flute. The entire image is simplified. The eyes, nose and mouth are showed with small round holes, with forceful way of cutting. There are two perforations separately on two sides of the waist of the middle ox for stringing.

The theme of this work is taken from the little cowboy, named the little boy pasture the caw. This kind of theme was popular from the Yuan Dynasty on, and appeared on the drawing, tooth carving(bamboo or wood), copper, and jade carving and even in the poem and drama, which reflected the posture in the countryside. This jade carving expresses the common life of posture and forms a special artistic conception. The two oxen crouch back to back quietly. The two oxen crouch back to back quietly. The babyish calf beside the old oxen leans to the mother. The manner that the cowboy leans to the middle ox and plays the flute makes people hear the minor scale of cowboy.

106. White Jade Pendant with Mandarin Ducks, Crane and Lotus Patterns

The jade pendant is molded with the technique of circular engravure with the positive side bulged and the reverse side slightly flat. The positive side is engraved with lotus and leave, on which there is a pair of mandarin duck swimming in the water with lotus seeds in the mouth, playing with each other. On the reverse side there is a crane turning its back and curling its neck. It is standing on the leave with a stem of lotus in the mouth and. Beside the crane stands a lotus seed. The manner of the crane and the mandarin are natural and vivid. The feathers are composed of rolling cloud patterns. The lotus and the leave are thick, unfolded, with clear veins.

The patterns on the jade pendant include two aspects of content. The image composed by mandarin duck and lotus is named "Mandarin Duck Playing with lotus". There is an old saying. "Only envy the mandarin but not the immortal". It means that people are willing to be the mandarin. while not the immortal because the harmony life between the husband and wife surpasses that of immortals. The crane and the lotus compose an image of "The crane screams in the broad marsh". Ancient people considered crane to be an auspicious bird. the Book of Songs Xiaoya says. "The crane screams in the broad marsh, and the voice can be heard far away." Poet Wang. Jian lived in the Tang Dynasty says. "Crane lives for thousands of years to enjoy its lives". Shuolinxun of Huainanzi records. "though the peach blossom comes out, it does not mean the spring; though the crane lives a long life, it is not divine". In addition, Nine Chapters of Statement for Qu, Yuan says. "groups of crane get together around the Pole Star" implied longevity and propitious omen.

107. Agate Pendant in the shape of Jujube

The red agate is engraved into three pendants in the shape of jujube. Two are bellow. and the other one is up. Several horizontal thin lines are carved on the body of the juiube, which shows the outline feature of a just ripe jujube. This pendant is molded by adopting the carving technique and employing the color and characteristic of the agate skin to engrave five jujube cores. A tiny concaved pit is carved on the core. The whole cutting is very simple and vivid.

108. Jade Hairpin

It is composed of silver hairpin body and jade hairpin head. The jade hairpin head is lice-shaped/ A magpie is bending down and raising its head, which is molded with the technique of double-faced engraving. Its sharp beak is open, tweeting for announcing good news. The wings are folded together at the back and its long tail is a little longer. The details of the bird body are carved with thin lines. The plum blossom under the bird head is blooming with leaves at the background. The counter of the plumblossom is composed of five connected arcs. calyx and the stamen of which are carved with slant grid patterns. The petals and leaves are engraved by intaglio lines. The space between the bird body and flowering branches are pierced with pipe-drilled technique, the surface of which is grinded meticulous, while the flank and the internal wall of the piercing part is coarse with obvious trace.

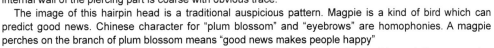

The image of this hairpin head is a traditional auspicious pattern. Magpie is a kind of bird which can predict good news. Chinese character for "plum blossom" and "eyebrows" are homophonies. A magpie perches on the branch of plum blossom means "good news makes people happy"

Jade hairpin is a kind of hair ornaments for woman; usually it is a decorating part for metallic ornaments.

After the Tang Dynasty, jade flowering hairpin was popular.

109. Jade Bracelet with the Motif of "Two dragons playing with a ball"

The bracelet is oval shaped, engraved with the pattern of Two Dragons Playing with a Ball. The dragons seem to be happy to meet with each other. With head to head, they have round balls in the mouths. It is proper to take round as the base materials. For the two dragons on the bracelet, only with their heads carved. The shape are the same, such as long mouths, wide noses, thick and long eyebrows, curled horns and two strands of hair are curved. The center part of the dragon body is decorated with a piece of cloud. The dragon head and cloud are carved finely and complicated. The five senses and the beard and hair are all polished well, while the internal wall of the dragon mouth pipe-drilled is not subjected to meticulous polishing.

Two Dragons Playing with a Ball is a common theme in the jade bracelet carving in the Ming Dynasty and the Qing Dynasty. In Chinese ancient legendary, dragon ball is the essence of the dragon, and is the element and spirit of the cultivation. Thus, in the art, people express their happy life by the theme of dragons striving for the ball.

Jade bracelet is a kind of arm decorates. It is appeared in Liang zhu Culture of the new stone period. The shape of jade bracelet in the early Qin Dynasty were influenced by Liangzhu Culture, therefore, the body is high and is in cylindric shape. The bracelet wall is slice-shaped with flat and straight rim, And then it developed into the shape of short body and thick wall. Till the Tang Dynasty and the Song Dynasty, the cylindric arm bracelet was appeared. There were several kinds of jade bracelet in the Ming Dynasty, such as type of cutting bamboo and type of hank knotting with the internal wall flat and straight and the external wall round and convex. Type of Two Dragons with Balls in the Mouths Separately or the jade which had the external wall engraved with images or auspicious language was popular in the Qing Dynasty.

110. Jade Double Beast Pendants

The pendant is in the shape of oval, engraved with three-dimensional circular engravure. The double beasts crouch face to face with each other. They have long mouths, with big ears closed backwardly, The long tails are covered with the head of the other one. The four eyes are looking with each other. They are having along ribbon in their mouths. Generally speaking, the image of jade bracelet is well fabricated, with excellent engraving craft.

The beast engraved on this bracelet is badger, an animal with brutal temperament and ferocity. With outstanding skills and employing traditional techniques such as intaglio, relief, circular engravure, piercing, etc, the carver molded the round bodies strong four limbs and big noses. The whole shape of the double badger is tender and lovely. The manner of reposing and the posture of eye to eye reflect a kind of care.

The Chinese character huan(badger) is the homophonic of happy. Changshou (ribbon) is the homophonic of longevity, which means that the couple is happy and longevity.

111. Jade Double Fish Pendants

The pendant is engraved to be a shape of double fish. The head of two fishes toward the same direction. One fish body is straight and the other one is curved. Each of the fish holds waterweeds with the mouth. The round eyes are pipe-drilled and the dorsal fin is carved with short line goes according to the body, beside which there are crossing patterns. The tail is unfolded as a bow, the outline of which is in the shape of connected arcs. Two sides are decorated with arc lines in radial pattern. The shapes of the two fishes shows the moment situation when fishes having waterweeds in the water, with rich joy and fun.

112. Jade Pendant with the Motif of Liuhai(a god in the Chinese legend) Playing with Toad

There is one boy climbing up the cucurbit, with one hand grasped the branches, and the other hand carried the threading belt fishing the golden toad under the cucurbit. The boy bends his knees and arches his back, with his head funnily slanted to one side. A bat is on his back. The name of this image is Liuhai Playing with Toad. This literary quotation is from Taoism, drawn a farfetched analogy by an intellectual man. The golden toad is a frog with three toes. In ancient times, people considered that toad can bring about fortune, thus, toad implies successive fortune and happiness, Bat is a mammal animal which can fly. "Bat" in Chinese is the homophonic of fortune. What a bat is flying in means the fortune is coming. Cucurbit is the magic weapon of Tieguaili, who is one of the eight immortals of the Taoism. It also is one of the secret eight treasures. Tieguaili usually takes care of the patients with the herbal medicine in the cucurbit and saves the lives of people and bring about happiness to people, This piece of jade pendant combined the golden toad, bat and cucurbit together to compose an auspicious picture.

113. Green Jade Board with Chi Dragon and Cloud Patterns

It is a ring-shaped pendant, with one hole in the center, one dragon lying inside of the hole, who's holding its head high, opening its eyes widely, four legs crouch and twist, and its long tail resting on the back. There are two dragons crawling outside the ring. One of the dragons is on upper side and the other lower. They are looking into the hole with four paws walking and long tails dragging. Beside the dragons, there are three floating clouds, which symbolize that the dragon is crawling in the clouds. The manners of three curled-

dragons are different. The one in the hole is curling up and having a rest, with head rose up. Its eyes are focusing on the front direction and seem to hide himself. The two outside are walking in the clouds, with two eyes watching with each other and looking at the one in the hole.

The three curl-up dragons are strong with powerful limbs, which show strong and vigorous sense. The one in the hole is resourceful and clear, while the two on the ring are searching for the hidden one. Seen from the manner of the eyes, they have found the left one. The ferocious animals are playing with the hide and seek as children. Due to rich imagination, the image is full of temperament and interest.

114. Jade Board with Kui Dragon Pattern

Kui Dragon sits erectly, turning its head back to see backward. Its eyes are round, nose broad, mouth big, hair on the forehead curled backward. The body is in the shape of "S", while the tail is holding up. The body of the dragon squats on the raised tail point, the entire body is decorated with successive clouds, Circular engravure, intaglio and piercing are adopted in the carving, which achieves a vivid legendary image.

In the Shang Dynasty and the Zhou Dynasty, Kui Dragon was as the decoration on the wares. It is very mysterious and horrible, and a symbol of power and status. The imperators in the Qing Dynasty were fond of antique, especially in Qianlong period, "The inferiors always copy the favor of the superiors and go further". Thus, modeling after the antique was popular in common people. This plate is an representation of that trend of modeling after the antique.

115. Jade Board with Parrot Pattern

A parrot in the ring with connected bead patterns are carved, with round eyes and hook-shaped beak. The long tail is drooping down. One of the feet is standing on the beam and the other foot is tied to a long belt which is around the beam. The connected bead ring and the beam are used to lock the parrot. The startled parrot is about to fly suddenly with feather folded, while the belt tied to the leg makes it impossible. Thus the parrot is turning its head back and walking back and forth to take precautions against unexpected attacking. With life-like manner, it produces a vivid image. Each of the connected beads on the ring is meticulously processed with long and thin belt around the beam, which is exquisite and delicate. The feathers on the whole body are white and clean without any flaw. It is excellent and wonderful.

Jade parrot plate ornament is a pendant worn on one's body and is very popular in common people, represented the jade engraving craft at the time, This piece of jade parrot plate belongs to the product after Qianlong times of Qing Dynasty.

116. Jade Square Board Symbolizing Happiness and Longevity

The plate is in the shape of rectangle and multilayer pierced. The frame of the plate is in the shape of bamboo joint, with the center piercing a character Shou in the seal character type. The place around the character are decorated with branches of plum blossoms and bamboo leaves, There is a bat in the right bottom corner. The flowering branches go outwardly, with branches turning reversely. The surface of the character strokes, petals and bamboo are hidden and sketched with intaglio lines. There is a bat flying with the wings unfolded. The joints of the bamboo are hidden and sketched with intaglio lines. The positive side is well polished and the back is smooth.

The patterns on the jade plate include several auspicious patterns. Shou implies longevity. "Bat" in Chinese is the homophonic of fortune. Plum blossom can stand the frost and resist the snow.

117. Jade Grasshopper

The grasshopper is thin and long, with double eyes bulge and long wings close to the body. Two hint legs fold at the side of the abdomen and is about to jump. The carving technique is simple, with details carved by smooth intaglio lines. The shape is vivid, with unity of form and spirit. Grasshopper livers in the later autumn, and is the symbolization of late autumn, expressed bleak morning in autumn, wilderness in the late autumn, withered trees and tweet of grasshopper, which increase the flavor of desolation.

During the period of Kangxi, Yongzheng and Qianlong Reign, the social stability and development of economy reaches a top position in the traditional society, and achieved a "Kang&Qian Flourishing Age", However, the ruling class's severe pressure policy in the "literary inquisition" had appealed the disappointment of the intellectuals. They expressed their feelings by describing the nature. This is piece of jade grasshopper is a reflection of sadness and disappointment of the times.

118. Jade Reclining Dog

The dog is in the prone position, with the head and mouth raised up, and two eyes opened. The big ears are drooping down and the four limbs crouch forwardly. The hind legs are carved with slant cutting. and the tail rolls up and closes to the buttock. There is a hole between the two legs for stringing. The small dog is exquisite and warning of surroundings. Few lines outline the eyes, nose, mouth and four limbs, with coordinate proportions.

Embedded Jade Articles

119. Jade Sword Finial with Grain Patterns

Both the two sword heads are cake-shaped, the section of which is trapezoid. The patterns and ornaments on the positive side are divided into inner area and outer area. A protuberant line is carved on the rim of both the inner and outer areas by intaglio lines to form inner outline and outer outline, Cloud patterns are carved smoothly and freely in the inner area, and diamond patterns are in the center part, with the plane leveled to the outer rim of the sword head. The outer layer is carved with grain patterns with the technique of reducing the base materials. Every grain pattern has the same size and end line, with sharp way of cutting. A round stage is protruding in the center part of the sword head, with slope stage around. There are mortise in the center of the round stage for inserting the handle of a sword. THere are three inclined perforations outside the mortise in the bigger one, which is used to hit into the wedge to fix the sword handle.

120. Jade Sword Finial with Hollow-carved Chi Pattern

The undersurface of the sword head is flat, with two round holes fixing the sword handle an d head. The positive side and two flanks are engraved with three-dimensional Chi Dragons in clouds. Some of them are climbing, some are flying on the clouds. Moreover, there are vivid monsters with different images. Three-dimensional carving, relief and hollowing carving are adopted to mold an image in the cloud, which set off the Chi Dragon in the clouds. The top one is on the peak of cloud, with eyes dilated widely, head toward one side and looking down and mouth open slightly. The forceful and solid forepaws are climbing the clouds, with bulging leg muscle and round body. It seems that a limitless power is hidden in the fluctuant belly and will burst forth at any time. There is another Chi Dragon climbing over the cloud, with the beard on the head top fluttering in the wind. The sharp paws is grasping the clouds and is about to jump. Other Chi Dragons are holding up the head with glaring eyes and are about to running. It looks like they are meeting with the opponent and are ready to fight with each other. Small monsters are hidden away because they are afraid with Chi Dragon. Meanwhile, they are worried of falling off, with head turning back and paws grasping the cloud. Generally speaking, it is a picture of groups of Chi Dragons which are playing together in the sky. The structure of Chi Dragons are all S-shaped, with the beauty of curving lines, as well as dynamic and fluctuant sense. The artist set off the Chi Dragons with rolling clouds, shows the situation of going to fighting with contrast technique.

121. Jade Xin(a sword ornament) with Grain Pattern

Jade Xin is hill-shaped. The upper part is sharp, while the lower part is indent. Seen from the flank, it is a diamond. The center part is unsymmetrical pierced. The upper part is pierced to be oval square shaped, only for crossing a sword handle. The lower part is pierced to be diamond to clip the shoulder part of the blade. The surface of Xin is filled with patterns. Jade Xin, usually named Jade Ge, is the ornament jade between the blade and the handle.

122. Jade Zhi(a sword ornament) with Chi Dragon Pattern

It is rectangle in vertical view, with the front and the back ends rolled inwardly. There is a hole in the shape of rectangle for installing a Cortical belt, A Chi Dragon is embossed on the positive side with the technique of removing the ambient materials. The body of Chi Dragon is hidden in the clouds, and turns back its body and place the head on the upper waist. The joints and bifurcate tails is decorated with arcs. The back and its vicinity are decorated with cloud patterns in thin intaglio lines, which show the brave and fierce manner of the dragon. The representation technique of carving thin lines on the body of Chi Dragon is one of the main characteristics of Chi Dragon in the Eastern Han Dynasty.

123. Jade Zhi(a sword ornament) with Chi Dragon Pattern

It is rectangle in vertical view, with the front and the back ends rolled inwardly. There is a hole in the shape of rectangle for installing a Cortical belt. A Chi Dragon is embossed on the positive side of the bottom of spade. The head and buttock are protruding to the level, The body of Chi Dragon is curled to S shape. The four limbs are in a walking position. The Zhi spade bottom is engraved with cloud patterns, The body of Chi Dragon is powerful and unfolded, and is not limited to the Zhi surface, molded a vivid manner of the dragon in the clouds.

124. Jade Zhi with Son Dragon and Mother Dragon Patterns

It is rectangle in vertical view, with the front and the back ends rolled inwardly. There is a hole in the shape of rectangle for installing a Cortical belt. High relief of a pair of son dragon and mother dragon are embossed in the positive side. The shapes and postures of the two are basically the same. They are looking at each other with the head toward another side and playing with each other. The mouths of the big dragon and the small dragon are pierced, and corners of the mouth are drilled. The eyeballs droop a little, while the eyebrows are upright and hook-shaped. There are two intaglio parallel arcs. The ears are like those of Pekingese, while the tail is crossing the cloud. The upper part of the head, shoulder, hip and tail are polished well, and the edges are outlined with thin intaglio lines in the type of "silk hair carving". There is sugar color locally in the material of the jade. The catver employs the technique of "artful" to show the sugar surface, and added beauty to the vivid and lifelike son dragon and mother dragon.

125. Jade Zhi with Animal Face and Cloud Patterns

It is rectangle in vertical view, with the front and the back ends rolled inwardly. There is a hole in the shape of rectangle for installing a Cortical belt. THe positive ornament is carved secretly with the technique of removing the ambient materials excluded the patterns. One end is engraved with beast face, with double horns, big eyes, mouth and nose. There are successive cloud patterns eudipleural to the axes on the upper side of the beast face. Parallel curve lines are decorated among them. The rim on each flank is outlined with an intaglio line. The other end is engraved with curved geometry patterns in intaglio lines. There is one intaglio line separately on the upper side and lower side as the boundary. It seems that the two ends of Zhi and the pattern of the center part are independent ones, in fact, it is one complete beast pattern. The beast face of one end is as the head and the axes are as the ridge and the cloud patterns is as the stripes on the body. The geometry on the other end is as the tail.

126. Jade Zhi with Animal Face and Cloud Patterns

It is rectangle in vertical view, while it is similar to the arch bridge ween from the flank. There is a hole in the shape of rectangle for installing a Cortical belt. The positive ornament is carved secretly with the technique of removing the ambient materials excluded the patterns. There are reversed beast face, with clear eyebrows, eyes and nose, in which there is a midcourt line represented the ridge. The left and the right places are decorated with could patterns. There are triangular overlapping curve in the middle of the other end.

127. Jade Bi(a sword ornament) with Chi Patterns

Jade Bi is in the shape of trapezoid, the section of which is in the shape of a long olive. Both the two sides are embossed with Li patterns. There is bas-relief of Chi Dragon on one side of the Jade Bi. The body of the dragon is S-shaped, with clouds crossing form the waist. The head of Chi Dragon is holding up, and the eyebrows are upright and hooked. The eyeballs droop a little. There are intaglio double arc lines on the nose ridge. The short ears are upright, and the long hair on the neck is curled. An intaglio lines from the neck to the tail is used to represent the ridge. The shoulder and the hip are decorated with rolling clouds and the tail is in filate. The place around th Chi Dragon is molded with the technique of removing the ambient materials excluded the patterns and is carved with several clouds. The outline of one side of the Jade Bis is a little thick. The other side is molded with high relief to be a big Chi Dragon and a small Chi Dragon with S-shaped manners which are similar with the former one. The two Chi Dragons are holding one ribbon in their mouth. The ribbon goes across the underneath of the body of the small Chi Dragon, with ribbon fluttering and dragons flying, which achieve a dynamic sense. There are intaglio lines on the place closed to the Rim of the three angles, which is used to show the outline. There is one mortise on the top of the Jade Bi, used for the connection between the pin and the sword Ting head.

128. Jade Sword Finial with Chi Dragon and Bird Patterns

The sword head is in the shape of trapezoid. There are three tooth-shaped strips edges on the upper and lower edges, and in the middle of the tooth-shaped strip there is a groove. The positive side and the reverse side are embossed with Chi Dragon pattern and phoenix pattern separately, and the place around are outlined with intaglio lines to form the frame of the trapezoid. The head of the Chi Dragon is oval-shaped. Its eyes are round and ears droop down. The chest is round and upright, the body is straight, and the tail is curled up. Both the forepaws stretch forward, while the two hind legs are with one in front of the other. The phoenix on the other side is standing and only its profile can be seen. The sharp beak is hooked slightly, and the corner of the eyes are a little longer. The long crown is close, the wings are unfolded and the tail is raised. The rolling clouds and the curling patterns are as the feathers. The patterns on this piece of sword head are all the imitations of the same kind of the Qin Dynasty and the Han Dynasty. However, seen from the outlines, it is sharp in the transition place and soft in the turning place. It is classical technique of the Qing Dynasty.

129. Jade Zhi with Animal Patterns

It is rectangle in vertical view, with the front and the back ends rolled inwardly. There is a hole in the shape of rectangle for installing a cortical belt. The positive side is engraved with two pairs of animal patterns with one being big and another small by a certain technique of embossment. The big one is in the middle and the small one is at two ends. The animals are chasing by pairs. There are four animals. All of them are with big head. U-shaped small body, without four limbs. Around them there are ripples. Thus it seems that they are playing with each other. The two pairs of animal patterns are similar with each other. The pairs on the left: the head of the big animal is like a bird head in profile, with oval eyes, long eye corners and sharp beak; the small animal has slightly square head. Its face, forehead, and horns are in shape of three level stages. The face is in shape of trapezoid, and a pair of round vortex is used to indicate the eyes. The forehead is flat, and is equal with the neck, while the two U-shaped horns used vertical. The pairs on the right: the head of the big animal is like a duck's head in profile, with round eyes and long beak, while the small animal has the similar manner with the left one, with face in triangle shape. With symmetrical arrangement, the entire image is dynamic. The powerful cutting and the fine polishing achieve a perfect combination between art and practice.

130. Jade Bi(a sword ornament) with Animal Patterns

Jade Bi is in the shape of trapezoid, the section of which is olive-shaped. Both the two sides are decorated with animal faces. The faces are a little square, with big face. The upper eye sockets are close to flat and the eye corners stretches outside the faces. The eyebrows are close to square, and the nose is garlic-shaped. There are intaglio process us mastoideus in the place of the two sides of the forehead, the place between the eyebrows and the cheeks, Its mouth is opened, with teeth exposed and faces are with grossly offensive features. The periphery of outline of the animal faces is grinded to be flat and the edge of the nose molded by the technique of removing the ambient materials excluded the patterns is outlined with intaglio lines, The eye frames and lips are ambient materials excluded the patterns is outlined with intaglio lines. The eye frames and lips are chamfered with slant cutting, which highlights the ferocious lips and opened mouth, thus, the horrible sense of the animal faces are strengthened. The upper part of the trapezoid-shaped Bi is double-faced chamfered, the top side and the two hypotenuses are polished. The nether plane of the trapezoid is in the shape of olive, with a perforation in the center part, at two sides of which there are two slanted perforations separately hit into the waist of the mortise, used for fixing the rabbet of the head of sword cortical belt.

131. Oval Shaped Jade Ornament with Wild Goose Pattern

The Jade plate is in the shape of oval, one side of which is engraved with a flying wild goose. The wild goose stretches the feather, with long beak, round eyes, long neck, clear feather carving and several clouds around. The outline of the wild goose is carved with the technique of removing the ambient materials excluded the patterns, and the feathers are represented with chamber cutting and intaglio lines. The clouds around are polished with chamfer cutting as well.

wild goose belongs to migratory bird, the living habit of which changes as the seasons. They are faithful to come and back from south to north. The feature keeps pace with the feeling of the contemporaries, thus the image of the wild goose is the expression of the infatuation and missing to the relatives far away.

The back of plate is flat and plane. There is a copper rivet left in the right perforation while in the left there is a slanted pierced arc perforation used for inlay and fixing up.

132. Round Jade Flake with Chi Dragon Pattern

There is a pair of jade slice with the same shape and pattern. The jade plate is in round slice. A Chi Dragon is carved with the technique of reducing the base materials on the positive side of the jade plate. The head of dragon is slightly square, and the snout is flat, The nose and eyes are close to the forepart of the face. The ears are like a cat's and the neck is concave. The body is turn to one side, with four forceful limbs and bifurcate and curled tail. A deep cutting with intaglio line on the back outlines the ridge. Several short and slant intaglio lines are carved at the rear side of the shank of hind leg. Though the shape a similar with that of the Han Dynasty, the cutting and the features of head and neck have the characteristics of the Yuan Dynasty. The plate is not smooth and there are shallow and round indenture left by the pipe-drilling tool. There is a pair of slanted pierced arc perforation used for wedge and inlay, one of which is big and the other is small.

133. Jade Wild Goose

The four swan gooses have different manners, which are separately fluttering its wings and is about to fly, spreading its wings and flying, raising the feathers and landing on, as well as standing on the land and overlooking. These are four acts for a swan goose to finish a whole flying course, and it seems that they are a group of animation from hopping off to landing on. The basic features of the four swan gooses are consistent. Each of them has a beak which looks like a duck's, round eyes, a long neck and a short tail. The feathers on the body are outlined with intaglio lines. The technique is skilled, the shape is vivid, and the polishing is excellent. The jade is in the white color, with soil leaching trace. This group of swan gooses is carved in single face and is embossment. The other side is smooth and plain, without perforation. In view of the above. it may be the ornament of a wooden implement.

134. Jade Board with Phoenix Pattern

This is a pair of slice-shaped jade phoenix, with similar shape and manner, toward oppsite direction and both are single-sided carving. The phoenixes unfold their feathers and turn back the heads, with hooked beaks, long eyes and high crowns. The top feathers are closed backward and curled up, and the neck feathers droop down and flutter. The long legs twist and long tails flutter in the wind. There is a piece of cloud carved in front of the feather, which represents that the phoenix is flying in the clouds. The shape of phoenix is exquisite and each part of the phoenix is showed in detail.

Phoenix is a kind of ornamentation pattern which synthesizes the bird manners in the nature and molded an image by ancient people according to the aesthetic consciousness. The early phoenix grain is actually pattern of common birds. It was until the Han Dynasty that the image character of phoenix became definite. The symbol meaning of the phoenix is rich of mystical color. And the shape of the phoenix is covered with a sense of happiness. Therefore, people like the phoenix patterns generation after generation.

135. Oval-shaped Board with Chi Pattern

The slice ornament is oval-shaped and double-sided carving. There are connected bead patterns around the outer edge. There is a Chi Dragon in the shaped of oval in the slice ornament, proper of climbing and crawling. The Chi Dragon holds up its head, with flat mouth and lifted nose. The ears are with rolling clouds, and the top of head are with fluttering hair. The body of Chi Dragon is thin and long, with the soft forelegs curled up. One of the hind legs is in front of the other. The joints of the four limbs are decorated with clouds. A line is carved on the curled body to represent the ridge; a thin and short line is carved on the shin of shank. The tail is curled body to represent the ridge; a thin and short line is carved on the shin of shank. The tail is curled up and bunch of flowers and decorated among them.

136. Roundish Jade Board with Plum Blossom Patterns

The jade plate is flat and round, multilayer pierced and dish-shaped in lateral view. There is a plum blossom with five petals in the middle of the plate, and there are five small plum blossoms on ring-shaped branches at another layer, corresponding with the five petals. Among the plum blossoms, there is a bunch of flowers stretched out aslant, and the separate petals are connected with the adjacent small plum blossoms. The stamen and pistil of the plum blossom is in the shape of trumpet. There are holes separately in the center for in laying the gems.

137. Jade Man

The jade man is a flat embossment craft. There is a crown on the head, and he wears a robe with cross collar and wide sleeve. A belt is tied to the waist and both the two hand s are superposed in front of the chest. The wide belt is fluttering before the abdomen and the two legs are twisted together. The eyebrows are like a falcate moon on the face, and the eyes are narrow. The small nose is like a green onion and also he has a small cherry-like mouth. The five senses are all outlined with intaglio lines. The gather showed by thin short straight lines and curved lines are natural and smooth. The clothing and headgear of the jade man were popular in the Song Dynasty. The images in the two works of Along the River during the Ch'ing-Ming Festival by Zhang. Zeduan and Lister to Sever-stringed Harp by Zhao. Ji in the Song Dynasty have clothing of this style. This jade man has a flat back, thus it may be an ornaments inlayed in a certain wear originally. For it is buried under earth, the positive side has been whitening.

138. Jade Hawk Head

The head of eagle is circular engravure, with thick eyebrows frowned and two eyes stared. The wing of nose concaves slightly, and the beak is broad and hooked. There are corresponding pipe-drilled round holes and wedge-shaped convex groove on the two sides of mouth. The waist is outlined with deflected cutting. The back part is molded with intaglio lines and rolling patterns, which represents the feathers on the neck. The back part of the eagle head is in the shape of square, on top of which there are five round holes. And there is a big pipe-drilled round hole at back. The hole at the back of top side is perforating to the big round hole at back. These holes may be used to fix the eagle head to the beam on the shaft of the carriage or other implements. The eagle head is molded with rectangle materials and processed primarily to form the outline. And then sketches the details such as eyes, beak and feathers. The lines are coarse and forceful, and it is grinded with stone roller with deep cutting. The middle part is thick and straight, and the end of the cutting is thin and forceful, concise and vivid.

139. Jade Dragon Head

The dragon head is similar to a rectangle. The eyebrow ends are curled up. The nose is wide, the mouth is broad and the teeth are bared. The upper lip turns out wardly, and the big ears are closed backwardly. The top head is flat. The top part is pierced and the long horns are bent backwardly. The back part of the dragon head and the bottom part are flat. There is rectangle groove in the center part of the dragon head. The bottom and one side of the groove are in the shape of half arc. And the other two sides are flat. Seen from the cutting saw kerf and inner core which were left after pipe-drilling, it should be drilled separately from horizontal direction and vertical direction and then cut the center part. There is a perforation in the middle of the two horns connected with the concave groove. The mouth, teeth, eyes and nose on th face are carved with thick intaglio lines. The beard and eyebrows are carved with thin intaglio lines. It is obvious that it is grinded by rolling stone. The cutting is forceful and the shape is vivid. The image is brave and fierce with a sense of sculpture. This dragon head was excavated from the relic of Da Tang Furongyuan. In view of the groove shape and perforation position, it belongs to the inlay ornament for pleasure-boat of the emperor. There are zinnober left at the teeth sew. lip edge, eye frame and auricle, which shows that these parts are decorated with zinnober.

Burial Jade

140. Jade Cicada

The cicada body is in the shape of oval, with sharp head and sharp tail. The two eyes are at two sides and are molded with the technique of removing the ambient materials excluded the patterns. The jagged lines are used to represent the neck of the cicada. The concave triangle is carved at the back with slanted cutting. Straight convex edges are at the behind. And on both the two sides there are double wings. The wing pulses are molded with connected clouds in S shape with intaglio lines. The abdomen is bulge and round. The nature of the jade is green with yellowing, fine and smooth. The image is simple and the shape is vivid. Based on the outline, intaglio lines are adopted to carve the neck and the wing pulses, to express the inner nature of the body, head and double feathers.

141. Jade Cicada

The head of Jade Cicada is arc-shaped. It's protruding eyes point to the left and right ends. Its folding wings are curved on the back, and there are two skew curves on both side of the abdomen to sketch the outline of the abdomen. The radial arc in the central epigastric which is connected with the cicada head is the tympanum; and the seven crossed slightly arc lines lin the lower abdomen symbolize the telescopic abdominal segments. This Jade Cicada's sculpture is realism and vivid; the curved lines are brief and strong. There are typical handicraft characteristics of the late Western Han Jade Cicadas. Meanwhile it's milling skill is very outstanding, especially the millstone techniques has been quite skills, and the sloping curved lines are milled very sleek and smooth, and have no any cracks. you can see the cicada is almost like the glass which is clear. It is crystal and has refraction light.

142. Jade Pig

This couple of jade pigs belongs to the circular engravure. They have same modeling and similar postures. The noses have flat end s and the nostrils were depicted by two holes. Their eyes in the olive shape are curved in a unique traditional Chinese relief skill. And their bias tails which are sticking to their hips are curved in the same way. The two asymmetrical lines composed the ear. There are several arc lines on the lower jaw, neck, shoulders and hips are well show the stout pig body. One pig gets down on its two front hoofs; the other one front hoof is stretching out and another front hoof is curled up. They both are trying hard to get up with their two back hoofs to eat foods. These two jade pigs are curved with same carving techniques. They look real, vivid, buxom and very lovely. The sculptures show the pigs 'desire to get up successfully and it is really a very high level of expression skill. They are rare art treasure of the Han Dynasty.

143. Jade Pig

This Jade Pig is sculptured in prostrate shape. Its eyes, ears, arms and legs are curved in the skewed knife method. Meanwhile its underpants mouth and tail was depicted as flat surface according the shape. The carving style is mild, distinctive, and powerful. Just several simple sculpture, the pig was vivid like alive. This skill was called "Chinese Eight Carving".

144. Jade Pig

This two-sided engraved Jade Pig has a flat body, diamond eyes, protruding mouth, exposed long sharp teeth on both side, two long and thin ears pointing to back. And the hair on the spine is standing and protracted to the front. The curving style of this jade pig is very concise. The intaglio method with the thin line outlined the mouth, eyes, hairs, arms and legs of the pig and it express very well the sharp-witted image when the pig get a rest.

Pig is one of the earliest animals which were domesticated by human beings. Even early in the legends of five sovereign's era, the pig was taken as the symbol of wealth. They are workable in the sacrifices and funerals. As a subject in jade article, it appears a lot in the West Zhou Dynasty and the Han Dynasty. Before the Shang Dynasty and the Zhou Dynasty, the top class always buried the live pigs with the dead. But in the Han Dynasty, people began to bury jade pigs with the dead. And this tradition to bury pig with dead has been kept till today.

145. Talcum Pig

This jade pig was engraved in the running status. With a fat head, wide mouth, snobby nose, dentation hair on its neck and back, short large body, long thick legs and upspring with four legs, the pig image is exaggerated, vivid, interesting. It shows well the heroic posture when the wild boar is running.

Jade Utensils and Displays

146. Jade Seal

This is a single side jade seal with four sloping sides back, and the button is like the helm roof which with a hole on it. And the three seal characters "Xu, Ri, Yue" was curved on the seal surface in the intaglio way.

147. Jade Seal

This is a single side jade seal with flat back and tile like button which is with a hole on it. And on the squared seal surface, there are three seal characters "Lecheng Chen" were engraved in intaglio way.

148. Jade Seal

This is a private single side with four sloping sides back, altar-shaped button, and there is a hole on the button. And on the squared seal surface, there are three seal characters "Song Heng Seal" were engraved in intaglio way.

149. Jade Seal

This is a single side private seal with four sloping sides bake, altar-shaped button which has hole on it. And there is continuous cloud sculpture on each sloping side. And on the squared seal surface, there are three seal characters "Yao Wei" were engraved in intaglio way.

150. Crystal seal

This is a single side seal with four sloping sides back, helm-roof button which has hole on it. And on the squared seal surface, Crystal body has even moire, there are three seal characters "Chen Qingshi" were engraved.

151. Jade Seal

This is a single side seal with four sloping sides back, helm-roof button which has hole on it. And on the squared seal surface, there are three seal characters "Chen Qingshi" were engraved.

152. Jade Seal

Single side seal with flat seal back, animal shape button. The head of the animal slightly turned to one side, and its tail touches the ground, just like the animal is making a dragon prance. There are two phoenixes engraved on the seal surface. The big one with long beak. high crown. expanding wings, and long tail, the small one is turning around his neck to watch sth. It belongs to animal image seal.

153. Jade Cup with High Stem

This Jade Cup was composed by the cup body and cup holder. The cup body has wide mouth and smaller end; the cup holder likes a jade bean. The brim of the cup was shaped by narrowing one circle of the cup diameter. The abdominal grains are separated into four layers by the three lines of double hook curving lines. The highest layer has a circle of four leafs and continuous cloud grains. The second layer is a circle of Guding hooked cloud grains. The third layer is a circle of geometry hooked cloud grain. The last layer is distorted cloud grains. There are five intaglio curved squared frame. And there is simplified phoenix like a "S" in each frame. The different figures continuously left and right curved to decorative the cup brim and base. But on the abdomen, there are 4 continuous figures spreading around to decorative it. The second Guding hooked cloud grain combined the unique Chinese relief skill and intaglio method. The Guding are curved first and the cloud grains. They are connected up and down, left and right. It's really a outstanding design in that time. The first three layers are bas-relief, very powerful. All in all, this jade cup is not only very bright and clear, but also very dedicated, It's color is green with a little yellow, and sparkling like the crystal. This cup excavated in the Qin Dynasty Efang Palace. From Its big body and outstanding article design, we can tell it belongs to emperor.

154. Pig-shaped Pillow

This Jade Pillow is pig-shaped, almost rectangular. The pig has a flat mouth with a "U" shaped hooked line to draw its lips. The slight sloping surface on the top of the mouth is the nose head with two holes to depict its nostrils. The two little circles curved by thin lines on both sides of its surface are pig eyes. Its ears was engraved in traditional Chinese relief way. Both the face and ears are little concaving. There is a cone-shape tail in middle of pig hips. Its arms and legs are outlined by several simple arc lines. The top of this jade pig is flat, so it can be used as a pillow. This pig-shaped pillow was sculpted in a bright, concrete style. It's very realism, without to much decoration. It's a representative of "Chinese Eight Curving".

155. Jade Square Powder Box

This powder box is octagonal square shaped. Its cap was connected with the body by a snap button. One side is mosaic up and down with gold ring o-like button; the opposite side has a handle. The cap and body are symmetry, and they have same decorations. Around of the positive side curved a blooming lotus in the octagonal frame. And it is surrounded by branches and leaves whose veins are curved in intaglio lines. And there are radical intaglio lines on the bottom of petals of leaves. The brass figures were engraved on the sloping side of the compact outline. On the handle, there is hollowed a couple of playing mandarin darks whose eyes, mouth, feather and tail are curved in intaglio lines. Over 3 curving methods are expressed in this jade compact. In one words, it is the superb of Tang Dynasty Jade curving applicants.

156. Agate Mortar

This mortar was sculpted by agate which is dark brown with milk white strip texture. It is in long oval shape. a little fatter in the middle, but thinner at the top and end. The inside bottom is very smooth, while the outside bottom is with a circle of short legs. Although the mortar has no any decoration on body, the natural agate texture is crossing and brightly sparking. The pestle and the mortar is as a pair to be the tools of making Chinese traditional medicine.

Agate is one of the chalcedony. It has different colors and distribute by layers. According its different texture and color, it was divided into striped agate, moss line agate, jade agate, coralline agate, water bile agate and so on. Its name "agate" comes from Buddhism. After the Buddhism came to China, Qiong Jade or Red Jade was renamed with Agate which is produced in Chinese northwest, north China, northeast, southwest, south China and a lot of other districts.

157. Lion-shaped Jade Incense Burner

It is made of pure white marble. The lion mouth is slightly opened, and there is a hole under its abdomen and goes to its mouth. The spice container has flat bottom, deep stomach, and contractive top. It's like a box with a hole on its positive side. The whole body is polished very fine and smooth.

158. Two Boys

This jade pendant is a slightly triangular body. It is composed of two playing boys who are fighting for one lotus stem. One half kneeling down boy is holding a lotus stem tightly with his two hands and turning his head to left. The other boy is riding on this boy's back with his two legs clamping tightly. His left hand is on the bellowing boy's forehead, while his right hand is grabbing the lotus stem. And his head is turning to the left, too. Their mouths are little opened; eyes are slightly closed. It seems they are very happy. With hairs on their round heads, they are both wearing long gown which has wide sleeves. Their hairs and pleats on the gowns are engraved in intaglio lines. The lotus stem is punched a hole for sling. This pendant includes the full relief, deep hollow sculpting method. The lines seem deep, strong and classical. The whole design is concise, but it fully show the naughty, nave, and restless of the two boys.

159. Jade Qilin(a divine beast in Chinese legends)

This jade Qilin is in a low-creeping posture with his lifting head, slightly opened mouth, exposed sharp teeth, lower jaw which is closed to its chest, protruding eyes, big nose, backward ears, double rolling horns, stretching wings expositing his chests, big dropping tail. The Qilin body is very strong, powerful and sturdy; its look is forceful and aggressive. Its curving beard and stretching wings make this Qilin seems more extraordinary. Different sculpture techniques including the hollowing curving, relieve, intaglio and skewed curving are applied on this art work. Its mouth is the hollowing curving; its eyes ears and horns are intaglio curving; its horns, wings, arms, legs and tail are relieve curving. The con caving line to separate the two wings, the parallel arc lines in front of the chest, rolling cloud grains in the cheeks and wings brim are skewed curving; the beard, wings, legs and claws are engraved intaglio lines. You must say the sculpture techniques are very dedicated; the mill skill is outstanding. After all, this smooth and glossy Qilin is narrow on top and wide in the end. Its carted of gravity is a little low; and it belongs to the furnishing articles.

160. Jade Bixie(talisman)

This jade Talisman is in a low-creeping posture with its full rounded head, slightly opened wide mouth, backward ears, double long horns, closed wings on his back, strong and powerful arms and legs, leftward rolling tail which is closed to his abdomen. Its look is very concentrative and alert. The wings, ears and horn are clinging to the neck and back of Talisman. Its upheaval shoulder, tightly contracting chest and abdomen are showing its aggressive temperament. It is made of red agate with a little yellow and brown color which is touched glossily and smoothly. The animal fur and hairs looks very real, and it brings this art work strong natural feeling.

Talisman is one of the sacred beasts in the old legend. It looks like lions but with short horns and wings. The ancestor says: "For getting rid of bad luck, it named Talisman." And the ancestor also says: "Talisman kill the Ba and other demons". "It is said that Talisman can drive the demon away." And it is said that the horns of Talisman can fight with the villain. Talisman appears a lot in the jade article works after the Han Dynasty for praying for the good luck.

This jade Talisman has obvious Han Dynasty style in its posture and curving techniques. But you can tell it is produced in the Ming Dynasty from its intaglio thin line and the incurving tools. In one word, it is a take Han Dynasty art work.

161. Jade Stove Roof with Hollow-carved Figure

This jade stove roof is nearly a cylinder with inclined roof. It applied the hollowing openwork techniques. With pine tree and Ganoderma Lucidum on the mountain rocks, there is the elderly and the arcane. The elderly has a wide protruding forehead, and long white beard; and he wears a "V" collar long gown which is with wide sleeves and belt. The arcane turns its neck facing to the elderly. It has a long beak round eyes, closed wings and dropping tail. And it is walking with its one leg in front and the other back. In the bottom, there is square prominence which has two holes on opposite sides for fixing the stove cap.

This stove roof combines the traditional wish for longevity and good luck. The five images are obbligato. The hollowing curving, skilled techniques make the five images vivid, real, and individualized. It is made of white jade. It touches warm, glossy and gives person happy, pleasant and comfortable feeling.

162. Jade Stove Roof with the Pattern of Hollow-carved Dragon

This stove roof is in slightly squared shape with flat bottom; and it its sculptured in the dragon theme. The dragon is a little squared image to fit for the X curving. Its face apply the deep curving style; and it has protruding eyes, snobby nose, upward nostrils, beards besides the nose, backward ears, stronghorns, fire ball behind his jaw, engraved inclined squared grains in intaglio way to express the scale, straight standing for legs, and with intaglio straight lines on its shanks. There is a oval hole in the center of its bottom which has a concaving circle around it. Stove roof is the cap of the censer. Gao, Lian of the Ming Dynasty said this name appeared in the jade article since the Tang and Song Dynasty in his book Zun Sheng Ba Jian.

163. Jade Cup with Plum Blossoms

The cup body is short and round: the cup mouth brim is slightly contracting; the inside bottom is a little protruding and there is an angle image composed by three concaving arc lines which is surrounded by four skewed curving petals. The cup mouth is in the circle of six plum blossoms which has mash stamen in the middle of stretching petals. The petals of the buds are also engraved very natural. The blossom branches are hollowing curved through the whole cup body form end to the top; they are not only decorate the cup body but also working as the handle. The design of this cup is very ingenious; the different images match with each other perfect and are curved in the right place. It is indeed a perfect combination of arctic and practical.

164. Jade Incense Burner with Hollow-carved Patterns

This sachet is a flat round box with hollow openwork, snap button, same modeling and decoration of the cap and box. Its decoration is divided by the raised line into the inside zone and the outside zone. There is an engraved lotus in the inside zone with a jewel box on the top of the flower; and a Ganoderma Lucidum is growing in the jewel box and open the jewel box. There is a phoenix with long beak, high crown, stretching wing flying above it; the phoenix is carrying a flower with its mouth Outside, there is a circle of flower to furnish them.

The Sachet belong s to the aromatherapy jade works. Its designs come from the aromatherapy warming stove before the Han Dynasty. The later generations copy its designs with jade materials but not for warming. It is for store the spices only. They put the osmanthus flowers, roses, jasmines and other flowers in it. If the sachet is big, it is used for decorating the lobby or desk, if the small one it will be hung in the belt of person. The potpourri will come out natural to make people feel pleasant. And then some people put importing India Sandal Wood spice, Persia (Iran) Benzoin, Jiaozhi (North Vietnam) Longnao Spice and other famous spices in it and light it up to keep brain vivid, get rid of the bad. After all, the sachet has not only practical value but also appreciation value.

165. Jade Quadripartite Boxes

The box is in square shape, and its four angles are a little convex, and the bottom has round legs according its shape. The cap and body was connected by snap button, and the cap is a little protruding. Four angles are decorated by four good-luck textures which is connected by straight lines. The inside images are composed by good-luck textures and deformation good-luck rolling cloud lines. All the lines is in relief sculpture to make the images have stereo effect. Good-luck cloud texture is the texture on the handle of Good-Luck Stick. They seem like Ganoderma Lucidum and cloud. Good-Luck Stick is a sacred instrument. In Sanskrit, it is called A Na Lv, This is recorded in the Neng Gai Zhai Fssay of Good-Luck Stick, Shi Shi Summary of Property both written by Zeng Wu of Song Dynasty. The Good-Luck stick was used to write the scriptures on by the Buddhist when they are preaching in case of they forget the scriptures. But in modern times, it means good-luck for appreciation. And the good-luck texture has changed into cloud images called good-luck cloud texture to be the representatives of getting better and better.

166. Jade Snuff Box with Gold Inlaid

This snuff box is curved according the jade's natural shape. It was engraved the inside part to make a hollow room and with a hole on to its mouth, and there is a circle of short feet on the bottom. The relief of mountains was sculpted on the surface and there are Chi Tiger, fierce leopards and wolves among the mountains; and the Ganoderma Lucidum is growing on the top of mountains. The Jade is fine. warm, clear white and with a little yellow outside. This Snuff Bottle just like a high peak surrounded by other lower mountains. Utilizing the natural color of the jade, by the comparison between the warm color (yellow flushed with red) and the cold color(white flushed with green), this art work well expresses the momentum of a mountain. The design is ingenious and the artistic conception is fresh. The relief of surrounded mountains calls a lot of fantasy. The green color just like clouds floating in the sky. The yellow and red color like the sunset landscape that all the objects seem red between the sky and earth. The aggressive and wild characters of the Chi Tiger, fierce leopards and wolves among the mountains are expressed very well.

Snuff comes to China in the late Ming Dynasty; in the Kangxi emperor of Qing Dynasty, the snuff bottle is invented. Then every workshop leaded by emperor operation department and the Jingdezhen imperial kilns, Suzhou, Yangzhou Jade workshops in charged by the emperor are begin to produce different material, workmanship snuff bottles after getting the order from emperor. The production quantity climax is in Qianlong period for not only the quantity is big and the designs are abundant but also the techniques are very high. Since the Jiaqing emperor, the production quantity bein reduced and some designs has stopped production, the other designs are kept till the perish of the Qing Dynasty. This is called th imperial snuff bottles. People always follow with the famous one. Since the Qing Dynasty, a lot of commons begin to use snuff bottles; so the snuff bottles appears in the local handcraft workshops. you can't imagine the how big of the quantity, how much of the kinds, and how outstanding of the snuff bottle. It's just a little snuff bottle, but it combines different of handcraftsmanship. This never happened in the history. To sum up, the snuff bottle can be divided into nine kinds. They are enamel, glass, ceramics, jade, lacquer ware, enamel with glass fetal painting, carving with bamboo knife, mosaic, inside painting and so on. And there are different techniques of every kind so. So if you classify the kinds in details, it will be thousands of kinds.

For the fresh artistic power of snuff bottle, all person including the emperor and the commons like it. After the Qing Dynasty, it becomes the art pieces from the practical appliance and the hot collections of people. So, during the period of Republic of China, the snuff is still in production even there is only a few people keep using it.

167. Jade Quadripartite Bottles

This appliance looks like four connected bottles; the surfaces of the bottle mouth, neck, abdomen and feet are in square shape which with convex round angles. In the center of the bottle was engraved a whole equal diameter empty cylindrical hole. This bottle has round mouth, long neck, hard folding shoulder, straight abdomen, and a circle of high feet. Along with four angles of the mouth, four rolling cloud texture was engraved in the intaglio way; and there is a circle of distorted Japanese banana leaves in the neck; the shoulder was decorated by cloud and thunder patterns; seven dragons was coiling on the above abdomen; low abdomen is decorated nu distorted Japanese banana leaves and good-luck cloud patterns. The color of jade material is dark green, and the jade is very fine, smooth and hard.

The quadri in the quadripartite bottles means spring. summer, fall and winter. The Chinese pronunciation of bottle is the same with Pingan(safe and well). So the quadripartite bottles are symbol of safety and well-being in four seasons. The cloud patterns, distorted Japanese banana leaves and coiling dragon texture imitate the decorative texture of brass ware in West Zhou Dynasty. The whole desigh looks new, classical, dignified and elegant.

168. Jade Yi-Shaped Cup

This cup has a flat body and deep cavity. The brim of the cup neck is very wide and there is a gap in one side. The cavity wall is slightly straight; and its lower part of the cavity is contractile; its bottom is nearly flat. The outside wall of the mouth a decorated by a circle and thunder patterns which is separated by vertical lines. The decorative patterns in the abdomen was divided into three parts including the top layer which is engraved with distorted Japanese banana leaves in its lower position, dragon texture on the both sides and distorted cicada image on the back; the middle layer is curved two couples balanced gluttonous faces; the last layer is finished by a circle of distorted Japanese banana leaves; The decorative patterns in the abdomen apply a special Chinese curving technique, and the thin part was outlined by straight knife and inclined knife method.

Yi was popular bronze washing applicant in the middle of the Western Zhou Dynasty till the Western Han period. But this jade cup imitates the early brass Yi modeling. The decorative images on it are the common patterns of the Shang and Zhou Dynasty while the techniques of the detailed characters and solid relief belong to the Qing Dynasty jade applicants obviously.

169. Jade Fu, Lu, Shou(the three gods in charge of good fortune, official career and longevity)

This applicant is in the mountain shape. The positive side is decorated by relief patterns and utilizes the tawny color to engrave the pine tree and standing crane which is turning its head back. There is a deer on the mountain slop and a big tree behind the mountain. Some bamboo and Ganoderma Lucidum are growing under the tree.

The crane, deer, pine tree and Ganoderma Lucidum all have implied meaning. The crane is the sacred animal of longevity which has legend of the immortal; if you ride it, you can meet the god in heaven. The deer is also the sacred animal of longevity which needs to be ride when you become an immortal. The pine can be taken as the leader of all woods which keep green in the whole year. And so is the bamboo which can keep green all the time. The Ganoderma Lucidum belongs to the fungi which are never rotted; it is said it could keep people from old and make dead people re-alive. In one words, these animals and plants all the symbol of good luck and longevity.

This mountain is molded by the techniques of stereoscopic full relief. The trees utilizing the tawny color to express their branches' strength and youth. The pine tree image is vivid and has strong impression. The white crane is standing on the bamboo rock and turning its neck back to see the deer. The body of deer is strong and the feather of crane is clear white. They look like vivid. With the bamboo leaves. Gannoderma Lucidum and cloud textures as background, the mountain are standing among the bamboo and grass. The whole landscape make people think of the slightly cloudy day of the cool autumn. All the decorative images are vivid, natural, and alive. They both show the scenery of mountain and woods in the later autumn.

170. Jade Toad with Three Legs

The toad has three legs; two legs is prostrating on the ground and one leg which is in the middle of tail is pedaling hard. The toad head is slightly upwards; wide mouth is a little closed; nostrils are in olive shape; round eyes are a little protruding; there is convex pine on the back; and there is decorated by flat hobnails; its legs are strong with muscles; mouth is engraved with one intaglio line; the angles of mouth are a little upwards like a smile; each claw has three toes. The body of this toad is very plim and with two holes on its face as eyes. Its eye socket nostrils pine on the back and flat decorative hobnails are engraved in intaglio way. So the toad outline is very stereo.

The toad with three legs is the legendary toad. Toad is amphibious animal with taupe body, and scraggy skin. They are good at catching and feeding on insects and small gecko and they are good to crops. Their secretion of hind behind the ear and the skin could be made into Chinese medicines. In reality, the toad with three legs doesn't exist. It was well known just because the story of Hai Liu (person name) Tease Toad. According the Shu X Wu Ji of early Qing Dynasty, it is said that Hai Liu tease toad and then Hai Liu became very famous. And it's more unbelievable in the Feng Xia Bi Tan written by Laifu Meng of Qing Dynasty. It is said in this book that Hai Liu got a toad with three legs when he lift water from the well; so he hung the toad with colorful strings and bear it on his shoulder; and he told others if this toad escape, it can be caught again in many years; then many people go to see the toad. Therefore, the toad with three legs became the good-luck symbol. And then, this story was printed on the Chinese New Year pictures and engraved as sculpture. Toad with three legs becomes the article image, too.

This piece of toad with three legs has a lively sculpt, bright eyes and interesting look. It has the pleasant green color and shows very high milling kills.

171. Jade Pendants with the Motif of Mandarin Ducks and Lotus Leaves Patterns

A mandarin duck is on the lotus leave with the lotus stem in its mouth. The lotus is curved before the chest. It is a rounded sculpture. The mouth, nose, eyes, feather, tail and leave veins are all carved in intaglio lines. The carving of the jade mandarin duck is according to the nature texture of the jade material and the distribution feature skillfully. The smart design makes the upper lip of the Mandarin Duck, the top of its head, the feather, as well as the petal and stem of the lotus are in the color of sugar. The molding and the material, as well as the color are consistent, which makes a masterpiece.

172. Jade Boy

This jade boy has a squabby body. He is wearing a gown with narrow sleeves and round collar. He sits on his twisted legs and turns his head to one side and looks towards the sky; he is holding a lotus stem with two hands and the lotus and leaves are on his back. A pinch of hairs was kept on the top of his head; the eyebrow, little eyes, small mouth and protruding nose are on his round face. The naive smile on his face is very lovely and he seems born with silver spoon in his mouth. All the organs on his face are applied the skewed lines, so the cheekbone and nose bridge looks a little high. His lips are slightly convex; the angles of eyebrows are connecting with the eye angles. The lines are strong and deep, but not very smooth. This modeling of jade by utilizes the natural color of the material. So the head of the boy is white and his body is tawny. This strengthens the article effect of the boy image.

시안시문물보호고고소(西安市紋物保護考古所) 유물창고에는 고대 옥기(玉器) 4천여 점이 소장되어 있으며 그중에는 몇 년 사이 새로 출토된 몇백 점도 포함된다. 오랫동안 창고에 숨겨져 있던 아름다운 이 고대 옥기들을 하루빨리 독자들에게 선보이기 위해 그중 가장 대표성을 띤 역대 옥기 수작 약 200여 점을 간추려 본서에 수록하였다.

『시안문물정화(西安文物精華)』「옥기」는 톈당성(田党生)이 기획하고 쑨푸시(孫福喜), 왕펑쥔(王鋒鈞)이 표제를 선정하고 체계를 세웠다. 유물 관련 설명은 왕펑쥔, 쑨푸시, 짜이룽(翟榮), 양훙이(楊宏毅), 장샹위(張翔宇)가 작성하였고 사진은 왕바오핑(王保平)이 촬영하였다. 엮는 과정에서 류윈후이(劉雲輝)가 일부 옥기의 이름 설정 및 연대 판단에 소중한 의견을 내놓았고 왕당룽(王檔榮)은 모든 옥기의 재질을 감정하였으며 시안시 문물국(文物局)의 리잉커(李穎科), 둥리췬(董立群), 샹더(向德), 리싱전(李興振), 장신(張新), 리톈순(李天順), 황웨이(黃偉) 또한 여러모로 힘을 보태었다. 이 자리를 빌려 감사를 표한다.

본서는 쑨푸시가 교열하고 최종 심사하였다. 중국도서수출입시안회사 우훙차이(武宏才)와 판신(樊鑫)도 본서의 출판에 도움을 주었다. 특히 감사드린다.

본서는 문화계 및 문물애호가를 위한 옥기전문서적으로 과학적인 체계 편성, 정확하고 알기 쉬운 설명, 미관을 고려한 디자인에 주력했다. 이는 본서를 통하여 시안지역 옥기 문화의 발전상을 보다 체계적으로 독자들에게 보여주기 위해서이다. 본서의 저자 모두 장기간 문물관리와 연구사업에 종사한 전문가이지만 수준의 한계로 잘못된 부분이 있다면 독자들의 소중한 의견을 바라는 바이다.

엮은이